Nigerian Pentecostalism and Development

This book examines the contributions, both intentional and unintentional, of Nigerian Pentecostal churches and NGOs to development, studying their development practices broadly in relation to the intersecting spheres of politics, economics, health, education, human rights, and peacebuilding. In sub-Saharan Africa, Pentecostalism is fast becoming the dominant expression of Christianity, but while the growth and civic engagement of these churches has been well documented, their role in development has received less attention. The Nigerian Pentecostal landscape is one of the most vibrant in Africa. Churches are increasingly assuming more prominent roles as they seek to address the social and moral ills of contemporary society, often in fierce competition with Islam for dominance in Nigerian public space.

Some scholars suggest that the combination of an enchanted worldview, an emphasis on miracles and prosperity teaching, and a preoccupation with evangelism discourages effective political engagement and militates against development. However, *Nigerian Pentecostalism and Development* argues that there is an emerging movement within contemporary Nigerian Pentecostalism which is becoming increasingly active in development practices.

This book goes on to explore the increasingly transnational approach that churches take, often seeking to build multicultural congregations around the globe, for instance in Britain and the United States.

Nigerian Pentecostalism and Development: Spirit, Power, and Transformation will be of considerable interest to scholars and students concerned with the intersection between religion and development, and to development practitioners and policy-makers working in the region.

Richard Burgess is Senior Lecturer in Theology, University of Roehampton, United Kingdom.

Routledge Research in Religion and Development

The *Routledge Research in Religion and Development* series focuses on the diverse ways in which religious values, teachings and practices interact with international development.

While religious traditions and faith-based movements have long served as forces for social innovation, it has only been within the last ten years that researchers have begun to seriously explore the religious dimensions of international development. However, recognising and analysing the role of religion in the development domain is vital for a nuanced understanding of this field. This interdisciplinary series examines the intersection between these two areas, focusing on a range of contexts and religious traditions.

Muslim Women in the Economy
Development, Faith and Globalisation
Edited by Shamim Samani and Dora Marinova

International Development and Local Faith Actors
Ideological and Cultural Encounters
Edited by Kathryn Kraft and Olivia J. Wilkinson

Nigerian Pentecostalism and Development
Spirit, Power, and Transformation
Richard Burgess

Nigerian Pentecostalism and Development

Spirit, Power, and Transformation

Richard Burgess

Routledge
Taylor & Francis Group
LONDON AND NEW YORK

First published 2020
by Routledge
2 Park Square, Milton Park, Abingdon, Oxon OX14 4RN

and by Routledge
605 Third Avenue, New York, NY 10017

First issued in paperback 2021

Routledge is an imprint of the Taylor & Francis Group, an informa business

Publisher's Note
The publisher has gone to great lengths to ensure the quality of this reprint but points out that some imperfections in the original copies may be apparent.

British Library Cataloguing-in-Publication Data
A catalogue record for this book is available from the British Library

Library of Congress Cataloging-in-Publication Data
A catalog record has been requested for this book

Typeset in Times New Roman
by Wearset Ltd, Boldon, Tyne and Wear

ISBN 13: 978-1-03-223730-5 (pbk)
ISBN 13: 978-1-138-05330-4 (hbk)

DOI: 10.4324/9781315167299

For Amy
and
in memory of Mary Templeton Burgess (1927–2017)

Contents

Illustrations

Figures

Tables

Preface

Most of the work reported in this book is the outcome of two research projects. Between 2007 and 2010, I was a member of the GloPent (European Research Network on Global Pentecostalism) research team within the NORFACE-funded research programme "Religion as a Re-emerging Social Force in Europe". The GloPent project, entitled "Transnational Southern Pentecostal Churches, Networks and Believers in Three Northern Countries: A Potential and Potent Social Force", was a collaborative venture shared jointly by three European universities (VU Amsterdam, Birmingham, and Heidelberg). I am grateful to André Droogers, Michael Bergunder, and Allan Anderson, who directed the project, and to my co-researchers, Kim Knibbe and Anna Quaas, for their friendship and support. Between 2010 and 2012, I was Principal Investigator on a research project within the Pentecostal and Charismatic Research Initiative, which was supported by a grant from the John Templeton Foundation and administered by the Center for Religion and Civic Culture (University of Southern California). I want to thank Donald Miller and the staff at the Center for Religion and Civic Culture, my co-researcher Naar M'fundisi, and my fellow scholars on the Pentecostal and Charismatic Research Initiative, for their encouragement and collegiality. Additional support came from a grant (2010–2011) from the Global Prayers – Redemption and Liberation in the City project, initiated by metroZones: Centre for Urban Affairs, Berlin, and jointly executed by Haus der Kulturen der Welt and the Europa-Universität Viadrina, financed by Forum Transregionale Studien. I am grateful to Stephan Lanz, academic director of the programme, and to Annalisa Butticci for advice offered during fieldwork in Lagos. My research was also supported by a fellowship (2012–2013) from the Religious Freedom Project, Georgetown University, funded by the John Templeton Foundation. I want to thank Timothy Shah and Allen Hertske, who directed the programme, and my co-researcher Danny McCain at the University of Jos, Nigeria.

The present study has benefitted from interactions with other scholars. In the Department of Theology and Religion at Birmingham University, I was fortunate to belong to the Centre for Pentecostal and Charismatic Studies, which provided a convivial research environment and opportunities to share my ideas with colleagues and students. I am particularly grateful to Allan Anderson and

Mark Cartledge for their encouragement and friendship throughout my time at Birmingham. In 2013, I moved to the Department of Humanities at Roehampton University, where I have continued to conduct research on African Pentecostalism. I am indebted to my colleagues Mark Garner, Daniel Eshun, Andrew Rogers, and David Muir for their kindness, support, and friendship. Special thanks go to Mark Garner, Allan Anderson, and Jörg Haustein for commenting on earlier chapter drafts of the book. My numerous conversations with Mark helped to sustain me during the writing process. I have also benefitted from interacting with students studying theology and religion at Roehampton, many of whom are members of African Pentecostal churches.

My fieldwork would not have been possible without the generous support of church leaders, congregants, and individuals in Nigeria and Britain, who provided hospitality, shared their stories, and allowed me to participate in their church activities. I am grateful to Pastors Enoch Adeboye (Redeemed Christian Church of God), Sam Adeyemi (Daystar Christian Centre), Paul Adefarasin (House on the Rock), Daniel Olukoya (Mountain of Fire and Miracles), Mike Okonkwo (The Redeemed Evangelical Mission), Poju Oyemade (Covenant Christian Centre), Tony Rapu (This Present House), and Elijah Olusheye (Christ Apostolic Church), who gave me access to their churches. I would like to thank those who provided hospitality and support throughout my fieldwork in Nigeria, especially Bishop Dapo and Mrs Harriet Asaju and Pastor James Oyetubo at Lagos State University, Bishop James and Mrs Lydia Odedeji, Rev. John Ojo, Sina Bamtefa, Philemon Ishaya, Salama Hassan, and Andy and Manuela Warren, whose assistance during my visits to Lagos and Jos proved invaluable. I am also indebted to Danny McCain, Musa Gaiya and the staff of the Nigeria Pentecostal and Charismatic Research Centre at the University of Jos. I am especially grateful to Danny for introducing me to some of the key Pentecostal leaders in Lagos and Jos. In Britain, my fieldwork would not have been possible without the assistance of Pastors Agu Irukwu (Redeemed Christian Church of God), James Oladimeji (Mountain of Fire and Miracles), and Michael Efueye (House on the Rock), who gave me access to their churches. Special thanks go to Pastor Ranti Oyewale and the community of RCCG Covenant Restoration Assembly in Birmingham for providing me with a church family during my sojourn in Birmingham. Many others, too numerous to mention, have contributed to this project. Some of their names are mentioned in the book itself. I hope I have captured in this work a little of their vision and experience.

Finally, I would like to express my gratitude to Leila Walker and Rosie Anderson at Routledge for their editorial advice. Above all, I thank my father for his support in various ways over the years, and my daughter, Amy, for her forbearance during the long time that it has taken to bring this project to completion. I dedicate this book to her and to the memory of my mother, Mary Burgess.

I need to acknowledge the previous publication of some of the material contained in the book. Part of Chapter 3 is printed from my 2015 article

Abbreviations

ACHPR	African Charter on Human and People's Rights
ACRWC	African Charter on the Rights and Welfare of the Child
AFREG	African Forum on Religion and Government
AiMP	Apostles in the Marketplace
ARHAP	Africa Religious Health Assets Programme
BME	Black and Minority Ethnic
CADAM	Christ Against Drug Abuse Ministry
CAFOD	Catholic Fund for Overseas Development
CAN	Christian Association of Nigeria
CFT	Christ Faith Tabernacle
CHAN	Christian Health Association of Nigeria
CNAL	Coalition of Nigerian Apostolic Leaders
CRA	Child Rights Act
CRC	Convention on the Rights of the Child
CRPD	UN Convention on the Rights of Persons with Disabilities
CRUDAN	Christian Rural and Urban Development Association of Nigeria
DFID	Department for International Development
FBO	Faith-based Organization
FISD	Fountain Initiative for Social Development
GAIN	Global Apostolic Impact Network
GBNC	God Bless Nigeria Church
HFY	Hope for You
IMC	Interfaith Mediation Centre
IPV	Intimate Partner Violence
KICC	Kingsway International Christian Centre
LEAP	Leadership, Effectiveness, Accountability and Professionalism
MDG	Millennium Development Goal
MFM	Mountain of Fire and Miracles Ministries
NAPTIP	National Agency for the Prohibition of Trafficking in Persons
NEEDS	National Economic Empowerment and Development Strategy
NGO	Non-governmental Organization
NNNGO	Nigeria Network of NGOs
NPE	National Policy on Education

NUC	National Universities Commission
PDP	People's Democratic Party
PEPFAR	President's Emergency Plan for AIDS Relief
PFN	Pentecostal Fellowship of Nigeria
PHC	Primary Healthcare
PJI	Pathfinders Justice Initiative
PLWHA	People Living With HIV/AIDS
PWDs	People With Disabilities
RAPAC	Redeemed AIDS Programme Action Committee
RCCG	Redeemed Christian Church of God
RCCGNA	Redeemed Christian Church of God North America
RUN	Redeemer's University
RWF	Real Women Foundation
SAP	Structural Adjustment Programme
SDG	Sustainable Development Goal
SME	Small and Medium Enterprise
SNG	Save Nigeria Group
TREM	The Redeemed Evangelical Mission
UNESCO	United Nations Educational, Scientific and Cultural Organization
UNICEF	United Nations Children's Fund
UBE	Universal Basic Education
UNDP	United Nations Development Programme
UPE	Universal Primary Education
USAID	United States Agency for International Development
WHO	World Health Organization
WIMBIZ	Women in Business, Management and Public Service
WOWWI	Women Without Walls Initiative
YACPIF	Young Ambassadors for Community Peace and Inter-Faith Foundation

Introduction

In sub-Saharan Africa, Pentecostalism is fast becoming the dominant expression of Christianity, contributing to the shift in Christianity's centre of gravity southwards. The public role of religion is at the centre of debates on global Pentecostalism, partly stimulated by developments in Africa, where the turn to democracy in many countries coincided with the rapid growth of Pentecostal churches. The combined effects of democratization and neoliberal economic reforms, associated with the rolling back of the state and the privatization of service provision, has opened up space for new civil society organizations and enabled Pentecostals to become significant players in the public sphere (Kalu 2008; Marshall 2009). The exponential growth of Pentecostal Christianity in developing countries is one reason for the increasing interest in religion among development scholars, practitioners, and policy-makers (Deneulin and Rakodi 2011; Tomalin 2015). In order to engage effectively with Pentecostal churches, it is important for individuals and bodies involved in development to understand the factors that influence Pentecostal development beliefs and practices.

This book examines the role of Nigerian Pentecostalism in development. Specifically, it studies the relationship between Pentecostal spirituality and development in Nigeria and the Nigerian diaspora in Britain and the United States. One of the book's aims is to elucidate the nature and significance of Nigerian Pentecostal development activities. Another aim is to investigate the contextual and cultural factors that shape the way that Nigerian Pentecostals understand development and engage in development activities. Nigerian Pentecostal churches are of interest for a number of reasons. First, the vibrant Pentecostal landscape in Nigeria is perhaps the most dynamic in the whole of Africa, often with a significant missionary impulse and exercising theological influence on other African Christians. Some of the largest Christian gatherings in the world occur in the campgrounds of these Nigerian churches, especially in the vicinity of Lagos, which is arguably the most Pentecostal city in the world. A significant development is the "Pentecostalization" of mainline denominations, facilitated by groups such as the Evangelical Fellowship of the Anglican Communion (EFAC) and the attendance of mainliners at Pentecostal events and church services. Second, Nigerian Pentecostal churches are increasingly assuming more prominent roles as they seek to address the social and moral ills of contemporary society. Third, there is fierce competition with Islam for dominance in Nigerian public space. Thus, the inter-religious factor is important. Finally, Nigerian Pentecostal communities are often transnational in nature, with aspirations to build multicultural congregations around the globe.

Nigerian Pentecostal pastors have come in for some bad press in recent years. They have been linked to financial misconduct,[1] human rights infringements connected to witchcraft accusations and deliverance practices, and abuse of women and children (Johnson 2010; Topping 2014; Adeoye 2019; Ellison 2019). Criticism has also been levelled against certain pastors who have purchased private jets despite the relative poverty of the majority of their members. The main thesis of this volume, however, is that there is an emerging sector within contemporary Nigerian Pentecostalism, which is becoming increasingly active in development initiatives geared towards poverty alleviation and human well-being. This shift in orientation is driven by a variety of theological, sociological, and contextual factors, including Pentecostalism's encounter with Islam. In Nigeria, an important feature of this movement is a focus on nation-building and national transformation through diverse forms of social, economic, and political engagement. In Britain and the United States, these progressive currents are also evident, though on a smaller scale. Nonetheless, Nigerian Pentecostal diaspora churches represent an increasingly potent social force, challenging the notion that religion in the West is losing its significance in public life.

The book is interdisciplinary in outlook, combining development studies with religious studies and the social sciences to explore the influence of African Pentecostal religion on development. Recently, there has been a growing interest among scholars in studying the relationship between religion and development (Tomalin 2013; Ter Haar 2011; Clarke and Jennings 2008; Clarke 2011).[2] The discipline of development studies, which emerged in the 1960s and 1970s, was originally founded on the belief that religion is not important to development. It was assumed that as societies developed and modernized, they would also undergo a process of secularization. The secular nature of post-1960 development theory was influenced by the secular global development industry that emerged in the wake of the Second World War (Deneulin and Rakodi, 2011; Tomalin 2013, 2015). However, as Haynes (2008) notes, religion has recently made a remarkable return to prominence in Western development circles. This is reflected in the number of development funding agencies that formed relationships with faith communities to achieve the Millennium Development Goals (MDGs), a set of eight international development goals, which the UN member states and various international organizations agreed to achieve by 2015. The rationale behind this "turn to religion" within some parts of development studies is the perceived closeness of faith communities to poor communities and their highly motivated staff and volunteers (Deneulin and Rakodi 2011). Séverine Deneulin and Carole Rakodi (2011) refer to three trends which have combined to bring religion back into development studies. These are the rise of political Islam; the continuing salience of religion in people's lives, associated especially with the growth of Pentecostal and Evangelical Christianity in developing countries; and recognition of the importance of non-government organizations (NGOs), including religious organizations, as mechanisms for delivering development in contexts where neoliberal reforms have resulted in the withdrawal of the state from welfare provision. It is now increasingly recognized that religion plays a significant role in relation to development outcomes, whether for good or for ill (Haynes 2008).

Within the growing field of religion and development are studies that examine the developmental role of African Pentecostalism. While some scholars emphasize the positive contributions of Pentecostal religion to development (Freeman 2012; Dilger 2009; Adogame 2016; Togarasei 2011), others are doubtful of Pentecostalism's potential to contribute to Africa's development (Gifford 2015; Obadare 2016). Although there are some exceptions (e.g. Burchardt 2013; Dilger 2009), most studies of African Pentecostalism and development focus on churches rather than Pentecostal NGOs. For example, Dena Freeman's edited volume on Pentecostalism and Development (2012) compares Pentecostal churches and secular NGOs as alternative types of development actors. According to Freeman (2015: 116), Pentecostal churches have been much slower than mainstream churches in establishing "development wings" and engaging in explicitly development-focused activities.

There are also a number of important studies of Nigerian Pentecostalism, which examine the movement from a variety of disciplinary perspectives. Matthews Ojo (2006) examined the origin and development of the movement with a particular focus on south-western Nigeria. My previous book (2008) told the story of the movement among the Igbo people of eastern Nigeria with its roots in the Nigerian civil war and the work of Scripture Union. Asonzeh Ukah (2008) provided a sociological analysis of the Redeemed Christian Church of God (RCCG), the largest Pentecostal denomination in Nigeria. Ruth Marshall (2009) and Ebenezer Obadare (2018) considered Pentecostalism's political significance in postcolonial Nigeria. Finally, writing from the perspective of virtue-ethics, the theologian Nimi Wariboko (2014) examined Nigerian Pentecostal spirituality in relation to politics, economics, social ethics, and epistemology.

This book builds on the current research context in a number of ways. Taking its cue from the post-2015 international development agenda and the Sustainable Development Goals (SDGs), which have a range of foci, it examines Pentecostal development practices broadly in relation to the intersecting spheres of economics, governance and democracy, human rights, healthcare, education, and peacebuilding. Furthermore, the scope of book encompasses both informal church ministries and Pentecostal NGOs. As we will see in Chapter 1, Nigerian Pentecostal churches are establishing faith-based NGOs in their quest for recognition and funding from donor organizations. Although most Pentecostal NGOs maintain links with their congregations or denominations of origin, some are independent, free-standing organizations. Finally, the book explores the transnational dimension by examining Pentecostal development activities in Nigeria and the Nigerian diaspora in Britain and the United States.

Contextualizing Nigerian Pentecostalism

There has been an ongoing debate about the appropriateness of "Pentecostalism" as an umbrella term for African movements and churches which stress the experience of the Holy Spirit. Western definitions that focus on historical continuity with the North American Azusa Street Revival or adherence to a doctrine of Holy Spirit baptism have proved inadequate due to the great variety of movements elsewhere. Here I follow Anderson (2000) by adopting a more inclusive definition which comprises any African church or movement that stresses the experience of the Spirit and the practice of spiritual gifts. In this book, the term "Pentecostal" is used to describe individuals who belong to mission-related classical Pentecostal denominations; those who belong to the older African-initiated churches (AICs), called "Pentecostal-type" churches by Anderson; and those who belong to independent Pentecostal churches of more recent origin (neo-Pentecostal). The term "Charismatic" is used to describe Christians in mainline churches who satisfy one of the following criteria: (i) they describe themselves as "Charismatic" or "Pentecostal" Christians; or (ii) they say they speak in tongues.[3]

Nigeria is Africa's most populous nation with an estimated 193 million people in 2016 (National Bureau of Statistics 2019).[4] It also has the largest Pentecostal/Charismatic constituency on the African continent and the fourth largest in the world (after Brazil, USA, and China), with approximately 7.6 million mission-related Pentecostals and 27 million neo-Pentecostals and Charismatics in 2011 (Johnson 2013). The country is more or less equally divided between Christians and Muslims: of the three main ethnic groups, the northern Hausa-Fulani are predominantly Muslim, the eastern Igbo are predominantly Christian, and the western Yoruba are divided between the two faiths.

Nigeria hosts some of the largest Pentecostal denominations in the world with multiple national and international branches. For example, the Redeemed Christian Church of God (RCCG), founded in 1952, has over 14,000 branches in Nigeria and branches in over 178 nations (RCCG 2017; Gledhill 2017). Deeper Life Bible Church has planted over 6,000 branches across Nigeria, and has multiple branches in other African countries, Europe, Asia, and the Americas (Burgess 2008). Mountain of Fire and Miracles (MFM), founded in 1989, has over 300 branches nationally, 131 branches in Europe, 111 in the USA, as well as multiple branches in other African countries and Asia (Adogame 2005; MFM USA 2016). And Living Faith Church Worldwide, popularly known as Winners Chapel, has over 6,000 branches in Nigeria and congregations in 147 countries in Africa, Asia, Europe, and the USA (Gifford 2015; Ojo 2006; Vanguard 2014).[5] There are also a multitude of smaller Pentecostal congregations and denominations in Nigeria, which exert significant social influence on their members and the wider society.

The transnational nature of Nigerian Pentecostalism raises the question of the interplay between the local and global. In the literature on religious transnationalism, there is a growing interest in the way African Pentecostal churches are resacralizing urban landscapes in the global North (e.g. Adogame 2013;

Garbin 2013; Gornik 2011). Transnational movements such as African Pentecostalism challenge the usual national frameworks for the scholarly study of religious movements. Some migrants remain strongly influenced by ties to their homelands or by social networks that transcend national borders (Wimmer and Glick Schiller 2003). The transnational character of Nigerian Pentecostal churches is sustained by migrants who increasingly move between home and host countries, visiting family, engaging in business, and attending religious conferences (Burgess, Knibbe, and Quaas 2010). Transnational networks are also reinforced by media technologies such as mobile phones, the Internet and Satellite TV.

Pentecostalism in Nigeria emerged in the first decades of the twentieth century as a revival movement in the South. This first wave was associated with indigenous efforts to break free of Western missionary control and cultural dominance. It produced a proliferation of African-initiated churches (AICs) collectively known as Aladura ("praying") or "prophet-healing" churches because of their emphasis on prayer, prophecy, and healing. During the 1930s, some of these churches established formal links with western Pentecostal missions such as the British Apostolic Church and the North American Assemblies of God (Burgess 2008). During the 1950s, they were joined by two other mission-related Pentecostal denominations, the Foursquare Gospel Church and the Apostolic Faith Church, both planted by missionaries from the United States (Ojo 2006). One of the most important early AICs was the Christ Apostolic Church, which seceded from the Apostolic Church in 1939 due to disagreements over the doctrine and practice of divine healing. More significant for Nigerian Pentecostal growth was the Redeemed Christian Church of God (RCCG), founded in 1952 by Josiah Akindayomi who broke away from the Aladura Cherubim and Seraphim Church. The Assemblies of God was the first Pentecostal denomination to penetrate northern Nigeria. By 1964, it had established churches in the northern townships of Jos, Lafia, Sokoto, Gusau, Maiduguri, and Gyom (Burgess 2008).

The second major Pentecostal wave arose in the aftermath of the Nigerian civil war (1967–1970), initially among students and young people from mainline and Pentecostal mission churches, the interdenominational Scripture Union and university campus fellowships. It has generated a multiplicity of indigenous Pentecostal churches and denominations, which together represent the dominant expression of Christianity in Nigeria (Ojo 2006; Burgess 2008; Marshall 2009). The post-civil war Pentecostal revival consisted of three distinct phases (Wariboko 2014; Marshall 2009). The first phase occurred prior to 1980 when neo-Pentecostal churches emerged in the South emphasizing holiness and urgent evangelism in preparation for the second coming of Jesus Christ. The most important new church was Deeper Life Bible Church which promoted strict holiness doctrines via a rigorous regime of Bible study and prayer. Southern (mainly Igbo and Yoruba) Pentecostals were responsible for carrying the revival into northern Nigeria (Burgess 2008; Ojo 2006). This period coincided with rapid economic growth fuelled by the oil boom (Wariboko 2014). From the mid-1980s, a second phase arose which "distinguished itself from the older 'holiness' wave by preaching to greater or lesser degrees the 'doctrine of prosperity' or 'faith gospel'" (Marshall 2009: 78). During this period, the Nigerian economy experienced serious decline due to the 1981 oil glut, the global economic recession, and rising corruption by political leaders (Wariboko 2014). A significant development was the accession of Enoch Adeboye as head of the RCCG, which propelled the church into a period of rapid expansion. Adeboye has been largely responsible for transforming the image and constituency of the church by his implementation of a series of innovative initiatives. The most important was the model parish system, initiated to stimulate the growth of the RCCG by attracting young, urban professionals, imitating the style of other Pentecostal churches that were growing fast at the time (Ukah 2008; Marshall 2009). Professionals such as the lawyer Tunde Bakare and the medical doctor Tony Rapu, who like Adeboye himself were successful in the "secular world", were instrumental in setting up these parishes and facilitating the spread of the RCCG. The third phase (1990 to the present) was a period of rapid expansion as new churches emerged and members of the socio-economic elite were attracted into the movement's ranks, enabling Pentecostals to move from the periphery to the centre of Nigerian society (Wariboko 2014; Obadare 2018). The Nigerian political and economic contexts in which Pentecostalism has flourished will be discussed further in Chapters 2 and 3.

The spread of Nigerian Pentecostal churches to Britain and the United States must be understood within the context of social and religious developments at home and in the host countries. Poor governance and a decline in educational standards at home, combined with a relatively liberal migration policy in Britain, resulted in a growing African immigrant community in that country, especially from former British colonies such as Nigeria and Ghana.[6] The first wave of African church-planting in Britain followed the increase in immigration in the 1960s and consisted of mainly Aladura-type churches from Nigeria, transplanted to cater for their members in the diaspora (Harris 2006). The second wave, which began in the 1980s, involved mainly Nigerian and Ghanaian neo-Pentecostals concerned with catering for members who had migrated to Britain at a time of economic decline at home. Church growth was stimulated by a conscious missionary agenda as African Christians, who had migrated in pursuit of education and employment, considered that God had given them a unique opportunity to bring the gospel back to those who originally brought it to them. Among the earliest transplants were Deeper Life Bible Church (1985) and the RCCG (1988). A more recent development saw individual Africans setting up their own independent congregations with no formal links to a sending denomination at home or in Britain. The majority were started by Nigerians or Ghanaians, and most were located in London (Burgess 2009). Significantly, seven out of the 12 largest churches in London were planted by Nigerians (Cartledge *et al.* 2019).[7] The RCCG is the fastest-growing Pentecostal denomination in Britain with over 850 branches in 2019 (RCCGUK 2019; Brierley 2017). There is also an increasing number of churches started by migrants from other African countries.

African Pentecostal church growth in the United States has also followed the contours of African immigration. The 1965 Immigration Reform Act and the Diversity Visa Program (often referred to as the "Visa Lottery"), introduced as part of the 1990 Immigration Act, contributed to an unprecedented wave of new immigrants during the twentieth century, including a substantial number of African immigrants (Olupona and Gemignani 2007; Adogame 2013). Like Britain, African diaspora churches in the United States are mainly the product of West African Pentecostalism (Hanciles 2008). The first phase of African Pentecostal church-planting began in the 1970s and consisted largely of Aladura churches from Nigeria. The second phase began in the 1980s with the founding of (mainly Nigerian and Ghanaian) neo-Pentecostal churches such as the RCCG (1992) and the Church of Pentecost (1992) (Hanciles 2008). African diaspora churches are now found in gateway cities such as New York, Washington, DC, Chicago, Atlanta, Houston, and Los Angeles, as well as smaller cities and towns across the United States. The fastest-growing is the RCCG with around 800 congregations in 2019 (RCCGNA 2019).

There is considerable diversity of theological emphasis and social orientation within contemporary Nigerian Pentecostalism. Various typologies have been suggested to navigate the territory. However, the churches are not easy to classify. Nigerian Pentecostal churches have not remained static but have been influenced by a succession of theological currents which have developed in response to global flows and changing local contexts. Deji Ayegboyin (2005: 36) identifies three broad theological categories: "Holiness Movements", "Prosperity Organizations", and "Deliverance Ministries", though there is substantial overlap between the three. Ruth Marshall (2009: 85) suggests that most Nigerian Pentecostal churches situate themselves in the middle ground of the "holiness-prosperity" spectrum. In terms of social orientation, Nigerian church historian Musa Gaiya (2015) distinguishes between "centripetal churches" and "centrifugal" churches. Centripetal churches "tend to be inward-looking, channeling human and financial resources into the church and not routinely using them for social and human development". Centrifugal churches are more outward-looking, employing resources for social and political improvement (2015: 63–64). Gaiya's centrifugal churches resemble Miller and Yamamori's "progressive" Pentecostals (2007). In contrast to the other-worldly spirituality of holiness churches and the this-worldly spirituality of prosperity churches, progressive Pentecostals emphasize a holistic gospel and view the world as a place they want to make better. This movement began to emerge in the 1990s and can be found in both classical Pentecostal and neo-Pentecostal churches (Miller and Yamamori 2007). Most of the churches that feature in this book correspond to Gaiya's centrifugal churches and Miller and Yamamori's progressive Pentecostals.

Religion and development

Religions have a long history of engagement in development by "supporting those experiencing poverty, through service delivery as well as the provision of spiritual resources that provide mechanisms for resilience at both the individual and community level" (Tomalin 2018: 1). Tomalin, Haustein, and Kidy (2019: 105) identify three historical phases of the engagement across religions and global development: (i) the colonial period, "when religion and development efforts were ideologically entwined in the Christian 'civilizing mission' "; (ii) the post-World War Two era of the secular global development industry, where the role of religion was marginalized in development studies; and (iii) the "turn to religion" by development policy-makers and practitioners from the early 2000s.

Mainstream development theory has undergone significant changes since the Second World War. This has had implications for the "conceptualization of the relationships between religions and development" (Deneulin and Rakodi 2011: 46). Until the 1980s, modernization theory held sway, presuming that developing countries would undergo democratization, industrialization, and secularization as they evolved into modern societies in the mould of Europe and the United States. The focus was on economic development only, and the concern was to create conditions conducive to economic growth (Deneulin and Rakodi 2011). According to Tomalin (2013: 27), from the "beginnings of this modern development project, underpinned as it was by modernization theory, religion and culture were given no place of importance". Religion was considered detrimental to economic growth and it was assumed that religious faith "would become less important to people as they experienced economic development" (Tomalin 2013: 27). However, as Bompani and Frahm-Arp (2010: 241) note, "rather than being perceived as an anti-modern agent in Africa, religion is often a vehicle of modernity per se".

By the late 1960s, it was becoming clear that modernization theory was not working as rapid economic growth was not trickling down to reduce poverty. It was superseded by dependency theory, "which, influenced by Marxism, sought to explain why developing countries remained underdeveloped" (Tomalin 2013: 27). Dependency theorists challenged many of the assumptions of modernization theory, insisting that capitalism was incapable of achieving development. In the 1980s, the debt crisis in the global South led to attempts by Western governments and international development agencies, including the World Bank and IMF (the so-called Washington Consensus), to encourage developing countries to restructure their economies in order to stimulate growth. Neoliberal policies and structural adjustment were the tools used to implement economic reform (Haynes 2007; Tomalin 2013).

In the 1990s, the failure of structural adjustment programmes to achieve their desired outcomes was partly responsible for a "shift towards thinking about development in terms of poverty reduction and inequality" (Tomalin 2013: 34). A significant change in development thinking occurred with the emergence of the notion of "human development", which emphasized that people's well-being is not solely dependent upon economic growth but includes health, education, social relationships, the realization of rights, physical and economic security, and access to services (Haynes 2007; Rakodi 2016). The idea of human development was influenced by the "capabilities approach" of Amartya Sen (1999). For Sen, the purpose of development was "to improve human lives by expanding the range of things that a person can be and do, such as to be healthy and well nourished, to be knowledgeable, and to participate in community life" (Fukuda-Parr 2003: 303).[8] The emphasis on human development gave rise to the United Nations Development Programme's Human Development Index (HDI), which measures sustainable development using a set of three indicators, reflecting human well-being: life expectancy (as a proxy for health achievement), adult literacy and educational enrolment (as a proxy for educational attainment) and per capita income (Neumayer 2001). The purpose of the HDI was to provide a measurement of development that does not rely solely on economic indicators. The idea of human development has become a key factor driving the work of development professionals (Haynes 2007). To some extent, it resonates with the holistic understanding of development embraced by Nigerian Pentecostals, as we will see later in the book.

The emphasis on poverty reduction and human development was reflected in the Millennium Development Goals (MDGs). As Fukuda-Parr (2004: 395) notes, the adoption of the MDGs reflected an "important endorsement of the central objectives of poverty and human well-being". The post-2015 Sustainable Development Goals (SDGs), which replaced the MDGs, are part of a broader agenda that includes environmental, social, and economic development as well as food security and gender equality (Fukuda-Parr 2016). While the MDGs included only eight goals with 21 targets, the SDGs comprise 17 goals with 169 targets. In contrast to the MDGs, which focused on meeting the basic needs of the poorest countries, the SDGs represent a global agenda for sustainable development that encompasses both developing and developed countries.

Various critical responses to conventional development models have arisen, stimulated by concerns that "economic growth is not happening quickly enough, that it was not reaching the poorest or that it was directed in ways that served the interests of northern economies" (Tomalin 2013: 37). Some scholars reject top-down approaches in favour of more participatory, locally relevant and people-centred models of development (Lunn 2009; Bompani and Frahm-Arp 2010). As Tomalin (2013: 38) notes, "bottom-up" approaches "opened up space for conceptions of development that differed from the mainstream and that could, among other things, be influenced by people's religions and culture".

A more radical response is post-development theory which emerged in the late 1980s and early 1990s, calling for "alternatives to development" based on "models of progress and improvement rooted in local traditions rather than Western capitalist forms" (Freeman 2012: 9). According to Freeman (2012: 9), the model of social change espoused by African Pentecostals is different from both the mainstream development and post-development views:

> While they [Pentecostals] embrace the mainstream capitalist "spirit of development" with its desire for wealth and commodity consumption, they maintain a magico-religious worldview in sharp contrast to mainstream development's rational secularism. And while they acknowledge the existence of traditional practices and values, they seek to break away from them, in

> stark contrast to the post-development theorists who seek to base new models of the future in these traditional pasts.

As I will show in the book, there are both commonalities and contrasts between Nigerian Pentecostal conceptions of development and mainstream development theory and praxis. Pentecostals and development practitioners find common ground in their focus on empowerment and transformation even if they pursue these goals differently. For Nigerian Pentecostals, however, development is not conceived exclusively in materialist terms but includes reference to an invisible world of spirits that can either hinder or hasten development. I will examine this further in Chapter 1.

In the field of international development, there has also been an increasing trend towards engagement with faith-based organizations (FBOs) which have featured strongly in UN policy agendas since the early 2000s (Tomalin, Haustein, and Kidy 2019). Clarke and Jennings (2008: 2) consider the Millennium Declaration (2000) and the MDGs to lie at the heart of the new engagement with religion, because "faith communities and organisations to which they give rise are … seen as important actors in galvanizing the moral commitment on which the MDGs depend and in popularizing them in local churches, mosques and synagogues". The UN Inter-agency Task Force on Religion and Development was established in 2010 to "facilitate knowledge exchange; provide a resource pool of experiences; and strengthen partnerships with faith-based organizations" (UN Environment 2018: 4). It played a leading role in engaging faith communities in the consultation process of the SDGs (Tomalin, Haustein, and Kidy 2019).

Research methodology

This study contributes to the field of religion and development by examining the relationship between popular forms of religiosity and social change through the lens of Nigerian Pentecostalism. The research on which the book is based is primarily qualitative in nature, drawing on ethnographic research conducted in Nigeria and Britain. It adopts an interpretivist approach in order to portray the motives and meanings attached to Pentecostal practices as much as possible from the perspectives of the participants themselves. During fieldwork, I conducted semi-structured interviews with Pentecostal pastors and members, political aspirants, educators, social activists, and leaders of a variety of development ministries and NGOs. In Nigeria, I interviewed 67 pastors and members (45 in Lagos, 18 in Jos, and four in Abuja) belonging to 33 different Pentecostal denominations and independent churches. I also interviewed nine leaders belonging to mainline mission churches in Nigeria. In Britain, I interviewed 62 Pentecostal pastors and members (42 in London and 20 in Birmingham) belonging to 11 different denominations and independent churches. However, most of my respondents in Britain belonged to the RCCG. I also engaged in participant observations of Pentecostal church meetings, conference events, and development initiatives in

Nigeria and Britain. In addition, I visited a number of Pentecostal healthcare, educational and rehabilitation initiatives and institutions.

Given the widespread use of media by Nigerian Pentecostals, data from oral interviews and observations was supplemented by the collection of media products. These included newspapers, church magazines, books, and Bible studies as well as CDs/DVDs of congregational worship services and conference events. Church websites proved an invaluable source of information, providing insight into the churches' self-understanding, theological beliefs, organizational structure, ministry outreaches, and development activities. Some congregational websites include sermons, blogs, articles, videos, and photos of Pentecostal worship services and social programmes. Content analysis of congregational websites was particularly important for my investigation of Nigerian diaspora churches in the United States and for exploring the transnational dimension of Nigerian Pentecostalism.

In 2011, I conducted a questionnaire survey in Nigeria which generated 906 usable questionnaires. These included 439 Nigerian Pentecostals and 467 Nigerian Charismatics. Henceforth, I will refer to it as the Nigeria Survey. Random sampling was not possible due to logistical and time restraints during fieldwork. It was decided to conduct the survey mainly in Pentecostal and mainline church theological institutions because the response from the congregations was poor. Most respondents were from south-western Nigeria, though questionnaires were also distributed in south-eastern and northern regions of the country. The sample included respondents from 97 different Pentecostal denominations and independent churches, and 22 different mainline denominations. However, the majority of respondents belonged to the following churches: Christ Apostolic Church, RCCG, Fountain of Life Church, The Redeemed Evangelical Mission (TREM), Anglican, Baptist, and Methodist. The demographic profile of respondents included roughly equal numbers of pastors and lay persons (52 per cent and 48 per cent respectively). However, there is a significant gender bias (85 per cent male and 15 per cent female), reflecting the predominance of male students in the seminaries.

The main research locations were Lagos, Jos, Abuja (Nigeria), London, and Birmingham (Britain). However, most of my fieldwork was conducted in Lagos and London.

Lagos is one of the world's largest cities, an increasingly fragmented and unregulated urban space characterized by a lack of basic infrastructure, traffic congestion, insecurity, and a growing gulf between rich and poor. This has made it especially fertile ground for Pentecostal churches with their social support networks and promises of power to overcome sickness, poverty, unemployment and evil forces (Ukah 2004). London is a global city with a multicultural and cosmopolitan character, reflected in the diversity of its ethnic and religious communities. Black Africans and Caribbeans account for a third of the city's churchgoers (Brierley 2017). It also has the highest concentration of Nigerian Pentecostal churches in Europe, occupying a variety of local spaces, ranging from former industrial warehouses and office spaces to cinemas and traditional church buildings. Not surprisingly, most churches are concentrated in areas where there are clusters of Nigerian immigrants.

During fieldwork, a range of Pentecostal denominations and independent churches were studied in order to gather material from the diversity of Pentecostal Christianity. These included representatives from the different types of Pentecostalism as well as churches with transnational networks. More detailed case studies included the RCCG, Winners Chapel, Fountain of Life Church, Covenant Christian Centre, Daystar Christian Centre, God Bless Nigeria Church, The Redeemed Evangelical Mission (TREM), House on the Rock, Mountain of Fire and Miracles, and Assemblies of God Nigeria.

It is important to consider positionality. My status as a European outsider presented potential problems related to gaining entry into the field and understanding Nigerian Pentecostalism from a participant point of view. However, my involvement in the British Charismatic movement since the early 1980s, and my experience as a theological educator in Nigeria, facilitated my access to Pentecostal churches and made it easier for me to become an active participant rather than a detached observer. Between 1990 and 2007, I spent nine years in Nigeria teaching in three different theological institutions, most recently in the city of Jos where I attended a Pentecostal church called the Redeemed People's Mission. On my return to Britain in 2007 to join the NORFACE-funded research project at Birmingham, I became a member of a RCCG congregation for three years.

Outline of the book

The next chapter examines the role of faith-based organizations (FBOs) in development, with a particular focus on the Nigerian context. Here I introduce some of the Pentecostal "ministries" and NGOs that feature in the book before discussing key characteristics of Nigerian Pentecostal churches that shape their understandings of development and their development activities. Chapters 2 to 8 each address one of the topics included in the 2030 agenda for sustainable development as expressed in the SDGs. Chapter 2 examines Nigerian Pentecostal engagement with the economic domain, with a particular focus on the prosperity gospel and initiatives geared towards economic empowerment and business entrepreneurship. Chapter 3 considers the intersection between Pentecostalism and governance in Nigeria and discusses some of the contextual and cultural factors influencing Pentecostal political behaviour.

The following two chapters focus on areas that have long been associated with faith-based social action in Africa: education and healthcare. Chapter 4 examines Pentecostal engagement with Nigeria's educational sector. Here I look at a range of educational initiatives including schools, universities, and capacity-building NGOs. Chapter 5 investigates Pentecostal approaches to healing and healthcare, paying particular attention to the influence of theology, culture, and context on Pentecostal health-seeking practices. It also explores Pentecostal responses to some of the major health challenges in Nigeria. The next two chapters both address human rights issues that feature prominently in the SDGs. Chapter 6 examines Pentecostal responses to human rights infringements against women, young people, and children. I examine some of the Pentecostal ministries and NGOs addressing the needs of street children, commercial sex-workers and trafficking victims. Chapter 7 considers Pentecostal responses to violence and violation of rights to religious freedom in northern Nigeria. Finally, Chapter 8 investigates the nexus between Nigerian Pentecostalism, migration and development with a particular focus on Britain and the United States where some of the largest Nigerian diaspora communities are located. The book is completed by a short conclusion, which summarizes the main research findings, examines various factors that account for the heterogeneity of African Pentecostal approaches to development, and discusses some of the implications for the engagement between African Pentecostalism and the development sector.

Notes

1 The issue of corruption was brought to the fore over allegations of money laundering directed against Chris Oyakhilome, senior pastor of Christ Embassy, one of the largest Pentecostal denominations in Nigeria. See Johnson (2010). Kingsway International Christian Centre (KICC), Winners Chapel, and Christ Embassy have all been investigated by Britain's Charity Commission for financial mismanagement.

2 Examples of recent research on religion and development includes the work carried out by the DFID funded "Religion and Development" project at the University of Birmingham and the "Religion and Global Development" program administered by the Berkeley Centre for Religion, Peace, and World Affairs at Georgetown University.

3 For discussions of the relationship between Pentecostalism and Aladura Christianity, see Wariboko (2014: 22–26) and Kalu (2008: 68–82). Kalu (2008) identifies two positions: those who emphasize the similarities between the two movements due to their shared worldview and pneumatic emphasis, and those who emphasize elements of discontinuity. Kalu (2008) criticized the former for sometimes ignoring the insiders' perspective and the demonization of AICs by the newer Pentecostal churches. In Nigeria, Christ Apostolic Church is the only Aladura church accepted by neo-Pentecostals (Marshall 2009). However, some of the other Aladura churches self-identify as Pentecostal on their congregational websites.

4 This figure is a projection from the last national census (2006), when the estimated population was 140 million.

5 Winners Chapel boasts the largest congregations in Ghana, Kenya, and Zambia (Gifford 2004, 2015).

6 Current estimates indicate that there were 191,183 Nigerian-born residents in the UK in 2011, up from 87,000 in 2001, with the large majority living in London (based on the 2001 and 2011 census data). This does not include undocumented migrants and British citizens of Nigerian descent.

7 These are Kingsway International Christian Centre, RCCG Jesus House, Winners Chapel, New Wine Church, Glory House, Victorious Pentecostal Assembly, and Christ Faith Tabernacle.

8 Sen's influence is reflected in the following excerpt from the UNDP's 2001 Human Development Report (HDR):

> The most basic capabilities for human development are to lead long and healthy lives, to be knowledgeable, to have access to the resources needed for a decent standard of living and to be able to participate in the life of the community.
>
> (United Nations Development Programme 2001)

References

Adeoye, Aanu (2019) "The Young Women Leading Nigeria's #MeToo Revolution", *Vice News*, 17 July, available at: www.vice.com/en_uk/article/xwnj77/nigeria-me-too-movement-biodun-fatoyinbo (accessed 26 September 2019).

Adogame, Afe (2016) "African Christianities and the Politics of Development from Below", *HTS Theological Studies* 72(4): 1–11.

Akintayo, Eribake (2014) "Winners Chapel Has Six Million Members Spread Across 147 Countries – Oyedepo", *Vanguard Nigeria*, 27 December, available at: www.vanguardngr.com/2014/12/winners-chapel-has-six-million-members-spread-across-147-countries-oyedepo/ (accessed 18 May 2018).

Anderson, Allan H. (2000) *Zion and Pentecost. The Spirituality and Experience of Pentecostal and Zionist/Apostolic Churches in South Africa*, Pretoria: University of South Africa Press.

Ayegboyin, Deji I. (2005) "'But Deliver us from Evil …' The Riposte of the MFM and its Implications for the 'Reverse' in Mission", *Orita. Ibadan Journal of Religious Studies* 37(1/2): 33–64.

Bompani, Barbara and Maria Frahm-Arp (2010) "Introduction: Development and Politics from Below: New Conceptual Interpretations", in Barbara Bompani and Maria Frahm-Arp (eds) *Development and Politics from Below. Exploring Religious Spaces in the African State*, Basingstoke: Palgrave Macmillan, pp. 1–22.

Brierley, Peter (2017) *UK Church Statistics, Number 3: 2018 Edition*, Tonbridge: ADBC Publishers.

Burchardt, Marian (2013) "'We Are Saving the Township': Pentecostalism, Faith-Based Organisations, and Development in South Africa", *The Journal of Modern African Studies* 51(4): 627–651.

Burgess, Richard (2008) *Nigeria's Christian Revolution. The Civil War Revival and its Pentecostal Progeny (1967–2008)*. Carlisle: Paternoster.

Burgess, Richard (2009) "African Pentecostal Spirituality and Civic Engagement: The Case of the Redeemed Christian Church of God in Britain", *Journal of Beliefs & Values* 30(3): 255–273.

Burgess, Richard, Kim Knibbe, and Anna Quaas (2010) "Nigerian-initiated Pentecostal Churches as a Social Force in Europe: The Case of the Redeemed Christian Church of God", *PentecoStudies* 9(1): 97–121.

Cartledge, Mark J., Sarah Dunlop, Heather Buckingham, and Sophie Bremner (2019) *Megachurches and Social Engagement: Public Theology in Practice*, Leiden: E. J. Brill.

Clarke, Gerard and Michael Jennings (2008) "Introduction", in Gerard Clarke and Michael Jennings (eds) *Development, Civil Society and Faith-based Organisations: Bridging the Sacred and the Secular*, New York: Palgrave Macmillan, 1–16.

Clarke, Matthew (2011) *Development and Religion: Theology and Practice*. Cheltenham: Edward Elgar Publishing.

Clarke, Matthew (2015) "Friend or Foe? Finding Common Ground Between Development and Pentecostalism", *PentecoStudies* 14(2):156–175.

..n, Séverine and Carole Rakodi, (2011) "Revisiting Religion: Development ..udies Thirty Years On", *World Development* 39(1): 45–54.

..ilger, Hansjörg (2009) "Doing Better? Religion, the Virtue-ethics of Development, and the Fragmentation of Health Politics in Tanzania", *Africa Today* 56(1): 89–110.

Ellison, Marc (2019) "Branded and Beaten. The Children Accused of Witchcraft and Murder", BBC News, available at: www.bbc.co.uk/news/resources/idt-sh/nigeria_children_witchcraft (accessed 25 September 2019).

Freeman, Dena (ed.) (2012) *Pentecostalism and Development: Churches, NGOs and Social Change in Africa*, London, UK: Palgrave Macmillan.

Freeman, Dena (2012) "The Pentecostal Ethic and the Spirit of Development", in Dena Freeman (ed.) *Pentecostalism and Development: Churches, NGOs and Social Change in Africa*, London: Palgrave Macmillan, pp. 1–38.

Freeman, Dena (2015) "Pentecostalism and Economic Development in Sub-Saharan Africa", in Emma Tomalin (ed.) *The Routledge Handbook of Religions and Global Development*, London: Routledge, pp. 128–140.

Fukuda-Parr, Sakiko (2003) "The Human Development Paradigm: Operationalizing Sen's Ideas on Capabilities", *Feminist Economics* 9(2–3): 301–317.

Fukuda-Parr, Sakiko (2004) "Millennium Development Goals: Why They Matter", *Global Governance* 10: 395–402.

Fukuda-Parr, Sakiko (2016) "From the Millennium Development Goals to the Sustainable Development Goals: Shifts in Purpose, Concept, and Politics of Global Goal Setting for Development", *Gender & Development* 24(1): 43–52.

Gaiya, Musa A. (2015) "Charismatic and Pentecostal Social Orientations in Nigeria", *Nova Religio: The Journal of Alternative and Emergent Religions* 18(3): 63–79.

Garbin, David (2013) "Visibility and Invisibility of Migrant Faith in the City: Diaspora Religion and the Politics of Emplacement of Afro-Christian Churches", *Journal of Ethnic and Migration Studies* 39(5): 677–696.

Gifford, Paul (2004) *Ghana's New Christianity. Pentecostalism in a Globalizing African Economy*, London: Hurst & Co.

Gifford, Paul (2015) *Christianity, Development and Modernity in Africa*, London: Hurst & Co.

Gledhill, Ruth (2017) "Enoch Adeboye Steps Down as Head of Redeemed Christian Church of God in Nigeria", 9 January, *Christianity Today*, available at: www.christiantoday.com/article/enoch-adeboye-steps-down-as-head-of-redeemed-christian-church-of-god/103720.htm (accessed 15 May 2018).

Gornik, Mark R. (2011) *Word Made Global: Stories of African Christianity in New York City*, Grand Rapids, MI: Eerdmans.

Hanciles, Jehu J. (2008) *Beyond Christendom. Globalization, African Migration, and the Transformation of the West*, Maryknoll, NY: Orbis.

Harris, Hermione (2006) *Yoruba in Diaspora. An African Church in London*, Basingstoke: Palgrave Macmillan.

Haynes, Jeffrey (2007) *Religion and Development. Conflict or Cooperation?* New York: Palgrave Macmillan.

Haynes, Jeffrey (2008) *Development Studies*, Cambridge: Polity.

Johnson, Bamidele (2010) "The Pastorpreneur's Fresh Scandal", *The News (Lagos)*, 20 December: 19–21.

Johnson, Todd (2013) "Global Pentecostal Demographics", in Donald E. Miller, Kimon H. Sergeant and Richard Flory (eds) *Spirit and Power: The Growth and Global Impact of Pentecostalism*, Oxford: Oxford University Press, pp. 319–328.

Kalu, Ogbu U. (2008) *African Pentecostalism: An Introduction*, Oxford: Oxford University Press.

Lunn, Jenny (2009) "The Role of Religion, Spirituality and Faith in Development: A Critical Theory Approach", *Third World Quarterly* 30(5): 937–951.

Marshall, Ruth (2009) *Political Spiritualities: The Pentecostal Revolution in Nigeria*, Chicago, IL: University of Chicago Press.

MFM UK (2019) "MFM Branches UK", available at: www.mountainoffire.org.uk/index.php/branches (accessed 12 September 2019).

MFM USA (2016) "MFM USA Branches", available at: http://mfmusa.org/branches/ (accessed 12 September 2019).

Miller, Donald E. and Tetsunao Yamamori (2007) *Global Pentecostalism: The New Face of Christian Social Engagement*, Berkeley: University of California Press.

National Bureau of Statistics (2019) "National Population Estimates", National Population Commission and National Bureau of Statistics Estimates, available at: http://nigerianstat.gov.ng/elibrary?queries[search]=population (accessed 23 September 2019).

Neumayer, Eric (2001) "The Human Development Index and Sustainability: A Constructive Proposal", *Ecological Economics* 39(1): 101–114.

Obadare, Ebenezer (2016) "'Raising Righteous Billionaires': The Prosperity Gospel Reconsidered", *HTS Theological Studies* 72(4): 1–8.

Obadare, Ebenezer (2018) *Pentecostal Republic. Religion and the Struggle for State Power in Nigeria*, London: Zed Books.

Ojo, Matthews A. (2006) *The End-time Army: Charismatic Movements in Nigeria*, Trenton, NJ: Africa World Press.

Olupona, Jacob O. and Regina Gemignani (2007) "Introduction", in Jacob O. Olupona and Regina Gemignani (eds) *African Immigrant Religions in America*, New York: New York University Press, pp. 1–26.

Pew Research Center (2011) "Global Christianity: A Report on the Size and Distribution of the World's Christian Population", available at: www.pewforum.org/2011/12/19/global-christianity-exec/ (accessed 15 September 2019).

Rakodi, Carole (2016) "A Framework for Analysing the Links Between Religion and Development", in Carole Rakodi (ed.) *Religion, Religious Organizations and Development: Scrutinising Religious Perspectives and Organisations*, London: Routledge, pp. 14–30.

RCCG (2017) "Welcome", available at: http://rccg.org/welcome/ (accessed 21 August 2019).

RCCG UK (2019) "RCCG Church Locator", available at: www.rccguk.church/rccg-church-locator/ (accessed 19 September 2019).

RCCGNA (2019) "USA Parishes", available at: https://rccgna.org/regions/parishes/usa-parishes/ (accessed 12 September 2019).

Sen, Amartya (1999) *Development as Freedom*, Oxford: Oxford University Press.

Ter Haar, Gerrie (2011) *Religion and Development: Ways of Transforming the World*, London: Hurst & Company.

Togarasei, Lovemore (2011) "The Pentecostal Gospel of Prosperity in African Contexts of Poverty: An Appraisal", *Exchange* 40(4): 336–350.

Tomalin, Emma (2007) *Religious Studies and Development: A Literature Review*, Birmingham: Religions and Development WP 6.

Tomalin, Emma (2013) *Religions and Development*, London: Routledge.

Tomalin, Emma (2015) "Introduction", in Emma Tomalin (ed.) *The Routledge Handbook of Religions and Global Development*, London: Routledge, pp. 1–14.

Tomalin, Emma (2018) "Religions, Poverty Reduction and Global Development Institutions", *Palgrave Communications* 4(1): 1–12, available at: www.nature.com/articles/s41599-018-0167-8 (accessed 14 October 2019).

Tomalin, Emma, Jörg Haustein, and Shabaana Kidy (2019) "Religion and the Sustainable Development Goals", *The Review of Faith & International Affairs* 17(2): 102–118.

Topping, Alexandra (2014) "Church Linked to Witchcraft Row Applies to Open UK School", *Guardian*, 22 August, available at: www.theguardian.com/education/2014/aug/22/church-witchcraft-row-uk-school (accessed 25 September 2019).

Ukah, Asonzeh (2004) "Pentecostalism, Religious Expansion and the City: Lessons from the Nigerian Bible Belt", in Peter Probst and Gerd Spittler (eds) *Between Resistance and Expansion: Explorations of Local Vitality in Africa*, Münster: Transaction Publishers, pp. 415–443.

Ukah, Azonzeh (2008) *A New Paradigm of Pentecostal Power. A Study of the Redeemed Christian Church of God*, Trenton, NJ: Africa World Press.

United Nations Development Programme (2001) *Human Development Report 2001: Making New Technologies Work for Human Development*, New York: Oxford University Press.

UN Environment (2018) Engaging with Faith-based Organizations, UN Environment Strategy, January, pp. 1–19, available at: https://wedocs.unep.org/bitstream/handle/20.500.11822/25989/UNEP%20Strategy%20Engaging%20FBOs.pdf?sequence=1&isAllowed=y (accessed 13 July 2019).

Wariboko, Nimi (2014) *Nigerian Pentecostalism*, Rochester, NY: University of Rochester Press.

Wimmer, Andreas and Nina Glick Schiller (2003) "Methodological Nationalism and Beyond: Nation-state Building, Migration and the Social Sciences", *Global Networks* 2(4): 301–334.

1 NGOs, faith-based organizations (FBOs), and churches

Introduction

Faith-based organizations (FBOs) are increasingly recognized as partners in development by the international community, including the UN. In January 2018, the United Nations Environment Programme (UN Environment), which coordinates the UN's environmental strategy, published a report entitled "Engaging with Faith-Based Organizations" in which it identified FBOs as "important players in eradicating poverty, improving people's health, protecting the environment and thus achieving sustainable development" (UN Environment 2018: 2).

The focus of this chapter is on Pentecostal FBOs of Nigerian provenance. The chapter begins with a general discussion of FBOs and their inclusion in the international development agenda. Here I engage with some of the issues and debates discussed in the literature on FBOs. Second, I examine the Nigerian context and the proliferation of NGOs and FBOs (including Pentecostal FBOs) in recent decades. Finally, the chapter explores some of the key characteristics of Nigerian Pentecostal churches that help to shape their understanding of development and their developmental activities. An awareness of the beliefs, practices and religious assets of Pentecostal FBOs is important if development actors are to engage with them effectively.

FBOs and development

The term "faith-based organization" began to feature in Western public policy discourse in the late 1990s. In the USA, where the term is most widely used, faith-based social service re-emerged on the political agenda during the Clinton and George W. Bush administrations. In 1996, the Republican Congress passed and President Clinton signed into law the Work Opportunity Reconciliation Act, as part of a neoliberal agenda to roll back the state and reform the social welfare system (Cnaan and Boddie 2006). Under the Charitable Choice provision of the Act, faith-based organizations "can compete for public funding on equal footing with secular providers without giving up their essential religious character" (McGrew and Cnaan 2006: 23). Charitable Choice provision had been proposed by Senator John Ashcroft, a Pentecostal Christian, to encourage the participation of non-profit organizations (including FBOs) in federally funded welfare service provision (Cnaan and Boddie 2002). More controversial was President Bush's "Faith-Based Initiative", introduced in 2001, which pledged to increase FBO involvement in publicly funded social service provision (Ebaugh *et al.* 2003). The "Faith-Based Initiative" represented a change in thinking about church-state relations and signified "a move away from strict separation towards greater accommodation of religion by government" (Segars 2003: 4).[1]

In Britain, FBOs have also become increasingly prominent in welfare provision and public policy in recent decades. Since the mid-1990s, successive governments have recognized the potential of faith communities to contribute to social capital and welfare provision, especially in urban contexts characterized by fragmentation, racial and religious tensions, and increasing crime levels. Faith communities are also seen as sources of volunteers and physical resources (Furbey and Macey 2005; Dinham and Lowndes 2009). The New Labour government (1997–2010) introduced a series of initiatives intended to strengthen the relationship between government and religious communities (Jochum, Pratten, and Wilding 2007). Since 2010, the Conservative-Liberal Democrat Coalition and successive Conservative governments have sought to develop a localism agenda, heralded by the introduction of former Prime Minister Cameron's notion of the "Big Society" and the 2011 Localism Act. The Big Society was intended to be contrasted with the big state of New Labour and to endorse the proactive role of the voluntary sector in fixing Britain's "broken society" (Alcock 2010: 380). A key aim of the localism agenda is to return power from the state to the citizen and place the responsibility of social change in the hands of the people (Dinham and Jackson 2012). It is seen as a potential opportunity for voluntary groups, including FBOs, to play a greater role in delivering social services to their communities. The British government also recognizes the important contribution made by faith communities to international development. In June 2011, the Department for International Development (DFID) formed the Faith Partnerships Working Group to strengthen its "collaboration with faith groups to transform poor people's lives and achieve the Millennium Development Goals" (DFID 2012: 2). DFID works with a variety of faith groups in Britain and around the world.[2]

Religious actors have a long history of development activity in Africa stretching back to the colonial era (Haustein and Tomalin 2017). However, the increased interest in FBOs by international development actors is linked to the "NGO-ization" of African society since the 1980s in response to structural adjustment and neoliberal reforms imposed by international donors and implemented by African governments (Freeman 2012; Burchardt 2012; Dilger 2009). Structural adjustment was accompanied by a change in international aid policy as funds were increasingly channelled through international and domestic NGOs rather than given directly to governments. As Freeman (2012) notes, this change in foreign aid policy led to an explosion of NGOs involved in a variety of development activities. International development agencies favoured NGOs because it was believed that, as grassroots organizations, they "would be able to stimulate the participation of local people in their own development and empower them to take up new activities that would increase their wellbeing and lead to economic growth" (Freeman 2012: 6). Initially, religious institutions had to accept constraints due to the secularism of development aid. Haustein and Tomalin (2017: 87–88) note that, even before the emergence of FBO terminology, some religious actors in Asia and Africa functioned as "gatekeepers to local communities to facilitate the entrance of NGOs", while others "made important modifications to gain NGO funding, by founding development wings or adjusting their project plans and funding applications to the required language". However, the recent re-emergence of religion in development policy and practice has meant that religious institutions are now encouraged to form FBOs to tap into funds reserved for religious organizations. Burchardt (2012: 15) refers to this as the FBO-ization of the religious field, the "expansion of activities in the cultural vicinity of churches that are carried out by church members, organized through voluntary non-profit organizations, and oriented towards social service provision and advocacy".

One reason that development donors have increasingly chosen to support FBOs is their perceived comparative advantage over not only state organizations but also secular NGOs in the achievement of development interventions (Tomalin 2016; Leurs 2012). Scholars refer to the added value of spiritual and cultural capital that religious groups can contribute to development, their ability to mobilize their members, their closeness to grassroots communities, their financial self-sufficiency, and their capacity to deliver services efficiently and cost effectively (Leurs 2012; Berger 2003; James 2011). However, as Tomalin (2016: 79) notes, there is "little evidence to support generalized claims that FBOs are distinctive and have a comparative advantage over secular NGOs". Most of the studies available are case studies of individual FBOs rather than comparative assessments of FBOs and secular organizations. Existing comparative studies show considerable overlap between the development aims and activities of FBOs and NGOs (e.g. Davis *et al.* 2001; Leurs 2012). Another challenge of assessing FBOs in development relates to whether a "presumed distinctive attribute of an FBO is a product of its faith identity" or other non-religious factors (Tomalin 2016: 78).

There is a lack of conceptual clarity in the literature about how we should define and classify FBOs working in development. An ongoing debate is whether local congregations or the denominational bodies that run them should be included in the category "FBO". Some scholars resist the inclusion of congregations and limit the definition of an FBO to registered organizations that resemble NGOs (e.g. Jeavons 2004). However, this runs the risk of excluding much informal faith-based development work with which donors might usefully engage (Tomalin 2016). Clarke and Jennings (2008: 6) argue for a broader definition which includes "any organization that derives inspiration and guidance for its activities from the teachings and principles of the faith or from a particular interpretation or school of thought within the faith". McGrew and Cnaan (2006: 28) suggest that a congregation be considered a subset of faith-based organizations, albeit one whose primary purpose is not to provide social services but religious services. The UN shares this more inclusive definition (UNHCR 2014).

In this book, I make a distinction between formal FBOs of the NGO variety and informal FBOs such as Pentecostal congregations that often include development initiatives among their outreach ministries. In any given African community, one may find a "complex web of initiatives", including programmes run by multiple faith-affiliated sources alongside an array of international faith-based and secular agencies (Olivier and Woden 2014: 54).

One challenge for Western donors and policy-makers seeking to engage with FBOs is the diversity of religious organizations involved in development activities. Various typologies of FBOs have been proposed to help researchers and development actors to navigate the terrain (Clarke 2008; Sider and Unrah 2004; Tomalin, Haustein, and Kidy 2019). Sider and Unrah (2004) categorize FBOs in terms of the extent to which faith is manifest in different aspects of their work. At one end of the spectrum are "faith-permeated" organizations, in which "the connection with religious faith is evident at all levels of mission, staffing, governance, and support". At the other end are secular organizations which have "no reference to religion in their mission or founding history" (2004: 119–120). They argue that classifying FBOs in this way helps funders choose appropriate organizations with which to work and also helps FBOs to understand and describe their religious character (2004: 132). In Africa, the complexity of faith-based development activity at local community level makes it difficult to classify FBOs into discrete types. As Olivier and Woden (2014: 68) note, "the bulk of community-level work often spontaneously emerges out of 'congregations' or is linked to individuals motivated by personal faith". These informal community initiatives are difficult to know, measure, and support.

Some scholars have questioned the usefulness of the FBO/secular NGO distinction, especially in contexts where religion permeates almost every aspect of people's lives (e.g. Tomalin 2013; Haustein and Tomalin 2017). As Tomalin (2013: 227) notes,

> the model of an NGO-like FBO does not capture all types of religious organizations engaged in development activities, and the term "faith-based" may reflect a largely Christian view of religion and a Western (mainly US) context characterised by particular forms of secularism.

She argues that the way in which the debate about the distinctiveness of FBOs is articulated "reflects political priorities as well as a desire to promote FBOs as viable development partners, worthy of donor support" (2013: 227). Tomalin, Haustein, and Kidy (2019: 105) identify seven types of "faith actor" engaged in development:

1 Large, formal international FBOs, often with strong links to the UN.
2 International apex bodies representing faith traditions.
3 Formal FBOs and networks such as inter-religious councils.
4 Smaller formal FBOs that may have transnational ties but are not necessarily linked to international development organizations.

5 FBOs engaged in local development work, which may be linked to local places of worship, and are less likely to have formal links to the UN and other international processes.
6 Religious leaders invited to participate in global and national policy debates.
7 Places of worship in the Global South that may also support development at a local level.

As we will see, most Nigerian Pentecostal faith actors involved in development work belong to types (4), (5) and (7). Many Pentecostal development initiatives are carried out by the social engagement arms of local places of worship. Increasingly, however, Pentecostal churches and individuals are establishing formal Pentecostal NGOs, sometimes with links to the UN and other international development organizations.

The Nigerian context

The growth of FBOs in Nigeria is closely connected to the proliferation of NGOs in recent decades. The dramatic rise of NGOs in postcolonial Nigeria began in the 1980s during military governments (Smith 2012). Scholars attribute this growth to three main factors. First, economic decline and gaps in service delivery arising from the oil glut and structural adjustment encouraged the emergence of NGOs. Second, the political context under successive military dictatorships prompted the emergence of pro-democracy and human rights civil society organizations. Finally, donor preferences for funding NGOs rather than the state, which was deemed incompetent and corrupt, created a conducive environment for NGO proliferation (Leurs 2012; Davis *et al.* 2011; Obadare 2007). NGOs in Nigeria are involved in a variety of areas including poverty-related issues, HIV/AIDS, youth development, democracy and governance, advocacy, health, education, research and policy, and environment issues.

FBOs have also played an important role in development, especially in the areas of health, education, community development, human rights advocacy, and conflict resolution (Odumosu, Olaniyi, and Alonge 2009; Leurs 2012). Christian FBOs include apex bodies such as the Nigerian Catholic Bishop's Conference, the Christian Association of Nigeria, and the Nigerian Supreme Council of Islamic Affairs; development organizations such as CRUDAN and CHAN; socio-political organizations such as the Justice Development and Peace Caritas Commission (Catholic); missionary organizations; and interfaith organizations such as the Interfaith HIV/AIDS Council of Nigeria (Odumosu, Olaniyi, and Alonge 2009). As Leurs (2012: 707) notes, many "are now labelled (and label themselves) FBOs and their development agendas have been influenced by international donor agendas and associated funding streams".

The rapid proliferation of NGOs in Nigeria has led to unhealthy competition for donor funds and to the perception of NGOs by the Nigerian public as corrupt and unaccountable (Smith 2012; Leurs 2012). The primary regulator of NGOs, including FBOs, is the Corporate Affairs Commission (CAC) via the Companies and Allied Matters Act (CAMA) 1990. FBOs that register with CAC are required to submit reports of annual activities. Under Nigerian law they are non-governmental organizations and non-profit in orientation. However, government regulatory mechanisms lack the capacity to hold NGOs accountable (Olarinmoye 2011). The alternative is self-regulation. In 1992, representatives from 60 Nigerian NGOs met with the Federal Ministry of Health and several international organizations such as USAID, UNICEF, the World Bank, the British Council, and UNESCO to discuss the organizational challenges facing disparate civil society organizations (NNNGO 2018a). Following the meeting, the Nigeria Network of NGOs (NNNGO) was established in order to support Nigerian NGOs in their developmental activities, encourage transparency in the sector, and enable collaboration with international and government agencies in the implementation of effective development programmes. Since then, it has become the largest network of NGOs in the country, representing over 2,400 organizations, including many FBOs (NNNGO 2018b).[3] Members must subscribe to the NNNGO code of conduct and conform with international best practices for the Third Sector. They do not necessarily have to be registered with the CAC but must have their ways of working, constitution, and bye laws written down in publicly available documents. The issue of NGO accountability was brought to a head with the proposed 2017 NGO Bill (HB585), intended to regulate the activities of non-profit organizations by making it compulsory for all NGOs to register with the government. However, it eventually failed in parliament following strong opposition from civic groups, activists, and faith groups (including the Pentecostal Fellowship of Nigeria) who believed that, if passed, the Bill would limit the freedom of civil society (Oluseyi 2018).

In the course of my research, I encountered a range of Pentecostal development initiatives, including feeding programmes for the poor, rehabilitation centres, orphanages, ministries to widows, prison ministries, health clinics, HIV/AIDS programmes, microfinance projects, water/borehole projects, peacebuilding initiatives, and political organizations. Many of these are informal "ministries" run by church congregations and denominations as part of their corporate social outreach. Pentecostal churches in Nigeria have also established institutions such as hospitals, schools, and universities. Some of the larger churches run multiple social ministries covering different development sectors. For example, the outreach programmes of Fountain of Life Church in Lagos include a feeding programme called the Lord's Kitchen, a rehabilitation programme for street boys called Grace Springs Home, a vocational skills centre, a hospital, a HIV/AIDS programme, a farm project, a prison ministry, and an educational support programme. Founded in 1992 by Pastors Taiwo and Bimbo Odukoya, the Fountain of Life Church has an estimated 8,000 members.[4]

Significantly, Pentecostal churches and individuals in Nigeria are also establishing FBOs of the NGO variety. Pentecostal NGOs often start out as informal ministries but assume more formalized structures in their quest for recognition and funding from donor organizations. Many are registered under Section C of CAMA 1990 and so take the form of trustee incorporated NGOs. Their websites include information about trustees, management structure, recognitions and awards, external partnerships and sponsorships. They also provide opportunities for people to donate funds and volunteer their service. Most Pentecostal NGOs are founded by pastors and maintain links with their congregations of origin, but others are established by lay church members as independent, free-standing organizations. Some Pentecostal pastors have established multiple NGOs. One example is Ituah Ighodalo, senior pastor of Trinity House, Lagos, who has founded at least eight NGOs. Most Pentecostal NGOs focus on one particular developmental sector, such as health, education, or economic development. However, some of the larger Pentecostal NGOs cover a range of sectors. Based on my research, the majority of Pentecostal NGOs focus on the following four areas: education, economic empowerment, rehabilitation/human rights, and healthcare (see Table 1.1).

In their development efforts, some Nigerian Pentecostals are engaging with development discourse and the international development agenda though further research is needed to gauge the extent of this engagement. As we will see in subsequent chapters, several Pentecostal NGOs make references to the MDGs/SDGs on their websites. One example is a blog posted on the website of the Freedom Foundation, entitled "The Case for the Nigerian Woman", which calls upon governments to address the issue of gender inequality and gender-based violence (GBV):

> Governments that have had any measure of success in addressing inequality and GBV have done so through sheer political will and activism. No change is complete or even possible without government. Studies have shown that any country that focuses on the empowerment of women has the potential to meet all Millennium Development Goals – none of which Nigeria has been able to meet in 15 years.
>
> (Nwakanma 2019)

Pentecostal engagement with development discourse is also evident in conferences hosted by Pentecostal NGOs and universities, such as the annual "Lagos Teachers Conference", organized by Covenant Christian Centre's Edu-Aid, and Covenant University's "Covenant – International Conference on African Developmental Issues" (see Chapter 4). As we will see, some Pentecostal NGOs have formal links with the UN and other international development organizations. Moreover, a number of Pentecostals are acting as advisers to the UN. One example is Tonye Cole, an ordained RCCG minister and a regular speaker at Pentecostal events. Cole is the co-founder of the Sahara Group, a leading African Energy company. In February 2017, Yemi Osinbajo, RCCG pastor and Vice-President of Nigeria, inaugurated the Nigerian Private Sector Advisory Group (PSAG) on Sustainable Development Goals aimed at achieving effective public-private partnerships for the SDGs. The Sahara Group is one of the members of the PSAG (Sustainable Development Goals Fund 2017). Tonye Cole is also a member of the Private Sector Advisory Group of the United Nations Sustainable Development Goals Fund (UNSDG-F).

Table 1.1 Selected Pentecostal NGOs in Nigeria

Category	*Name of NGO*	*Church or independent*
1. Education (schools support, child sponsorship, capacity-building, leadership training)	Courage Educational Foundation	Trinity House
	Edu-Aid	Covenant Christian Centre
	Incubator Africa	Independent
	Institute for National Transformation	Independent
2. Economic empowerment (poverty eradication, microfinance, entrepreneurship education)	Covenant Capital	Covenant Christian Centre
	LEAP Africa	Independent
	Olumide Emmanuel Foundation	Calvary Bible Church
	Success Power International	Daystar Christian Centre
	Fountain Initiative for Social Development	Fountain of Life Church
3. Women empowerment	WIMBIZ	Independent
	Awesome Treasures Foundation	Independent
	Funke Felix Adejumo Foundation	Agape Christian Ministries
4. Youth empowerment	Nehemiah Youth Empowerment Initiative	Independent
	David Oyedepo Foundation	Winners Chapel
5. Orphanage care/child support (orphanages, adoption services, mentoring)	Heritage Homes	Trinity House
	Love Homes Orphanage	Daystar Christian Centre
	Bethesda Child Support Agency	This Present House
6. Community development	Changing our World Foundation	Guiding Light Assembly
7. Rehabilitation/human rights (street children, human trafficking victims/sex workers, drug addicts)	Freedom Foundation	This Present House
	Habitation of Hope	RCCG
	CADAM	RCCG
	Wholistic Outreach	RCCG
	Real Women Foundation	Daystar Christian Centre
	Rock Foundation	House on the Rock
	PBO Foundation	Fountain of Life Church
	Lydia Grace Foundation	Trinity House

continued

Table 1.1 continued

Category	*Name of NGO*	*Church or independent*
8. Healthcare (HIV/AIDS, medical assistance, mental health, reproductive health)	RAPAC	RCCG
	Edensfield Health Initiative	Trinity House
	ELPIS Mental Health Initiative	Trinity House
	Mental Health Foundation	Independent
	Ibidunni Ighodalo Foundation	Trinity House
9. Conflict resolution (relief, victim support, peacebuilding)	YACPIF	Assemblies of God
	Interfaith Mediation Centre	Independent
	Macedonian Initiative	Living Waters Unlimited Church
	Women Without Walls Initiative	Jos Christian Missions International
10. Governance and democracy (election monitoring, political protest, capacity-building)	Save Nigeria Group	Independent
	International Centre for Reconstruction and Development	Latter Rain Assembly

Source: Author

Spiritual and religious capital

We now turn our attention to some of the characteristics of Nigerian Pentecostal churches that influence their understanding of development and their development activities. Baker (2009: 112) distinguishes between "religious capital", defined as "the concrete actions and resources that faith communities contribute", and "spiritual capital" which is the "motivating basis of faith, belief and values that shapes the concrete actions of faith communities and individuals". Drawing on Baker's distinction, I assess the added value of Pentecostal spiritual and religious capital in relation to development beliefs and practices.

Rupture, transformation, and power for service

An important element of Pentecostal spirituality is the focus on rupture and transformation (Meyer 1998; Anderson 2018; Freeman 2012). This is associated with the experience of personal conversion, and an emphasis on ongoing holiness and individual progress. African Pentecostalism has long been associated with personal transformation, and Pentecostals commonly consider conversion as the key to social change (Kalu 2008; Marshall 2009). To some extent, this resonates with the emphasis on social transformation and empowerment in the development sector (Clarke 2015; Ter Haar 2011). However, Pentecostals emphasize the role of the Holy Spirit and divine grace in pursuit of these goals. According to Freeman (2012: 13, 25), the key element of this "transformation of subjectivity" is a "shift from seeing oneself as a victim to seeing oneself as a victor", enabling Pentecostals to "reject passive, fatalistic beliefs and reclaim their agency". Freeman suggests that this sense of empowerment leads to new forms of conduct and social relations, both of which "enhance economic development and foster upward social mobility" (2012: 25).

The main context for encountering the Spirit is congregational worship, which Miller and Yamamori (2007) regard as the root of Pentecostal social engagement, empowering people to help their neighbours and engage in community-building activities. Worship meetings function as important socialization mechanisms, enabling pastors to mobilize and motivate their members. Participation in communal worship and prayer is also an important element of Pentecostal development initiatives, both as a source of empowerment for volunteers and as a means for recipients of social care to break from their former lifestyles and addictions. The worship services I attended often lasted for several hours and included extended periods of congregational singing, interspersed with offerings, testimonies and prayers. This was followed by the sermon, usually preached by a male pastor. Worship services also include "altar calls" for salvation and invitations to receive prayer for Holy Spirit baptism.

In 2011, I attended a Sunday worship service on Kuramo Beach (Lagos) organized by RCCG's Habitation of Hope, an outreach to street children and youth. The majority of the congregation were homeless boys and girls living on the beach. During the service, one of the pastors prayed:

> You complain of homelessness, no food; plead to God to have mercy on Kuramo. Every unrighteousness in the lives of everyone in Kuramo, may it be blotted out by the blood of Jesus. Let there be transformation in the lives of everyone. Let there be change for the better in the lives of everyone.

Here the Kuramo residents' experience of homelessness and poverty is framed in moral and religious terms, and the redemptive work of Jesus is presented as the means of individual and community transformation. At the end of the service, seven young people received prayer for salvation. I will say more about the ministry of Habitation of Hope in Chapter 6. On another occasion, I attended Sunday worship at RCCG Christchurch in Lagos. The theme of the service was "The Ministry of Helps",[5] and the pastor's sermon focused on neighbour love, based on the parable of the Good Samaritan and the Christian great commandment to love God and love neighbour as self. During the sermon, the pastor spoke about the church's social ministries and encouraged members to volunteer their service. The meeting ended with prayer for people to receive the Spirit's anointing for the gift of "helps" and for the church to be filled with believers "who know how to love neighbour as self and to love in deed and truth".

However, these services were by no means typical. Many of the sermons and prayers I witnessed during Pentecostal worship meetings focused on individual problem-solving and the expectation of miracles such as healing and prosperity. Here there are continuities with traditional religious rituals. For example, in Yoruba culture, prayer is highly pragmatic, and worship is expected to bring tangible benefits in terms of the "good things" of this life: children, prosperity, health and longevity (Peel 2000). Marshall (2009: 151) describes Nigerian Pentecostal prayer as a "central technique of the self, in which, through a personal communication or discussion with God, the convert articulates both desires and fears, plenitude and lack, and is brought to envision an imagined future". During one meeting I attended, the pastor based his sermon on the Old Testament story of Queen Esther and explained Esther's change in fortunes in terms of the favour bestowed upon her by King Xerxes. He then applied this to his mainly Yoruba audience by linking personal progress with divine favour. "When favour comes your way, it can change your life around", by giving you "uncommon provision", "moving you from the gutter to the best place", and making you "the most important person in that place". "This month multiple promotions will come your way…. People will come and serve you, bow down to you…. This year, some will move from obscurity and be celebrated". However, the enjoyment of divine favour is conditional upon faith. The pastor encouraged us to repeat out loud statements such as "favour must come my way this morning" and "this is my month of favour", and ended by leading us in prayers to this effect.[6]

In Nigerian Pentecostal discourse, Spirit baptism is associated with power for service. As Matthew Clarke (2015: 164) notes, Pentecostals believe they are empowered by the Holy Spirit to "serve God, the Church, the world, and to engage in the wider society". This is reflected in Guiding Light Assembly's statement of beliefs: "Every believer should seek and expect to be baptised in the Holy Spirit as a distinct experience of empowering for Christian life and service and as a gateway into the supernatural gifts of the Holy Spirit" (Guiding Light Assembly n.d.). RCCG's Adult Sunday School manual describes Spirit baptism as the "endowment with power for effective Christian service.... It makes the believer spirit-filled, spirit-motivated, spirit-controlled and spirit-empowered" (RCCG 2010: 19–20). During interviews, pastors referred to Spirit baptism as a pivotal event in their Christian experience and one that propelled them into intense missionary activity. Usually this added a new dimension to their ministry and an expectation that supernatural "signs and wonders" such as healing and deliverance would accompany the preaching of the gospel.

The link between empowerment by the Holy Spirit and service is reflected in a sermon preached by Sam Adeyemi, senior pastor of Daystar Christian Centre in Lagos. For Adeyemi, the purpose of the "anointing of the Holy Spirit" is to influence people by solving their problems: "The proof, the evidence that the Holy Spirit is in your life is not just speaking in tongues. It has to do with the capacity to solve problems for people." In keeping with the wider Pentecostal tradition, Adeyemi employs a restorationist hermeneutic that seeks to retrieve and reappropriate the biblical way of life as recorded particularly in Luke's Gospel and the Acts of the Apostles (Yong 2010). The mandate given to Jesus and his disciples, according to Adeyemi, was to solve the problem of poverty, restore broken lives, dispel ignorance, and destroy "yokes of oppression" through the power of the Holy Spirit. He calls on Christians to emulate Jesus and the early church by using their experience of the Spirit's power to change people's lives for the better (Adeyemi 2010).

Nigerian Pentecostals also associate the spirit-filled life with prophecy. Here I use the term "prophecy" in a broad sense to include visions and dreams which are not necessarily expressed in oracular speech. For Nigerian Pentecostals, the Holy Spirit distributes charismatic gifts of wisdom and knowledge in response to prayer, guiding them in their missionary and social outreaches. As Clarke (2015: 164) notes,

> Pentecostals believe that because believers have intimacy with God, arising out of his immanence, this empowerment also comes in a more direct form of hearing God's "heart/voice", wanting passionately to fulfil this "calling" to see spiritual/physical/social salvation, and being directed specifically to particular tasks.

Poloma and Lee (2013: 281) refer to prophecy as an "often-overlooked key to spiritual empowerment", a particular experience of the Spirit in divine guidance, which can play a "significant role in compassionate service". Some of the Pentecostals I interviewed referred to dreams, visions, inaudible "voices" and other forms of divine communication that they had experienced in the course of their lives. Sometimes these prophetic revelations were features of conversion narratives, calls to ministry, and testimonies of healing. A common context for prophecies is the Pentecostal worship service though they also take place in private settings during prayer. In the Nigeria Survey, significant numbers stated that they had heard God through a vision or dream in the previous six months (38 per cent), felt led by God to perform a specific action (35 per cent), and given or interpreted a prophecy (28 per cent).

Nigerian Pentecostal churches emphasize "miracles", especially healing, and this is a major reason for their appeal. The popularity of divine healing arises from poverty in communities plagued by the collapse of state healthcare systems. Pentecostal pastors with gifts of healing attract large followings. For example, the week-long Holy Ghost Congress in Nigeria, organized by the RCCG, attracts several million people, largely due to the expectation of miracles associated with the ministry of Pastor Enoch Adeboye. When I attended in 2010, Adeboye frequently interrupted his sermon with divine "revelations" regarding miracles taking place in the auditorium. These included physical healings, deliverances from barrenness and other ailments, and promises of financial breakthroughs. In the Nigeria Survey (2011), most Pentecostals stated that God grants health to all believers who have enough faith (91 per cent of Nigerian Pentecostals and 85 per cent of Nigerian Charismatics). However, as we will see in Chapter 5, Pentecostal understandings of illness and health can sometimes discourage church members from seeking medical intervention and perpetuate the stigmatization of people living with conditions such as HIV/AIDS and physical/mental disability.

Prosperity teaching, which associates God's blessings with the expectation of material prosperity and success, is pervasive among the churches I studied. The most influential in this respect is Winners Chapel, which spreads its message of prosperity through church-planting, conference events, and print and electronic media. In the Nigeria Survey (2011), 82 per cent of Nigerian Pentecostals and 65 per cent of Nigerian Charismatics stated that God grants prosperity to all believers who have enough faith. Critics of African prosperity teaching regard it as incompatible with positive development outcomes (e.g. Gifford 2015). Yet generalizations are sometimes made which fail to take into account the different meanings attached to it in different contexts. Most of churches that feature in this book have embraced a moderate form of prosperity doctrine. While some Nigerian pastors continue to grow rich at the expense of their churches' impoverished members, others have adopted a different understanding: the purpose of wealth is for the common good rather than for personal enrichment. Increasingly, Nigerian Pentecostal churches are channelling their financial resources into development projects in the wider society. Another emerging trend is the shift away from a miraculous approach to prosperity to an emphasis on work and entrepreneurial skills. We will return to the important subject of the prosperity gospel and its significance for Pentecostal economics in Chapter 2.

Despite the prominence of prosperity teaching, holiness remains a key characteristic of Pentecostal self-identity and an important feature of the spirit-filled life. The Nigeria Survey (2011) asked respondents to identify the main emphasis of their church. A significant majority (53 per cent) said "holiness" (compared to 24 per cent "missions/evangelism", 10 per cent "worship", 5 per cent "deliverance", and 2 per cent "prosperity"). As well as positive values such as honesty, purity and love, Pentecostals promote holiness taboos such as modest dress codes, and abstinence from alcohol and sexual immorality. Pentecostals refer to these character traits as the "fruit of the Spirit" and link them to Spirit baptism. This is reflected in another excerpt from RCCG's Adult Sunday School Manual: "The fruit of the Holy Spirit stands as evidence of a spirit-filled life. They are gracious and godly habits produced in the life of a consecrated believer who has been baptized with the Holy Spirit." (RCCG 2010: 23). Historically, the separatist tendencies associated with an emphasis on holiness have discouraged Nigerian Pentecostal engagement in social and political activism (Marshall 2009). However, what is now being stressed by some churches is holiness expressed as obedience to Christ's command to love one's neighbour in the wider society. This is the added value of spiritual capital associated with the Pentecostal holiness. It is also a form of bridging social capital, as it drives Pentecostals to create new relationships with people from other religious traditions. Invariably when asked about their motivation for social engagement, respondents referred to the importance of emulating Christ's example and to Bible texts which exhort Christians to show compassion towards others. Other core values linked to Pentecostal holiness, which have implications for civic engagement, include integrity, peaceability, and respect for human life. However, I also came across accounts of Pentecostal moral misdemeanours, which have damaged the reputation of the movement and weakened its capacity for effective civic engagement.

Deliverance is another important practice, often associated with holiness in Nigerian Pentecostal discourse. Deliverance practices are popular in Nigeria, partly because of the influence of one megachurch, Mountain of Fire and Miracles, and its charismatic Pastor Daniel Olukoya. Another factor is the widespread circulation of Christian video films, which often feature Pentecostal deliverance rituals and discourses. From an initial focus on holiness and healing, deliverance theology in Nigeria has been extended to include economic circumstances, geographical localities, people groups, and socio-political structures (Ojo 2006). For Nigerian Pentecostals, development is not formulated in exclusively materialist terms but includes reference to an invisible world inhabited by spiritual entities. In the literature, this "enchanted" worldview is sometimes regarded as a hindrance to development, encouraging fear and distrust, and diminishing human responsibility (Gifford 2004, 2015; Marshall 2009). Wariboko (2014: 241) refers to the Pentecostal tendency to explain national poverty in spiritual terms by blaming Nigeria's economic underdevelopment on demons and the devil. For Pentecostals who adopt this approach, the key to development is "intercessory prayer and deliverance" to "redeem the land" rather than direct political engagement. One of the consequences is that politicians "who made wrong economic policies or looted the nations' treasuries are not held personally accountable for the deplorable situation of the continent" (Wariboko 2014: 242). However, a focus on deliverance and spiritual warfare does not necessarily detract from civic engagement. For example, Christ Livingspring Apostolic Ministry in Lagos combines an emphasis on deliverance with a commitment to social engagement, especially in the areas of healthcare, education, and community development. Deliverance also serves as an important ritual of rupture for recipients of social care, enabling them to break free from destructive lifestyles such as prostitution, drug addiction, and criminality.

The appeal of deliverance theologies is obvious in a hostile economic environment like Nigeria, where access to social services and state funds is severely restricted. Their popularity also stems from their close affinity to biblical and African cosmologies. Unlike many Westerners, Nigerian Pentecostals are reluctant to divest the Bible of its supernatural character and are particularly drawn to the Gospels and Acts, where healing and exorcism occur regularly. The focus of deliverance is on problems that beset African Christians in particular, such as witchcraft, ancestral covenants, and idol worship. Symptoms associated with demons and targeted during deliverance sessions include bad dreams, sickness, mental illness, poverty, unemployment, business failure, and immoral behaviours.

Pentecostal deliverance beliefs and rituals suggest both continuity and rupture with African indigenous cosmologies. Ontological beliefs in a "spirit-filled" world permeate African societies and persist within African Pentecostalism (Anderson 2018). Despite a tendency to demonize traditional culture, and present themselves as modern individuals, Nigerian Pentecostals interpret Christianity

Figure 1.1 Billboard for the November 2010 Great Deliverance service at Mountain of Fire and Miracles' Prayer City.

Source: author.

through the lens of existing religious categories and especially the traditional search for spiritual power, a pervasive theme in societies such as the Yoruba (Peel 2000). Wariboko (2014: 5–6) refers to this as the "spell of the invisible" in Nigerian Pentecostalism. He argues that Nigerian Pentecostals' ability to "extract information from the spiritual, invisible realm for productive application in the phenomenal world reveals their disposition of simultaneously being inside and outside African traditional religions". For Wariboko, understanding how this spell works is vital for "reaching the heart of the movement and comprehending its creativity, diversity, and resilience in addressing the embodied needs, questions, desires, and hopes of millions of Nigerians". One of the key elements of Yoruba traditional spirituality, for example, is the belief that an invisible world (*orun*) of benevolent and malevolent powers is constantly interacting with the visible material world (*aye*). Because of the activity of these powers, and their potential manipulation by human agents, this world is a dangerous and precarious place (Ray 1993). Religious rituals, such as prayer (*adura*), divination and sacrifice, are intended to attract benevolent powers and repel malevolent ones. As Adogame (2005: 399) notes,

> This tendency has continued in the Pentecostal churches although the medium and object has changed. The benevolent powers of the indigenous worldview become translated as malevolent forces in the new Pentecostal rhetoric. They argue that the Bible clearly portrays human life as lived in a context of continual warfare between the kingdom of God and the kingdom of Satan.

While Pentecostal deliverance is viewed in negative terms as the removal of the effects of past religious and social associations, it is oriented towards the present and the future in ways that seem to resonate with modernity's notion of the autonomy of the self and its call to make a break with the past (Meyer 1998; Marshall 2009). Nigerian Pentecostals promote deliverance as a means of severing ties with social and religious pasts, thus removing obstacles to personal progress. Yet the goal is primarily ethical rather than social, and the result is not so much increased autonomy and individuality but a new commitment to Christ and a new set of communal relationships.

Motivations for service

What motivates Nigerian Pentecostals to engage in development activities? It is important to consider why people serve, not just how they serve. Here I draw upon interviews with pastors as well as material from church publications, websites and conferences talks. Two primary themes emerged from my research which provide insights into their understanding of development. First, Nigerian Pentecostals are driven by a desire to show the love of God (or Christ) through practical care. A London-based pastor explained the rationale behind his church's community engagement:

> We want to express that love by showing people irrespective of who they are, we love them, we care for them, and we care about their community. So those are some of the real driving forces behind what we are trying to do. If the church wants to be relevant in the UK, we've got to care, we've got to have that passion and hunger to reach out to people and show them the love of God.

The link between loving God and loving other people is reflected in a talk given by Pastor Nike Adeyemi during Daystar Christian Centre's 2010 "Excellence in Leadership" Conference, where she refers to her ministry to young people living on the streets of Lagos:

> If we love God, we will love humanity and we will want to help. Jesus has given us a commission: Mark 16.15 – go into all the world and preach the gospel and make disciples of men. It's a commission; it's an assignment of rescue. It's an assignment of reconciling people back to God. So if I see young people on the street living their lives anyhow, I should want to help them.
>
> (Nike Adeyemi 2010)

Here we see that the urge to show God's love to others is a response to Jesus' mandate to his followers to preach the gospel (Mk 16:15).[7] The narrative also indicates another motivation for service: the encounter with human suffering, poverty and alienation (from God and the community). The responsibility to show God's love is also evident in Pentecostal mission statements and publicity material. For example, Daystar Christian Centre refers to the church's responsibility "to impact society by showing the love of Jesus in practical terms" (Daystar Christian Centre n.d.). The mission statement of Fountain of Life Church's Grace Springs Medical Centre in Lagos is: "Demonstrating the love of Jesus through the provision of quality healthcare" (see Figure 5.2). And an article in Jesus House London's *Outflow* magazine refers to the church's duty to "touch this dysfunctional world with the love of Christ" and to "show the love of God in a practical way" through prayer, charitable giving and participation in social welfare programmes (Irukwu 2008). Another example is RCCG's Fountain of Love church, who's commitment to serve others is expressed in its mission statement: "To reach out with the love of God to a world that is hurting and insecure and to get ready for the coming of our Lord and Saviour Jesus Christ" (Fountain of Love 2019). Nigerian Pentecostals model their development activities on the ministry of Jesus, as reflected in the following extract from the website of the Festival of Life, RCCG's flagship conference in London:

> As Jesus identified with the poor, the afflicted, the oppressed and the marginalised, we believe that we are called to serve those in need, to improve and alleviate poverty and play a role in transforming communities. We believe that God created and loves everyone and we also endeavour to love as Christ loves.
>
> (RCCG Festival of Life 2016)

When Pentecostals speak about reaching out with the love of God, they are referring to a quality with divine origins and with the potential to energize altruistic behaviour towards others. Margaret Poloma and Ralph Hood (2008: 2, 65–70) refer to this as "godly love" in their study of Pentecostal faith-based social ministry and link it to Spirit baptism and the exercise of spiritual gifts. Godly love is the experience of "a loving God through glossolalia and the spiritual gifts that accompany it", which in turn "empowers compassion and loving behaviour" (2008: 115–116). It includes the elements of "receiving God's love" and "working with others in benevolent ways" (Poloma, Lee, and Post 2013: 15). The emerging study of Godly Love involves interdisciplinary dialogue among social scientists and theologians (Poloma, Lee, and Post 2013). It has helped to explain the ways in which Pentecostals have lived out the commandment to love God and love neighbour at the heart of the Christian tradition.

The emphasis on showing the love of God through practical care reflects the merging of development with evangelism in Nigerian Pentecostal practice. This integrated approach to development is reflected in the following interview excerpts:

> We've been trying as much as possible to do what we can to reach out to others. Apart from doing works it certainly is about spreading the gospel as well. So a lot of the community projects are two-pronged in the sense that we are providing a service and at the same time using that as an opportunity to touch people with the love of Christ, preach to them.[8]
>
> We believe strongly that if we come into any community, we should affect the community positively for the kingdom. Souls are very important, but then their social lives should be affected. That's what informs most of what we are doing. We consider their social wellbeing, we heal them, provide food for them, visit the poor and needy, the sick in hospital, those in prison. So these are the things that have informed the ministry. From the moment we came in, we started evangelising, going around telling them Jesus loves them.[9]

There are parallels here with Erica Bornstein's concept of "lifestyle evangelism" in her study of evangelical NGOs in Zimbabwe (Bornstein 2002, 2004). Bornstein (2002: 27) refers to the way NGO employees articulated "the logic of development" through two concepts: "lifestyle evangelism" and "holism". Lifestyle evangelism entails "living a life in a manner of Christ, providing an example, and showing non-believers Christianity through the life that was led" (Bornstein 2002: 11). Holism refers to a holistic notion of development which combines spiritual and material transformation (2002: 9). However, the priority given to evangelism in Nigerian Pentecostal practice has the potential to bring Pentecostals into conflict with secular-based donor organizations and NGOs. As Rick James (2011: 111) notes, international donors are reluctant to engage with Christian FBOs that they perceive as using development activities as a means of evangelization and religious proselytizing.

The second primary motivation arises from this holistic understanding of development. Some churches are intentionally seeking to bring about social transformation in their communities. A London-based pastor stated:

> I believe in the idea of social transformation.... The gospel is more than individual salvation, it involves saving cities and nations; the kingdom of God in society ... I believe in community transformation.[10]

The theme of social transformation is also reflected in Jesus House London's logo, displayed on its website and in its publicity material: "Loving God, Impacting Lives, Transforming communities" (Jesus House 2016). The mission statement of the Freedom Foundation in Lagos also mirrors this holistic approach to development: "Our Mission is to reach out, give hope, rehabilitate, educate and empower impoverished persons in Nigeria through community-based programs and initiatives in order to achieve individual and community transformation" (Freedom Foundation 2019).

A recent development among some Pentecostals in Nigeria is a focus on nation-building and national transformation in response to the underperformance of political leaders and the state's failure to deliver on its promises of development and democratization. This is an ecclesiocentric vision which regards the church, rather than government, as the "redemptive agent of society".[11] One of the leading Pentecostal voices in Nigeria calling for the Church to take responsibility for national transformation is Tony Rapu, senior pastor of This Present House in Lagos. Rapu formerly led the Apapa parish of the Redeemed Christian Church of God, but left the church in 1997, disturbed by what he perceived to be its overemphasis on miracles and prosperity to the detriment of the holiness doctrine (Marshall 2009). In a newspaper article, Rapu calls on Christians to take responsibility for Nigeria:

> We can reverse the decay in governance, politics, society, the economy, business, law, health, education, the family, etc. It is our mandate and calling. It is to this end that the Church must discard our church-building mentality, roll up our sleeves and get involved in the restorative processes for National Transformation.
>
> (Rapu 2005)

Rapu belongs to a growing network of younger, educated Pentecostal pastors in Nigeria, whose focus on national transformation is influenced by the Nigerian Pentecostal Sunday Adelaja, founder of the Embassy of God in the Ukraine, and by a version of "kingdom" or dominion theology, called "Seven Mountain" theology, associated with the late C. Peter Wagner's New Apostolic Reformation and the Religious Right in the United States (McCain 2013b; Christerson and Flory 2017). Kingdom theology represents a significant departure from the "two kingdoms" theology inherited from the early missionaries, who followed the Western enlightenment tradition by separating religion and politics into two distinct spheres (Ellis and Ter Haar 1998). It includes both the idea of divine sovereignty – God's present rule on earth through the church – and the presence of transformational leaders carrying biblical principles and "kingdom" values into the key culture-shaping spheres of society: the seven "mountains" of government, family, media, business, education, arts and culture, and religion (Enlow 2008; McCain 2013b). Adelaja is credited with introducing kingdom theology to Nigeria during a meeting organized by a group of pastors in Lagos in 2004 (McCain 2013a: 177). Following Adelaja's visit, the pastors eventually formed themselves into a loose network, called the National Transformation Council (later renamed Church for Change).[12]

The focus on national transformation and kingdom theology represents only one strand of Nigerian Pentecostalism, albeit an increasingly influential one. Those associated with the movement include megachurch pastors, denominational overseers, national leaders of the Pentecostal Fellowship of Nigeria (PFN), university professors, business entrepreneurs, politicians, and social activists. While the Nigerian pastors have embraced some of the ideas associated with Wagner's New Apostolic Reformation, especially the mandate to influence the key culture-shaping spheres of society, they have distanced themselves from the emphasis on total submission to "apostolic leaders" and the more triumphalist and theocratic versions of dominion theology (Marshall 2014).

Lay participation and leadership

The effectiveness of religious organizations in engendering change is partly contingent upon the social capital they are able to generate (Bompani 2015; Ter Haar 2011). Lack of trust in society is considered a major obstacle to development, especially in countries dominated by corruption and violence such as Nigeria. One of the strengths of Pentecostal churches in African societies is their closeness to poor communities, with members embedded in networks of relationships that are dependent on trust and reciprocity. Another is their organizational culture which is designed to mobilize the laity and foster participation (Freeman, 2012; Bompani 2015; Clarke 2015; Kalu 2008). As Clarke (2015: 168–169) notes, Pentecostalism "instils participation and personal investment as part of Pentecostal practice", which makes it "ripe for leveraging development initiatives that will improve the physical wellbeing of local communities".

Nigerian Pentecostal churches and institutions represent strong networks of religious capital capable of generating considerable numbers of volunteers for community engagement. In mainstream development theory, community participation and empowerment are considered essential components of successful development outcomes (Clarke 2011). Clarke (2011: 10) refers to the way that self-worth is restored and traditional structures of power and domination overturned when people are allowed to run and take control of development interventions. According to Dena Freeman (2012: 24–25), the ability of Pentecostal churches to foster participation is one reason why they seem more successful than secular NGOs in bringing about effective and sustainable social change. Freeman points to the way that Pentecostal churches are embedded in local communities and to the ability of Pentecostal pastors to enable their members to become involved in church activities from the outset. Thus, Pentecostal churches are "locally owned organizations, run by people for the people, in a way that development NGOs simply are not" (Freeman 2012: 25). Similarly, Donald Miller and Tetsunao Yamamori (2007) refer to the highly active lay leadership within Pentecostal churches which gives them a competitive edge over more traditional congregations that are mired in bureaucracy. The role of Pentecostal pastors, according to Miller and Yamamori (2007: 186), is to enable church members to discover their gifts and to become actively engaged in the work of the ministry. However, African Pentecostalism suffers from an unstable base due to the tendency of believers to move from one church to another (Kalu 2008; Marshall 2009). As Marshall (2009: 133, 135) notes, with a few exceptions, Nigerian Pentecostal pastors have little real control over their congregations, partly because of the "egalitarian access to spiritual power and knowledge", but also because they have a "high degree of dependence, in terms of both their authority and the financial success, on their followers".

There is considerable diversity of organizational structures among Nigerian Pentecostal churches. Many are laity-driven institutions, in which individuals are empowered to pursue their vision without excessive interference from bureaucracy. This is facilitated by the creation of small groups, characterized by affirming and supportive relationships. While the time spent in service to their churches can restrict their participation in the community, many Pentecostal development initiatives are led by lay volunteers rather than salaried pastors. For example, the RCCG has a category of lay "workers", who volunteer their time for service in the church and the wider society. Another church with a strong focus on lay ministry is Daystar Christian Centre. Daystar's church slogan is "Every member a minister" and its vision statement is to "raise men and women who will become role models in the society by applying Bible-based principles and fulfilling their own destinies" (Daystar Christian Centre 2011). In order to progress to the level of lay ministers, members are required to attend a series of training programmes culminating in the Daystar Advanced Training Academy and the Evangelism & Missions School. They are also expected to join one of the many congregational "service groups" which offer opportunities to serve the church in different capacities. But it is the cell group system that provides the main context for the development of the Pentecostal subject through the acquisition and enactment of techniques of the self (Marshall 2009), such as prayer, Bible study, and acts of service. Kevin O'Neill (2010: 62–63) refers to this as "cellular forms of citizenship", where Pentecostals act upon themselves for the sake of the nation. According to O'Neill (2010: 62), cells enable believers "to craft a sense of self" and "to link that self to the fate of their nation", allowing "Christian contemplation to constitute Christian action". Daystar Christian Centre has established approximately 3,000 cell groups across the city of Lagos (Daystar Christian Centre 2018). These encourage the development of social capital by providing opportunities for members to build relationships based on trust, and develop leadership and ministerial skills. They also provide a context for congregants to discuss Adeyemi's sermons, ponder and pray over the issues of the day, and engage in various forms of civic action.[13]

Another important element of Pentecostal religious capital is leadership, which can either encourage or hinder development, depending upon the character and orientation of the leader. As Ter Haar (2011: 23) notes, "Whether a faith-based organisation has the ability to play a constructive role in development depends to a large extent on the capability and outlook of its leaders." Bompani (2015: 104) refers to the effects of religious leadership on the vision, regular functioning and decision-making of religious organizations, "especially in forms of religious expression that are not strongly hierarchical, such as Pentecostal-Charismatic Christianity". In the case of African Pentecostalism, an historical perspective is important. The early post-1970 Pentecostal revival was characterized by an egalitarian ethos, as youthful revivalists "deployed the concept of the priesthood of all believers as a strategy to pry open the ecclesiastical space, challenge the elders, and contest the monopoly and control mounted by the old mission churches" (Kalu 2008: 138). However, a significant shift in ecclesiology has occurred in recent years towards more authoritarian leadership styles, which mirror neopatrimonial and "Big Man" models in the wider society (Gifford 2004; Kalu 2008; Marshall 2009; McCauley 2012). According to Kalu (2008: 138), this is largely taking place at the top, "while the base leadership remains intensely egalitarian and prominently lay". To some extent, it is an inevitable consequence of church growth and the rise of Pentecostal megachurches. However, the emphasis on charismatic power has encouraged the elevation of unaccountable, "anointed" leaders who have used their position as power-brokers for monetary gain rather than to serve the needs of the poor and marginalized. To counter this, some Nigerian Pentecostals are teaching models of "servant" and transformational leadership deemed more conducive to successful development outcomes.

There is a plurality of leadership styles among Nigerian Pentecostal churches. Many are characterized by independent, charismatic forms of leadership, but others have a polity where leaders are appointed on the basis of constitutional guidelines rather than personal charisma. In organizational studies, a distinction is made between transactional and transformational styles of leadership. Whereas transactional leaders cater for their followers' immediate self-interests by offering material incentives, transformational leaders cause their followers to become committed to the leader's mission and make personal sacrifices on behalf of others (Bass 1999). Pentecostal pastors who have embraced a transformational model of leadership combined with a commitment to civic engagement have tended to foster churches with a strong social outlook. The Nigeria Survey (2011) showed that Pentecostals rate church leaders, alongside print and electronic media and congregational meetings, as the most important socialization mechanisms for helping them understand their civic responsibilities. Pastors often possess healing gifts, organizational skills, and teaching abilities, enabling them to motivate and mobilize their members. Education is another factor influencing Nigerian Pentecostal leadership styles. Most of the men and women leading the new wave of progressive Pentecostalism have been educated in public universities and include former medical doctors, architects, lawyers, accountants, engineers, bankers, and business people. This stands in contrast to older classical Pentecostals churches, such as Assemblies of God and Foursquare Gospel Church, whose senior leaders have mostly passed through Nigerian Pentecostal seminaries (McCain 2013a). McCain (2013a: 175) suggests that those educated in traditional theological seminaries "have been so shaped in the traditional way of doing things that they have difficulty seeing alternatives". However, without the constraints of traditional theological education, the new leaders are able to approach social problems in innovative and creative ways.

The Pentecostal emphasis on transformational leadership has the potential for developing human capital, which is essential for sustained economic growth.[14] Leadership training institutes aimed at raising transformational leaders for public life are becoming increasingly popular in Nigeria. Examples include RCCG's Redeemer's International Leadership Academy (RILA), Vincent Anigbogu's Institute for National Transformation, Sam Adeyemi's Daystar Leadership Academy, and David Ogbuele's Dominion Leadership Institute. RILA's vision is to be "a global Christian center of excellence for raising transformational leaders for ministry and the marketplace" (RILA n.d.). Amongst RILA alumni are church pastors, business leaders, military officers, traditional rulers, and government leaders, including the current Vice-President, Yemi Osinbajo. Anigbogu's Institute for National Transformation runs courses on transformational leadership for church leaders, government workers, business entrepreneurs, academics, and young people.[15] Adeyemi's Daystar Leadership Academy aims "to raise exceptional leaders who will transform their families, organizations and communities globally" (Daystar Christian Centre 2019). Adeyemi has a doctorate in Strategic Leadership from Regent University in the United States. Daystar Christian Centre hosts an annual leadership conference which attracts participants from a wide variety of Christian denominations. The 2010 "Excellence in Leadership" conference included sessions led by experts in the fields of politics, education, social welfare, media, and business.[16]

Adeyemi also uses the pulpit to challenge dominant models of leadership in church and society. In one service I attended, Adeyemi's sermon, entitled "Love and Leadership", was essentially a treatise on servant leadership. Lacing his messages with scripture references, he contrasted the traditional "Big Man" concept of leadership in Nigeria, based on unequal power relations and a culture of fear and domination, with the style of leadership portrayed in the New Testament, based on love. Love is the best way to motivate others, Adeyemi insisted, and if leaders neglect it, they will miss the opportunity to influence people's lives for the better. His message ended in typical Pentecostal style with a prayer for the congregation to experience God's love through a fresh baptism of the Holy Spirit.

Ecumenical networks, external connections, and the media

Pentecostal networks are important sources of religious capital. Through their participation in national ecumenical networks, such as the Pentecostal Fellowship

Figure 1.2 Billboard for the 2010 Excellence in Leadership Conference, hosted by Daystar Christian Centre in Lagos.

Source: author.

of Nigeria (PFN) and the Christian Association of Nigeria (CAN), Pentecostal churches in Nigeria have been relatively successful in developing bonding capital as well as interethnic and interdenominational bridging capital. This has helped them to present a united front in the political arena and to mobilize their members for democratic engagement. At state level, member churches of PFN also collaborate in development projects and relief programmes. However, PFN has been less successful in developing interfaith bridging capital capable of forging links between communities divided by religion.

More important for Nigerian Pentecostal engagement in development are networks of like-minded church leaders such as Church for Change, Apostles in the Marketplace (AiMP), the Institute for National Transformation, and the Coalition of Nigerian Apostolic Leaders (CNAL). Their relatively flat and flexible ecclesiology, their use of digital technology, and their focus on leadership training, enables the mobilization and empowerment of members for engagement in the different spheres of public life. They also allow more space for creativity and innovative practice outside the constraints of denominational structures. Several recent studies have focused on the significance of networks for Pentecostal organizational culture (Kay 2007; Christerson and Flory 2017). William Kay (2007: 20) charts the rise of apostolic networks in Britain, which he describes as "centred around the guiding ministry of an apostle". He contrasts the hierarchical nature of bureaucratic authority with apostolic networks, which "set their faces against bureaucracy" and are characterized by flat organizational structures (2007: 288–289). In their book *Network Christianity*, Christerson and Flory (2017: 11) introduce the term "Independent Network Charismatic" (INC) Christianity to describe this new form of Christianity composed of networks of strong leaders who "know each other and combine and recombine for specific projects, but who are functionally independent of one another". They suggest that this "subset of neo-Charismatic Christianity is one of, if not the, fastest-growing subset of Christianity in the United States and around the world" (2017: 147). According the Christerson and Flory, INCs are "not primarily focused on building congregations in the traditional sense, but rather seek to influence the beliefs and practices of followers regardless of congregation or affiliation". They also "seek to transform society as a whole rather than saving individual souls and building congregations" (2017: 147).

Apostles in the Marketplace (AiMP) was founded in 2003 by John Enelamah, senior pastor of World Revival Church in Lagos, as a network of Christian professionals and leaders. AiMP defines a marketplace apostle as "an agent of change" and a "nation builder who through personal commitment to Christ and the disciplined application of biblical principles to all areas of life is able to transform society" (AiMP 2015). Members of AiMP include professionals working in the different spheres of politics, business, education, law, and medicine as well as Pentecostal pastors and leaders of parachurch organizations. The network seeks to mobilize and support Christians in the marketplace through its "Nation Building" workshops, "Leadership and Governance" seminars, and "Working for God in the Marketplace" training programme. It also engages in advocacy for reform in education and politics. Its monthly e-newsletter, entitled "Nation-Builders", carries information about AiMP programmes and articles on marketplace ministries. As well as facilitating cooperation within its own network, it collaborates with other networks and NGOs in Nigeria such as Church for Change and the Institute for National Transformation. Members of AiMP and Church for Change also have international links with networks in Europe and the USA such as Adelaja's Embassy of God in the Ukraine, the International Coalition of Apostolic Leaders (ICAL) associated with C. Peter Wagner in the United States, and Hugh Osgood's Churches in Community in Britain.

The International Coalition of Apostolic Leaders (formerly International Coalition of Apostles) was founded in the USA by C. Peter Wagner and John P. Kelly in 1999 (Christerson and Flory 2017). In 2002, Wagner, Kelly and Chuck Pierce began to convene a series of apostolic summits around the world aimed at sparking apostolic alliances like ICAL within different geographical regions. The 2002 Nigerian Apostolic Summit was hosted by RCCG's Enoch Adeboye and attended by leading Pentecostals pastors such as William Kumuyi and David Oyedepo (Wagner 2004). In 2011, Kelly began to establish national convenors of indigenous apostolic leaders within their nation. The Coalition of Nigerian Apostolic Leaders (CNAL) is an affiliate member of ICAL. It was established in 2012 following the appointment of Pastor Adewale Adefarasin as the convening apostle for Nigeria at the 2011 ICAL Annual Conference (CNAL 2015b). Adefarasin is the senior pastor of Guiding Light Assembly in Lagos and a founding member of Church for Change. CNAL's vision is to establish a network of apostles across Nigeria "to work together for the purpose of advancing God's Kingdom and aligning Nigeria with godliness" (CNAL 2015a). CNAL organizes annual pastors' conferences, and members of CNAL regularly attend ICAL conferences in the USA. International speakers at CNAL conferences have included ICAL members Chuck Pierce, Randy Clark, and Bill Johnson, all leaders of INC groups in the USA.

Another apostolic network is the Global Apostolic Impact Network (GAIN), a group of church leaders, Christian entrepreneurs and professionals linked to Tunde Bakare's Latter Rain Assembly in Lagos. The Latter Rain Assembly was founded in 1989, after Bakare left the RCCG, and the church has an average attendance of 5,000 members at its Sunday services. Most of GAIN's member churches are located in Nigeria but it also has partners in South Africa, Ghana, Britain, the USA, Canada, and Australia. Bakare is a cosmopolitan pastor, who divides his time between Nigeria, Europe, and the United States. He is also an astute operator, sensitive to changing cultural trends and familiar with the dynamics of the global network society. He styles himself as the "serving overseer" of a loose network of churches rather than the head of a denomination.[17] The network started in 1992 as an association of independent church leaders before metamorphosing gradually into the Global Apostolic Impact Network. GAIN's organizational culture echoes some of the features of Manuel Castells' network society (Castells 2010). Castells discerned the rise of the network society as a key component of the Information Age. In his analysis of contemporary global society, Castells (2010: 501) understands a network as a "set of interconnected nodes". Networks are "open structures, able to expand without limits, integrating new nodes as long as they are able to communicate within the network, namely as long as they share the same communication codes (for example, values or performance goals)". GAIN's flexible and flat organizational structure allows freedom for "new developments, ideas, and new styles of ministries". GAIN churches share a common set of "codes" or "corporate culture" (core values, beliefs, and practices), patterned after the New Testament, which enable them to communicate and cooperate in the pursuit of a common vision: the extension of "God's Kingdom on earth" and the creation of "governing churches to influence the city and impact the nations" (GAIN n.d.). Latter Rain Assembly's penchant for information technologies is reflected in its e-learning discipleship programme called the Apostolic Training School online, and the use of the Internet to live stream its worship services and provide online access to Bakare's sermons.

External connections with individuals and institutions beyond the church are also an important source of religious capital. Pastors with large constituencies, such as RCCG's Enoch Adeboye, have used their wealth and status as spiritual authorities not only as access to the state but also as a means of political influence, establishing close relationships with certain politicians (Marshall 2009; Obadare 2018). Government ministers, public sector workers, and civil society activists are sometimes invited as speakers at Pentecostal conferences. Pentecostal NGOs also collaborate with state and national government agencies. Other partners and sponsors include local hospitals, schools, banks, and businesses as well as international donors and transnational corporations, and international NGOs. They also use transnational religious networks to appeal for funds and to publicize their development initiatives.

Media use is another source of religious capital for Nigerian Pentecostals. The rapid deregulation of the media, which coincided with the turn to democracy in many African countries (de Witte 2003; Meyer 2004), has generated a lively debate about the media, democracy, and the role of the state. Many commentators celebrate the media's potential to promote democratic principles of openness, pluralism, and participation, all characteristics of a healthy civil society. Yet some lament the increasing commercialization of the media, which has allowed those who have money to hijack the airwaves for personal profit rather than use it for the common good. The expansion of the media sphere also exacerbates inter-religious tensions, especially in countries with large Muslim and Christian communities such as Nigeria (Hackett 2003). This has serious political ramifications and threatens regional and national stability.

Those African Pentecostals with sufficient funds at their disposal have shown themselves adept operators in this new public space created by the media (Asamoah-Gyadu 2004; Meyer 2002). This is especially so in Nigeria, where media presence has raised the profile of the Pentecostal elite, including those with political ambitions. Nigerian Pentecostals use print and electronic media to mediate transcendental ideas, such as holiness and prosperity doctrines, and to socialize their members. Books, magazines, CDs and DVDs, featuring Pentecostal sermons and Bible teaching, are sold in bookshops and on the Internet. Newspaper columns, written by Pentecostal pastors, figure prominently in the national press.[18] Mostly these consist of short Bible studies on such topics as the Christian discipleship, family relationships, and prayer. However, sometimes they include opinion pieces on social and political issues. Newspapers also publish interviews with Pentecostal social activists and leaders of Pentecostal NGOs as well as solicit the opinion of prominent Pentecostal pastors on matters of public interest. Some churches run their own newspapers and magazines,[19] and pastors host programmes on government-owned and private television stations. Nigerian Pentecostals also use the media to articulate their social vision and advertise their development activities. One example is the Freedom Foundation, which uses its website, Facebook, Twitter, and YouTube to publicize its activities, engage in advocacy, and appeal for donations. Interviews with Freedom Foundation staff members have featured in several national newspapers, and in 2018, "My Lagos Diaries", a documentary series showcasing the ministry of Freedom Foundation, was screened in the cinema and broadcast on television. It is also available on YouTube. According to Pastor Tony Rapu, the Director of the Freedom Foundation, the aim of the documentary is to "sensitise the general public about the struggles of the less privileged while providing an opportunity for interested individuals and organisations to support Freedom Foundation's vision via donations and funding" (*Guardian Nigeria* 2018).

Financial assets, buildings, and campgrounds

An important element of Pentecostal religious capital is the capacity to generate considerable financial resources due to the emphasis on prosperity teaching, mandatory tithing, and the generosity of the churches' more prosperous members. This has enabled some of the larger churches to embark on ambitious building projects such as Winners Chapel's Covenant University and House on the Rock's Rock Cathedral in Lagos. Funds for these projects, as well as for some of the Pentecostal development initiatives I studied, are largely raised internally from the membership. Pentecostal worship services include "offering times" where members are encouraged to give generously with the promise of receiving material blessings in return. While most of the money is used to pay congregational running costs and pastors' salaries, funds are also channelled into mission and development initiatives in the wider community.

Buildings in particular are important sources of Pentecostal religious capital, sometimes combining as places of worship and centres of civic engagement. Across Nigeria, the urban religious landscape is littered with Pentecostal institutions occupying warehouses, office spaces, cinema houses, and purpose-built structures (Ukah 2004). The five largest Pentecostal church auditoriums in the world are located in Nigeria.[20] Church buildings are important identity markers and provide congregations with a measure of visibility in public space. For African Pentecostals, they are often multi-functional spaces, operating as social support mechanisms on behalf of local communities. Some of the larger churches are also building schools, universities, rehabilitation centres, health clinics, and hospitals. These are either situated on the church premises or in separate locations, depending upon the availability of land and the purpose of the building. Schools, for example, are often housed in church premises, while rehabilitation centres are usually located away from the bustle of city life, making it easier for clients to break from their former lifestyles.

In November 2010, I visited the international headquarters of The Redeemed Evangelical Mission (TREM) in Lagos to attend the church's annual Kingdom Life World Conference. TREM was founded in 1981 by Bishop Mike Okonkwo, a former president of the Pentecostal Fellowship of Nigeria. The conference took place in TREM's 2,000-seater auditorium and featured guest speakers from Nigeria, Zimbabwe, and Zambia. Decorating the outside walls of the church were banners displaying TREM's mission statement:

> This is a place where we gather together in quality praise and worship of the true and living God, equipped with the Word of God for growth and fellowship with one another in covenant relationship and released to make a formidable impact in our world for the Kingdom.

Adjacent to the auditorium, TREM's new "Cathedral" was still under construction. The church premises also housed the administrative offices of "We-Care Ministry" (TREM's community outreach programme), the Power in the Word bookshop, and Rehoboth Microfinance bank.

I also visited House on the Rock's Rock Cathedral, said to be the largest building in Lagos State. House on the Rock was started in 1994 by former architect Paul Adefarasin as a house fellowship in his mother's home. Since then it

Figure 1.3 TREM Cathedral, Lagos.
Source: author.

has grown to around 7,000 members in its Lagos headquarters, with branches in 26 Nigerian states, the Democratic Republic of Congo, South Africa, the Netherlands, Dublin, and London. The Rock Cathedral's formal opening in 2012 was attended by President Goodluck Jonathan and former British Prime Minister Tony Blair. The Rock Cathedral combines as a place of worship and a "Centre for Social Justice and National Transformation". It currently hosts a hospital and mobile clinic for delivering primary healthcare across Lagos. It also has facilities for a primary school, a secondary school, a skills acquisition centre, a Bible school, and a "Centre of African Economy and Governance". The church's social initiatives include an "urban alternative church" for drug addicts and gang members, a prison rehabilitation ministry, and a feeding programme for the poor. These come under the umbrella of the Rock Foundation, an NGO committed to social reformation, education, provision of healthcare, and relief work.[21]

Pentecostal campgrounds have become an increasingly common phenomenon. One example is Bishop David Oyedepo's Canaan Land situated in the town of Ota, Ogun State, adjacent to Lagos. Canaan Land consists of the international headquarters of Winners' Chapel, the 50,000-capacity church auditorium known as Faith Tabernacle, Covenant University, Faith Academy Secondary School, and Kingdom Heritage Nursery/Primary School. Various businesses owned by the church also operate within Canaan Land. The Canaan Land complex also has restaurants, stores, banks, and residential estates that cater for church employees and university students (Iherika and Okon 2015).

A popular location for Pentecostal campgrounds is the 120-km-long Lagos-Ibadan Expressway. There are several camps along the expressway owned by Pentecostal megachurches, including Deeper Life Bible Conference Center, Gospel Faith Mission International's Gospel City, Foursquare Gospel Church Camp, MFM's Prayer City, and RCCG's Redemption Camp (or Redemption City).

These are gated communities providing refuge from the daily traumas of urban life. Their main function is to host a range of conference events and retreats for those seeking spiritual solace and sustenance through socializing with fellow believers and engaging in extended periods of communal prayer, worship, and Bible teaching. They also contribute to Pentecostal civic engagement by enabling churches to advertise their social projects, generate funds, and recruit volunteers.

By far the largest campgrounds are MFM's Prayer City and RCCG's Redemption Camp. MFM's Prayer City was purposively created "to accommodate massive crowds of prayer warriors and to shape the emotional, sensory, physical and collective experiences of prayer" (Butticci 2013: 54). Its open auditorium, which is said to accommodate 500,000 people, is the heart of Prayer City where the altar is located. This is considered the place where believers encounter God's presence through prayer and worship. In addition to the auditorium, Prayer City provides accommodation for visitors seeking spiritual aid. It also hosts MFM's Mountain Top University, the Deliverance Conference Centre, a medical centre, a bank, a restaurant, and a housing estate.

RCCG's 850-acre Redemption Camp hosts three conference events: the monthly Holy Ghost Service, the Annual Convention, and the Holy Ghost Congress. At the centre of the camp is the Congress Arena with a seating capacity of three million people (Iherika and Okon 2015). To accommodate the crowds attending these events, RCCG provides various administrative, commercial and municipal facilities including offices, guest houses, electricity and water supplies, a post office, a health clinic, several banks, supermarkets, and restaurants. The camp is home to the RCCG's international headquarters and to various ancillary institutions such as the Redeemed AIDS Programme Action Committee (RAPAC), the Wholistic Outreach (RCCG's outreach to victims of prostitution and trafficking), Redeemer's High School, the Redeemed Christian Bible College, and, until its recent relocation to its own site, the Redeemer's University (RUN). It also features residential housing estates where members can either build their own houses or purchase prebuilt houses constructed by a developer (Osinulu 2014). Close to the Camp is the rehabilitation centre of Habitation of Hope, RCCG's social outreach to street children and youth.

Nigerian Pentecostal campgrounds are being replicated in the United States and Britain though on a much smaller scale. In 2003, RCCG North America (RCCGNA) acquired 400 land hectares near Dallas, Texas, to build a replica of Redemption Camp in the United States. Currently, it houses RCCGNA's administrative headquarters, the 10,000-seat "Worship Pavilion", the Dayspring Conference Center, RCCGNA's Bible College and Redeemer's Leadership Institute, and a hotel complex called Redemption Resorts (Iherika and Okon 2015; Herrpich 2016). Examples in Britain include the European headquarters of Winners Chapel and KICC's "Prayer City", both located in Kent (Cartledge *et al.* 2019). Some Nigerian diaspora churches host conference events which attract large crowds. One example is RCCG's Festival of Life (FOL), which has helped to raise the RCCG's profile in the national public sphere. Held in

London's ExCel centre, the FOL attracts over 30,000, mainly African, participants during one night of praise, prayer, and preaching. It also provides a platform for a variety of public figures, including church leaders, politicians, and senior members of the Metropolitan Police Service, as well as space for different civic organizations, including Nigerian Pentecostal NGOs, to advertise their activities and raise financial support.[22]

Conclusion

The chapter began by discussing the nature of FBOs and their inclusion in Western public policy and the international development agenda. It then examined the Nigerian context and the proliferation of NGOs and FBOs (including Pentecostal FBOs) in recent decades. Many Pentecostal FBOs are informal ministries run by church congregations and denominations as part of their corporate social outreach. Increasingly, however, Nigerian Pentecostals are establishing FBOs of the NGO variety in their quest for recognition and partnership with donor organizations. Pentecostal development programmes cover a range of areas including education, healthcare, rehabilitation, economic empowerment, human rights, politics, and peacebuilding.

The chapter considered the spiritual and religious capital that Nigerian Pentecostals contribute to their development activities. The focus on rupture, transformation and empowerment resonates with the emphasis on modernization and progress in the development sector. However, Pentecostals emphasize the role of the Holy Spirit in pursuit of these goals. Participation in Pentecostal rituals, such as deliverance and Spirit baptism, is an important element of Pentecostal development initiatives, both as a source of empowerment for volunteers and as a means for recipients of social care to break free from their former lifestyles and addictions. Yet the "enchanted" worldview associated with Pentecostal approaches to development can potentially pose an obstacle to positive development outcomes, encouraging fear and distrust, and diminishing human responsibility. The chapter identified two primary motivations driving Pentecostal development activities: a desire to show God's love through practical care and a commitment to engendering social transformation. Together these reflect the holistic nature of Pentecostal development activities which combine spiritual and material transformation. For most of the churches discussed in this book, the division between religion and development is an artificial construct, reflecting the influence of Western understandings of development and modernity. As we will see in subsequent chapters, Pentecostal development activities are closely tied to religious visions and practices. However, this holistic approach has the potential to bring Pentecostals into conflict with secular-based donor organizations and NGOs.

The capacity of Nigerian Pentecostal churches to bring about positive development outcomes is partly contingent upon their organizational culture. One of their strengths is their ability to mobilize volunteers and foster participation. Another variable is leadership which can either encourage or hinder development, depending upon the character and orientation of the leader. The Pentecostal emphasis on charismatic power and egalitarian access to the "gifts" of the Spirit has encouraged the elevation of unaccountable leaders who have used their position for financial gain rather than to serve the needs of the poor. In response, Pentecostals such as Sam Adeyemi and Vincent Anigbogu, and leadership institutes such as RILA and Daystar Leadership Academy, are promoting alternative models of "servant" and transformational leadership deemed more conducive to positive development outcomes. A significant development is the emergence of Pentecostal networks of like-minded church leaders, such as Church for Change and Apostles in the Marketplace, which seek to mobilize and empower church members for engagement in public life. Church buildings and campgrounds are also important sources of Pentecostal religious capital, sometimes combining as places of worship and centres of civic engagement. Some of the larger churches are building schools, universities, rehabilitation centres, and hospitals. Other important resources for Pentecostal civic engagement are media technologies, ecumenical relationships, transnational networks, and external partnerships with government, banks, and businesses as well as secular NGOs and international donors.

Notes

1 In 2009, the Obama Administration retained the OFBCI and renamed it as the Office of Faith-Based and Neighborhood Partnerships.
2 These include Christian Aid, CAFOD, Tearfund, the Church of England, World Jewish Relief, and the Muslims Charities Forum (DFID 2012).
3 The NNNGO hosts an annual conference attended by policy leaders, regulators, business executives, and NGO leaders to address issues related to national development.
4 Interview, Pastor Taiwo Odukoya, Fountain of Life Church, Lagos, 9 December 2010.
5 The gift of "helps" is listed in 1 Corinthian 12:28 as one of the gifts of the Holy Spirit, alongside healing, administration, and tongues.
6 Sermon preached at the Sunday Service, RCCG House of Praise, Birmingham, 5 October 2008.
7 Mk 16:15: "And He said to them, 'Go into all the world and preach the gospel to all creation' ".
8 Interview, Pastor Sola Adeaga, Jesus House, London, 22 July 2008.
9 Interview, Pastor Taiwo Odukoya, Fountain of Life Church, Lagos, 9 December 2010.
10 Interview, Pastor Sola Fola-Alade, RCCG Trinity Chapel, London, 22 July 2008.
11 Interview, Pastor Kemela Okara, This Present House, Lagos, 12 December 2010.
12 Interview, Bishop Abraham Olaleye, Abraham's Evangelistic Ministry, Lagos, 20 September 2010. Pastors who belong to Church for Change include Wale Adefarasin (Guiding Light Assembly), Paul Adefarasin (House on the Rock), Tony Rapu (This Present House), Sam Adeyemi (Daystar Christian Centre), Abraham Olaleye (Abraham's Evangelistic Ministry), John Enelamah (End Time Revival Ministries), Ladi Thompson (Living Waters Unlimited Church), and Yemi Osinbajo (RCCG pastor and incumbent Vice-President of Nigeria).
13 Interview, Pastor Sam Adeyemi, Daystar Christian Centre, Lagos, 7 October 2011.
14 A recent World Bank assessment of 192 countries in 1998 revealed that human capital contributes as much as 64 per cent towards economic development while physical infrastructure and available natural resources account for 16 per cent and 29 per cent respectively (Olayemi 2012).

15 Interview, Prof. Vincent Anigbogu, Institute for National Transformation, Abuja, 25 May 2012.
16 Interview, Pastor Sam Adeyemi, Daystar Christian Centre, Lagos, 7 October 2011.
17 Interview, Pastor Tunde Bakare, Latter Rain Assembly, Lagos, 2 October 2011.
18 For example, a recent edition of the *Guardian Nigeria*'s Sunday Magazine featured 14 pieces written by Nigerian Pentecostal pastors, including William Kumuyi (Deeper Life Bible Church), Bishop Francis Wale Oke (Sword of the Spirit Ministries), Austen Ukachi (He's Alive Chapel), and Chide Okoroafor (General Superintendent of Assemblies of God Nigeria). See *Guardian Nigeria* (2019).
19 Examples of Pentecostal newspapers and magazines include This Present House's *TPH Review*, God Bless Nigeria Church's *Urban Times*, Pastor Ituah Ighodalo's *Timeless Newspaper*, and RCCG's *Redemption Light*.
20 These are Salvation Ministries (Port Harcourt, 120,000-seater), Dunamis International Gospel Centre (Abuja, 100,000-seater), Winners Chapel (Lagos, 50,000-seater), Word of Life Bible Church (Warri, 35,000-seater), and Deeper Life Bible Church (Lagos, 30,000-seater). Estimates are based on human sitting capacity in a single service. RCCG's three million capacity auditorium at the Redemption Camp is not included as it is not a completely enclosed building.
21 Interview, Pastor Paul Adefarasin, House on the Rock, Lagos, 11 October 2011.
22 The Festival of Life is now held in other regions of Britain in order to cater for people who are unable to attend the London event.

References

Adeyemi, Nike (2010) "Anti-Corrupt Heart", Talk delivered at the 2010 Excellence in Leadership Conference: Leadership and Change, Daystar Christian Centre, Lagos, 10 November 2010.

Adeyemi, Sam (2010) "Anointing for Leadership", Talk delivered at the 2010 Excellence in Leadership Conference: Leadership and Change, Daystar Christian Centre, Lagos, 10 November.

Adogame, Afe (2005) " 'A Walk for Africa': Combating the Demon of HIV/AIDS in an African Pentecostal Church: The Case of the Redeemed Christian Church of God: The Challenge of HIV/AIDS to Christian Theology", *Scriptura: International Journal of Bible, Religion and Theology in Southern Africa* 89(1): 396–405.

AiMP (2015) *Nation-builders: An E-Newsletter of AiMP*, March, available at: https://aimpnetwork.org/newsletters/ (accessed 15 August 2019).

Anderson, Allan H. (2018) *Spirit-filled World: Religious Dis/Continuity in African Pentecostalism*, New York: Palgrave Macmillan.

Baker, Chris (2009) "Blurred Encounters? Religious Literacy, Spiritual Capital and Language", in Adam Dinham, Robert Furbey, and Vivien Lowndes (eds) *Faith in the Public Realm: Controversies, Policies and Practices*, Bristol: The Policy Press, pp. 105–122.

Bass, Bernard M. (1999) "Two Decades of Research and Development in Transformational Leadership", *European Journal of Work and Organizational Psychology* 8(1): 9–32.

Berger, Julia (2003) "Religious Nongovernmental Organizations: An Exploratory Analysis", *Voluntas: International Journal of Voluntary and Nonprofit Organizations* 14(1): 15–39.

Bompani, Barbara (2015) "Religion and Development in Sub-Saharan Africa: An Overview", in Emma Tomalin (ed.) *The Routledge Handbook of Religions and Global Development*, London: Routledge, pp. 101–113.

Bornstein, Erica (2002) "Developing Faith: Theologies of Economic Development in Zimbabwe", *Journal of Religion in Africa* 32(1): 4–31.

Bornstein, Erica (2004) *The Spirit of Development: Protestant NGOs, Morality, and Economics in Zimbabwe*, New York: Routledge.

Burchardt, Marian (2012) "Faith-based Humanitarianism: Organizational Change and Everyday Meanings in South Africa", *Sociology of Religion* 74(1): 30–55.

Butticci, Annalisa (2013) "Crazy World, Crazy Faith: Prayer, Power and Transformation in a Nigerian Prayer City", in Guiseppe Giordan and Linda Woodhead (eds) *Prayer in Religion and Spirituality*, Leiden: E. J. Brill, pp. 244–261.

Cartledge, Mark J., Sarah Dunlop, Heather Buckingham, and Sophie Bremner (2019) *Megachurches and Social Engagement: Public Theology in Practice*, Leiden: E. J. Brill.

Castells, Manuel (2010) *The Rise of the Network Society*, Chichester: Wiley-Blackwell.

Christerson, Brad and Richard Flory (2017) *The Rise of Network Christianity*, Oxford: Oxford University Press.

Clarke, Gerard (2008) "Faith-based Organizations and International Development: An Overview", in Gerard Clarke and Michael Jennings (eds) *Development, Civil Society and Faith-based Organizations: Bridging the Sacred and the Secular*, Basingstoke: Palgrave Macmillan, pp. 17–45.

Clarke, Matthew (2011) *Development and Religion: Theory and Practice*, Cheltenham: Edward Elgar.

Clarke, Matthew (2015) "Friend or Foe? Finding Common Ground Between Development and Pentecostalism", *PentecoStudies* 14(2): 156–175.

Clarke, Gerard and Michael Jennings (2008) "Introduction", in Gerard Clarke and Michael Jennings (eds) *Development, Civil Society and Faith-based Organisations: Bridging the Sacred and the Secular*, Basingstoke: Palgrave Macmillan, pp. 1–16.

Cnaan, Ram A. and Stephanie C. Boddie (2002) "Charitable Choice and Faith-based Welfare: A Call for Social Work", *Social Work* 47(3): 224–235.

Cnaan, Ram A. and Stephanie C. Boddie (2006) "Setting the Context: Assessing the Effectiveness of Faith-based Social Services", in Stephanie C. Boddie and Ram A. Cnaan (eds) *Faith-based Social Services: Measures, Assessments, and Effectiveness*, Binghamton, NY: Haworth Press, pp. 5–18.

CNAL (2015a) "About Us", available at: www.cnaleaders.com/about_us (accessed 5 August 2019).

CNAL (2015b) "History of CNAL", available at: www.cnaleaders.com/history-of-cnal (accessed 5 August 2019).

Davis, Comfort, Ayodele Jegede, Robert Leurs, Adegbenga Sunmola, and Ukoho Ukiwo (2011) *Comparing Religious and Secular NGOs in Nigeria: Are Faith-based Organizations Distinctive?* Birmingham: Religion and Development Research Programme WP 56.

Daystar Christian Centre (n.d.) "Community Impact", available at: https://daystarng.org/community-impact/ (accessed 19 August 2019).

Daystar Christian Centre (2011) *Daystar Christian Centre ... Raising Role Models*, Lagos: Daystar Christian Centre.

Daystar Christian Centre (2018) "Sharing God's Love in Brothels & Beyond with Nike Adeyemi", available at: www.daystar.com/news-updates/general-updates/sharing-gods-love-in-brothels-and-beyond-with-nike-adeyemi/ (accessed 16 November 2019).

Daystar Christian Centre (2019) "Our Mission & Vision", available at: http://dlaonline.org/index.php/about-us/our-mission-vision (accessed 19 August 2019).

Department for International Development (2012) *Faith Partnership Principles: Working Effectively with Faith Groups to Fight Global Poverty*, London: DFID.

de Witte, Marleen (2003) "Altar Media's Living Word: Televised Charismatic Christianity in Ghana", *Journal of Religion of Africa* 33(2): 172–202.

Dilger, Hansjörg (2009) "Doing Better? Religion, the Virtue-ethics of Development, and the Fragmentation of Health Politics in Tanzania", *Africa Today* 56(1): 89–110.

Dinham, Adam and Robert Jackson (2012) "Religion, Welfare and Education", in Linda Woodhead and Rebecca Catto (eds) *Religion and Change in Modern Britain*, London: Routledge, pp. 272–298.

Dinham, Adam and Vivien Lowndes (2009) "Faith and the Public Realm", in Adam Dinham, Robert Furbey and Vivien Lowndes (eds) *Faith in the Public Realm: Controversies, Policies and Practices*, Bristol: Policy Press, pp. 1–20.

Ebaugh, Helen R., Paula F. Pipes, Janet S. Chafetz, and Martha Daniels (2003) "Where's the Religion? Distinguishing Faith-based from Secular Social Service Agencies", *Journal for the Scientific Study of Religion* 42(3): 411–426.

Ellis, Stephen and Gerrie Ter Haar (1998) "Religions and Politics in Africa", *Journal of Modern African Studies* 36(2): 175–201.

Enlow, Johnny (2008) *The Seven Mountain Prophecy: Unveiling the Elijah Revolution*, Lake Mary, FL: Creation House.

Fountain of Love (2019) "Mission Statement", available at: www.fountainoflove.org.uk/mission-statement/ (accessed 20 August 2019).

Freedom Foundation (2019) "About Us", available at: www.freedomfoundationng.org/about-us/ (accessed 21 August 2019).

Freeman, Dena (2012) "The Pentecostal Ethic and the Spirit of Development", in Dena Freeman (ed.) *Pentecostalism and Development: Churches, NGOs and Social Change in Africa*, Basingstoke: pp. 1–40.

Furbey, Robert and Marie Macey (2005) "Religion and Urban Regeneration: A Place for Faith?", *Policy and Politics* 33(1): 95–116.

GAIN (n.d.), "Membership Spotlight", available at: www.gainglobal.org/index.php?option=com_content&view=article&id=52&Itemid=41 (accessed 23 July 2013).

Gifford, Paul (2004) *Ghana's New Christianity: Pentecostalism in a Globalizing African Economy*, London: Hurst & Co.

Gifford, Paul (2015) *Christianity, Development and Modernity in Africa*, London: Hurst & Co.

Guardian Nigeria (2018) "Again, Freedom Foundation Releases its Docu-series, 'My Lagos Diaries' ", *Guardian Nigeria*, https://guardian.ng/saturday-magazine/again-freedom-foundation-releases-its-docu-series-my-lagos-diaries/

Guardian Nigeria (2019) "Ibru Ecumenical Centre", *Guardian Nigeria*, 20 October, available at: https://guardian.ng/category/sunday-magazine/ (accessed 24 October 2019).

Guiding Light Assembly (n.d.) "What We Believe", available at: www.glawebchurch.net/what-we-believe.html (accessed 4 September 2019).

Hackett, Rosalind I. (2003) "Managing or Manipulating Religious Conflict in the Nigerian Media", in Jolyon P. Mitchell and Sophia Marriage (eds) *Mediating Religion: Conversations in Media, Religion, and Culture*, Edinburgh: T & T Clark, pp. 47–63.

Haustein, Jörg and Emma Tomalin (2017) "Religion and Development in Africa and Asia", in Pedro Amakasu Raposo, David Arase, and Scarlett Cornelissen (eds) *Routledge Handbook of Africa–Asia Relations*, London: Routledge, pp. 76–93.

Herrpich, Bergit (2016) "Redeemed Christian Church of God, North America", in George T. Kurian and Mark A. Lamport (eds) *The Enclopedia of Christianity in the United States*, Volume 5, London and New York: Rowman & Littlefield, pp. 1911–1913.

Iherika, Walter C. and Godwin B. Okon (2015) "Mega Churches and Megaphones: Nigerian Church Leaders and Their Media Ministries", in Jonathan D. James (ed.) *A Moving Faith: Megachurches Go South*, Los Angeles: Sage, pp. 62–82.

Irukwu, Agu (2008) "In the Crucible with Pastor Agu: Our Corporate Social Responsibility", *Outflow Magazine*, October, p. 5.

James, Rick (2011) "Handle with Care: Engaging with Faith-based Organisations in Development", *Development in Practice* 21(1): 109–117.

Jeavons, Thomas H. (2004) "Religious and Faith-based Organizations: Do We Know One When We See One?" *Nonprofit and Voluntary Sector Quarterly* 33(1): 140–145.

Jesus House (2016) *The Evolving Church: The Jesus House Annual Report 2016.* London: Jesus House.

Jochum, Véronique, Belinda Pratten, and Karl Wilding (2007) *Faith and Voluntary Action: An Overview of Current Evidence and Debates*, London: NCVO.

Kalu, Ogbu U. (2008) *African Pentecostalism: An Introduction*, Oxford: Oxford University Press.

Kay, William K. (2007) *Apostolic Networks in Britain: New Ways of Being Church*, Milton Keynes: Paternoster.

Kwabena J. Asamoah-Gyadu (2004) "Pentecostal Media Images and Religious Globalization in Sub-Saharan Africa", in Peter Horsfield, Mary Hess, and Adan Medrano (eds), *Belief in Media: Cultural Perspectives on Media and Christianity*, Aldershot: Ashgate, pp. 65–79.

Lee, Matthew T., Margaret M. Poloma, and Stephen G. Post (2013) *The Heart of Religion: Spiritual Empowerment, Benevolence, and the Experience of God's Love*, Oxford: Oxford University Press.

Leurs, Robert (2012) "Are Faith-based Organisations Distinctive? Comparing Religious and Secular NGOs in Nigeria", *Development in Practice* 22(5–6): 704–720.

Marshall, Ruth (2009) *Political Spiritualities: The Pentecostal Revolution in Nigeria*, Chicago: University of Chicago Press.

Marshall, Ruth (2014) "'Dealing with the Prince over Lagos': Pentecostal Arts of Citizenship", Mamadou Diouf and Rosalind Fredericks (eds) *The Arts of Citizenship in African Cities: Infrastructures and Spaces of Belonging*, New York: Palgrave Macmillan, pp. 91–114.

McCain, Danny (2013a) "The Metamorphosis of Nigerian Pentecostalism: From Signs and Wonders in the Church to Service and Influence in Society", in Donald Miller, Kimon Sergeant, and Richard Flory (eds) *The Spirit and Power: The Growth and Global Impact of Pentecostalism*, Oxford: Oxford University Press, pp. 160–181.

McCain, Danny (2013b) "Addressing Urban Problems Through Kingdom Theology: The 'Apostles in the Market Place' Model in Lagos, Nigeria", *Africa Journal of Evangelical Theology* 32(1): 61–80.

McCauley, John F. (2012) "Africa's New Big Man Rule? Pentecostalism and Patronage in Ghana", *African Affairs* 112(446): 1–21.

McGrew, Charlene and Ram Cnaan (2006) "Finding Congregations: Developing Conceptual Clarity in the Study of Faith-Based Social Services", in Stephanie C. Boddie and Ram A. Cnaan (eds) *Faith-based Social Services: Measures, Assessments, and Effectiveness*, New York: Routledge, pp. 19–38.

Meyer, Birgit (1998) "'Make a Complete Break with the Past': Memory and Postcolonial Modernity in Ghanaian Pentecostalist Discourse", *Journal of Religion in Africa* 28(3): 316–349.

Meyer, Birgit (2002) "Pentecostalism, Prosperity and Popular Cinema in Ghana", *Culture and Religion* 3(1): 67–87.

Meyer, Birgit (2004) "'Praise the Lord …' Popular Cinema and Pentecostalite Style in Ghana's New Public Sphere", *American Ethnologist* 31(1): 92–110.

Miller, Donald E. and Tetsunao Yamamori (2007) *Global Pentecostalism: The New Face of Christian Social Engagement*, Berkeley: University of California Press.

NNNGO (2018a) "Our History", available at: https://nnngo.org/our-history/ (accessed 15 August 2019).

NNNGO (2018b) "NGOs Directory", available at: https://nnngo.org/list-of-ngos-on-our-database/ (accessed 15 August 2019).

Nwakanma, Amabelle (2019) "The Case for the Nigerian Woman", available at: www.freedomfoundationng.org/the-case-for-the-nigerian-woman/ (accessed 23 October 2019).

O'Neill, Kevin (2010) *City of God: Christian Citizenship in Postwar Guatemala*, Berkeley: University of California Press.

Obadare, Ebenezer (2007) "Religious NGOs, Civil Society and the Quest for a Public Sphere in Nigeria", *African Identities* 5(1): 135–153.

Obadare, Ebenezer (2018) *Pentecostal Republic: Religion and the Struggle for State Power in Nigeria*, London: Zed Books.

Odumosu, Olakunle, Rasheed Olaniyi, and Sunday Alonge (2009) *Mapping the Activities of Faith-based Organizations in Development in Nigeria*, Birmingham: Religion and Development Research Programme, WP 38.

Ojo, Matthews A. (2006) *The End-Time Army: Charismatic Movements in Modern Nigeria*, Trenton, NJ: Africa World Press.

Olarinmoye, Omobolaji (2011) *Accountability in Faith-based Development Organizations in Nigeria: Preliminary Explorations*, Oxford: Global Economic Governance Programme, WP 67.

Olayemi, Simon-Oke O. (2012) "Human Capital Investment and Industrial Productivity in Nigeria", *International Journal of Humanities and Social Sciences* 2(16): 298–307.

Olivier, Jill and Quentin Wodon (2014) "Increased Funding for Aids-engaged Faith-based Organizations in Africa?" *The Review of Faith & International Affairs* 12(1): 53–71.

Oluseyi, Oyebisi B. (2018) "A New Policy for Civil Society in Nigeria", Commonwealth Foundation, 29 January, available at: https://commonwealthfoundation.com/making-law-work-civil-society-nigeria/ (accessed 19 October 2019).

Osinulu, Adedamola (2014) "The Road to Redemption: Performing Pentecostal Citizenship in Lagos", in Mamadou Diouf and Rosalind Fredericks (eds) *The Arts of Citizenship in African Cities: Infrastructures and Spaces of Belonging*, New York: Palgrave Macmillan, pp. 115–135.

Peel, John D. Y. (2000) *Religious Encounter and the Making of the Yoruba*, Bloomington, IN: Indiana University Press.

Poloma, Margaret M. and Matthew T. Lee (2013) "Prophecy, Empowerment and Godly Love", in Donald E. Miller, Kimon H. Sergeant, and Richard Flory (eds) *Spirit and Power: The Growth and Global Impact of Pentecostalism*, New York: Oxford University Press, pp. 277–297.

Poloma, Margaret M. and Ralph W. Hood, JR. (2008) *Blood and Fire. Godly Love in a Pentecostal Emerging Church*, New York: New York University Press.

Rapu, Tony (2005) "Nigeria: Where Will We Be in 15 Years?" THISDAY (Lagos), 4 June, available at: http://allafrica.com/stories/200506060745.html (accessed 15 September 2014).

Ray, Benjamin C. (1993) "Aladura Christianity", *Journal of Religion in Africa* 23(3): 266–291.

RCCG (2010) *Sunday School Student's Manual, 2010/2011*, UK, Ireland & Europe Edition. London: Delta Publishers.

RCCG Festival of Life (2016) "CSR", available at: www.festivaloflife.org.uk/about/csr (accessed 16 October 2019).

RILA (n.d.) "Redeemer's International Leadership Academy", available at: www.rila-ng.com/ (accessed 26 June 2019).

Segars, Mary C. (2003) "Introduction", in Jo Renee Formicola, Mary C. Segers, and Paul Weber (eds) *Faith-based Initiatives and the Bush Administration: The Good, the Bad and the Ugly*, Lanham, MD: Rowman & Littlefield Publishers, pp. 1–23.

Sider, Ronald J. and Heidi R. Unruh (2004) "Typology of Religious Characteristics of Social Service and Educational Organizations and Programs", *Nonprofit and Voluntary Sector Quarterly* 33(1): 109–134.

Smith, Daniel J. (2012) "AIDS NGOs and Corruption in Nigeria", *Health & Place* 18(3): 475–480.

Sustainable Development Goals Fund (2017) "Inspired by SDG Fund, Nigeria Launches the First Country Level Private Sector Advisory Group", 27 March, available at: www.sdgfund.org/inspired-sdg-fund-nigeria-launches-first-country-level-private-sector-advisory-group (accessed 15 April 2019).

Ter Haar, Gerrie (2011) *Religion and Development: Ways of Transforming the World*, London: Hurst & Company.

Tomalin, Emma (2016) "Thinking About Faith-based Organisations in Development: Where Have We Got to and What Next?", in Carole Rakodi (ed.) *Religion, Religious Organisations, and Development*, London and New York: Routledge, pp. 69–83.

Ukah, Asonzeh F.-K. (2004) "Pentecostalism, Religious Expansion and the City: Lessons from the Nigerian Bible Belt", in Peter Probst and Gerd Spittler (eds) *Between Resistance and Expansion: Explorations of Local Vitality in Africa*, Münster: Lit Verlag, pp. 415–443.

UN Environment (2018) Engaging with Faith-based Organizations: UN Environment Strategy, January, pp. 1–19, available at: https://wedocs.unep.org/bitstream/handle/20.500.11822/25989/UNEP%20Strategy%20Engaging%20FBOs.pdf?sequence=1&isAllowed=y (accessed 13 July 2019).

UNHCR (2014) *On Faith-based Organizations, Local Faith Communities and Faith Leaders*, Geneva: United Nations.

2 Pentecostal economics, entrepreneurship, and capacity-building

Introduction

On Nigerian Independence Day, following the 2011 presidential elections, I attended The Platform, a bi-annual Pentecostal conference hosted by Covenant Christian Centre and attended by Christians from all over Lagos. Covenant Christian Centre was founded in 1994 by Pastor Poju Oyemade, a graduate of the University of Lagos. The 2011 edition of The Platform was entitled "Enterprise and Governance" and featured speakers from Nigeria, the United States, and Colombia, including pastors, business entrepreneurs, bankers, and politicians. The event began with a rendition of the Nigerian National Anthem, which set the tone for the rest of the conference. Its focus was on nation-building through value-based education, business enterprise, and good governance, and the event was broadcast live on television and the Internet (see Figure 2.1). The Platform was established to address issues related to Nigeria's economic development, to empower Nigerians in their places of work, and to encourage a culture of entrepreneurship.[1] Other conference themes have included "Beyond Politics: The New Tribe of Africans Fighting Poverty and Changing the Face of the Continent", "Understanding the New Global Economy: How the Internet, Social Media and Technology is Driving Business & Entrepreneurship", and "Entrepreneurship, Small and Medium Scale Businesses as the Vehicle for Economic Growth". A particular emphasis of The Platform is on cultural reformation and the reorientation of societal values as a strategy for tackling Africa's underdevelopment.

This chapter examines Nigerian Pentecostal engagement with the economic sphere. It begins, first, by discussing the role of business enterprise in development and its inclusion in the post-2015 sustainable development agenda. Second, it sets the context by tracing the contours of Nigeria's economy since independence with a particular focus on the government's economic policies during the Fourth Republic. Third, it engages with current debates on Pentecostalism and economic development in Africa. Pentecostal beliefs impinge upon the economic domain, alternatively motivating or discouraging the pursuit of wealth and its employment for the benefit of others. Finally, the chapter examines a range of Nigerian Pentecostal initiatives geared towards economic empowerment and capacity-building, including programmes directed at women entrepreneurs and Nigerians in the diaspora. It also investigates Pentecostal efforts directed at reforming cultural values and changing institutional structures and economic policies considered an obstacle to positive development outcomes.

Enterprise, SMEs, and development

The post-2015 sustainable development agenda comprises a commitment to inclusive economic growth, addressing inequalities, and initiatives aimed at encouraging more ethical business practices (Sheyvens, Banks, and Hughes 2016). The UN has adopted a multi-stakeholder approach for the achievement of the SDGs which includes national and local governments, civil society organizations, businesses, academia, and development partners. A significant shift with the development of the SDGs has been the "foregrounding of the private sector" and the inclusion of business as an important development partner, partly driven by the fallout from the 2007/8 global financial crisis, which led to a reduction in public development budgets, along with the scale of global development challenges (Scheyvens, Banks, and Hughes 2016: 372).

There is a now a growing recognition within the international development community of the important contribution of Small and Medium Enterprises (SMEs) to developing economies (Ugwuegbe, Urama, and Iloh 2018; Grater, Parry, and Viviers 2017). As Abor and Quartey (2010) note, they are often perceived as efficient job creators, seeds of big businesses, and the fuel of economic growth. The SME sector plays a significant developmental role in African neoliberal economies, exemplified by structural adjustment, privatization, and diminished public sectors, especially since the 2007/8 global financial crisis. However, despite the potential of SMEs to foster economic growth and job creation, their development is hampered by financial constraints, deficiencies in managerial and marketing skills, poor regulatory environment, and lack of access to international markets (Igwe *et al.* 2018). Hence, government, financial institutions, and NGOs (including FBOs) have an important role to place in the capacity-building of SMEs. As we will see later, Pentecostal churches and NGOs are involved in building the capacity of the SME sector in Nigeria through microfinance initiatives, business schools, entrepreneurship education, use of print and electronic media, and conference events.

The Nigerian context

The rapid expansion of the petroleum sector made Nigeria the wealthiest country in Africa during the 1970s. However, as Falola and Heaton (2008) note, rather than contributing to national development and improved conditions for Nigerian citizens, this wealth was distributed unequally, mainly benefitting those who had access to state power. Government mismanagement and pervasive corruption resulted in economic decline, despite abundant natural resources and high-level manpower. Economic mismanagement and corruption were linked to prebendalism or neo-patrimonialism, a system of government dominated by patron-client relationships and the use of public office for private gain. But Osaghae (1998: 15–16) refers to the larger crisis of "extraversion which resulted from the country's peripheral location in the global system". As a rentier state, Nigeria's revenues accrued from taxes or rents on production of minerals by multinational corporations rather than directly from productive activity. This left it vulnerable to fluctuations in the world market and made it economically unstable. Dependence on oil discouraged agricultural development (the mainstay of the rural economy) and the growth of non-state capitalism (Osaghae 1998). Oil revenues had reached a peak in 1980, and by 1983, the economy was in serious decline due to the 1981 oil glut and the global economic recession (Badru 1998). Ihonvbere and Shaw (1998: 106) refer to the massive scale of government plunder between 1979 and 1983, where the "criteria of success escalated from Mercedez-Benz to personal jets for 'big men' and from stereos to VCR's for the middle class". Economic recession, austerity measures, and gross government mismanagement led to severe problems of unemployment and inflation. While politicians continued to enrich themselves, the urban poor and rural peasants bore the brunt of economic neglect.

The Structural Adjustment Programme (SAP), instituted in 1986 under General Ibrahim Babangida as a means of rescheduling Nigeria's debts and restructuring the Nigerian economy, caused serious hardships for Nigerian citizens and failed to achieve many of its anticipated results. There was little improvement in general living standards and unemployment levels increased (Falola and Heaton 2008). Writing in 1998, Julius Ihonvbere and Timothy Shaw (1998: 105) described the country's oil-dependent rentier economy as a case of economic growth without development. In 1999, Olusegun Obasanjo became the first civilian president of the Fourth Republic, inheriting a fragile state and economy characterized by dependence upon oil, poor industrial support infrastructure, and indebtedness. Obasanjo's economic policies in many ways "served as a continuation of the SAP measures" (Falola and Heaton 2008: 235). His adoption of neoliberal principles and a policy of privatization, encapsulated in the National Economic Empowerment Development Strategy (NEEDS), was an attempt to attract foreign investment and reduce Nigeria's external debts (Alao and Alao 2013).

Successive civilian regimes have continued to promote neoliberal policies and implement programmes directed at economic reform and transformation. President Umaru Yar'Adua's Seven-Point Agenda, introduced in 2007, focused on infrastructure (particularly energy and transport), food security and agriculture, human capital development and education, national security, land tenure and home ownership, and wealth creation (Alao and Alao 2013). In 2009, Nigeria adopted the "Nigeria Vision 2020" (NV 20: 2020) strategy, an ambitious plan to improve the living standards of its citizens and enable the country to become one of the top 20 economies in the world by 2020. The NV 20: 2020 included eight objectives based on the MDGs: eradicate extreme hunger and poverty; enhance access to quality healthcare; provide sustainable access to potable water and basic sanitation; provide accessible and affordable housing; build human capacity for sustainable livelihoods and national development; improve access to micro-credit; promote gender equality and empower women; and foster a culture of recreation and entertainment for enhanced productivity (National Planning Commission 2009).

In May 2011, President Goodluck Jonathan introduced the "Transformation Agenda", a developmentalist strategy for transforming the Nigerian economy (Alao and Alao 2013; Gyong 2012). The Transformation Agenda focused on three key areas: "strong, inclusive and non-inflationary growth; employment generation and poverty alleviation; and value re-orientation of the citizenry" (Gyong 2012: 98). However, it was greeted with cynicism by many Nigerians who suspected that it would go the way of its predecessors unless it succeeded in changing the political culture of corruption which continued to feed injustice and inequality. While it achieved a measure of success in key sectors such as job creation, power, education, and employment, poverty levels continued to rise (Alao and Alao 2013). The Jonathan administration also promised to fight corruption, engender a culture of responsible leadership, and campaign for an ethical reorientation of Nigerian society (Gyong 2012). Yet accusations of corrupt practices dogged the administration throughout his presidency (Awofeso and Odeyemi 2014). The developmentalist approach to politics has continued under President Muhammadu Buhari, whose five-point Change Agenda, introduced in 2015, aims at combating insecurity, tackling corruption, and addressing unemployment through economic diversification, education oriented towards a knowledge economy, and improving the environment for enterprise and entrepreneurship (*The Nation* 2015).

Each of these government development strategies included policies geared towards supporting SMEs by mobilizing and deploying microfinance funding. SMEs constitute a significant proportion of Nigerian businesses and characteristically belong to the informal sector. The 2015 World Bank enterprise survey in Nigeria indicated that SMEs had increased to over 90 per cent of enterprises in the country (Ugwuegbe, Urama, and Iloh 2018). In 2016, after more than a decade of economic growth, the Nigerian economy dipped into recession, partly brought about by the decline in oil prices since mid-2014, along with a failure to diversify the economy (Igwe *et al.* 2018). In 2017, the Buhari government introduced the Nigeria Economic Recovery and Growth Plan (ERGP). The top three priorities of the ERGP are food and agriculture, energy and power, and industrialization (with a particular focus on SMEs) (Yedder and Kantai 2017). Despite experiencing growth in the service sector and industry, the Nigerian economy is characterized by sluggish growth, high inflation, low oil prices, and depreciating exchange rate (Nevin and Omomia 2019).

Pentecostal economics and the prosperity gospel

The affinity between Pentecostalism and neo-liberalism in terms of entrepreneurial initiative, the generation of capital and the focus on the self raises questions concerning its capacity to encourage socio-economic mobility and development. Recent debate in discussions of Pentecostal economic culture concerns the extent to which the movement plays a role in establishing a "Protestant ethic" similar to the one played by Calvinism in Weber's account of capitalism (Robbins 2004; Freeman 2012; Gifford 2015; Drønen 2015). A key question regarding the impact of Pentecostalism on development in Africa is whether Pentecostal churches help to build, intentionally or otherwise, some of the economically significant beliefs, attitudes, and behaviours that can be loosely described as the Protestant ethic (Freeman 2012).

Scholars of African Christianity are divided over this. Dena Freeman (2012: 22) argues that "Pentecostalism does indeed bring about a Pentecostal Ethic, similar to Weber's Protestant Ethic, which supports and legitimates the spread of capitalism". Weber's key point, according to Freeman, was that in order for capitalism to develop, there had to be a shift in people's "values and subjectivity in order to motivate new behaviours and to make the new economic system seem moral, and that Protestantism unintentionally did this" (2012: 20). Pentecostalism is a form of Protestantism that "not only fits with African sensibilities, but also stimulates a transformation of behavior that can lead to success, or at least upward mobility, in the contemporary neoliberal economy" (2012: 20). Other scholars disagree, arguing that Pentecostalism's "enchanted" worldview and miraculous approach to wealth does not promote the classic Protestant ethic (e.g. Gifford 1998, 2015; Obadare 2016). Ebenezer Obadare (2016: 7–8) contends that Pentecostalism "offers no realistic path out of the economic crisis in Africa", because its emphasis on personal transformation renders it blind to "structure and social facts". Contrary to the Protestant ethic's emphasis on "personal industry and frugality", wealth is understood by African Pentecostals as something that occurs "miraculously, and not necessarily issuing from prior investment in terms of individual preparation" (2016: 6). However, as we will see later, some Nigerian Pentecostal pastors are challenging dominant attitudes and behaviours in church and society, such as corruption, excessive consumption, and unaccountable leadership styles, by promoting values of hard work, frugality, and altruism.

Scholarly debates on Pentecostalism and development in Africa usually make reference to the prosperity gospel, which links faith and prayer with the expectation of material prosperity and success (e.g. Wariboko 2012; Gifford 2015).[2] Much criticized by both Western and African scholars (Ayegboyin 2006; Obadare 2016; Gifford 2004; Ogungbile 2014), African prosperity theologies must be understood within the particular contexts they arise. In the case of Nigerian Pentecostal appropriations, existing religious preoccupations, local socio-economic context, and global forces all came into play. To use an agricultural metaphor, there needed to be a fertile soil, a favourable climate, and access to a ready supply of seed. Nigerian societies, such as the Yoruba and Igbo, traditionally associate the deities with prosperity. In Yoruba culture, the "good life" is summed up in the state of *alafia* or "peace", which embraces protection, practical guidance, health, fertility, success, and material prosperity, all fruits of power looked for in Christianity (Peel 2000: 91, 219). Related to this is an emphasis on achievement, progress, and prestige, in which status and moral standing in the community are associated with symbols of success acquired through religious power, and the redistribution of wealth for the benefit of others (Okorocha 1987). Thus, there are close affinities between traditional religious aspirations and prosperity teaching, with its emphasis on material acquisition through faith, and this facilitated its assimilation into Nigerian soil. As Kalu (2008) notes, one of the reasons for the popularity of the prosperity message is its resonance with African indigenous concepts of salvation, abundant life, and the goals of worship.

There are also discontinuities between Pentecostal prosperity teaching and traditional concepts of wealth accumulation. In indigenous cultures, such as the Yoruba and Igbo, the rich are bound by obligations of reciprocity, which require them to redistribute their wealth to kin and community of origin through patronage networks (Smith 2001). There is also a link in the popular imagination between the achievement of wealth and power, on the one hand, and human sacrifice, on the other. Iheanyi Enwerem (2003) refers to this as "money-magic", which he suggests has resurfaced in contemporary Nigeria in an environment characterized by economic decline and increasing poverty. This has resulted in the widespread belief that wealthy people, especially those who fail to redistribute their wealth for the benefits of others, must have acquired their money through engaging in occult ritual practices and witchcraft.

There is a growing anthropological literature exploring the way that emerging inequalities in sub-Saharan Africa, brought about by the penetration of global capitalism, are expressed in discourses about the occult or what Geschiere calls "the modernity of witchcraft" (Geschiere 1997; see also Meyer 1998). The paradox of the processes of globalization, according to Geschiere, is that they appear to reinforce cultural heterogeneity rather than erode it. One example is the "ease with which witchcraft discourses in Africa incorporate the money economy, new power relations, and consumer goods associated with modernity …" (1997: 8). Daniel Smith (2001) suggests that the inequality that gives rise to modern discourses of the occult in relation to wealth accumulation in Africa is marked simultaneously by resentment of the wealthy and the desire to benefit from their patronage. He explores the relationship between occult practices and prosperity churches by examining the role of religion in a crisis which erupted in September 1996 following the discovery of incidents of ritual killing in the city of Owerri, south-eastern Nigeria, allegedly committed in pursuit of "fast-wealth". Smith argues that what the town's *nouveau riches* did with their money shaped popular interpretations of how this wealth was acquired. Because they flouted their wealth and failed to "fulfil the reciprocal obligations of patrons prescribed by a morality rooted in kinship" (2001: 593), they became targets of popular resentment, resulting in the destruction of their property. It was generally believed that their acquisition of "fast-wealth" was achieved through satanic rituals.

What was unusual in the case of the Owerri crisis was that the premises of several prosperity churches were also burned by the rioters, suggesting that they too were implicated in the rumours of occult activity. Smith notes the paradoxical position of Nigerian Pentecostalism in this respect. While it offers a critique of inequality and "illegitimate wealth" acquired through witchcraft and the occult, the movement "has also produced its own inequalities and embodies the very materialism that motivates so much discontent" (2001: 608). Thus, Pentecostalism is "positioned in somewhat contradictory ways in relation to Nigeria's patronage-oriented political economy". Pentecostal leaders preach against state corruption and the distribution of wealth through patron-client networks based on ethnicity and kinship. Nonetheless, they, too, have their own patronage networks and hierarchical social structures, which have allowed some of them to accumulate wealth on an unprecedented scale (2001: 589–590). One way of explaining the popularity of Pentecostal prosperity teaching in Nigeria, according to Smith (2001: 602), is that it provides a moral justification for individual ambition and accumulation, free from the obligation to kin and community.

Smith's analysis is a convincing account of why prosperity detached from the obligations of reciprocity, as portrayed in some sectors of the Nigerian Pentecostal constituency, has elicited apparently conflicting popular reactions. However, as I have argued in Chapter 1, not all Nigerian Pentecostals have neglected their reciprocal responsibilities. Some Nigerian Pentecostal churches and individuals, while adhering to a doctrine of prosperity, are redistributing their wealth through development projects and charitable giving. The impulse behind this, from the participants' point of view, is not only traditional concepts of reciprocity and redistribution of wealth, but obedience to the biblical mandate to love one's neighbour.

To return to our agricultural metaphor, two other conditions contributed to the absorption of prosperity teaching into Nigerian soil. These were a suitable socio-economic climate and access to a ready supply of seed, in this case the message itself. Matthews Ojo (2006: 208) states that in Nigeria prosperity and success as religious ideas were "developed as a response to the socio-economic changes of the 1980s". Contrary to Gifford (1990), who stresses the American origins of prosperity teaching in Africa, Ojo (2006) insists that Nigerian Pentecostals read their Bibles for themselves and appropriated its message to suit local contexts, suffering from economic decline caused by corrupt political regimes and IMF-inspired Structural Adjustment Programmes. Wariboko (2014: 35) also stresses the role of indigenous agency in the development of prosperity theology. Drawing upon David Martin's argument that Pentecostal recourse to the "power of Jesus" provides an alternative to the occult economy (Martin 2008), Wariboko (2014: 236, 35) suggests that prosperity preachers "motivate believers to become agents of their own personal economic improvement", crafting a "theology of hope to deal with the exigencies of everyday existence, to imaginatively transform dire socioeconomic conditions of ordinary Nigerians, and to offer their followers a robust sense of dignity". However, global flows through media, transnational exchanges of ministry, and theological education were crucial in shaping Nigerian prosperity theology. While it resonated with traditional piety, and satisfied local religious demands, it was expressed in standard American form. Perhaps the best example of this is the principle of

"seed faith", lifted directly from American Word of Faith teaching, which encourages Christians to expect financial returns from their giving.

Prosperity teaching has been criticized for discouraging Christians from productive economic activity and hindering African development. In the case of Ghana's charismatic churches, Gifford (2004: 155–158) suggests that the focus on faith, giving, deliverance, and the pastor's gifts leaves insufficient room for the place of work in achieving "victorious prosperity". Rather than transforming Ghana's economic situation, Gifford argues, faith teaching may have the opposite effect by encouraging Christians to pray for prosperity rather than engage in productive activity. More recently, Gifford (2015: 60) has turned his attention to Nigeria and the prosperity theology of Bishop David Oyedepo of Winners Chapel: "Oyedepo stresses the need to work, but victory and success in business, in getting jobs, in health and in life, do not depend on work" (2015: 60). For Gifford, Oyedepo's faith gospel, exemplified by the logic of seed faith, is the antithesis of Weber's spirit of capitalism (2015: 60).

In Nigerian Pentecostal discourse, nonetheless, hard work and entrepreneurship are often promoted alongside faith as necessary conditions for success and material prosperity. This is reflected in the following extract from a book written by William Okoye, General Overseer of All Christians Fellowship Mission:

> If you till your land, work hard, and you are disciplined in your work habit; if you are not a lazy person that likes dozing and sleeping all the time, God will bless the work of your hands and prosper you.
>
> (Okoye 1993: 125)

And a sermon preached by RCCG's Enoch Adeboye states: "When you ask God to prosper you, what He will do is that He will give you work to do that will bring in money" (Adeboye 2002: 74). According to David Oyedepo (2007: 215),

> The works of our hands are the primary channel through which God blesses us. So if you are not a worker, you are not a candidate for His prosperity. If your hands are idle, God has a problem of finding how to bless you, no matter how much you give.

For Oyedepo, work is the way to "bring down God's blessings" and "eradicate poverty from the nations" (2007: 217). The Nigeria Survey showed that a variety of factors, from background to work ethic to government policies, are regarded by Pentecostals as key to determining economic success or failure. However, the factors deemed most important are faith in God, hard work, and education (Nigeria Survey 2011).

Scholars acknowledge the diversity of African Pentecostal approaches to prosperity and success (Obadare 2016; Wariboko 2014; Gifford 2015). Gifford (2015) compares the developmental effects of two different forms of Christianity in Africa, an "enchanted Christianity that operates from a belief in pervasive spiritual forces", represented by Pentecostalism, and a "disenchanted and internally secularized Christianity that operates on a totally different plane, that of human development", typified by Roman Catholicism (2015: 157). Gifford (2015: 48) identifies six different registers on which Pentecostal success is played: motivation, entrepreneurship, practical skills for personal living and business success, the faith gospel, the anointing of the pastor, and blocking the spirits impeding one's progress. Not all are incompatible, and many churches combine these registers. A positive assessment of Pentecostalism's economic potential arises from a focus on the first three registers. For Gifford, however, it is the last three that are more prevalent: "To the extent that African Pentecostalism builds on the faith gospel, a pastor's anointing, and the enchanted religious imagination, the effects seem far less positive" (2015: 55).

Wariboko (2014) outlines five basic theological paradigms that "frame the discourse on Africa's economic development among Pentecostal pastors" (2014: 233). These are not discrete categories, according to Wariboko, but Weberian ideal constructs. Wariboko's covenant paradigm, exemplified by Oyedepo, sees poverty as a religious problem caused by lack of faith in God's promises. The Spiritualist paradigm, which often undergirds the covenant paradigm, advocates spiritual warfare to engender national prosperity. Wariboko's Leadership paradigm attributes Africa's underdevelopment to immoral leadership and to "unjust, unpatriotic, and exploitative social structures" (2014: 242).[3] Wariboko's other Pentecostal paradigms are the Developmental paradigm (exemplified by the RCCG), which "sees churches as agents of economic development in their local communities", helping the poor, providing public services, and engaging in development projects (2014: 244–245); and the Most-Favored Nation Status paradigm, a "geographical theology" whose proponents believe that Nigeria is destined by God to play a crucial role in the development of the black race (2014: 246).

Recently, critics of Nigerian Pentecostal prosperity doctrine have emerged from within the movement itself. Marshall (2009: 240) refers to Tony Rapu, senior pastor of This Present House, who has

> condemned prosperity preachers, moral laxity, and rampant materialism, arguing that the majority of Born-Again Christians have found themselves in a new form of bondage, and that as church growth has exploded, so have injustice, violence, poverty, sickness, corruption and death.

We will return to Rapu later in the chapter. As was discussed in Chapter 1, two emerging trends can be discerned with regard to Nigerian Pentecostal approaches to prosperity: first, a shift from reliance on "miracles" to an emphasis on work and entrepreneurship; and second, a new understanding that the purpose of wealth is for it to be used for the common good rather than for personal enrichment. The latter trend is reflected in the following interview excerpts:

> We are now teaching the purpose of wealth, not just to multiple cars, houses, but to increase in financial prosperity in turn to be used for the expansion of God's kingdom. Religion is not really affecting society in

> Nigeria as its very corrupt. What is the purpose of that prosperity? It is imperative to teach the church that the purpose of abundance is to abound for every good work and charitable donation. God is not saying it is not good to be wealthy, provided that the purpose of that wealth is that you help the poor. We cannot afford to keep seeking God for what we can get, but for what we want to do for God and for humanity.[4]
>
> People are beginning to see prosperity in terms of it putting you in a position where you are more useful to your community; that is the perspective in which it is being framed now, not how much you can demonstrate personal wealth. In fact, I think it is becoming quite embarrassing for you to say you personally have this amount of money when there is so much poverty around.[5]

In the remainder of the chapter, I consider some of the ways that Nigerian Pentecostals are seeking to alleviate poverty and contribute to people's economic prosperity. First, I examine Pentecostal programmes geared towards economic empowerment and entrepreneurship education, focusing particularly on the SME sector. These initiatives correspond to Gifford's first three registers: motivation, entrepreneurship, and practical skills for personal living and business success. Second, I investigate Pentecostal efforts directed at reforming cultural values and changing institutional structures and economic policies deemed inimical to positive development outcomes. Finally, I consider the transnational dimension by examining Pentecostal entrepreneurship in the diaspora.

Economic empowerment and entrepreneurship

Nigerian Pentecostal churches and NGOs are increasingly involved in building the capacity of the SME sector through microfinance initiatives, conference events, business schools, and entrepreneurship education. Pentecostals also publish books and magazines articles, and present TV and radio programmes, on entrepreneurship and Christian engagement with the financial sector. Business enterprise has become a popular profession for Nigerian Pentecostals in response to increasing unemployment, especially among the youth. Pentecostal pastors sometimes combine church ministry with business initiatives to supplement their income.

Some Nigerian Pentecostal churches and individuals have founded NGOs aimed at economic empowerment and entrepreneurship education. Here I return to Covenant Christian Centre's 2011 Platform event introduced at the beginning of the chapter. In his opening address, Pastor Poju Oyemade, senior pastor of Covenant Christian Centre, emphasized the importance of business entrepreneurship for Nigeria's development. According to Oyemade, business enterprise creates employment opportunities, reduces the gap between the rich and the poor, and encourages the growth of the middle class. Covenant Christian Centre has established an NGO called Covenant Capital which aims to build the capacity of entrepreneurs and fledgling businesses by providing microfinance assistance,

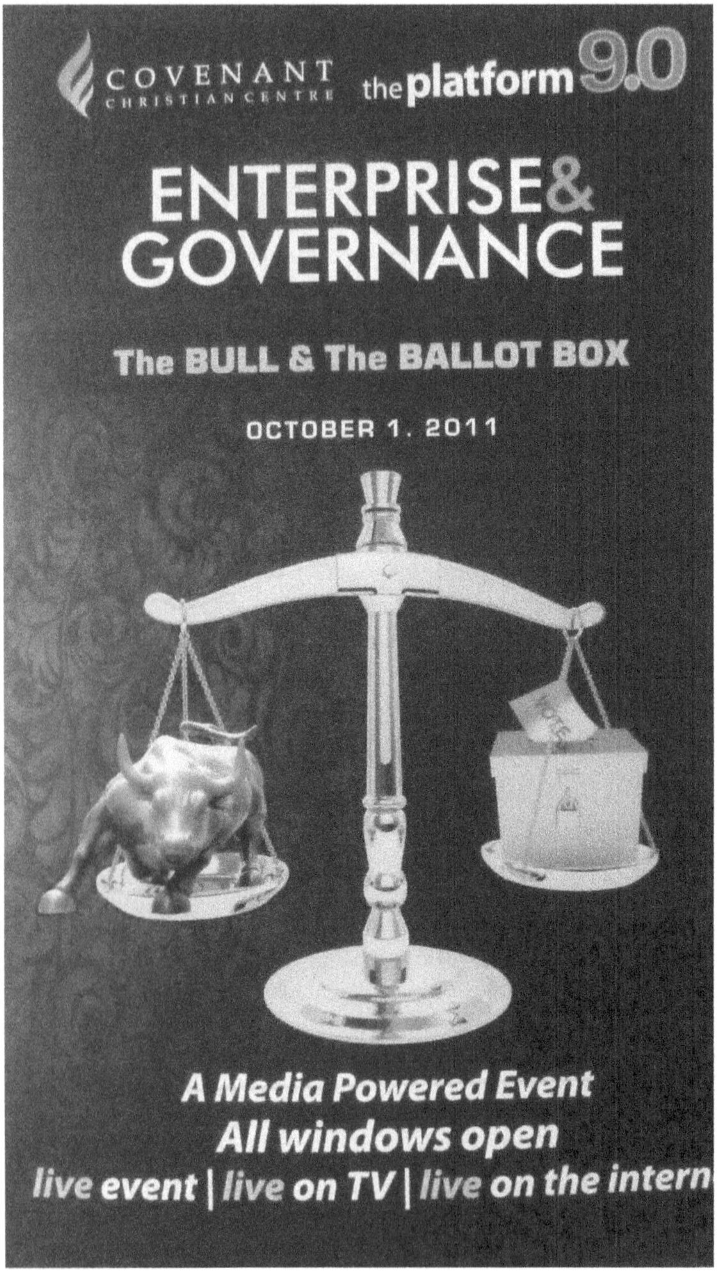

Figure 2.1 Flyer advertising the October 2011 edition of The Platform, hosted by Covenant Christian Centre, Lagos.

Source: author.

advisory services, and entrepreneurship education (Covenant Capital 2016a). Covenant Capital's capacity-building programmes include an annual SME Fair for business owners, an Economic Empowerment Summit, an Internet-based SME hub and business directory, a vocational skills training centre called the Formal and Vocational Employment Program, and Covenant Capital Business School (CCBS). CCBS focuses on "equipping entrepreneurs by teaching them requisite business skills to better manage and grow their businesses" (Covenant Capital 2016b).

Fountain of Life Church in Lagos runs an NGO called Fountain Initiative for Social Development (FISD). FISD's founder is Pastor Nomthi Odukoya, married to Taiwo Odukoya, senior pastor of Fountain of Life Church. One of FISD's capacity-building initiatives is the Entrepreneurship Development Programme, which provides business skills training and information about accessing finance for SME owners through its Enterprise Academy. Other FISD initiatives include the Career Development and Employability Programme, the Women Entrepreneurship Programme, and the Vocational Skills Programme (FISD 2016). In 2015, about 5,000 members of the National Youth Service Corps attended the Enterprise Funding Fair in Lagos, organized by FISD to encourage entrepreneurship (Kukogho 2015).

Another Pentecostal NGO is the Olumide Emmanuel Foundation (OEF), named after its founder, Olumide Emmanuel, senior pastor of Calvary Bible Church in Lagos.[6] The OEF is a Pentecostal NGO geared towards poverty alleviation and development. Olumide Emmanuel is also a business entrepreneur, author, conference host, and radio presenter. His bestselling book *The Pathway to Wealth* (2008) serves as a practical manual on biblical economic principles and wealth creation strategies. The OEF engages with the MDGs and SDGs which are listed on its website and in its newsletter (Emmanuel 2016). It has developed a seven-point agenda to tackle poverty in Nigeria, loosely based on the MDGs, which focuses on food, clothing, shelter, education, health, entrepreneurship, and investment (Olumide Emmanuel Foundation 2019). In 2012, Calvary Bible Church opened the Entrepreneurship Academy, aimed at "raising a new generation of entrepreneurs who will drive the nation's economic development" (Nzeako 2017).

Some of the most successful Pentecostal entrepreneurs in Nigeria are women. Studies of entrepreneurship in sub-Saharan Africa show the significant role played by women, especially within the SME sector (Richardson, Howarth, and Finnegan 2004; Halkias *et al.* 2011; Mwobobia 2012). One reason for this is that the sector provides sustainable employment opportunities for those at the margins of the economy, including women, the poor, and people with disabilities. However, women entrepreneurs encounter significant challenges and constraints in developing their businesses. These include negative cultural attitudes to women in business, gender bias in accessing financial resources, the time pressures of juggling business and family responsibilities, and a lack of entrepreneurial training (Richardson, Howarth, and Finnegan 2004; Mwobobia 2012). Despite these challenges, many African women are running successful businesses that employ others and help to support their families.

Among the keynote speakers at the 2011 Platform event was Ibokun Awosika, an ordained pastor in the Fountain of Life Church. Awosika is the founder of The Chair Centre Ltd and co-founder of the Sokoa Chair Centre Ltd, as well as the current Chairman of First Bank Nigeria Plc. She is also an author and TV presenter.[7] Her career as an entrepreneur began in the 1990s when, in partnership with an architect, she started a small business manufacturing furniture which eventually evolved into The Chair Centre. Since then, The Chair Centre has become one of the market leaders in the Nigerian office furniture industry. In 2000, Awosika co-founded Women in Business, Management and Public Service (WIMBIZ), a faith-based capacity-building NGO which seeks to "inspire, empower and advocate for greater representation of women in leadership positions in the public and private sector" (WIMBIZ 2017a). WIMBIZ hosts an annual conference which attracts over 1,000 women working in the corporate, business, and public sectors. It also runs a mentoring programme designed to empower young girls in public schools with life skills and leadership capacity, and a graduate internship and mentoring programme that aims to address the unemployment crisis in Nigeria by equipping unemployed female undergraduates with workplace skills (WIMBIZ 2017b). In Awosika's account of her life, published in her book *The "Girl" Entrepreneurs. Our Stories So Far* (2008), she refers to the spiritual and social capital provided by her family, her Christian faith, and her membership of Fountain of Life Church, which have enabled her to persevere and develop as an entrepreneur despite the challenges posed by a hostile business environment, especially for women.

Another leading Pentecostal woman entrepreneur is Ndidi Nwuneli, a member of Apostles in the Market Place's Leadership Forum. Born and raised in eastern Nigeria, Nwuneli received an MBA from Harvard Business School. In 2000, she returned to Nigeria to become the pioneer Executive Director of FATE Foundation, an NGO established to promote wealth creation and entrepreneurship in Nigeria through education and enterprise support (FATE Foundation 2019). In 2002, she founded another NGO called LEAP Africa. LEAP is an acronym for Leadership, Effectiveness, Accountability and Professionalism. Since its inception, LEAP Africa has trained thousands of entrepreneurs, young people, teachers, and community organizers across Nigeria. Nwuneli is also co-founder of Sahel Capital, a company focused on agriculture, a sector which is attracting increasing interest from public and private investors since the downturn in the global economy and the rapid decline in oil prices (Foodtank 2019). Nwuneli is an author (Nwuneli 2016), conference speaker, and consultant. She has addressed the United Nation's Commission for Social Development, the World Economic Forum, and the Clinton Global Initiative, and is a member of USAID's advisory committee on Voluntary Foreign Aid.

In August 2017, Nwuneli delivered a TED Talk entitled "The Role of Faith and Belief in Driving Social Change in Africa" in which she called on faith groups to take responsibility for securing Africa's future:

> Now there are many things, I believe, that we can control – some we cannot. I believe that God is all-powerful, but he's not a micromanager. He has sent us here as his change agents, and we must stop making excuses and using him.

Nwuneli appealed to faith communities to utilize their resources and assets for social impact, and to partner with other stakeholders (Nwuneli 2017).[8] In October 2017, Nwuneli was one of the speakers at a Women's MSME (Micro, Small, and Medium Enterprises) Conference in Lagos, hosted by Covenant Christian Centre. The conference theme was: "Equipping the Female Entrepreneur with Ideas, Concepts and Insights to Thrive in the Nigerian Economy and Beyond". The keynote address was delivered by Dr Jumoke Oduwole, Senior Special Assistant to the President on Industry, Trade, and Investment (Office of the Vice-President) (*Government and Business Journal* 2017).

Cultural and structural reform

Some Nigerian Pentecostals are intentionally seeking to implement a reformation of culture by confronting popular conceptions of faith and prosperity within their ranks and inculcating values such as hard work, integrity, self-discipline, and servant leadership. Another speaker at the 2011 edition of The Platform was Prof. Yemi Osinbajo, RCCG pastor and current Vice-President of Nigeria. Osinbajo's talk, entitled "The Value Systems Upon Which Successful Enterprises Are Built", focused on the influence of values on enterprise and development. According to Osinbajo, a nation's economic development is dependent upon its cultural value system more than its innate talent or natural resources. Nigeria has remained poor, he told us, despite its rich natural resources. He proceeded to outline various values that Nigerian citizens need to nurture in order to build successful enterprises and engender national development. These include discipline and timeliness in the workplace; a culture of savings, investment, and frugality; integrity and trust in business; and the value of meritocracy where government and business appointments are based on merit.

Significantly, some Pentecostal pastors in Nigeria define Africa's economic problems in terms of social and political structures, recognizing that economic prosperity will only be attained if the structural and environmental causes of poverty and inequality are addressed. These pastors fit the profile of Wariboko's Leadership paradigm. As Wariboko (2014: 243) notes, this paradigm is distinctive because it "not only explains the Nigerian economic predicament by focusing on exploitative socioeconomic injustice, but it also raises serious leadership questions relating to social justice". Exemplars of this paradigm include Pastors Tony Rapu, Sam Adeyemi, and Tunde Bakare. Because these pastors also address political issues, we will return to them in Chapter 3, when we examine the political dimensions of Pentecostal Christianity. In 2012, roughly a year after the launch of President Jonathan's Transformation Agenda, Tony Rapu wrote an article, entitled "Agents of Change", in which he discerned a shift in orientation among Nigerian Pentecostals away from a miraculous approach to prosperity towards addressing the social and political causes of poverty.

> Slowly but surely, the seeds of a new consciousness are sprouting in the Church. It is the idea that the gospel must not only cause an inward change in the individual, but also inform a transformation of society. Over the past three decades, the message of personal prosperity – the notion that the individual will continue to prosper even as communities unravel – has resounded from pulpits. Now the limits of this message have become apparent. Insecurity, crime, infrastructural decay and general instability threaten to make us prisoners within our framework of God's blessings. We are discovering that individual prosperity and God's supposed blessings do not necessarily protect us from the problems that afflict society as a whole. As a result, in the Church, we are seeing the first tender shoots of a resolve to engage more holistically with society. In theological terms, we are moving from the selfish pursuit of blessings to the place where we become blessings to our communities.... The potential to positively transform our society is immense. There also remains the engagement of the structures of government. The Church should encourage members to seek active participation in public office.
>
> (Rapu 2012)

In 2016, Sam Adeyemi of Daystar Christian Centre was one of the speakers at the October edition of The Platform. His talk, entitled "Unleashing the Potentials for Wealth Creation", began with the words: "If we want to prosper and see Nigeria develop, we must ensure some deep changes in our economic and political institutions" (Adeyemi 2016). In his address, which was broadcast on national television, there was no mention of the Faith Gospel. Instead he spoke about the need for the legislature to change the laws on land and property rights; for politicians to be more accountable to the electorate, to increase the ease for running businesses in the country, and to spend money on infrastructure rather than on enriching themselves; and for banks to be more willing to loan money to business entrepreneurs (Adeyemi 2016). Adeyemi then proceeded to encourage members of his audience to get involved in the political process:

> Let us join the political parties *en masse* now for the sake of our future and that of our children and grandchildren. Change must begin within the parties and if it is possible when you get in there, contest for the primaries.

Like Osinbajo, Adeyemi also addressed the issue of cultural values, with a particular focus on leadership:

> I believe that we cannot prosper collectively without a change in our collective values. The likelihood is that most of us will behave exactly like those who are in control of our political and economic institutions if we had the opportunity to control those institutions. I will challenge you as I

> challenge myself to practice accountable leadership where we are.... Submit to the principles, the laws and the policies of the institution you are helping to build. Focus on service because service is the essence of leadership. Focus on meeting needs, focus on adding value to people's lives.
>
> (Adeyemi 2016)

Adeyemi's prescription for economic development includes an emphasis on entrepreneurship education. Early in his ministry, he began to teach financial principles to his congregation. In 1995, he founded "Success Power International", an educational NGO designed to motivate Nigerians to be successful in their lives and businesses (Success Power International 2019). Adeyemi encourages his church members to become business entrepreneurs because he believes that government is unable to create jobs for all its citizens. His venture into entrepreneurship education followed his discovery that successful nations usually build their prosperity on small businesses. Businesses stimulate the economy, according to Adeyemi, by creating jobs and by enabling business owners and their employees to spend money and pay taxes.[9]

My final example is Tunde Bakare, General Overseer of the Latter Rain Assembly and one of the most prominent political activists in Nigeria. Wariboko's analysis of Bakare's views on economic development, gleaned from his political speeches, identifies four key points "oriented around the development of individuals and federating units". First, Bakare advocates skills development which will ensure everyone will have a trade. Second, "every federating unit in the country should be given a chance to develop at its own pace according to the resources of its area". Third, distribution of the country's resources should benefit all its citizens. Finally, "he reasons that none of these will actually work without reforms (e.g. to social structures, the constitution, and the justice system)" (Wariboko 2014: 243). Significantly, Bakare also engages with the international development agenda. In a 2009 political speech, entitled "There is Hope in our Future", he criticized the United Nations MDGs as a western development pattern imposed on developing nations for the benefit of those who designed it. According to Bakare, God's plan is for every nation "to develop at her own pace" rather than copy the Western world.

> What Nigeria has spent so far and what we still need to spend to attain the MDGs could have been put into some productive use in developing vital domains of our society and by now we would have something to show for credible governance.
>
> (Bakare 2009)

Diaspora and transnational entrepreneurs

There is also a transnational dimension to Nigerian Pentecostal engagement with the economic domain. Most of the pastors discussed in this chapter make regular ministry trips to Europe and the United States, and their books and CDs/DVDs are available to buy online or are on sale during conference events and church services.[10] As we will see in Chapter 8, churches in the diaspora send collective remittances and charitable donations to support development work in Nigeria and other parts of Africa. Nigerian Pentecostals in Britain are also engaged in small and medium business enterprises. The context for this is an entrepreneurial spirit, a preference for self-employment, racial discrimination in the labour market, immigrant social and economic disadvantage, and a large co-ethnic social network which is both a potential source of labour and a customer base (Fadahunsi, Smallbone, and Supri 2000; Nwankwo, Gbadamosi, and Ojo 2012). Recently, it has also been played out against a backdrop of economic recession, which has adversely affected the lives of many African Pentecostal migrants. Starting a business returns agency to the individual and in the case of Pentecostal pastors enables them to devote more time to Christian ministry without being dependent upon their churches for financial support.

Research on labour market changes in Europe has shown the increasing prominence of ethnic minority self-employment and business ventures (Barrett, Jones, and McEvoy 1996). Studies of transnational entrepreneurship, which examine immigrant entrepreneurship through the theoretical lens of transnationalism, have posed a challenge to conventional ethnic entrepreneurship studies, which have mainly focused on immigrants' entrepreneurial activities within the host country (Chen and Tan 2009; Portes, Haller, and Guarnizo 2002). Transnational entrepreneurs are immigrant entrepreneurs "who conduct border crossing business activities" (Chen and Tan 2009: 1080). While most transnational entrepreneurs operate between the host and home country, border-crossing entrepreneurial activities may sometimes involve multiple countries.

There is a growing literature on black African entrepreneurship in Britain. Research has focused on the characteristics of black African entrepreneurial activity, the importance of diaspora social networks for ethnic business ventures, the challenges posed by government policy and regulatory regimes, the transition from enclave to transnational entrepreneurship, and the contributions of diaspora communities to economic development in Africa (Nwankwo, Gbadamosi, and Ojo 2012; Nwankwo and Gbadamosi 2013; Ojo 2019). Ethnic entrepreneurship is a growing phenomenon among Nigerian immigrants. Nigerian businesses engage mostly in retail, consumer, and professional services such as selling Nigerian foods, health products, clothes and videos, hair and beauty salons, information technology and medical services. Often this involves some kind of export-import activity, for example the importation of various goods from Europe into Nigeria (Fadahunsi, Smallbone, and Supri 2000).

A number of studies analyse the religion-entrepreneurship connection among black Africans in Britain, including the entrepreneurial activities of Pentecostal Christians (Nwankwo and Gbadamosi 2013; Ojo 2017, 2019). Nwankwo and Gbadamosi (2013:18) argue that African-Caribbean Pentecostals in Britain employ their faith to "reconstruct their entrepreneurial values", improve their entrepreneurial learning and "exploit the cultural resources of faith-based networks to promote and sustain their entrepreneurialism". Sanyo Ojo (2017: 262) describes African Pentecostalism as a "nurturing platform for entrepreneurship" which alleviates impediments to ethnic business enterprise in the UK. According to Ojo, African Pentecostalism "motivates people with the idea that their lives can be changed", Pentecostal pastors provide practical advice to members on how to save money and start small businesses, and the "social capital advantages" in African Pentecostal entrepreneurship are probably more robust than in other forms of ethnic entrepreneurship (2017: 266, 264). Religious entrepreneurship, which mixes enterprise with spiritual themes, also underlines the transnational nature of ethnic entrepreneurship as business models and commercial exchanges "are communicated with faith by the African Pentecostal movements globally" (2017: 266).

In Britain, conferences and seminars on business enterprise and marketplace ministries are regular events within the Nigerian Pentecostal community. Churches such as KICC and Winners Chapel run business seminars which include biblical teaching on Pentecostal themes such as tithing and the prosperity gospel alongside practical training in business management and investment. Another example is the "Christians in the Marketplace" conference, a three-day event organized by Olatunji Adebayo, senior pastor of RCCG's Central London Fellowship. Pastor Adebayo explained why he started the conference:

> The idea behind it is basically to create a platform where we enlighten and educate believers to understand their position in the secular world, that is the marketplace. Because a lot of Christians are very active in the church, but when they get out there, they are not as strong as they should be.[11]

The theme of the 2010 conference was "Succeeding in the current economic crisis", and included sessions on "Foundations for business success", "Faith and social enterprise", "How to run your business from a Christian perspective", and "How to maintain your character in the marketplace".

In 2010, I attended the Business Professional Breakthrough Conference (BPBC), organized by the Watford branch of Mountain of Fire and Miracles, which combined prayer sessions for financial "breakthrough" with talks by Nigerian pastors, business professionals, and local politicians on such topics as debt management, business start-up, career success, and investment. The BPBC is an annual three-day conference first held in 2007. In keeping with MFM's emphasis on spiritual warfare, the first day of the conference is devoted to prayer where delegates come together to "break the backbone of debt, poverty and economic crunch". The 2010 conference handbook contained a list of prayers designed to liberate Christians from demonic powers and remove obstacles to individual progress and prosperity (David 2010).

Conclusion

This chapter has examined Nigerian Pentecostal engagement with the economic sphere. Business enterprises are increasingly recognized by the international community as important partners in economic development. During Nigeria's Fourth Republic, successive civilian regimes have implemented policies and programmes directed at economic reform, including policies geared towards supporting SMEs. While these have achieved a measure of success, poverty levels in Nigeria have continued to rise. Pentecostal churches and NGOs are involved in building the capacity of the SME sector through microfinance initiatives, business schools, entrepreneurship education, use of the media, and conference events. They are also engaged in programmes geared towards the economic empowerment of women entrepreneurs. Transnational entrepreneurship, involving border-crossing entrepreneurial activities, has become an important occupation for Nigerians in the diaspora. In Britain, Nigerian Pentecostal churches run seminars and conferences which provide contexts for members to engage in prayer for financial success as well as practical advice on business management and wealth creation.

Some Nigerian Pentecostal pastors have rightly been criticized for growing rich at the expense of their churches' impoverished members. However, the chapter identified two emerging trends with regard to Nigerian Pentecostal approaches to prosperity: first, a shift from reliance on "miracles" to an emphasis on work and entrepreneurship; and second, a new understanding that the purpose of wealth is for it to be used for the common good rather than for personal enrichment. Some Nigerian Pentecostals are confronting corruption and popular conceptions of prosperity teaching within their ranks by inculcating values and behaviours such as hard work, self-discipline, altruism, and accountable leadership. Significantly, influential pastors such as Tony Rapu, Sam Adeyemi, and Tunde Bakare are defining Africa's economic predicament in terms of social and political structures, recognizing that collective prosperity will be attained only if the structural and environmental causes of poverty and inequality are addressed. In church sermons, conference talks, and political speeches, they are challenging government economic policies and institutional arrangements that they deem to be an obstacle to positive development outcomes. They are also encouraging their members to get involved in the political process by joining political parties and standing for political office. The next chapter examines the political dimensions of Nigerian Pentecostalism and the strategies employed to influence the political sphere.

Notes

1 Interview, Pastor Poju Oyemade, Covenant Christian Centre, Lagos, 26 September 2011.

2 For a recent treatment of the prosperity gospel in Africa, see Heuser (ed.) (2015), which includes chapters on Nigeria, Ghana, Burkina Faso, Tanzania, Cameroon, and South Africa.

3 Elsewhere, Wariboko (2012: 47–48) divides the Leadership paradigm into two models: the Prophetic model, exemplified by Bakare, which defines Africa's economic problems in terms of social structures, and the Transformational engagement model which sees Africa's problems as caused by immoral leadership.

4 Interview, Bishop Abraham Olalaye, Abraham's Evangelistic Ministry, Lagos, 20 September 2010.
5 Interview, Pastor Poju Oyemade, Covenant Christian Centre, Lagos, 26 September 2011.
6 Calvary Bible Church also has branches in Abuja and Houston, Texas. Olumide Emmanuel studied business at the University of Huddersfield (UK) and the Harvard Business School. He counts among his spiritual mentors MFM's Daniel Olukoya and Winners Chapel's Bishop David Oyedepo.
7 Awosika is the host of a popular TV programme called "Business – His Way".
8 TED is a non-profit organization devoted to spreading ideas, usually in the form of short conference talks by experts in the fields of education, business, science and technology, which are then posted online.
9 Interview, Pastor Sam Adeyemi, Daystar Christian Centre, Lagos, 7 October 2011.
10 Covenant Christian Centre, Fountain of Life Church, Daystar Christian Centre, This Present House, Winners Chapel, and MFM all have branches in London.
11 Interview, Pastor Olatunji Adebayo, RCCG Central London Fellowship, London, 18 August 2010.

References

Abor, Joshua and Peter Quartey (2010) "Issues in SME Development in Ghana and South Africa", *International Research Journal of Finance and Economics* 39: 218–228.

Adeboye, Enoch A. (2002) *Sermons of the 2001 Holy Ghost Services*, Lagos: The Book Ministry.

Adeyemi, Sam (2016) "Unleashing the Potentials for Wealth Creation", Paper presented at The Platform, 1 October, available at: www.youtube.com/watch?v=aTcX8FuqEI0 (accessed 22 September 2019).

Alao, David O. and Ifeoluwa O. Alao (2013) "A Mid-term Evaluation of President Goodluck Ebele Jonathan's Transformation Agenda (May 2011–May 2013)", *Journal of Research and Development* 1(1): 53–69.

Awofeso, Olu and Temitayo Odeyemi (2014) "The Impact of Political Leadership and Corruption on Nigeria's Development since Independence", *Journal of Sustainable Development* 7(5): 240–253.

Awosika, Ibokun (2008) *The "Girl" Entrepreneurs. Our Stories So Far*, Lagos: Grace Springs Africa Publisher.

Ayegboyin, Deji I. (2006) "A Rethinking of Prosperity Teaching in the New Pentecostal Churches in Nigeria", *Black Theology: An International Journal* 4(1): 70–86.

Badru, Pade (1998) *Imperialism and Ethnic Politics in Nigeria*, Trenton, NJ: Africa World Press.

Bakare, Tunde (2009) "There is Hope for our Future". Independence Day Live Broadcast, 1 October 2009, available at: https://lraglobal.org/mediacast/nigeria-theres-hope-future/ (accessed 4 April 2014).

Barrett, Giles A., Trevor P. Jones, and David McEvoy (1996) "Ethnic Minority Business: Theoretical Discourse in Britain and North America", *Urban Studies* 33(4&5): 783–809.

Chen, Wenhong and Justin Tan (2009) "Understanding Transnational Entrepreneurship Through a Network Lens: Theoretical and Methodological Considerations", *Entrepreneurship Theory and Practice* 33(5): 1079–1091.

Covenant Capital (2016a) "Welcome to Covenant Capital", covenant-capital.org/ (accessed 15 June 2019).

Covenant Capital (2016b) "Covenant Capital Business School", available at: http://covenant-capital.org/?page_id=2048 (accessed 15 June 2019).

David, Humphrey (2010) "Kingdom Prosperity", *BPBC 2010 Programme Brochure*.

Drønen, Tomas (2015) " 'Now I Dress Well. Now I Work Hard': Pentecostalism, Prosperity, and Economic Development in Cameroon", in Andreas Heuser (ed.) *Pastures of Plenty: Tracing Religio-Scapes of Prosperity Gospel in Africa and Beyond*, Frankfurt am Main: Peter Lang, pp. 249–265.

Emmanuel, Olumide (2008) *The Pathway to Wealth*, Lagos: Commonsense Publishing.

Emmanuel, Olumide (2016) "From MDGs to SDGs", *Good Report. A Quarterly Newsletter of the Olumide Emmanuel Foundation*, available at: http://oefng.org/good-report/ (accessed 18 June 2019).

Enwerem, Iheanyi M. (2003) " 'Money-Magic' and Ritual Killing in Contemporary Nigeria", in Jane I. Guyer, LaRay Denzer, and Adigun Agbaje (eds) *Money Struggles in Ibadan and Other Urban Centers in Southern Nigeria 1986–1996*, Ibadan: Bookbuilders, pp. 189–205.

Fadahunsi, Akin, David Smallbone, and Salinder Supri (2000) "Networking and Ethnic Minority Enterprise Development: Insights from a North London Study", *Journal of Small Business and Enterprise Development* 7(3): 228–240.

Falola, Toyin and Matthew M. Heaton (2008) *A History of Nigeria*, Cambridge: Cambridge University Press.

FATE Foundation (2019) "About", available at: https://fatefoundation.org/about/ (accessed 13 May 2019).

Foodtank (2018) "Ndidi Nwuneli: Unlocking the Potential of Agriculture and Nutrition in West Africa", available at: https://foodtank.com/news/2018/01/ndidi-nwuneli-interview-leap-africa/ (accessed 13 May 2019).

Fountain Initiative for Social Development (2016) "Welcome to FISD", available at: https://fisdng.com/index-2.html (accessed 22 May 2019).

Freeman, Dena (2012) "The Pentecostal Ethic and the Spirit of Development", in Dena Freeman (ed.) *Pentecostalism and Development: Churches, NGOs and Social Change in Africa*, London, UK: Palgrave Macmillan, pp. 1–38.

Geschiere, Peter (1997) *The Modernity of Witchcraft. Politics and the Occult in Postcolonial Africa*, Charlottesville: University Press of Virginia.

Gifford, Paul (1990) "Prosperity: A New and Foreign Element in African Christianity", *Religion*, 20: 373–388.

Gifford, Paul (1998) *African Christianity: Its Public Role*, London: Hurst & Co.

Gifford, Paul (2004) *Ghana's New Christianity. Pentecostalism in a Globalizing African Economy*, Bloomington: Indiana University Press.

Gifford, Paul (2015) *Christianity, Development and Modernity in Africa*, London: Hurst & Co.

Grater, Sonya, Ali Parry, and Wilma Viviers (2017) *Realising the Potential of Services SMEs in Developing Economies*, Geneva: International Centre for Trade and Sustainable Development.

Gyong, John E. (2012) "A Social Analysis of the Transformation Agenda of President Goodluck Ebele Jonathan," *European Scientific Journal* 8(16): 95–113.

Halkias, Daphne, Chinedum Nwajiuba, Nicholas Harkiolakis, and Sylva M. Caracatsanis (2011) "Challenges Facing Women Entrepreneurs in Nigeria", *Management Research Review* 34(2): 221–235.

Haynes, Naomi (2012) "Pentecostalism and the Morality of Money: Prosperity, Inequality, and Religious Sociality on the Zambian Copperbelt", *Journal of the Royal Anthropological Institute* 18(1): 123–139.

Heuser, Andreas (ed.) *Pastures of Plenty: Tracing Religio-scapes of Prosperity Gospel in Africa and Beyond*, Frankfurt am Main: Peter Lang.

Igwe, Paul Agu, Oyedele M. Ogundana, Odafe M. Egere, and Juliana A. Anigbo (2018) "Factors Affecting the Investment Climate, SMEs Productivity and Entrepreneurship in Nigeria", *European Journal of Sustainable Development* 7(1): 182–200.

Ihonvbere, Julius and Timothy Shaw (1998) *Illusions of Power: Nigeria in Transition*, Trenton, NJ: Africa World Press.

Kalu, Ogbu U. (2008) *African Pentecostalism: An Introduction*, Oxford: Oxford University Press.

Kukogho, Samson (2015) "Entrepreneurs to Get Capital at NYSC Enterprise Funding Fair, 5000 Corps Members Expected", *Pulse NG*, 30 September, www.pulse.ng/communities/student/national-youth-service-corps-entrepreneurs-to-get-capital-at-nysc-enterprise-funding/xkhgp15 (accessed 15 July 2019).

Meyer, Birgit (1998) "The Power of Money: Politics, Occult Forces, and Pentecostalism in Ghana", *African Studies Review* 41(3): 15–37.

Mwobobia, Fridah M. (2012) "The Challenges Facing Small-Scale Women Entrepreneurs: A Case of Kenya", *International Journal of Business Administration* 3(2): 112–121.

National Planning Commission (2009) "Nigeria Vision 20: 2020. Economic Transformation Blueprint", available at: https://nairametrics.com/wp-content/uploads/2013/06/nigeria-vision-20_2020_draftetb.pdf (accessed 4 October 2019).

Nevin, Andrew S. and Omomia Omosomi (2019) "Nigeria Economic Outlook: Top 10 Themes for 2019", PricewaterhouseCoopers Nigeria, available at: www.pwc.com/ng/en/publications/nigeria-economic-outlook.html (accessed 6 October 2019).

Nwankwo, Sonny and Ayantunji Gbadamosi (2013) "Faith and Entrepreneurship Among the British African-Caribbean: Intersections Between Religious and Entrepreneurial Values", *Journal of Small Business and Enterprise Development* 20(3): 618–633.

Nwankwo, Sonny, Ayantunji Gbadamosi, and Sanya Ojo (2012) "Religion, Spirituality and Entrepreneurship: The Church as Entrepreneurial Space Among British Africans", *Society and Business Review* 7(2): 149–167.

Nwuneli, Ndidi O. (2016) *Social Innovation in Africa. A Practical Guide for Scaling Impact*, London: Routledge.

Nwuneli, Ndidi O. (2017) "The Role of Faith and Belief in Driving Social Change in Africa", TED Talk, available at: www.ted.com/talks/ndidi_nwuneli_the_role_of_faith_and_belief_in_modern_africa/transcript?language=en (accessed 26 October 2019).

Nzeako, Ikechi (2017) "We Are Raising New Generation of Entrepreneurs – Olumide", *Independent (Nigeria)*, 16 June, available at: www.independent.ng/we-are-raising-new-generation-of-entrepreneurs-olumide/ (accessed 15 August 2019).

Obadare, Ebenezer (2016) "'Raising Righteous Billionaires': The Prosperity Gospel Reconsidered", *HTS Theological Studies* 72(4): 1–8.

Ogungbile, David (2014) "African Pentecostalism and the Prosperity Gospel", in Clifton R. Clarke (ed.) *Pentecostal Theology in Africa*, Eugene, OR: Pickwick Publications, pp. 132–149.

Ojo, Matthews A. (2006) *The End-time Army, Charismatic Movements in Modern Nigeria*, Trenton, NJ: Africa World Press.

Ojo, Sanya (2017) "The 'Gospel' of Pentecostalism and Entrepreneurship: A Market Configuration", in Sanyo Ojo (ed.) *Diasporas and Transnational Entrepreneurship in Global Contexts*, Hershey PA: IGI Global, pp. 252–273.

Ojo, Sanya (2019) "The Confluence of Religion and Ethnic Entrepreneurship in the Informal Economy", in Veland Ramadani, Leo-Paul Dana, Vanessa Ratten, and

Abdylmenaf Bexheti (eds) *Informal Ethnic Entrepreneurship: Future Research Paradigms for Creating Innovative Business Activity*, Cham: Springer, pp. 45–62.

Okorocha, Cyril C. (1987) *The Meaning of Religious Conversion in Africa. The Case of the Igbo of Nigeria*, Aldershot: Avebury.

Okoye, William (1993) *Youth with a Purpose*, Enugu: Gospel Communications International.

Olumide Emmanuel Foundation (2017) "About Us", available at: http://oefng.org/ (accessed 17 August 2019).

Osaghae, Eghosa E. (1998) *Crippled Giant: Nigeria Since Independence*, Bloomington: Indiana University Press.

Oyedepo, David (2007) *Winning the War Against Poverty*, Lagos: Dominion Publishing House.

Peel, John D. Y. (2000) *Religious Encounter and the Making of the Yoruba*, Bloomington: Indiana University Press.

Portes, Alejandro, William Haller, and Luis E. Guarnizo (2001) *Transnational Entrepreneurs: The Emergence and Determinants of an Alternative Form of Immigrant Economic Adaptation*, WPTC-01–05, February.

Rapu, Tony (2012) "Agents of Change", 17 April, available at: www.facebook.com/notes/tony-rapu/agents-of-change/343533495707769 (accessed 15 August 2014).

Richardson, Pat, Rhona Howarth, and Gerry Finnegan (2004) *The Challenges of Growing Small Businesses: Insights from Women Entrepreneurs in Africa*, Geneva: International Labour Office.

Robbins, Joel (2004) "The Globalization of Pentecostal and Charismatic Christianity", *Annual Review of Anthropology* 33: 117–144.

Scheyvens, Regina, Glenn Banks, and Emma Hughes (2016) "The Private Sector and the SDGs: The Need to Move Beyond 'Business as Usual' ", *Sustainable Development* 24(6): 371–382.

Smith, Daniel J. (2001) " 'The Arrow of God': Pentecostalism, Inequality, and the Supernatural in South-Eastern Nigeria", *Africa* 71(4): 587–613.

Success Power International (2019) "Who We Are", available at: https://successpower.org/about-us/who-we-are/ (accessed 20 August 2019).

The Nation (2015) "2015: My Five-point Agenda, by Buhari", *The Nation*, 1 January 2015, https://thenationonlineng.net/2015-five-point-agenda-buhari/ (accessed 12 January 2020).

Ugwuegbe, Ugochukwu, Nathaniel E. Urama, and Emeka C. Iloh (2018) "Meeting the 2030 SDG in Nigeria: The Role of Entrepreneurship Development", AfriHeritage Policy Brief No. 16, May, pp. 1–4.

Wariboko, Nimi (2012) "Pentecostal Paradigms of National Economic Prosperity in Africa", in Katherine Attanasi and Amos Yong (eds) *Pentecostalism and Prosperity. The Socio-economics of the Global Charismatic Movement*, New York: Palgrave Macmillan, pp. 35–62.

Wariboko, Nimi (2014) *Nigerian Pentecostalism*, Rochester, NY: University of Rochester Press.

WIMBIZ (2017a) "About WIMBIZ", available at: https://wimbiz.org/who-we-are/ (accessed 25 August 2019).

WIMBIZ (2017b) "Our programs", available at: https://wimbiz.org/our-programs/ (accessed 25 August 2019).

Yedder, Omar Ben and Parselelo Kantai (2017) "The Big Interview with Okechukwu Enelamah", *New African Magazine*, 14 March, available at: http://newafricanmagazine.com/big-interview-okechukwu-enelamah/ (accessed 15 June 2019).

3 Pentecostals, governance, and development

Introduction

In 2011, an unprecedented 15 African countries held presidential elections, among them Nigeria. The institutionalization of regular multi-party elections in the African political landscape is evidence of the progress that has been made towards democratic consolidation on the continent. However, only four of the 2011 elections brought about a change of regime and many were marred by violence and allegations of election fraud. In Nigeria, post-election violence followed the victory of the Christian President Goodluck Jonathan over his Muslim rival Muhammadu Buhari. The persistence of election fraud and ethno-religious violence in Africa threatens to undermine the gains made over the past decades towards establishing sustainable democratic institutions. Significantly, two of the candidates who contested the presidential elections in Nigeria were Pentecostals.

The role of governance is increasingly recognized as important for international development. Peace, stability, human rights, and effective governance, based on the rule of law, are crucial for achieving sustainable development (UNDP 2014). This chapter examines the political dimensions of Pentecostalism in Nigeria. It explores Pentecostal political engagement in broad terms to include Pentecostalism's influence on direct political behaviour and electoral politics, as well as the structures and practices of civil society and their effect on political culture.

Nigerian Pentecostals have employed a variety of strategies to influence the political sphere, ranging from conventional methods such as electoral politics to more implicit strategies such as prophecy and prayer. Recently, some Pentecostal leaders have adopted more long-term strategies by establishing new institutions, and hosting conferences and training programs geared towards reforming cultural values and practices and raising transformational leaders who will influence the political sphere. I argue that these initiatives offer the most potential to reshape politics and achieve a democratic culture, even if it may be some time before the wider society feels their impact.

The return to democracy in Africa over recent decades has enabled Pentecostals to assume more prominent roles in the political sphere (Kalu 2008; Ranger 2008). One issue raised in the literature is whether African Pentecostalism contributes to movements of democratization (Gifford 1998, 1995; Marshall 2009; Wariboko 2014). Ruth Marshall (2009: 204, 208) is ambivalent, referring to Nigerian Pentecostal ambitions to redeem the nation through converting its citizens and replacing a corrupt political regime with "righteous" authority. On one hand, she claims, "Pentecostal discourse involves a critique which delegitimates the authoritarian use of power." However, "despite the potential force of the Born-Again political critique", God is definitely not a democrat:

> the model of "democracy through conversion" may be projected at the national level; however, the community of the saved must be led by divine authority, embodied in leaders of churches and organizations and legitimated by the word of the Holy Ghost.
>
> (Marshall 2009: 211)

For Marshall (2009: 165), Nigerian Pentecostalism, with "its emphasis on individual salvation, interiority, and affectivity, coupled with its incipient messianism", has great difficulty "creating the foundations of a political community". Taking issue with Marshall, the theologian Nimi Wariboko shifts the discourse from a political science emphasis on sovereignty to that of "practices of and virtues for creating and sustaining a Pentecostal form of community" (2014: 172). Pentecostalism can create political communities, according to Wariboko (2014: 172), as long as we are not insisting that they must have sovereign rulers or only sovereign rulers can make and sustain communities. Wariboko's study of Nigerian Pentecostalism focuses on the Pentecostal intimacy and desire for the Holy Spirit "who can nurture practices and virtues for commitment to an emancipatory collective" (Wariboko 2014: 172).

Another question discussed in the literature is whether African Pentecostal culture leads to political conservatism. According to Paul Gifford (1998: 111), Africa's Pentecostal churches

> have tended to be coopted fairly easily by government, and their Faith Gospel, their nearly exclusive emphasis on church growth, and the increase of deliverance thinking combine to prevent them from challenging the government, or from even seeing that as their task.

Ebenezer Obadare (2018: 64) refers to the "courting" of the Pentecostal elite by Nigerian politicians during Nigeria's Fourth Republic. While Nigerian Pentecostalism "has affected the socio-political order in Nigeria", it has "largely shied away from challenging it" (Obadare 2018: 5). However, as I will show in this chapter, there are a diversity of Nigerian Pentecostal political postures ranging from political acquiescence to public expressions of political protest and dissent.

The main focus of the chapter is the "third democratic revolution" involving the struggle for sustainable democracy; the first two were the anti-colonial struggle that brought independence and the challenge to one-party states and military rule during the 1980s and 1990s (Ranger 2008). The role of the churches was different during these three transition periods. According to Gifford (1995: 5), mainline churches generally have opposed Africa's dictators, while "the newer evangelicals and Pentecostal churches" have provided support. Ranger (2008) suggests, however, that Pentecostals have played a more central role in the struggle for sustainable democracy. The chapter begins by discussing the role of governance in development and its inclusion in the post-2015 sustainable development agenda. Second, I set the context by tracing the contours of Pentecostal political engagement in Nigeria since independence. Third, I examine contemporary Pentecostal strategies to influence the political sphere. I give attention to socio-economic and political contexts while considering the significance of theology in shaping Pentecostal political behaviour (Gifford 1998; Freston 2001).

Governance and development

One of the criticisms of the MDGs was that they paid insufficient attention to the influence of national and international politics on development outcomes (Aucoin and Donnenfeld 2016). Although the Millennium Declaration, adopted by the UN General Assembly in September 2000, outlined the importance of governance as a development priority, the notion of a standalone governance goal did not become an MDG (Edwards and Romero 2014).

In July 2012, the UN member states reaffirmed "democracy, good governance and the rule of law" as essential for sustainable development (UN General Assembly 2012: 2). Promoting good governance for human development is a crucial part of the SDGs (Biermann *et al.* 2014). While all the goals contain elements related to governance, they appear most directly in SDG 16 on "peaceful, just and inclusive societies". During the drafting of the SDGs, "Africa's assertive stance on the importance of adopting a dedicated goal on governance and peace was instrumental in forging a global consensus on SDG 16" (Laberge 2019: 13). Goal 16 addresses the challenges of global governance in targets 16.3 (rule of law), 16.6 (institutions at all levels), 16.7 (decision-making at all levels), and 16.8 (participation of developing countries in global governance).

Good governance "encapsulates values such as enhanced participation, transparency, accountability, and public access to information" (Biermann *et al.* 2014: 2). Such values are often associated with liberal democratic political institutions. Discussion about the definition of good governance has centred on two broad governance issues. The first pertains to institutions of governance, including public administration and public services. The second is concerned with "concepts of democracy and the rule of law" (UN System Task Team on the Post-2015 Development Agenda 2012: 4). UN Member States consider progress in these areas to be essential for the achievement of sustainable development.

Nigerian politics and the shift to political Pentecostalism

Nigerian Pentecostals have adopted a variety of political postures in response to the changing socio-political landscape. The nature and extent of their engagement has been influenced by theological orientation, organizational structure, and social location. In the 1970s, Pentecostals generally were apolitical due to their location on the margins of society, other-worldly orientation, and radical holiness ethic. The last of these led to the view that politics is linked to corruption and violence and is tainted by its perceived association with pre-Christian religion and "occult" forces (Ojo 2006; Burgess 2008).

The formation in 1977 of the Christian Students' Social Movement marked the beginnings of a more politically engaged Pentecostalism (Ojo 2006). The Movement has sought to inform Charismatics of their potential influence on national life "by linking prophecy with politics", increasing prayer for the nation and encouraging Christians to speak out on political issues (Ojo 1998: 27). The Movement's influence declined in the late 1980s, however, following the dispersal of its founders (Ojo 2006).

During the military regime of Muslim President Ibrahim Babangida (1985–1993), Pentecostal political activity escalated, in response to two interrelated issues: fear of Islamization, and frustration over the failure of the democratization program, which culminated in the annulled 1993 elections and military takeover of Muslim dictator General Sani Abacha (1993–1998). Christians challenged Babangida's 1986 decision to make Nigeria a full member of the Organization of the Islamic Conference (OIC) and the attempt to extend the jurisdiction of sharia courts in the 1988–1989 Constituent Assembly. They believed that the OIC undermined the nation's secular status, in contravention of the 1979 Constitution, and feared it would enlarge Muslim monopoly of public space. They also accused Babangida's government of failing to protect Christians in the north from Muslim attacks (Burgess 2015; Haynes 1996).

Ecumenical relations under the auspices of the Christian Association of Nigeria (CAN), which was founded in 1976, also contributed to a political reorientation of Pentecostalism. By 1985, the organization's leaders were publicly criticizing the military and demanding a return to civil rule, and in 1987 they "resolved that Christians must be directly involved in politics" (CAN 1987, cited in Falola 1998: 224). Their 1988 manifesto encouraged Christians to become politically aware, expose corruption among political leaders, and vote for leaders of their choice without allowing their votes to be influenced by bribery, ethnic sentiments, or religious intolerance (CAN 1987, cited Obadare 2006: 668). The Pentecostal Fellowship of Nigeria (PFN), founded in 1986, became an influential voice within CAN and in July 2010 enhanced its power base when Ayo Oritsejafor, senior pastor of Word of Life Bible Church, was elected CAN's first Pentecostal president.

In 1989, CAN issued a statement urging "properly born-again Christians, filled with the Holy Spirit" to "come and contest elections" (CAN 1989, cited in Obadare 2006: 668). Christian-Muslim rivalry in northern Nigeria, exacerbated by Sheikh Abubakar Gumi's public declaration that Muslims would never allow non-Muslims to rule Nigeria, stimulated Pentecostal participation in electoral politics. In the northern city of Kaduna, state capital of Kaduna State, Pentecostals allied with other Christians to field candidates and eventually Christians won the majority of seats in the 1988 local government elections (Ojo 2006). In the south, pastors with large constituencies used their wealth and status as spiritual authorities as a means of political influence (Marshall 2009). Marshall (2009) refers to the example of Benson Idahosa, Archbishop of Church of God Mission, who became a major power broker in the politics of Edo State. In 1992, Rev. Peter Obadan, a pastor in Idahosa's church, was elected deputy governor. The popular perception was that Idahosa used his influence among his followers to tilt the election in Obadan's favour.

During the 1990s, there was a more overtly critical stance by Pentecostals towards the Nigerian state. In January 1993, Rev. William Okoye of All Christians Fellowship Mission preached a sermon, broadcast on Nigerian television and radio, castigating political leaders who oppressed and exploited others while using their power to silence them (Okoroafor 1996). While it is doubtful that Pentecostals significantly influenced, except through prayer, the transition process during the Babangida regime, the annulment of the 1993 elections, and Abacha's subsequent intervention stimulated them into action. As the church became a major pro-democracy group within society, Pentecostals began to play a more active role in the politics of transition. Ogbu Kalu (2010) suggests that Pentecostals "radicalized" the politics of mainline churches during the 1990s. In 1994, a group of mainly Pentecostal and Charismatic leaders, alarmed at the "flood of corruption inundating Nigerian society", established the Congress of Christian Ethics in Nigeria. In 1997, the movement produced the "Nigeria Covenant", referring to the church as the "conscience of the nation", and sent copies to Christians and political leaders throughout the nation. The covenant called upon Christians to respect and obey their leaders, encouraged active participation in politics, and recognized the validity of non-violent civil disobedience and passive resistance, pledging to resist all forms of injustice and corruption in society (Congress on Christian Ethics in Nigeria 1997: 3, 5, 16).

In 1999, the return to multi-party democracy and the presidency of Olusegun Obasanjo (1999–2007) on the platform of the People's Democratic Party (PDP) ushered in Nigeria's Fourth Republic. Obadare (2018) traces the ascendance of Pentecostalism as the major Christian political force in Nigeria to this period. The declaration of sharia in some northern states united Christians across the Pentecostal-mainline church divide in vehement protests (Imo 2008: 41, 43–44). Other factors were the movement's numerical growth and demographic change as the socio-economic elite were attracted into its ranks. Obadare (2006: 665) refers to the "Pentecostalization" of governance: a Christian "theocratic class" surrounding the Obasanjo presidency further politicized religion while paying lip service to Nigeria's secularity. What seems to be new with this theocratic class is the "determination (as part of a project of 'winning Nigeria for Jesus') to embed the New Christianity into the heart of the state" signifying a congruence in the attitudes of Islamism and Pentecostalism toward (state) power (Obadare 2006: 665). This shift to the centre of society, however, has made Pentecostal leaders vulnerable to state co-option. Despite allegations of corruption and political manipulation, powerful Pentecostals such as Enoch Adeboye (Redeemed Christian Church of God) and David Oyedepo (Winners Chapel) endorsed Obasanjo's presidency and provided it with a sense of divine legitimization (Ukah 2008; Obadare 2006, 2018). Two notable exceptions to this Pentecostal co-option were Tunde Bakare (Latter Rain Assembly), who predicted the president's demise, and Chris Okotie (Household of God Church), who himself competed against Obasanjo in the 2003 presidential elections.

In 2006, Obasanjo's unconstitutional quest for a third term threatened to rupture the alliance between the state and Pentecostal leaders. He was eventually persuaded to retire, and handed power to Umaru Yar'Adua, his moderate Muslim successor in the PDP, who won the 2007 presidential election. Cyril Imo (2008: 66) suggested that this democratic handover of power from a Christian southerner to a Muslim northerner would defuse tensions between the two faiths, and enable Christians to channel their political activism into other areas important to sustainable democracy, such as the struggle against corruption. Nevertheless, Nigerian political culture continues to unfold against a backdrop of Muslim-Christian rivalry.

In November 2009, Yar'Adua travelled to Saudi Arabia for medical treatment of an illness that later claimed his life, and his failure to hand over power to Vice-President Goodluck Jonathan plunged Nigeria into a constitutional crisis that threatened national cohesion. One of the leading voices calling for the power transfer was Tunde Bakare, whose Save Nigeria Group (SNG), founded in January 2010, became the main vehicle for political agitation. The Group organized street protests in Lagos and Abuja that on 9 February forced the National Assembly to declare Jonathan the acting President.[1] He became the substantive President on 6 May following the death of Yar'Adua. The scale and nature of the protests led by the SNG marked a significant departure for Pentecostals, and since then the group has become a leading civil society group in Nigeria, earning Bakare the popular Nigerian magazine Newswatch's 2010 "Man of the Year" award (Ekpu 2010). Marshall (2014: 24) describes the SNG as a "broad-based civil coalition of pro-democracy groups set up to encourage popular political mobilization".

In April 2011, Goodluck Jonathan was elected to a second term despite strong opposition from the former Muslim head of state Muhammadu Buhari, who was competing on the Congress for Progressive Change platform. Although the election was judged by international observers as the fairest in decades, it was followed by a wave of violence across the predominantly Muslim north that resulted in destruction of churches and mosques and extensive loss of lives. In response, Pentecostal leaders such as Enoch Adeboye and Ayo Oritsejafor publicly condemned the violence and called upon Nigerians to accept the result as the will of God (Eghaghe 2011). Like Obasanjo, Jonathan solicited the support of the Pentecostal elite. In the run-up to the April 2011 presidential elections, Jonathan attended the penultimate night of the Redeemed Christian Church of God's annual Holy Ghost Convention, which attracted an estimated one million people. The following Sunday, several Nigerian newspapers carried frontpage photographs of the Jonathan kneeling to receive a prayer blessing from Adeboye. Bakare was Buhari's vice-presidential running mate. It is likely that Buhari's choice of Bakare was a pragmatic strategy aimed at shedding his reputation as an Islamic fundamentalist and winning the support from the Christian-dominated south (Iherika 2012; Onapajo 2012). Despite the alliance, however, Buhari failed to win any state in the south.

Buhari went on to win the 2015 presidential elections on the platform of the newly created All Progressives Congress. This marked a significant step in the road to democratic consolidation as it was the first time since independence that an opposition party had won a national election. Buhari's vice-Presidential running mate in this election was Yemi Osinbajo, a RCCG pastor and one-time attorney-general of Lagos State. Obadare (2018: 139) describes Buhari's choice of Osinbajo as a "political masterstroke" because it succeeded in easing Christian anxieties about "religious marginalization or Islamic domination". Significantly, Buhari won by a large majority in the Yoruba Pentecostal heartland even though CAN and PFN supported Jonathan, his main rival for the presidency. The elections were held in the shadow of huge security, economic, and social uncertainties which have continued to plague Nigerian society during Buhari's tenure as President. In 2019, Buhari and Osinbajo were re-elected to a second term.

Prayer, prophetic politics, and political protest

African Pentecostal discourse on politics is typically framed as a religious contest between good and evil, reflecting the dominance of supernatural ideas in African political culture (Ellis and Ter Haar 2004). Popular criticisms focus on the (im)morality of power, which for many Africans is generated not through the democratic process but rather by use of the occult (Meyer 1998b). For example, it is public knowledge that former dictator Sani Abacha employed Muslim clerics to offer daily sacrifices of live rams to maintain the leader's power (Kalu 2008). In this context, Pentecostals employ spiritual warfare in what Gifford (2004) has called an "enchanted" approach to politics, wherein demons are held responsible for adverse political circumstances and whose power must be broken through prayer.

According to Ogbu Kalu (2008: 219), Pentecostal prayer in Africa is a form of political praxis, a strategy of "political dissent", and "an exercise of political power at the level of infrapolitics", reflected in the Pentecostal tendency to organize prayer retreats at critical moments in the life of their nations. Obadare (2007) suggests that prayer should be regarded not only as an instrument of public intervention but as a form of narrative rhetoric exposing the nation's condition. In Nigeria, Pentecostal prayer meetings are often public occasions intended to capture the attention of the wider society. National prayer bodies addressing political issues have multiplied in recent years. They include Intercessors for Nigeria, Watchman Ministries, Gethsemane Prayer Ministries, Prayer for the Nation, and Nigeria Prays. According to its mission statement, Nigeria Prays aims to

> mobilize all Nigerians to regular, fervent and result-oriented prayers for the healing and transformation of the nation through prayer rallies and seminars; and to promote the virtues of patriotism, transparency, and incorruptibility in leadership, governance and in the entire citizenry.
>
> (Aransiola 2008a: vi)

In contrast to Bakare and the Save Nigeria Group, the national coordinator of Nigeria Prays, Moses Aransiola, believes that the proper Christian response to political grievance is prayer rather than protest:

> Other people may take to the streets to express their grievances over bad leadership and ungodly decisions, but Christians must take to prayer. God on several occasions had saved us from war in Nigeria through the persistent intercession of the saints.
>
> (Aransiola 2008a)

Emeka Nwankpa, founder of Intercessors for Nigeria, suggests that Christians can "redeem the land" from Satan through strategies gleaned partly from American Pentecostal literature (Nwankpa 1994), which has a strong ethical element and emphasizes holiness and reconciliation as necessary conditions for effective intercession. Nwankpa promotes spiritual warfare to wrest control of governments from malign spirits, and believes that ordinary Christians can change the destinies of nations through "prophetic" prayer. "When you pray prophetically, you are in the place of governmental authority.... Prophetic praying is very powerful. It can change laws. It can cancel what politicians have said" (Nwankpa 1994: 65, 69). As well as organizing prayer retreats and conferences, often at crucial moments in Nigeria's history, the leaders of these organizations publish books and pamphlets on prayer which invariably include social commentary on the state of the nation (see Aransiola 2008b).

Pentecostals' belief that they can improve society through prayer and spiritual warfare is consistent with African and biblical cosmologies and supported by anecdotal evidence, but such claims are difficult to prove. Gifford suggests that the Pentecostal tendency to spiritualize politics contributes little to the debate on modern government and diverts attention from "the mundane plane on which political issues have been most fruitfully addressed" (Gifford 2004: 172, 169). It would be wrong, however, to assume such initiatives are incompatible with more conventional forms of political activism. In the Nigeria Survey, 89 per cent of Pentecostal/Charismatics stated that Christians should combine prayer with participation in electoral politics (Nigeria Survey 2011).

Prayer is sometimes associated with prophecy in Pentecostal political discourse. Some Nigerian Pentecostals aspire to a prophetic role by projecting prophetic revelation into the public sphere and speaking on political issues. Amos Yong (2010: 11) refers to this as "prophetic politics" in which Pentecostals are "indirectly political, but nonetheless political for all that". As we have seen, the first Pentecostal group in Nigeria to link prophecy with politics was the Christian

Students' Social Movement, whose monthly Prayer Bulletin contained many prophecies regarding the state of the nation. These bulletins were intended mainly for Christian consumption, to sensitize and encourage the church to pray for Nigeria. In the 1990s, prophecies took on a wider public significance (Ojo 2006: 183), and several Pentecostal pastors gained reputations for their political prophecies. Tunde Bakare, pastor of the Latter Rain Assembly, attracted criticism from politicians and some Pentecostals for the antithetical nature of his prophecies directed against leading politicians.[2] Immediately prior to the 29 May 1999 elections which resulted in the presidency of born-again Olusegun Obasanjo, Bakare declared:

> Rejoice not, oh land, for your joy is temporary. I am bringing your rulers, your judges, your governors, your prophets to my threshing floor. After I have threshed them, I will give you permanent joy. Obasanjo is Agag,[3] he is the ram kept for slaughter, he is not your messiah. And the prophetic axe is coming upon his head before May 29.[4]

Not surprisingly, this prophecy generated considerable controversy among Pentecostals, many of whom regarded Obasanjo's ascendancy as an answer to prayers for a Christian president after two decades of Muslim political dominance. The prophecy was placed on the Internet and circulated to Nigerians in the diaspora, drawing comment from the secular press and soliciting several contradicting prophecies from other Pentecostal leaders (Ojo 2006; Obadare 2018).

On a second level, "prophetic politics" involves the "antithetical political stances" of Pentecostal public pronouncements (Yong 2010: 12). In Nigeria, this has generally centred on debates around political leadership and inter-religious conflict. Yong (2010) refers to anti-Islamic rhetoric among Nigeria's Pentecostals as an example of the boldness which sometimes characterizes Pentecostal discourse; however, from a Pentecostal perspective, public criticism of Islam is primarily a response to recurring violence against Christians by Muslim extremists, or a reaction against the imposition of sharia upon Christians in the north (Kalu 2008; Imo 2008). Criticism of government has escalated since the return to multi-party democracy, which has opened up space for political dissent, and some Nigerian Pentecostal leaders now head up large organizations with global links, making them less susceptible to intimidation. Bishop Mike Okonkwo, a former President of Pentecostal Fellowship of Nigeria, made several public statements in the run-up to the 2003 and 2007 elections. He criticized Nigeria's political structures that make it difficult for "good people" to be elected. "Let the votes of the people count and you will see that violence on the day of election will become a thing of the past" (Balogun 2010: 57).

Sometimes public criticism has spilled into the streets. I have already mentioned Save Nigeria Group's role in the 2010 street protests that forced the National Assembly to declare Goodluck Jonathan acting President. In January 2012, SNG was the main catalyst behind the countrywide mass protests against the removal of fuel subsidies by the Nigerian government, which threatened to plunge the economy into crisis and further impoverish its people. On New Year's Day, January 2012, the Christian President Goodluck Jonathan, under pressure from the IMF, announced the removal of subsidy on fuel, raising the price of petroleum from 65 naira per litre to 141 naira. The scale of the nationwide demonstrations that greeted the announcement was unprecedented in terms of political activism in the country. SNG was one of the first groups to protest against this policy. On 2 January, it mobilized Nigerians who began gathering at the famous Gani Fawehinmi Freedom Park in Lagos, named after the human rights lawyer and social activist (Awoyinfa, Okpi, and Attah 2012). This marked the beginnings of the Occupy Nigeria movement, which spread rapidly as SNG was joined by other civil society organizations, and similar street protests were organized in cities across the nation. On 4 January, Nigeria's main labour unions joined the protest, calling for a general strike, mass rallies, and street protests by its members (Abimboye 2012). The indefinite strike, which began on 11 January, threatened to bring down the government of Goodluck Jonathan. Occupy Nigeria engaged all segments of society throughout the country, from the affluent to the poor, from Muslims to Christians and traditionalists.

Although the protest was triggered by local concerns over the economic consequences of fuel subsidy removal, it gained inspiration from the global Occupy movement and the Arab Spring (Aziken 2013), and like them, gave a prominent role to social media and the Internet in rallying support and disseminating information (Howard and Parks 2012; Allagui and Kuebler 2011). Occupy Nigeria was led by SNG and its allies, but was largely driven by young people mobilizing themselves via social media, mobile phones, and word-of-mouth (Amaefule 2012). Social media played a leading role in generating the massive crowds that gathered in cities such as Lagos and Kano during Occupy Nigeria. Use of the Internet and mobile phones also created a constant stream of social commentary, which helped to maintain the momentum of the movement. Nigerians used Twitter, blogs, and phone texts to provide live coverage of the protests and posted press releases, photographs, and videos on the Internet. Media scholars and practitioners refer to this as "citizen journalism", in which a range of web-based practices are employed by "ordinary" users to engage in journalistic practices (Goode 2009: 1289). Citizen journalism has a potential democratizing effect, shifting the power of news production from professional journalists and government-owned media to the ordinary citizen. While the Nigerian press was generally supportive of Occupy Nigeria, the government used the state-owned Nigerian Television Association to stir up opposition. This prompted SNG to engage in citizen journalism by posting regular press releases on its website to disseminate information and counter government censorship and propaganda (Save Nigeria Group 2012).

Bakare and Save Nigeria Group were largely responsible for shifting the focus of the protests from fuel subsidies to the wider issue of government corruption (Bakare 2014a). In press releases and speeches, Bakare and his colleagues consistently drew attention to corruption in the Nigerian oil industry which enabled politicians to grow rich at the expense of the majority of citizens.

They also coined the slogan "Kill Corruption not Nigerians" which was worn on T-shirts and written on placards carried by protesters. The protests forced the government to make concessions by reducing the price of fuel to 97 naira per litre. It also gave rise to the Farouk Lawan Committee, which exposed the level of corruption in the oil industry. However, it did not succeed in curbing the culture of impunity and corruption in Nigeria.

There is also a transnational dimension to SNG activities. In January 2010, members of SNG from throughout Britain and Europe joined other Nigerian political groups in an "Enough is Enough – Save Nigeria" protest rally in London, demanding good governance in Nigeria and to know the whereabouts of President Umaru Yar Adua (Adejumo 2010). In July 2010, the launch of SNG (UK) was hosted by Tunde Bakare and attended by pro-Nigeria groups, journalists, politicians, and professionals (Sahara Reporters 2010). In 2012, Occupy Nigeria organized a rally outside the Nigerian Embassy in London protesting the removal of the fuel subsidy in Nigeria by President Goodluck Jonathan.

Electoral politics and political pastors

In the Nigeria Survey, 72 per cent of Pentecostals/Charismatics said Christians should engage in participatory politics to solve social problems, and 61 per cent said they voted in the April 2011 elections (Nigeria Survey 2011). The survey revealed a significant shift in Pentecostal political theology. Respondents were moving away from separatist tendencies and other-worldly spirituality associated with the early revival period, toward obedience to Christ's command to love one's neighbour by engaging in social and political action. In the run-up to the 2011 elections, pastors used the pulpit and the media to encourage their members to vote,[5] and SNG campaigned across Nigeria for free and fair elections, in which they encouraged Nigerians to take part. Ecumenical organizations, such as the Pentecostal Fellowship of Nigeria (PFN), claim to be non-partisan, preferring to advise Pentecostals to vote for "righteous" candidates rather than vote along religious or ethnic lines. In northern Nigeria, however, PFN encourages its members to vote for Christian candidates as a form of resistance to the perceived Islamist agenda of Muslim politicians.

The quest for political office by Pentecostal pastors has met with a mixed response. In 2003, Chris Okotie (Household of God church) competed for the presidency under the banner of the Justice Party, coming in eighth out of 20 aspirants (Ajayi 2006). His actions were opposed by many Pentecostals who felt that a pastor should not abandon the ministerial role for political office. They also questioned his motives for running against "born-again" President Olusegun Obasanjo. Okotie subsequently founded the Fresh Democratic Party as a platform for those wanting to run for office without being involved in political parties tainted by corruption (see Figure 3.1).[6] In Okotie's unsuccessful 2007 and 2011 presidential bids, the PFN withheld its support, insisting that he was ill-equipped for office.[7] Another example is Tunde Bakare: some Pentecostals expressed concern that he was using the apparatus of the SNG to support his

Figure 3.1 Election billboard for Pastor Chris Okotie and the FRESH Democratic Party in the run-up to the 2007 Nigerian presidential elections.

Source: author.

vice-presidential campaign. They also questioned his alliance with a former Muslim head of state.[8] Osinbajo's successful bid as Buhari's vice-presidential running mate was received more favourably, possibly because of his previous experience as Lagos State attorney-general and his status as a leading pastor of the RCCG.

Despite their relative inexperience in politics, the pastors' political ventures reflect their strong belief in their ability to rule and their self-image as the sole solution to Nigeria's problems. It is appropriate here to recall Paul Freston's identification of two Pentecostal traits detrimental to democracy: "triumphalism", the idea that the "people of God" have been chosen to rule their countries, and a "sense of moral superiority", which makes it difficult to accept that it is one player amongst many (Freston 2001: 306).

National transformation and the reformation of culture

Some Pentecostals have established new institutions for more long-term, sustainable political strategies, and have organized conferences and training programmes to raise transformational leaders and reform cultural values and practices. As discussed in Chapter 1, a recurring theme in Nigerian Pentecostal discourse emphasizes national transformation in response to the under-performance of existing political leaders and government failure to deliver on promises of economic development. One Pentecostal who has embraced this model is Tony Rapu, senior pastor of This Present House. His political theology is based on a holistic soteriology that moves beyond individualism to include societal and national redemption. Responding to the social chaos brought about by a "tragic overdependence on government", he believes the Holy Spirit's new agenda for the church as an "agent of change" will "transform social, economic and political" reality.

> The order of Moses that brought the Church into its present position out of Egypt will have to give way to the order of Joshua that will take the Church into the next level of relevance in issues of politics, economics and governance.

This will involve "a new post-Pentecostal, non-denominational order of ministers" who will model "the alternative government of the Kingdom of God" and mobilize their members to address "the real-life human crises afflicting the land" through divinely directed and empowered social ministries (Rapu 2007).

The Exodus motif and the biblical metaphor of the Kingdom of God suggest similarities with liberation theology, but Rapu's political agenda is different. He seeks to engender change not through revolutionary struggle advocated by some expressions of liberation theology, but through a gradual reformation of cultural practices and the raising up of new leaders who will run for political office and seek employment in the public sector. As Ruth Marshall (2009: 204) points out, this entails the projection into public space of a highly political agenda dependent upon the conversion of individuals rather than "a revolution to create a new institutional order, found a new constitution, or elaborate new laws". Miller and Yamamori (2007: 215) refer to this as a "trickle-up" model of social change in which "people with strong moral values move into positions of authority" and bring about gradual change in the institutions they lead. Miller and Yamamori contrast Pentecostal imagery, which tends "to be organic in tone, emphasizing harmony and purity", with liberation theology, which tends "to use metaphors that conjure images of opposition, conflict, and struggle, reflecting its Marxist orientation".

Pentecostal leaders seek to implement this political project through sermons, leadership training programs, conferences, and the media. One initiative is Governance 500, a political training and networking program launched in 2010 by Leke Alder, a member of Household of God Church, and Poju Oyemade, senior pastor of Covenant Christian Centre. As well as undergoing training, participants are encouraged to gain experience as volunteers attached to various political parties and organizations before embarking on a career in politics. Several members of the 2010 Governance 500 class went on to contest the 2011 elections, including Pentecostal Pastor Kemela Okara (This Present House), who ran for the governorship of Bayelsa State on the platform of the Action Congress of Nigeria.[9]

The African Forum on Religion and Government (AFREG) was founded in 2006 by Rev. William Okoye as an institution "committed to transforming Africa into a premier continent shaped by God-centred values" (AFREG 2006).

Figure 3.2 Signboard for All Christians Fellowship Mission's Cathedral of Compassion, Abuja.

Source: author.

Okoye, a Biafran army veteran and former trader in eastern Nigeria, is the General Overseer of All Christians Fellowship Mission, which now has 150 congregations throughout Nigeria. In 1978, he experienced a dream which he interpreted as God leading him to move his ministry to Abuja. Okoye was a product of the post-1970 Pentecostal revival in eastern Nigeria and is regarded as one of the pioneers of neo-Pentecostalism in northern Nigeria (Burgess 2008; McCain 2013). In 1999, he was invited to become assistant chaplain to President Obasanjo, a post he held until 2006 when he was appointed senior chaplain. During his tenure, Okoye published a series of booklets addressing issues of governance and development which were distributed to religious and political leaders throughout the nation (Okoye 2000). Initially, Okoye's vision was for AFREG to serve as a platform for President Obasanjo to bring his Christian influence to bear on other leaders throughout the African continent. AFREG's inaugural 2006 conference in Abuja, organized in collaboration with CAN, was attended by participants from 27 African countries including two heads of states (Nigeria and Burundi), government ministers, business leaders, and church leaders (Okoye 2008; McCain 2013). Delegates also included leaders from the African diaspora in the United States. Subsequent conferences were held in Kenya (2009), Uganda (2013), and Ghana (2017).[10] The Abuja Declaration, developed by delegates at the Abuja conference, expressed a commitment to "more proactive and collective leadership in addressing holistically the issues of development, governance and justice", and to promote a "spirit of oneness and cooperation between Africans on the continent and the Africans in the Diaspora", "foster a climate of working with people of other faiths", and "develop theologies and ministries that liberate Africans from spiritual superstition, deception and oppression" (AFREG 2006). One of the outcomes of AFREG was the publication of the Nigeria Christian Creed on Governance, a 37-page document which states in clear terms what is required of political leaders as well as what is expected of citizens. Copies were presented to President Umaru Yar'Adua and other political leaders in the country (Agbiji and Swart 2015).

Another Pentecostal initiative, founded by Vincent Anigbogu, is the Institute for National Transformation, introduced in Chapter 1. Apart from its Nigerian headquarters, it operates in several other African countries as well as the United States and Britain. While most of its students are pastors, the institute also runs courses for government officials and business entrepreneurs. Anigbogu's philosophy of education combines knowledge acquisition with character formation, spiritual empowerment, and practical application of biblical principles.[11] Nigeria's neopatrimonial political system encourages a transactional leadership with material incentives for loyal service and support (Joseph 1987; Smith 2007). Political scientists refer to this as "big man" or "personal" rule, where the "big man" as patron provides material resources, security, and opportunities to a client in exchange for loyal political support (Hyden 2006; Jackson and Rosberg 1984; McCauley 2012). Anigbogu's ambition, however, is to produce leaders who will transform organizations, communities and nations (see Figure 3.2).[12] Course modules include "Establishing Basic Infrastructure for National Development", "The Role of Values and Ethics in National Development", and "Understanding Leadership and Management Systems". The influence of "Seven Mountains" theology on Anigbogu's social vision is reflected in the institute's objective to raise "integrity leaders" in the spheres of "government, education, celebration (arts and culture, music and entertainment, sports), social services, communication media, and religion" (Institute for National Transformation n.d.).[13] Anigbogu is also a close associate of Sunday Adelaja in the Ukraine, whom he credits with introducing him to "kingdom" theology.

Such initiatives are designed to affect politics at the cultural level by replacing corruption and poor leadership with values that respect human life, hard work, and integrity. In his analysis of Pentecostalism's political role in Ghana, Paul Gifford (2004: 181) draws upon David Martin's argument that in contexts where politics are dominated by corrupt elites, and Pentecostals are unable to confront political issues directly, the latter nonetheless may function very politically "by slowly and subtly transforming cultural values in areas like power and gender relations" (Martin 1992: 22).

Sam Adeyemi and Daystar Christian Centre

One Pentecostal leader addressing the issue of culture is Sam Adeyemi, senior pastor of Daystar Christian Centre. Adeyemi, who mentors other pastors in

Figure 3.3 Banner for the Institute for National Transformation, Abuja.

Source: author.

Nigeria, holds sway over large numbers of people both within his church and in the wider community. On a typical Sunday, his sermons to an estimated 20,000 congregants are broadcast on national and satellite television, and the church's conferences and Sunday services are streamed live on the Internet.

Founded in 1995 and currently meeting in a converted warehouse in Lagos, Daystar Christian Centre encourages acquisition and enactment of personal development techniques such as prayer, Bible study, and service (Marshall 2009). Like Anigbogu, Adeyemi is concerned about the perennial problem of leadership in Nigeria, and he has outlined what amounts to a manifesto for national development through the renewal of culture and the formation of Christian citizens (Adeyemi 2010a, 2010b). Rather than blame external forces such as colonialism or capitalism, Adeyemi has identified indigenous cultural patterns and practices as the main causes of Nigeria's present predicament. Concerned with changing the way Nigerians think about themselves, their culture, and the nation itself, Adeyemi responded to a World Bank report that 70 per cent of Nigerians live below the poverty line by highlighting the importance of the mind and imagination in shaping self-identity and national development:

> Nigeria is not poor. It is richly loaded with some of the world's best mineral resources. Our poverty is that of the mind.... That is where you experience freedom from your past and current limitations and become all you can dare to become. And that is where we are creating the new Nigerian.... With a new dream of Nigeria, we have a new Nigerian who is a citizen of the greatest country in the world.
>
> (Adeyemi 2010a: 20–25)

Adeyemi's prescription for national transformation focuses on a citizen's ability to govern the self. "People make government too powerful in our country. They do not realize that the most powerful form of government is self-government. When God gives you a revelation of who you are, that is where change begins" (Adeyemi 2010b: 7). And again, "The key that unlocks the power in you is self-discipline.... The man who does not exercise self-control will end up a victim of circumstances and of other people" (Adeyemi 2010b: 11). Adeyemi (2010a: 31–33) draws a connection between national development and one's imagination and actions: "The day most Nigerians buy into the vision of a developed Nigeria, there will be changes in our behaviour.... We have been praying for change in Nigeria. Now we must add courageous action to our prayer."

Adeyemi's remarks echo those of O'Neill who, drawing on Michel Foucault's notion of governmentality (that is, the mentality of governance), argues that neo-Pentecostalism provides a "range of cultural practices through which citizens are both constituted and governed". As such, it functions as a kind of political rationality "that promotes self-governing subjects—citizens whom governments do not have to rule because these men and women manage themselves". For O'Neill, neo-Pentecostals exhibit a moral responsibility based on "a causal logic where the thoughts and feelings of an individual form his or

Figure 3.4 The main auditorium of Daystar Christian Centre, Lagos.
Source: author.

her actions, and actions congeal into habits, molding character and, ultimately, the nation" (O'Neill 2010: 5). Ruth Marshall also employs a Foucauldian analytical framework, arguing that Nigerian Pentecostalism has given rise to "new modes of governing the self and others" through which it seeks to reshape its subjects' conduct and fulfill its political ambition of redeeming the nation by "replacing a corrupt regime with a new form of righteous authority". This vision of citizenship involves rupture – overcoming the past – and reconstruction – "building up the old waste places and thus redeeming them" (Marshall 2009: 125).

The moral dimension of self-governance is evident in Adeyemi's emphasis on the practice of Christian values such as respect for human life and compassion for others. Making an oblique reference to Marxist ideology, he calls for a "cultural revolution" based on love rather than armed struggle.

> Love is the platform for cultural revolution in Africa. The mere sight of the deprivations and devastations in Africa should trigger compassion and a drive to help people.... Our understanding of love and the expression of human value is not just going to be by words of mouth. We must enact and enforce life protecting legislation. We need to look around our nation and continent and find ways of alleviating the hardships that our people are experiencing.
>
> (Adeyemi 2010a: 45–47)

This is an inherently nationalistic project, echoing the "national unity" and "Nigeria is one" approach adopted by political parties in recent years. For example, one of the aims of the People's Democratic Party is to "Uphold the integrity and sovereignty of the Federal Republic of Nigeria as one united indivisible political entity" (People's Democratic Party 2012: 7). In the new Nigeria of Adeyemi's imagination, citizens will "have equal rights to live, work, vote and be voted for wherever they choose to live in the country" (Adeyemi 2010a: 58), and they will put the interest of Nigeria first and work together to build a nation based on peace and justice (Adeyemi 2010a: 59).

Tunde Bakare and the Save Nigeria Group

Apart from Vice-President Yemi Osinbajo, the most significant Pentecostal figure in Nigerian politics today is Tunde Bakare, former vice-presidential running mate of Muhammadu Buhari and convener of the SNG. Like other Pentecostals discussed in this chapter, Bakare is a firm advocate of kingdom theology and its role in national transformation. However, he takes a more liberationist and emancipatory approach than some of his colleagues. Bakare's focus on national transformation is reflected in his annual "State of the Nation" address, which is broadcast live on television and radio and posted on the Internet. In his 2009 broadcast, Bakare begins by identifying "government by cronyism" and political corruption as the main causes of Nigeria's present predicament before outlining "God's template for national transformation, development and greatness" based on biblical principles. He then calls upon the church to move beyond criticism by participating in constitutional reform:

> We cannot continue to criticize.... We must bring alternatives to the table and present them to everyone that matters because any constitution that cannot bend will break. The people of this nation will rise up and begin to demand their rights as freedom and liberty is proclaimed over our land.
>
> (Bakare 2009)

The focus on national transformation is also reflected in Save Nigeria Group's political manifesto, entitled "A Contract to Save and Transform Nigeria", published in January 2011. Far from eschewing structural issues in favour of focusing on individual transformation, it challenges existing political structures and sets out a clear agenda in the public sectors of politics, the economy, law and order, education, and health and social security. It challenged the politics of exclusion exacerbated by military dictatorship, fraudulent elections and religious polarization, and called for genuine electoral democracy. Against a background of pervasive corruption, it calls for a commitment to transforming the political culture and to growing a new crop of leaders with public and personal morality. Its stated goal is the "empowerment" of citizens and communities, as well as the "transformation of Nigeria as a nation" in order to bring about the "liberty, security and prosperity" of all Nigerians (Save Nigeria Group 2011).

The inclusive nature of the SNG's political activism, and Bakare's efforts to align himself with Muslim clerics and political leaders (Marshall 2014),[14] represent a departure from the predominantly antagonistic stance adopted by Nigerian Pentecostals towards Muslims. One of the criticisms levelled against Nigerian Pentecostals is that their missionary practices and militaristic rhetoric can reinforce conceptions of the religious "other" as the enemy, resulting in an erosion of trust and a heightening of inter-religious tensions (Ojo 2007; Ukah 2009; Marshall 2009; Kalu 2008; Akinade 2014). As Marshall (2010: 217) rightly observes, their tendency to identify the demonic within the unconverted other and overcome it through conversion inhibits the stabilization of a coherent community based on trust.

Bakare's hermeneutical approach that moves from the context of the poor to the biblical text, his advocacy of non-violent civil disobedience, exemplified by the Occupy Nigeria street protests, and his willingness to confront government over its treatment of the poor suggest important points of intersection with liberation hermeneutics and praxis. There are also similarities between Bakare's kingdom theology, with its emphasis on justice and equality, and the liberationist doctrine of the Kingdom of God. For liberationists, such as Gustavo Gutiérrez, the Kingdom of God is about liberation and justice, a powerful symbol of social change which "requires us to change our present reality, reject the abuses of the powerful, and develop relationships that are fraternal and just" (Gutiérrez cited in Nickoloff 1996: 174). For Bakare, the metaphor of the Kingdom of God symbolizes the rule of God and the inauguration of a just society, liberated from oppressive states, through the agency of "kingdom" citizens (Bakare 2012). Bakare's use of the Exodus narrative and his employment of liberationist rhetoric also suggest affinities with liberation theology. For example, in a public lecture entitled "Nigeria at Centenary. A Nation under Bondage", Bakare compares Nigeria's history to the "liberation" of the people of Israel from bondage in Egypt. In his reading of Nigerian colonial and postcolonial history, Bakare refers to the early Nigerian nationalists as "liberators" who "challenged the oppressive policies of the British", and to the subsequent "liberation struggle" against "military oppression" by civil rights activists, which revived "the Nigerian ideal of liberty and brotherhood" and helped to return the nation to civilian rule. However, Nigeria has yet to experience "full liberty", according to Bakare, because a "culture of corruption, impunity and sectional interest" continues to pervade "every sector and every level of the social cadre" (Bakare 2014b).

There are also important differences between Bakare's theology and liberation theology as espoused by Latin American liberationists. Bakare's political theology is influenced by "Seven Mountains" theology and its focus on transforming the different spheres of society through the presence of moral citizens carrying "kingdom" values:

> The successful reconstruction of the social, economic and political landscape of the nations of the earth must be preceded by the manifestation of light through the carriers of the glory of God. These carriers of the light of

> His glory must permeate the seven mountains of society: Arts and Entertainment, Media, Education, Family, Religion, Business and Government with the light that they carry.
>
> (Bakare 2012)

Thus, there seem to be two strands to Bakare's political theology: a liberationist strand that seeks to overturn existing political structures in order to create a just and equitable society, and a reformist strand which seeks to transform existing structures through the gradual infiltration of "kingdom" citizens into the public sphere.

Conclusion

Nigeria's mix of Islamic resurgence and Pentecostal revivalism makes it unique in terms of evangelical politics. The shift to a more politically engaged Pentecostalism was precipitated negatively by fear of Islamization and frustration over the failed democratization program, political corruption, and military intransigence, and positively by the movement's exponential growth and ecumenical relations. The development of a political theology based on a holistic soteriology that encompasses national redemption further motivated Pentecostal political engagement.

Pentecostals have a mixed record in the move toward democratization. They played an active role in the political transition following General Sani Abacha's 1993 military takeover, but their support for beleaguered Christian President Olusegun Obasanjo after he diverted from democratization tainted their record of critical activism. Nonetheless, Tunde Bakare's Save Nigeria Group marked a significant departure for Pentecostal political engagement; pastors have used the media to call for free and fair elections; and programs have emerged to prepare Pentecostals for civic responsibilities. Chris Okotie's unsuccessful incursion into politics shows the dangers of seeking routes to office without preparation and training. And while only in their nascent phase, organizations and churches such as Governance 500, AFREG, the Institute for National Transformation, and Daystar Christian Centre offer a more long-term potential of transforming Nigeria's political culture. To maintain their credibility and avoid exacerbating Christian-Muslim tension, however, they may need to distance themselves from the more triumphalist and theocratic versions of dominion theology associated with the religious right in the United States. Significantly, Bakare's liberationist version of kingdom theology has closer affinities to Latin American liberation theology than it does to the American brand of dominion theology.

Whether Nigerian Pentecostalism can develop viable political communities for nation-building and social reformation remains to be seen. If it depends upon instituting sovereignty by maintaining pastoral authority over its disparate groups of believers, then I agree with Marshall that the difficulties may be unsurmountable. However, like Wariboko, I am more hopeful about Pentecostal prospects of forming such communities, based on their shared experience of the Holy Spirit and their common commitment to acts of discipleship and service.

The initiatives discussed in this chapter, which are seeking to develop "communities of character" and civic responsibility, hold out promise for the future, even if their impact is not felt in the wider society for some time to come.

Nigeria faces severe challenges in the quest for sustainable democracy. Muslim-Christian rivalry continues to dominate its political culture and represents a serious obstacle to the creation of viable democratic institutions and the conduct of peaceful elections. The inclusive nature of the SNG's political activism provides a public space for interaction between religious groups and is at odds with the predominantly anti-Muslim stance adopted by Nigerian Pentecostals. Meanwhile, with urban prayer projects multiplying across the country it is difficult to assess their contributions to the democratic process, and it would be wrong to assume such initiatives are incompatible with more conventional forms of political activism. For those at the grassroots who bear the brunt of suffering caused by government corruption and mismanagement, prayer and a belief in the possibility of miracles remain the principal tools of Pentecostal political engagement.

Notes

1 Interview, Pastor Tunde Bakare, Latter Rain Assembly, Lagos, 2 October 2011.
2 Interview, Pastor Tunde Bakare, Latter Rain Assembly, Lagos, 2 October 2011. For example, Bakare allegedly prophesied the fall of President Babangida's military dictatorship in 1993, the death of Chief Moshood Abiola (who ran for the presidency in 1993), and the demise of President Sani Abacha in 1999.
3 Agag was the Amalekite king mentioned in the Hebrew Bible. Agag was spared by Israel's King Saul but later executed by the prophet Samuel, who regarded Saul's clemency as a defiance of the will of God. Bakare's reference to the "prophetic axe" echoes the prophet Samuel's method of execution. See1 Samuel chapter 15: 32–33.
4 Interview, Pastor Tunde Bakare, Latter Rain Assembly, Lagos, 2 October 2011.
5 Interview, Pastor Kemela Okara, This Present House, Lagos, 12 December 2010. For example, This Present House in Lagos organized a special Sunday service around the theme "God and Government: the Role of the Church", and invited guest speakers to address congregants on such topics as "Registering and Protecting Your Vote", "Becoming a Member of a Political Party", and "Becoming an Election Observer".
6 The acronym "FRESH" stands for Faith, Responsibility, Equality, Security, and Hope.
7 Interview, Pastor Wale Adefarasin, Guiding Light Assembly, Lagos, 22 September 2011.
8 Interview, Pastor Tunde Bakare, Latter Rain Assembly, Lagos, 2 October 2011.
9 Kemala Okara, an indigene of Bayelsa State, came a creditable third behind the PDP candidate. In 2017, he was appointed Secretary to the State Governor, Seriake Dickson.
10 AFREG's 2013 conference in Lusaka was entitled "Empowering Leadership for Transforming Africa".
11 Interview, Professor Vincent Anigbogu, Institute for National Transformation, Abuja, 25 May 2012.
12 By 2014, over 1,600 Nigerians had graduated from the institute's programmes, including church pastors, denominational leaders, government officials, and leaders in the educational and business sectors (Institute for National Transformation n.d.).
13 Significantly, one of the core textbooks on the programme is Enlow's *The Seven Mountain Prophecy* (2008).
14 One of Bakare's close friends is Mallam Nasir El-Rufai, the incumbent governor of Kaduna State, who allegedly persuaded Bakare to run alongside Buhari in the 2011 presidential elections.

References

Abimboye, Demola (2012) "The War, Its Leaders", *Newswatch*, 23 January, available at: www.newswatchngr.com/index.php?option=com_content&task=view&id=3843&Item id=1 (accessed 2 April 2013).

Adejumo, Akintokunbo (2010) "The Save Nigeria Protest March in London, Friday 15th January 2010", *Vanguard*, 16 January, available at: http://community.vanguardngr.com/profiles/blogs/the-save-nigeria-protest-march (accessed 4 April 2013).

Adeyemi, Sam (2010a) *Nigeria of my Dream*, Lagos: Pneuma Publishing.

Adeyemi, Sam (2010b) *We are Government*, Lagos: Pneuma Publishing.

AFREG (2006) "AFREG 1 Abuja Declaration", available at: http://transformingleadership.com/about_ilf/partnerships/afreg/afreg_reports/afreg_1_abuja_declaration (accessed 26 June 2013).

Agbiji, O. M. and I. Swart (2015) "Christian Religious Leadership and the Challenge of Sustainable Transformational Development in Postmilitary Nigeria: Towards a Reappraisal", *KOERS – Bulletin for Christian Scholarship* 80(1): 1–13.

Ajayi, Kunle (2006) "Security Forces, Electoral Conduct and the 2003 General Elections in Nigeria", *Journal of Social Sciences* 13(1): 57–66.

Akinade, Akintunde (2014) *Christian Responses to Islam in Nigeria*, Basingstoke: Palgrave Macmillan.

Allagui, Ilhem and Johanne Kuebler (2011) "The Arab Spring and the Role of ICTs. Editorial Introduction", *International Journal of Communication* 5: 1435–1442.

Amaefule, Everest (2012) "Rage as Nigerians Fuel Protests on Social Media", *Punch Nigeria*, 15 January, available at: www.punchng.com/business/close-up-on-ict/rage-as-nigerians-fuel-protests-on-social-media/ (accessed 13 July 2013).

Aransiola, Moses (2008a) *The Prophetic Destiny of Nigeria: God's Plan for the Nation*, Ibadan: Gethsemane Publications.

Aransiola, Moses (2008b) *Praying for National Transformation: Securing Divine Visitation for Nigeria*, Ibadan: Gethsemane Publications.

Aucoin, Ciara and Zachary Donnenfeld (2016) "Unlocking Africa's Potential: The Relationship Between Effective Governance and Poverty", *Institute for Security Studies Papers* 2016(21): 1–28.

Awoyinfa, Samuel, Allwell Okpi, and David Attah (2012) "N1.7trn Fuel Subsidy Loot: Save Nigeria Group Mobilises for Mass Protest in Lagos, Others", *Punch Nigeria*, 22 April, available at; www.punchng.com/news/n1-7trn-fuel-subsidy-loot-save-nigeria-group-mobilises-for-mass-protest-in-lagos-others/ (accessed 18 July 2013).

Aziken, Emmanuel (2013) "One Year After Fuel Subsidy Protests: Who is Occupying Nigeria Now?", *Vanguard*, 7 January, available at: www.vanguardngr.com/2013/01/one-year-after-fuel-subsidy-protests-who-is-occupying-nigeria-now/ (accessed 8 July 2013).

Bakare, Tunde (2009) "There is Hope in Our Future", State of the Nation Broadcast, Latter Rain Assembly, 1 October.

Bakare, Tunde (2012) "Establishing the Kingdom of God Through Christians' Involvement in National Politics", available at: http://babatundebakare.com/site/2012/10/establishing-the-kingdom-of-god-through-christians%e2%80%99-involvement-in-national-politics-4/ (accessed 15 September 2013).

Bakare, Tunde (2014a) "Occupy Nigeria: Corruption and the Soul of Nigeria", 13 January, available at: http://saharareporters.com/2013/01/13/occupy-nigeria-corruption-and-soul-nigeria-pastor-tunde-bakare (accessed 12 July 2013).

Bakare, Tunde (2014b) "Nigeria at Centenary: A Nation under Bondage?", Speech Given by Tunde Bakare at the 10th Late Chief Gani Fawehinmi's Annual Lecture, The Nigerian Bar Association (NBA), Ikeja Branch, 15 January, available at: http://babatundebakare.com/site/2014/01/nigeria-at-centenary-a-nation-under-bondage/ (accessed 14 March 2014).

Balogun, Olusola (2010) "Bishop Mike Okonkwo Warns: Expect Explosion", *Sunday Sun (Lagos)*, 14 November, p. 57.

Biermann, Frank, Casey Stevens, Steven Bernstein, Aarti Gupta, Ngeta Kabiri, Norichika Kanie, Marc Levy, Måns Nilsson, Lásztó Pintér, Michelle Scobie, and Oran R. Young (2014) *Integrating Governance into the Sustainable Development Goals*, Policy Brief #3, Tokyo: United Nations University Institute for the Advanced Study of Sustainability.

Burgess, Richard (2008) *Nigeria's Christian Revolution: The Civil War Revival and its Pentecostal Progeny* (1967–2008). Carlisle: Paternoster.

Burgess, Richard (2015) "Pentecostalism and Democracy in Nigeria: Electoral Politics, Prophetic Practices, and Cultural Reformation", *Nova Religio: The Journal of Alternative and Emergent Religions* 18(3): 38–62.

Congress on Christian Ethics in Nigeria (1997) *Nigeria Covenant*, Jos: CAPRO Media Print Production.

Edwards, Martin S. and Sthelyn Romero (2014) "Governance and the Sustainable Development Goals: Changing the Game or More of the Same?" *SAIS Review of International Affairs* 34(2): 141–150.

Eghaghe, Richard (2011) "Accept Defeat as the will of God, Adeboye tells Buhari, Bakare", *National Mirror (Lagos)*, 28 April, available at: http://nationalmirroronline.net/news/10945.html (accessed 5 May 2012).

Ekpu, Ray (2010) "Man of the Year: Courage Is It", *Newswatch (Lagos)*, 28 December.

Ellis, Stephen and Gerrie Ter Haar (2004) *Worlds of Power: Religious Thought and Political Practice in Africa*, London: Hurst and Company.

Enlow, Johnny (2008) *The Seven Mountain Prophecy: Unveiling the Elijah Revolution*, Lake Mary, FL: Creation House.

Falola, Toyin (1998) *Violence in Nigeria: The Crisis of Religious Politics and Secular Ideologies*, Rochester, NY: University of Rochester Press.

Freston, Paul (2001) *Evangelicals and Politics in Asia, Africa and Latin America*, Cambridge: Cambridge University Press.

Gifford, Paul (1995) "Introduction: Democratisation and the Churches", in Paul Gifford (ed.) *The Christian Churches and the Democratisation of Africa*, Leiden: E. J. Brill, pp. 1–13.

Gifford, Paul (1998) *African Christianity: Its Public Role*, London: Hurst & Co.

Gifford, Paul (2004) *Ghana's New Christianity: Pentecostalism in a Globalising African Economy*, London: Hurst & Co.

Goode, Luke (2009) "Social News, Citizen Journalism and Democracy", *New Media Society* 11(8): 1287–1305.

Haynes, Jeff (1996) *Religion and Politics in Africa*, London: Zed Books.

Howard, Philip and Malcolm Parks (2012) "Social Media and Political Change: Capacity, Constraint, and Consequence", *Journal of Communication* 62(2): 359–362.

Hyden, Goran (2006) *African Politics in Comparative Perspective*, Cambridge: Cambridge University Press.

Iherika, Walter C. (2012) "From Televisuality to Social Activism: Nigerian Televangelists and Their Socio-Political Agenda", in Pradip N. Thomas and Philip Lee (eds) *Global and Local Televangelism*, Basingstoke: Palgrave Macmillan, pp. 173–198.

Imo, Cyril (2008) "Evangelicals, Muslims, and Democracy: With Particular Reference to the Declaration of Sharia in Northern Nigeria", in Terence O. Ranger (ed.) *Evangelical Christianity and Democracy in Africa*, Oxford: Oxford University Press, pp. 37–66.

Institute for National Transformation (n.d.) "Developing Transformational Leaders", available at: intinternational.org/site/images/int-brochure.pdf (accessed 30 March 2014).

Jackson, Robert H. and Carl G. Rosberg (1984) "Personal Rule. Theory and Practice in Africa", *Comparative Politics* 16(4): 421–442.

Joseph, Richard A. (1987) *Democracy and Prebendal Politics in Nigeria: The Rise and Fall of the Second Republic*, Cambridge: Cambridge University Press.

Kalu, Ogbu U. (2008) *African Pentecostalism: An Introduction*, Oxford: Oxford University Press.

Kalu, Ogbu U. (2010) "Faith and Politics in Africa: Emergent Political Theology of Engagement in Nigeria", in Wilhelmena J. Kalu, Nimi Wariboko, and Toyin Falola (eds) *Religion in Africa: Conflicts, Politics and Social Ethics*, The Collected Essays of Ogbu Uche Kalu, Trenton: Africa World Press, pp. 11–30.

Laberge, Marie (2019) *Is Africa Measuring Up to Its Goal 16 Commitments? The Road to HLPF 2019 and Beyond*, Oslo: United Nations Development Programme.

Marshall, Ruth (2009) *Political Spiritualities: The Pentecostal Revolution in Nigeria*, Chicago: University of Chicago Press.

Marshall, Ruth (2014) " 'Dealing with the Prince over Lagos': Pentecostal Arts of Citizenship", in Mamadou Diouf and Rosalind Fredericks (eds) *The Arts of Citizenship in African Cities: Infrastructures and Spaces of Belonging*, New York: Palgrave Macmillan, pp. 91–114.

Martin, David (1992) "Faiths Escaping the Hierarchies", *Times Literary Supplement*, 18 December: 22.

McCain, Danny (2013) "The Metamorphosis of Nigerian Pentecostalism: From Signs and Wonders in The Church to Service and Influence in Society", in Donald E. Miller, Kimon H. Sargent, and Richard Flory (eds) *Spirit and Power: The Growth and Global Impact of Pentecostalism*, Oxford: Oxford University Press, pp. 160–181.

McCauley, John F. (2012) "Africa's New Big Man Rule? Pentecostalism and Patronage in Ghana", *African Affairs*, 112(446): 1–21.

Meyer, Birgit (1998) "The Power of Money: Politics, Occult Forces, and Pentecostalism in Ghana", *African Studies Review* 41(3) December: 15–37.

Miller, Donald E. and Tetsunao Yamamori (2007) *Global Pentecostalism: The New Face of Christian Social Engagement*, Berkeley, CA: University of California Press.

Nickoloff, James B. (ed.) (1996) *Gustavo Gutierrez: Essential Writings*, London: SCM Press.

Nwankpa, Emeka (1994) *Redeeming the Land: Interceding for the Nations*, Achimota, Ghana: Africa Christian Press.

Obadare, Ebenezer (2006) "Pentecostal Presidency? The Lagos-Ibadan 'Theocratic Class' & the Muslim Other", *Review of African Political Economy* 33(110): 665–678.

Obadare, Ebenezer (2007) "Religious NGOs, Civil Society and the Quest for a Public Sphere in Nigeria", *African Identities* 5(1): 135–153.

Obadare, Ebenezer (2018) *Pentecostal Republic: Religion and the Struggle for State Power in Nigeria*, London: Zed Books.

Ojo, Matthews A. (1998) "The Church in the African State: The Charismatic/ Pentecostal Experience in Nigeria", *Journal of African Christian Thought* 1(2): 25–32.

Ojo, Matthews A. (2006) *The End-time Army: Charismatic Movements in Nigeria*, Trenton, NJ: Africa World Press.

Okoroafor, Peter (1996) *William Okoye: Called to Serve*, Abuja: Whole Gospel Publications.

Onapajo, Hakeem (2012) "Politics for God: Religion, Politics and Conflict in Democratic Nigeria", *The Journal of Pan African Studies* 4(9): 42–66.

O'Neill, Kevin (2010) *City of God: Christian Citizenship in Postwar Guatemala*, Berkeley: University of California Press.

People's Democratic Party (PDP) (2012) Constitution of the People's Democratic Party, available at: http://peoplesdemocraticparty.com.ng/wp-content/uploads/2018/08/PDP-CONSTITUTION-2012-AMENDMENT1.pdf (accessed 20 January 2020).

Ranger, Terence O. (2008) "Introduction: Evangelical Christianity and Democracy in Africa", in Terence O. Ranger (ed.) *Evangelical Christianity and Democracy in Africa: Evangelical Christianity and Democracy in the Global South*, Oxford: Oxford University Press, pp. 3–35.

Rapu, Tony (2007) "The Joshua Generation", THISDAY (Lagos), 13 February.

Sahara Reporters (2010) "Save Nigeria Group (UK) Launch – Champions for Nigeria Took the Front Seat", *Sarara Reporters*, 21 July, available at: http://saharareporters.com/2010/07/21/save-nigeria-group-uk-launch---champions-nigeria-took-front-seat (accessed 5 September 2018).

Save Nigeria Group (2011) *A Contract to Save and Transform Nigeria (A Manifesto for Liberty, Security and Prosperity for All Nigerians)*, January, Lagos: Save Nigeria Group.

Smith, Daniel J. (2007) *A Culture of Corruption: Everyday Deception and Popular Discontent in Nigeria*, Princeton: Princeton University Press.

Save Nigeria Group (2012) "SNG Ojota Rally Day 4: Press Release by the Convener of Save Nigeria Group", 13 January, available at: http://tundebakare.com/sng-ojota-rally-day-4-press-releaseby-the-convener-of-save-nigeria-group/ (accessed 26 September 2018).

Ukah, Asonzeh F.-K (2008) *A New Paradigm of Pentecostal Power: A Study of the Redeemed Christian Church of God in Nigeria*, Trenton, NJ: Africa World Press.

Ukah, Asonzeh F.-K (2009) "Contesting God: Nigerian Pentecostals and Their Relations with Islam and Muslims", in David Westerlund (ed.) *Global Pentecostalism: Encounters with Other Religious Traditions*, London: I. B. Tauris & Co., pp. 93–114.

UNDP (2014) *Discussion Paper: Governance for Sustainable Development – Integrating Governance in the Post-2015 Development Framework*, New York: United Nations Development Programme.

UN General Assembly (2012) *The Future We Want: Resolution Adopted by the General Assembly*, Rio de Janeiro: United Nations.

UN System Task Team on the Post-2015 UN Development Agenda (2012) *Governance and Development: Thematic Think Piece*, UNDESA, UNDP, UNESCO, May.

Wariboko, Nimi (2014) *Nigerian Pentecostalism*, Rochester, NY: University of Rochester Press.

Yong, Amos (2010) *In the Days of Caesar: Pentecostalism and Political Theology*, Grand Rapids, MI: Eerdmans.

4 Pentecostals, education, and development

Introduction

This chapter examines Pentecostal educational initiatives in Nigeria and their contributions to development. Pentecostal churches are responding to declining standards in Nigeria's educational system by engaging in a variety of educational enterprises geared towards national transformation. There is a growing literature on Pentecostal education in different global contexts, including Africa. Most research has focused on Pentecostal theological education and its role in ministerial formation (e.g. Alvarez 2000; Kärkkäinen 2012; Castleberry 2004; Anderson 2004; Asamoah-Gyadu 2018; Johns 1993). My focus in this chapter is on the intersection between Pentecostalism and Nigeria's education sector. It begins with a general discussion of the developmental role of education and its inclusion in the UN's sustainable development agenda. It then sets the context by examining Nigeria's educational system with a particular focus on developments since independence. The remainder of the chapter explores the diversity of Pentecostal educational initiatives including NGOs, schools, and universities.

Education and development

Education is recognized as an important contributor to development in the globalizing economy (Bloom, Canning, and Chan 2006; Haynes 2007). As Antoninis, Delprato, and Benavot (2016: 63) note, "Education is essential to economic growth, poverty reduction, gender equality, public health, conflict resolution and the transformation to sustainable production and consumption." The MDGs included two education-related goals: the achievement of universal primary education (Goal 2) and the elimination of gender disparity in all levels of education (Goal 3). However, one of the criticisms levelled against the MDGs was their neglect of the contribution of higher education to development (Boni, Lopez-Fogues, and Walker 2016). One reason for this neglect was that the international development community considered primary and secondary education as more important than tertiary education for poverty reduction and economic growth. This encouraged African governments to prioritize basic education over tertiary education. Universities were considered "high priced privileged enclaves" whose returns did not "warrant the investment and continuing costly support" (Samoff and Carrol 2003: 4).

In recent decades, organizations such as the World Bank and major donor governments have begun to reconsider their stance on higher education, recognizing its benefits in terms of generating tax revenue, increasing savings and investments, and engendering a more entrepreneurial and civic society (Bloom, Canning, and Chan 2006; Cloete, Bunting, and Maassen 2015). The World Bank has published a series of policy reports on higher education. Along with UNESCO, it convened a Task Force on Higher Education and Society, which brought together experts from 13 countries to explore the future of higher education in developing countries. In 2000, the Task Force published its report "Higher Education in Developing Countries: Peril and Promise", which argued that higher education is essential to national social and economic development in the new knowledge economy (The Task Force on Higher Education and Society 2000). Other World Bank reports on higher education include "Constructing Knowledge Societies: New Challenges for Tertiary Education" (2002) and "The Challenge of Establishing World Class Universities" (2009). Among the themes addressed in the World Bank reports are the problems of access and equity, the need for government involvement but also institutional autonomy, the so-called brain drain, the issue of quality, and the relevance of higher education curricula (Ewen 2018).

Education is more centrally positioned in the post-2015 sustainable development agenda. Ambitions for education are captured in SDG Goal 4 which aims to "ensure inclusive and equitable quality education and promote lifelong learning opportunities for all". The SDG agenda retains the emphasis of the MDGs on universal primary education and gender parity in all levels of education. In addition, five of the SDG-4 targets are related directly or indirectly to higher education. In contrast to the MDGs, vocational education and training is also a central aspect of Goal 4. Education is also linked with other SDG goals. As Rambla and Langthaler (2016: 8) note, sustainable progress in SDG 4 needs "decent social conditions regarding at least poverty (SDG 1), hunger (SDG 2), health (SDG 3), gender equality (SDG 5), work (SDG 8) and economic equality (SDG 10)".

In 2015, following the World Education Forum in Incheon, Republic of Korea, the Incheon Declaration for Education 2030, and the Education 2030 Framework for Action were adopted by the 184 member states of the United Nations as a new vision for education for the following 15 years. The Incheon Declaration recognizes the importance of education for development: "Our vision is to transform lives through education, recognizing the important role of education as a main driver of development and in achieving the other proposed SDGs" (UNESCO 2015).

The Nigerian context

Christian missionaries were largely responsible for introducing Western education into Nigeria. Education was used by Christian missions as an instrument of evangelization, creating intense competition between Protestant and Catholic denominations to establish schools. In 1942, 97 per cent of Nigeria's student population were enrolled in mission schools (Berman 1974). However, private participation in the provision of education in Nigeria was undermined when the military government took over all Christian mission schools in 1972. This was unpopular with Christians and had negative implications for education in Nigeria, because government schools were often poorly managed, with inadequate infrastructure, low standards of discipline, and poor learning outcomes (Gaiya 2014). In the immediate postcolonial period, the Nigerian government allocated significant resources to education, believing that schools were key to national unity. However, optimism gradually faded following the Nigerian civil war and subsequent fluctuations in the economy, resulting in a decline in government spending on schools (Moland 2015). Today, private schools run by churches and secular organizations have proliferated, partly in response to the decline in the quality of government schools.

In 1976, the Universal Primary Education (UPE) programme was established, an overambitious plan to bridge the educational gap by giving all children free primary education (Daniel-Kalio 2018: 258). The 1977 National Policy on Education was the first policy on education formulated by Nigeria's post-independence government. The policy was geared towards addressing the needs of Nigerian citizens, promoting national unity, and meeting the developmental needs of the nation (Daniel-Kalio 2018). Since then, the NPE has undergone a series of revisions to ensure that the educational sector is supportive of the government's developmental goals.[1] The 1998 revised NPE prescribed a Universal Basic Education (UBE) programme, which replaced the UPE and was launched in 1999 (Moja 2000; Daniel-Kalio 2018). Though the policy prescribed a compulsory UBE, it was not enforced effectively. Primary education is officially free and compulsory, yet Nigeria ranks as having the highest number of out-of-school children in the world (about 13.2 million) (Adedigba 2018). The main barrier to school enrolment is economic. Due to reduced federal government spending on education, local governments are increasingly charging school fees, resulting in a decline in enrolment rates (Moland 2015). The situation in the north of the country is particularly severe, with a net attendance rate of 53 per cent. In northern Nigeria, in addition to the economic barriers, socio-cultural norms and practices discourage attendance in formal education, especially for girls (UNICEF n.d.). Education deprivation is further exacerbated by the closure of schools brought about by Islamic insurgence.

The 2013 reviewed policy is the 6th edition of the NPE. The impetus for the changes derived from the government's commitment to such international protocols as the Education for All (EEA) and the UN MDGs, as well as the National Economic Empowerment and Development Strategy (NEEDS), the Roadmap for the Development of the Nigerian Education Sector (2009), and President Jonathan's Transformation Agenda (Federal Republic of Nigeria 2013). The purpose of the 2013 NPE was to engender "an expanded role for education as an investment for economic, social and political development" (FRN 2013: ii).

Nigeria has one of the oldest and largest higher education systems in Africa, with the second highest student enrolment, behind Egypt. It also has the largest number of HE institutions in Africa (Teferra and Altbachi 2004). From 1948 to 1999, university education was the sole responsibility of federal and state governments. University education in Nigeria started in 1948 with the creation of University College, Ibadan, which was affiliated to the University of London. This was followed by federal universities established in Lagos, Ile-Ife, Zaria (1950), Nsukka (1960), and Benin (1970). These represented the first generation of Nigerian universities. The second generation of federal universities was founded between 1974 and 1977, and included Jos, Maiduguri, Kano, Sokoto, Ilorin, Calabar, and Port Harcourt. These universities were established to meet the demand for higher education during the oil boom years. The third generation of universities was founded between 1980 and 1992, and included federal and state universities (Gaiya 2014; Ajayi and Ekundayo 2008).

The collapse of the oil economy in the 1980s posed a challenge to higher education. During Nigeria's military regimes, funding allocation for universities was low. The structural adjustment policies of the World Bank compounded the problem by putting pressure on African governments to prioritize expenditure on basic education at the expense of higher education (Carpenter 2017; Gaiya 2014). This began to change in 2000, when higher education "was identified as a major agent of development and social change" (Gaiya 2014: 29). However, the sector faces many challenges, including inadequate funding, resources, and infrastructure; inequity in the system; a decline in quality of education due to the rapid expansion of student numbers; irrelevant curricula; the exodus of academic staff overseas; and student protests (Moja 2000; Asiyai 2013). In addition, cultism has had a negative impact on learning and discipline in public universities (Aigboje 2013; Gboyega 2005).

The contemporary context for Christian (including Pentecostal) higher education in Africa is an increasing demand for education, dwindling government resources, the privatization of higher education, and a strong moral discourse (Kalu 2008; Carpenter 2017; Gaiya 2014). The provision of higher education by private institutions is a growing phenomenon in Africa (Levy 2007; Teferra and Altbachl 2004; Mabizela 2007; Thaver 2008). Kenya, Nigeria, and Zimbabwe were the first African countries to accredit private institutions (Levy 2007). Many private universities in Africa are owned by Christian organizations. As Joel Carpenter (2017) notes, this is partly driven by Christian groups seeking to consolidate and conserve the huge gains in Christian adherence on the continent. Churches often start universities to cater for their own people. But they also aim to contribute to their nation's development (Carpenter 2017). A significant trend is the rise of Pentecostal universities, founded by educational entrepreneurs attuned to market economics and with a strong sense of civic responsibility (Hittenberger 2004; Kalu 2008). Levy (2007) refers to the dominance of Pentecostal universities in Africa, compared to other religious traditions such as the Catholic Church. One reason for this is the growth of Pentecostal churches on the continent.

The introduction of private higher education in Nigeria followed the deregulation of the Nigerian economy in 1999 under the civilian regime of President Obasanjo. The aim of the Federal Government was to encourage private-public competition in the sector. However, it was also a response to the increasing demand for higher education and the declining capacity of public institutions (Obasi 2015; Gaiya 2014). Many private universities in Nigeria are owned by religious organizations. For example, Gaiya (2014) lists 41 approved private universities in Nigeria: 21 Christian, three Islamic, and the rest secular. The number of accredited private universities had increased to 79 in 2019, compared to 95 state and federal universities (NUC 2019a, 2019b, 2019c). Of Nigeria's private universities, at least 32 are owned by religious organizations: six Catholic, six Protestant mainline, 15 Pentecostal, and five Islamic (Funmilola 2019).

Funding for private universities in Africa comes from two main sources: student tuition fees and grants from sponsoring organizations (Thaver 2008). In the case of Christian universities, sponsorship includes donations from parent churches. The cost of education in private institutions is generally higher than in public universities, as student tuition fees are their main source of revenue (Teferra and Altbachi 2004). Critics point out that some private universities are run as personal business enterprises, preoccupied with profits (Gaiya 2014; Levy 2007). However, most Christian universities claim to be non-profit organizations.

Pentecostal perspectives on education in Nigeria

Nigerian Pentecostal churches are responding to the perceived collapse of morality and declining standards in Nigeria's educational system by engaging in capacity-building programmes in public schools, establishing educational NGOs, and opening private schools and universities. These initiatives are shaped by memories of former days when Nigeria was one of the leading providers of education in sub-Saharan Africa, as well as by Pentecostal ambitions to contribute to national development through high quality, value-based education. The dominant narrative is of an educational system in decline following the government takeover of Christian mission schools, the exodus of academics overseas (the so-called "brain drain"), and the squandering of oil revenues due to corruption. Pentecostals regard education as means of lifting people out of poverty. In the Nigeria Survey, 84 per cent of Pentecostals and 82 per cent of Charismatics said that education is very important for people's economic success (Nigeria Survey 2011). Pentecostal discourse on education is framed in ethical terms as an expression of the church's social and moral responsibility to bring about national transformation. In an article entitled "Rebranding Nigeria. Christian Education to the Rescue", Pastor Ezekiel Odeyemi, RCCG's Assistant General Overseer for Education and Training, explains the rationale behind the church's schools' movement:

> Despite all the contributions our nation has made to the world, there is a popular feeling that we are not supposed to be at the level we find ourselves either politically or economically.... This is where Christian education comes in. If we are going to truly change this nation, our education cannot target just the soul, but it must be total in order to lead to the emergence of

> the total person … Christian education is not just about teaching and preaching, but also about the development of Christian virtues and godliness in the subject … Christian education is the only hope of this society, bearing in mind the contributions of the mission schools before and after our independence, and the formation of the total person they were able to achieve which helped our nation to jumpstart her freedom from the shackles of colonialism.… Since education is a social good, that is, a product that is not profit-oriented, the church must see education as an investment and part of our social responsibility. This is the founding motive of Christ the Redeemer's Schools Movement.
>
> (Odeyemi 2009: 62, 78)

Here we see references to the contribution of mission schools to the nationalist struggle for independence, the holistic nature of Christian education, and its role in development. For Odeyemi, education is the social responsibility of the church, to be pursued as a non-profit venture and an investment for the future. The emphasis on holistic education and character formation is reflected in an excerpt from an interview with a staff member of Winners Chapel's Covenant University:

> When the chancellor of the university, the bishop [David Oyedepo], looked at the Nigerian educational system, he found out there was a lot of decay. Around the 1980s and 1990s, decadence set into the Nigerian university system. Overpopulation, people going out to other African countries, Europe and America. Our graduates were no longer doing well; they were not well-trained. So he got a vision to set up a university. That's how Covenant University came about. He also felt that morality was in decline. The kind of certificate you get in Nigeria says that after schooling you are not found wanting in character and learning. But only learning was emphasized; character went down. So here we are now emphasizing character as well as learning.[2]

Churches, NGOs, and capacity-building

As part of their Christian social responsibility, some Pentecostal churches are engaged in capacity-building programmes in public schools. One example is Sam Adeyemi's Daystar Christian Centre. Adeyemi believes that education is the basic foundation that people need to escape poverty, and that it is the church's responsibility to support the government in improving the quality of public-school provision in Nigeria. Daystar's "Community Impact" programme has completed a number of schools-related projects. In January 2002, a fire started in the Ikeja Military Cantonment, located in a densely populated area of Lagos. Over 1,000 people died and hundreds of homes, businesses, and schools were destroyed or damaged. Neither the military nor the government could muster the resources to repair or replace the buildings destroyed in the fire. Six years later, Adeyemi visited one of the public-school clusters near the military base. He discovered that four of the five schools in the cluster were destroyed and one was severely damaged. Adeyemi told his members that the church was going to replace those schools. The project was completed within ten months (McCain 2013).[3] Daystar's annual "Back to School" initiative provides school materials free-of-charge to underprivileged children across Lagos. In 2017, the event attracted 20,000 children (Agbo 2017). In a post on Daystar's website, Adeyemi explained the rationale behind this venture: "We believe government alone cannot fix the societal problems, hence the church.... If our nation must advance economically, the educational system must be restored with quality teaching materials which have been lacking in our government schools" (Daystar Christian Centre 2016).

Pentecostals have also established educational NGOs. Trinity House is an independent congregation on Lagos' Victoria Island, founded by Pastor Ituah Ighodalo. An accountant by profession, Ighodalo was the pastor of RCCG's Christchurch parish before he left RCCG in 2009. Trinity House runs two educational initiatives: Teachers for Change and Courage Education Foundation. Teachers for Change is a capacity-building project, providing support and training for school teachers in Lagos. It works in partnership with Lagos State government and employs teachers in well-performing schools to conduct the training. Courage Education Foundation is an NGO providing educational assistance and mentoring to children from indigent families whose access to formal education is hindered by poverty (Courage Education Trust 2017).[4]

Another Pentecostal NGO is Edu-Aid (Educational Aid Global Initiative), founded in 2005 by Poju Oyemade, senior pastor of Covenant Christian Centre, to improve the quality of public primary education in Lagos by supporting selected schools within the vicinity of the church's three congregational locations. Edu-Aid runs educational programmes for primary school children and training conferences for teachers (Edu-Aid 2017). It also hosts the annual "Lagos Teachers Conference", which is designed to build capacity and empower teachers as a means of realizing SDG-4. The conference attracts teachers from across the city. The theme of the 2017 maiden conference was "The Teacher Revolution" and featured lectures on the following themes: "The Transformative Role of the Teacher in National Development", "Child Rights and Protection Issues in Nigerian Schools", "Active Learning in the 21st Century Classroom", and "The Teacher and the 2030 Agenda for Sustainable Development" (Insights for Living 2013).

My final example is Alero Ayida-Otobo, a founding director of Apostles in the Marketplace and adviser to three federal ministers of education. In 2006, Ayida-Otoba joined the "Transformation Task Team" of the former Minister of Education, Dr Oby Ezekwesili. This experience developed in her a determination to reform Nigeria's educational systems. In 2011, she established Incubator Africa, a capacity-building development NGO which works across three key sectors: Education & Training, Health, and Governance. She also founded the Young Reformers Programme in 2013 to encourage and equip young people to become social reformers and entrepreneurs. Ayida-Otobo is a graduate of

Oxford University, who describes herself as a social reformer, "Transformation Strategist", and "Education Reform Specialist". She lists among her mentors leading Nigerian Pentecostals such as Tony Rapu, Paul Adefarasin, and Sunday Adelaja, as well as Johnny Enlow, one of the prime advocates of seven mountains theology (Ayida-Otobo 2017). She divides her time between Nigeria and London, where she is on the Board of Trustees of RCCG's Jesus House.

During the first five years of its existence, the focus of Incubator Africa was on education. Its mission was to "transform educational systems and enhance the learning outcomes in schools", and it successfully partnered with government agencies and private education providers to improve schools (Incubator Africa 2019a). In 2013, Incubator Africa established The Education Hub at Lagos City Hall to serve as a physical location for active reformers to congregate and develop innovative projects geared towards sustainable development. Among the successful educational initiatives birthed at the Education Hub is Teach for Nigeria, a NGO which recruits "promising future leaders from varied disciplines to teach in Nigeria's underserved schools in low-income communities through a highly selective, two-year Fellowship".[5] Its aim is to develop a "movement of leaders across the nation who are committed to putting an end to educational inequity" (Teach for Nigeria 2019). Another educational NGO is the Street to School Initiative, founded by Tosin Taiwo following her participation in Incubator Africa's Young Reformers Programme, which provides free education to out-of-school children on the streets. Ayida-Otobo and Incubator Africa also support the Slum2School Initiative, founded in 2012 by Otto Orondaam, which aims to improve access to education for children in hard-to-reach slums across Nigeria (Incubator Africa 2019b).

Pentecostal schools and universities

Pentecostal churches are also responding to Nigeria's educational crisis by establishing schools and universities. In the Nigeria Survey, a significant majority supported the private ownership of schools by churches (85 per cent of Nigerian Pentecostals and 88 per cent of Nigerian Charismatics). One perspective is to regard these institutions as driven by market concerns to generate economic capital, similar to secular-based private institutions. However, the educational impulse is also linked to the churches' social and economic outlook. A recurring theme in popular discourse is that Africa's problems stem from a lack of leaders with integrity (Kalu 2008). By establishing school and universities with an emphasis on academic excellence and character formation, Pentecostals aspire to raise a new generation of leaders for national transformation. The challenge facing Pentecostal educational institutions is to maintain a Christian perspective within a highly competitive marketplace, dominated by secular and Westernized epistemologies.

Some Pentecostal denominations own a range of institutions, providing education at primary, secondary, and post-secondary levels. For example, RCCG's educational institutions include Christ the Redeemer's Schools Movement,

Redeemed Christian Bible College, Redeemed Christian School of Missions, the School of Disciples, and Redeemer's University (RUN). Winners Chapel operates Kingdom Heritage Model schools (a network of nursery and primary schools), Faith Academy secondary schools, the Word of Faith Bible Institute, Covenant University, and Landmark University. Another Pentecostal denomination with multiple educational institutions is Living Word Ministries (LWM), founded in south-eastern Nigeria by Emmanuel Okorie. LWM owns a Bible school (Living Word Training Centre), Living Word Academy primary and secondary schools, and Rhema University.

Pentecostal schools are a common feature of Nigeria's urban landscape, especially in the south. During fieldwork, I visited several schools in Lagos and Jos. Church pastors and staff members I spoke to insisted that their schools are social enterprises providing equitable access to quality education rather than profit-making business ventures. Often the fees of children from poorer families are subsidized by the churches. One pastor in Jos stated:

> We are aware that there are children who should have basic primary education whose parents cannot afford to send them to private school. We feel it is our responsibility as a church to give such children opportunity for education. And that's how we got involved in this effort. Most of the children come from the local community. Some of the children, their parents cannot afford, so we pay for that child.[6]

There is also a strong emphasis on holistic models of education which include intellectual, moral, and spiritual development. A Deeper Life Bible Church pastor said that the church's schools programme is aimed at raising "children with distinction" who are not just "brilliant academically", but who acquire "Christian principles and lifestyles so as to be outstanding leaders of tomorrow".[7] This holistic approach to education is reflected in the vision statement of Living Word Academy: "Here the child is properly exposed and guided early enough to develop mentally, socially, emotionally and above all spiritually, hence our school motto – Education Under The Shadow of the Cross" (Living Word Ministries 2015). There is also an interfaith dimension to Pentecostal education as some schools cater for both Muslim and Christian children despite their strong Christian ethos.

At the tertiary level, Nigerian Pentecostal churches have traditionally favoured practical ministerial training over academic preparation. Increasingly, however, they are offering theological degree programmes and seeking affiliation with government universities. Pentecostal Bible colleges and seminaries are numerous, especially in cities where most Pentecostal denominations have their headquarters. One of the earliest Pentecostal Bible colleges was Assemblies of God Divinity School in Umuahia, Abia State, which was established in 1940 and affiliated to the University of Uyo in 1984 (Mbamalu 2014). A recent trend is the rise of Pentecostal universities. In 2002, Covenant University and Benson Idahosa University became the first Pentecostal universities to receive approval by the

National Universities Commission (NUC). By 2019, the number of NUC-accredited Pentecostal universities had grown to 15, which represents by far the largest number on the continent (NUC 2019a). The Times Higher Education World University Rankings 2019 listed Covenant University alongside the University of Ibadan as the best universities in West Africa and equal sixth in the whole of Africa (Times Higher Education 2019). This is a remarkable achievement and reflects not only the financial assets of Winners Chapel but also its investment in higher education. Covenant University was also ranked the best Pentecostal university in the world in the 2018 uniRank university ranking (above Vanguard University, Southeastern University and Evangel University in the United States) (uniRank 2018).[8] The student enrolment of Covenant University has grown from about 7,300 in 2008 to 15,000 in 2017 (Carpenter 2017). The 2019 uniRank ranking of 160 Nigerian universities listed five Pentecostal universities in the top 80 (Covenant University, Landmark University, Redeemer's University, Benson Idahosa University, and Mountain Top University) (uniRank 2019).

In 2011, I visited the campus of Covenant University, located at the international headquarters of Winners Chapel in Ota, Ogun State. In the morning, I attended the university's chapel service, held in the 3,500-seater university chapel. The meeting consisted of prolonged periods of worship, prayer, testimonies, and preaching. The sermon, delivered by the university chaplain, was part of a series of messages entitled "Destiny Advance". God has a "glorious destiny" for us, he insisted, but to succeed in life, we need to know how to tap into the "power of God" to combat the forces of Satan arraigned against us, opposing our progress. This was typical African Pentecostal fare, an eclectic mix

Table 4.1 List of NUC-accredited Pentecostal Universities

Name	*Church*	*Year of accreditation*
Covenant University	Winners Chapel	2002
Benson Idahosa University	Church of God Mission International	2002
Joseph Ayo Babalola University	Christ Apostolic Church	2004
Redeemer's University (RUN)	Redeemed Christian Church of God	2005
Crawford University	Apostolic Faith Church	2005
Rhema University	Living Word Ministries	2009
Samuel Adegboyega University	Apostolic Church	2011
Landmark University	Winners Chapel	2011
McPherson University	Foursquare Gospel Church	2012
Mountain Top University	Mountain of Fire and Miracles	2015
King's University	Kingsway International Christian Centre	2015
Hezekiah University	Living Christ Mission	2015
Evangel University	Assemblies of God Nigeria	2016
Anchor University	Deeper Life Bible Church	2016
Precious Cornerstone University	Sword of the Spirit Ministries	2017

of the motivational and the miraculous. The service ended with a celebration of the bishop's 57th birthday led by the Vice-Chancellor, Professor Aize Obayan, a deaconess in Winners Chapel. After the service, I was given a tour of the university and spoke to some members of staff. Strategically positioned around the campus were banners displaying the university's core values: spirituality, possibility mentality, capacity-building, integrity, responsibility, diligence, and sacrifice. At the time, I was staying at Lagos State University (LASU) so was able to compare the two institutions. Covenant University's state-of-the-art buildings and its strong emphasis on spiritual formation and moral discipline contrasted sharply with LASU's neglected infrastructure and its record of staff corruption, strikes, student indiscipline and cultism.[9]

The reasons given for establishing Pentecostal universities are to address the "decadence" in Nigeria's educational system, to raise "God-fearing" and ethical leaders and citizens, and to contribute to national development by delivering high quality education. This is reflected in the programme notes of an event organized by Redeemer's University (RUN):

> It has always been the desire of the RCCG to make a positive impact on university education in Nigeria, convinced that university education can play a significant role in the social and technological development of a

Figure 4.1 Billboard for Covenant University, Ota, Ogun State.
Source: author.

> nation.... The objective of the RCCG in initiating the university project is not only to increase the number of Nigerian youths seeking higher education, but also to arrest the decay in the educational system through appropriate training. This is in line with the vision of Pastor E. A. Adeboye, the GO of RCCG for the Redeemer's University. Pastor Adeboye longs for the return to the glorious days of mission schools, where students acquire high quality education with the fear of God, and become useful citizens. We have a vision for a future generation of creative, innovative, inventive entrepreneurs. We want to mould a generation of kind, thoughtful and gentle adolescents, who are motivated to build and sustain a better Nigeria where peace, justice, fairness and godliness reign.
>
> (RUN 2006)

Similar aspirations are expressed in Pentecostal mission statements displayed on their university websites and in their promotional literature. RUN's mission is to "continuously impact the society through commitment to excellence in education, research, creativity, innovation, entrepreneurship and raising global leaders as change agents imbued with God-fearing attributes" (Redeemer's University 2019a). Covenant University aspires to be a "leading world-class Christian mission University, committed to raising a new generation of leaders" (Covenant University 2008: 4). Benson Idahosa University shares a similar focus on leadership and national development:

> We are committed to the mission of raising leaders for the nation, who are complete in spirit, mind and body, thus contributing to the production of high-level leadership and quality manpower for the nation and the world.
>
> (Benson Idahosa University 2019)

To some extent, these mission statements are similar to those of public and private secular universities, especially their focus on the role of education in development. The University of Ibadan, for example, aspires to be a "world-class institution for academic excellence geared towards meeting societal needs" (University of Ibadan 2019). The vision of the University of Calabar is to be "a centre of excellence producing globally competitive graduates and contributing significantly to development through research" (University of Calabar 2019). And Igbinedion University, the first privately owned university in Nigeria, aims to be a "center of academic excellence through teaching, research and knowledge production in response to contextualized national and global needs" (Igbinedion University 2019). What sets Pentecostal universities apart, however, is their holistic approach to education, which combines academic learning with spiritual development and character formation. This is exemplified by Covenant University's integrative "Total Man Concept" (TMC) which informs its curricula and campus activities. TMC is described as a "holistic concept of human development", which focuses on students' physical, mental, and spiritual needs (Covenant University 2019a).

Other Pentecostal universities echo this holistic vision. Evangel University (Assemblies of God) aims to offer

> total education for the liberation of the total man for total service to God, humanity, the individual and the society at large, through scientific inquiry, academic integrity, tolerance to diverse views and opinions, coupled with faith in the Bible as God's Word.
>
> (Evangel University 2019)

Crawford University (Apostolic Faith Church) aspires to be "an international institution of learning for training the mind, body and spirit into a total personality to serve God and humanity" (Crawford University 2010).

The spiritual life of Pentecostal universities is sustained by their chaplaincies, under the direction of chaplains who are normally ordained pastors in the church that owns the university. The university chapel is often situated in the centre of the campus, reflecting symbolically the premium placed on the spiritual development of students and staff. Apart from regular chapel services, other activities run by chaplaincies include counselling services, workshops and conferences, group Bible studies, and community outreaches (Covenant University 2008). An excerpt from RUN's student handbook shows the value it places in its chaplaincy and the connections it makes between holistic education, spiritual development, and national transformation:

> One of the uniqueness of this University is the type of services offered by the Chaplaincy. It is the goal of this unit to produce godly character in every student. Since the spiritual life of the student is an important element in the formation of the total person, the University will make available all the resources necessary to enhance it. As a Christian University committed to the transformation of the Nigerian society through the provision of total quality education, the development of the total person will depend largely on the spiritual climate of the institution.
>
> (Redeemer's University 2018: 20)

Public universities also cater for the religious needs of students and staff. As non-sectarian institutions, however, they do not typically employ full-time chaplains unless they are ordained members of the teaching staff. Nor do they regard spiritual formation as integral to their educational goals (Kukah 2013). Public universities are required to provide worship facilities that cater for students and staff from different religious traditions. For example, the University of Ibadan, in south-western Nigeria, has four main designated places of worship: three Christian chapels (interdenominational Protestant, Baptist, and Catholic) and a mosque. It also provides facilities for campus fellowships run by Pentecostal/evangelical churches as well as non-denominational groups such as the Student Christian Movement, Scripture Union, the Nigerian Federation of Catholic Students, the Ibadan Varsity Christian Union, and the Muslim Students Society.

In contrast, universities in the core northern states have sometimes denied Christians land to erect chapels. Christians also face insecurity and violation of their rights to religious freedom, epitomized by the 2012 killings of church worshippers by Boko Haram terrorists on the campus of Bayero University Kano (*Sahara Reporters* 2012).

Like public HE institutions, Pentecostal universities publish codes of conduct for students and staff which cover areas such as dress styles, anti-social and criminal behaviour, violent conduct, sexual harassment and abuse, punctuality, and academic malpractice. Misconduct usually attracts disciplinary sanctions. Pentecostal universities, however, tend to have stricter regulations regarding dress codes, use of mobile phones, and sexual ethics than public universities. Most Pentecostal universities also insist on compulsory chapel attendance for students and staff. These regulations have sometimes attracted complaints from students over the infringements of their human rights, including their rights to religious freedom, especially from those who belong to more liberal Christian traditions or other faiths, such as Islam (*Daily Post* 2012).

The range of academic programmes offered by Nigeria's Pentecostal universities varies. Most private HE institutions in Africa are quite narrow in their programme coverage (Teferra and Altbachl 2004). Research on African private universities suggest a preference for commercially viable and job-oriented courses targeted to the needs of the market, such as business management, computer science, accounting, banking and finance (Mabizela 2007; Ajadi 2010; Thaver 2008). In Nigeria, most Pentecostal universities run programmes on business management, finance, accounting, and computer science. However, they also offer programmes in the natural sciences, social sciences, arts and humanities. Redeemer's University, for example, is divided into six colleges (Humanities, Management Sciences, Natural Sciences, Basic Medical Sciences, Law, and Postgraduate Studies); Covenant University has five colleges (Business and Social Sciences, Engineering, Leadership Development Studies, Science and Technology, and Postgraduate Studies); and Benson Idahosa University has five faculties (Agriculture, Arts and Education, Science, Law, and Social and Management Science). Some universities also run religious studies programmes.

Entrepreneurship education is an important emphasis in Pentecostal universities, reflecting their aspirations to contribute to economic development. MFM's Mountain Top University has a Centre for Entrepreneurial Skills, Crawford University has a Centre for Entrepreneurship and Innovation, and RUN has a Centre for Entrepreneurship Development. The latter's mission is to "produce job-makers and not job-seekers", and to empower graduates entrepreneurially so that they are able to "contribute significantly to national economic development" (Redeemer's University 2015: 5). Covenant University runs an Entrepreneurial Development Studies programme, which is compulsory for all students regardless of their chosen field of study.

One of the criticisms levelled against Africa's private universities is their limited research capacity (Thaver 2008). Like public universities, they face challenges such as weak research infrastructure, scarcity of equipment, lack of access to good library resources, and declining research funding. Some of the larger Nigerian Pentecostal universities, however, are developing growing research cultures and attracting research grants from international funding bodies. Redeemer's University (RUN) and Covenant University are the leading Pentecostal research-driven universities in Nigeria. In 2013, RUN was awarded a $1.5 million grant to support research and capacity-building of Africans in the field of genomics under the Human, Hereditary and Health in Africa (H3Africa) Programme, jointly funded by the United States National Institutes of Health and the UK's Welcome Trust (Redeemer's University 2019b). In 2014, RUN was one of ten Nigerian universities selected for the World Bank-sponsored project, African Centres of Excellence. The World Bank approved a grant of $80 million for Nigeria to fund its ten Centres of Excellence (Redeemer's University 2019c). RUN's award is funding its African Centre of Excellence for Genomics of Infectious Diseases.

Research conducted at Covenant University encompasses a broad range of fields including renewable energy, biotechnology, medical research, engineering, chemical and food processing, and town planning. During the 2007–2008 academic session, Winners Chapel's World Mission Agency donated ₦50 million to support research and spent about 1.1 million naira on research equipment (Covenant University 2008). In keeping with its ambitious vision to become one of the world's leading universities,[10] its publication profile increased from 396 outputs in 2012 to 3340 in 2018 (Covenant University 2019c). Significantly, Covenant University's research agenda is influenced by the post-2015 Sustainable Development Goals. In 2019, it hosted two international conferences on sustainable development: The Covenant Model UN Conference, themed "Restructuring the Future Through Innovative Ideas", and the 2019 International Conference on Sustainable Development in Africa, entitled "Africa's Development Agenda: Prospects and Challenges" (Covenant University 2019b). One of the keynote speakers at the Covenant Model UN Conference was the UN Secretary-General Antonio Guterres. It also runs an annual conference called the Covenant – International Conference on African Developmental Issues. The theme of the 2018 conference was "The Challenge of Leadership: Driving Africa's Future", and conference sub-themes included the following: "Governance and Democracy"; "Education"; "Strategic Business Management"; "Science, Technology, Engineering and Mathematics"; "Gender Issues"; "Peace and Security"; "Food Security and Agriculture"; "Environment and Climate Change"; and "SDGs and Transformational Leadership in Africa". The keynote speaker was Her Excellency Mrs. Joyce Banda, former President of the Republic of Malawi (Covenant University 2018).

Pentecostal universities are helping to meet the increasing demands for higher education in Nigeria. They are also contributing to development by offering a broad range of undergraduate and postgraduate programmes and by conducting research in areas such as the natural sciences, medicine and health, education, business and finance, and computer science. However, some Pentecostal universities have been charged with elitism, non-participatory and authoritarian governance, harsh disciplinary regimes, and violations of the rights to religious freedom. For example, Covenant University's high tuition fees compared to public institutions make it difficult for most church members to attend. This has caused resentment among some pastors and members because most of the finances for the university buildings have come from within the church. Moreover, questions have been raised regarding Oyedepo's autocratic leadership style, which has caused discontent among some members of the faculty and student body.[11]

Conclusion

This chapter has investigated Pentecostal educational initiatives and their contribution to development in Nigeria. Pentecostals are responding to the perceived collapse of morality and declining standards in Nigeria's educational system by engaging in capacity-building programmes in public schools, establishing educational NGOs, and opening private schools and universities. Some of the larger churches have invested considerable financial and human resources into supporting these ventures. One perspective is to regard Pentecostal educational institutions as driven by market concerns to generate economic capital, similar to secular-based private institutions. However, Pentecostal discourse on education is invariably framed in ethical terms as an expression of the church's social and moral responsibility for national transformation.

Pentecostal educational institutions vary considerably in the quality of their infrastructure, teaching and research. Some of the larger universities, such as Covenant University and Redeemer's University, compare favourably with government and secular private institutions. The predominant educational model embraced by Pentecostal schools and universities is holistic, combining academic learning with spiritual development and character formation. Pentecostal institutions seek to inculcate Christian virtues and values through their strict disciplinary regimes, their chaplaincy services, and by providing contexts for communal worship, Bible study and prayer. This distinguishes them from secular schools and higher education institutions in Nigeria.

Notes

1 The NPE underwent revisions in 1981, 1990, 1998, 2004, 2007, and 2013.
2 Interview, Dr Nnamdi Ekeanyanwu, Director of International Relations, Covenant University, 27 September 2011.
3 Interview, Pastor Sam Adeyemi, Daystar Christian Centre, Lagos, 7 October 2011.
4 Interview, Pastor Ituah Ighodalo, Trinity House, Lagos, 9 December 2010.
5 Teach for Nigeria is part of the Teach for All global network which includes Teach for America, Teach First UK, Teach for Ghana, and Teach for India.
6 Interview, Pastor Isaac Oyebamiji, Chapel of Mercy, Jos, 15 May 2012.
7 Interview, Pastor Jerry Asemota, Deeper Life Bible Church, Lagos, 10 October 2011.
8 Other Nigerian Pentecostal universities listed in the top 20 included Landmark University, Redeemer's University, Benson Idahosa University, Samuel Adegboyega University and Joseph Ayo Babalola University.

9 While I was staying at LASU the staff were on strike. I was also told by a member of staff that the former Vice-Chancellor was dismissed for corruption after he embezzled large sums of money given by the state government towards buildings.
10 According to its Vision 10:2022, developed in 2012, Covenant University aims to be one of the top ten universities in the world by 2022.
11 Interview, Dr Joseph Obe, London, 20 March 2012. Obe is a former member of Covenant University's academic staff.

References

Adedigba, Azeezat (2018) "Nigeria Now Has 13.2 Million Out of School Children – UBEC", *Premium Times*, 4 October, available at: www.premiumtimesng.com/news/top-news/288344-nigeria-now-has-13-2-million-out-of-school-children-ubec.html (accessed 23 May 2019).

Agbo, Agbo (2017) "Daystar and the Poverty Challenge", *The Nation*, 14 September, available at: https://thenationonlineng.net/daystar-poverty-challenge/ (accessed 22 September 2018).

Aigboje, Clement D. (2013) "Students' Perception on the Development and Eradication of Cultism in Tertiary Institutions in Nigeria: Implications for Educational Managers", *International Journal of Innovative Research and Development* 2(7): 34–40.

Ajadi, Timothy O. (2010) "Private Universities in Nigeria: The Challenges Ahead", *American Journal of Scientific Research* 7: 15–24.

Ajayi, I. A. and Haastup T. Ekundayo (2008) "The Deregulation of University Education in Nigeria: Implications for Quality Assurance", *Nebula* 5(4): 212–224.

Alvarez, Miguel (2000) "Distinctives of Pentecostal Education", *Asian Journal of Pentecostal Studies* 3: 282–293.

Anderson, Allan A. (2004) "Pentecostal-Charismatic Spirituality and Theological Education in Europe from a Global Perspective", *PentecoStudies* 3(1): 1–15.

Antoninis, Manos, Marcos Delprato, and Aaron Benavot (2016) "Inequality in Education: The Challenge of Measurement", in ISSC, IDS, and UNESCO, *World Social Science Report 2016, Challenging Inequalities: Pathways to a Just World*, Paris: UNESCO, pp. 63–67.

Asamoah-Gyadu, J. Kwabena (2018) "Rooted in the Spirit: Pentecostalism and Theological Education", in Lord E. Donkor and Clifton R. Clarke (eds) *African Pentecostal Missions Maturing: Essays in Honor of Apostle Opoku Onyinah*, Eugene, OR: Wipf and Stock, pp. 196–212.

Asiyai, Romina I. (2013) "Challenges of Quality in Higher Education in Nigeria in the 21st Century", *International Journal of Educational Planning & Administration* 3(2): 159–172.

Ayida-Otobo, Alero (2017) *Reformers Arise: Calling Out a People of Destiny to Influence and Action*, St Albans: Panoma Press.

Benson Idahosa University (2019) "Our Mission, Vision and Core Purpose", www.biu.edu.ng/about-biu/mission-vision-and-core-purpose/ (accessed 22 May 2019).

Berman, Edward H. (1974) "African Responses to Christian Mission Education", *African Studies Review* 17(3): 527–540.

Bloom, David E., David Canning, and Kevin Chan (2006) *Higher Education and Economic Development in Africa* (Vol. 102). Washington, DC: World Bank.

Boni, Alejandra, Aurora Lopez-Fogues, and Melanie Walker (2016) "Higher Education and the Post-2015 Agenda: A Contribution from the Human Development Approach", *Journal of Global Ethics* 12(1): 17–28.

Carpenter, Joel (2017) "Christian Universities Grow in Africa", *International Higher Education* 88: 25–26.

Castleberry, Joseph (2004) "Pentecostal Seminaries are Essential to the Future Health of the Church", *Pneuma* 26(2): 346–354.

Cloete, Nico, Ian Bunting, and Peter Maassen (2015) "Research Universities in Africa: An Empirical Overview of Eight Flagship Universities", in Nico Cloete, Peter Maassen, and Tracy Bailey (eds) *Knowledge Production and Contradictory Functions in African Higher Education*, African Minds Higher Education Dynamics Series Vol. 1, Cape Town: African Minds, pp. 18–31.

Courage Education Trust (2017) "Our Vision/Objectives", available at: http://courageeducation.org/our-visionobjectives/ (accessed 23 May 2019).

Covenant University (2008) *Covenant University: Raising a New Generation of Leaders*. Ota: Covenant University.

Covenant University (2018) "4th Covenant – International Conference on African Developmental Issues", available at: https://cicadi.covenantuniversity.edu.ng/ (accessed 18 May 2019).

Covenant University (2019a) "Total Man Concept", available at: https://covenantuniversity.edu.ng/About-Us/Unique-Programmes/TOTAL-MAN-CONCEPT#.XMbjPPZFzIV (accessed 22 May 2019).

Covenant University (2019b) "Covenant Economics Policy and Development Research", available at: http://cepder.covenantuniversity.edu.ng/2019-international-conference-on-sustainable-development-in-africa/ (accessed 22 May 2019).

Covenant University (2019c) "The Power of a Vision: Covenant's Research Output Increases by 906.36%", available at: https://covenantuniversity.edu.ng/News/The-Power-of-a-Vision-Covenant-s-Research-Output-Increases-by-906.36#.XMmu9_ZFzIU (accessed 19 May 2019).

Crawford University (2010) *Programme of 2nd Convocation Ceremony*, 19 November, Lagos: COFA Press.

Daily Post (2012) "Private Christian Universities: Faith in Deception?" *Daily Post*, 11 May, available at: https://dailypost.ng/2012/05/11/private-christian-universities-faith-in-deception/ (accessed 5 May 2019).

Daniel-Kalio, Blessing (2018) "Historical Analysis of Educational Policies in Nigeria: Trends and Implications", *International Journal of Scientific Research in Education* 11(2): pp. 247–264.

Daystar Christian Centre (2016) "Daystar Fetes Over 12,000 School Children, Students", Back to School, 1 June, available at: http://daystarng.org/blog/daystar-fetes-over-12000-school-children-students/ (accessed 2 May 2019).

Edu-Aid (2017) "Who We Are", available at: www.edu-aid.org/ (accessed 22 April 2019).

Evangel University (2019) "About EUA", available at: www.evangeluniversity.edu.ng/about.php (accessed 23 May 2019).

Ewen, Amy H. (2018) "The Changing Concerns of Higher Education: Examining the World Bank's Papers on Higher Education Since 1994", *Global University Network for Innovation*, available at: www.guninetwork.org/articles/changing-concerns-higher-education-examining-world-banks-papers-higher-education-1994 (accessed 22 September 2019).

Federal Republic of Nigeria (2013) *National Policy on Education, 6th edition*, NERDC Press: Lagos.

Funmilola, Bolaji (2019) "Full List of all Private Universities in Nigeria as Released by NUC", *Campusbiz Journal*, 10 April, available at: https://campusbiz.com.ng/private-universities-nigeria/ (accessed 22 June 2019).

Gaiya, Musa (2014) "Revolution in Higher Education in Nigeria: The Emergence of Private Universities", in Joel Carpenter, Perry L. Glanzer, and Nicholas S. Lantinga (eds) *Christian Higher Education: A Global Reconnaissance*, Grand Rapids, MI: William B. Eerdmans Publishing Company, pp. 24–42.

Gboyega, Ilusanya (2005) "Cultism and Violent Behaviours in Tertiary Institutions in Nigeria", *The Zimbabwe Journal of Educational Research* 17(1): 39–53.

Haynes, Jeffrey (2007) *Religion and Development. Conflict or Cooperation?* New York: Palgrave Macmillan.

Hittenberger, Jeffrey S. (2004) "Globalization, 'Marketization', and the Mission of Pentecostal Higher Education in Africa", *Pneuma* 26(2): 182–215.

Igbinedion University (2019) "Vision and Mission Statement", available at: www.iuokada.edu.ng/igbinedion-university-vision-statement/ (accessed 22 May 2019).

Incubator Africa (2019a) "Who We Are", available at: http://incubatorafrica.org/who-we-are/ (accessed 15 August 2019).

Incubator Africa (2019b) "Success Stories for Incubator Africa", available at: http://incubatorafrica.org/success-stories-for-incubator-africa/ (accessed 15 August 2019).

Insights for Living (2013) "2017 The Lagos Teachers' Conference: The Transformative Role of Teachers in National Development", available at: http://elibrary.insightsforliving.org/library/messages/search/page:1/keyword:Lagos%20teachers%20 (accessed 25 August 2019).

Johns, Cheryl B. (1993) *Pentecostal Formation: A Pedagogy Among the Oppressed*, Sheffield: Sheffield Academic Press.

Kalu, Ogbu U. (2008) *African Pentecostalism: An Introduction*, Oxford: Oxford University Press.

Kärkkäinen, Veli-Matti (2010) "Pentecostal Theological Education in a Theological and Missiological Perspective", *Journal of the European Pentecostal Theological Association* 30(1): 49–62.

Kukah, Mathew H. (2013) "The Chaplaincy and University Administration in Nigeria", Paper Presented at the Inauguration of the Members of the Governing Councils of Federal Universities Organized by the Nigerian Universities Commission, NUC, 8–9 July, Abuja, available at: http://cbcn-ng.org/newsdetail.php?tab=211 (accessed 20 July 2019).

Levy, Daniel (2007) "A Recent Echo: African Private Higher Education in an International Perspective", *Journal of Higher Education in Africa* 5(2–3): 197–220.

Living Word Ministries (2015) "LW Academy N/P Int'l", available at: http://lwmng.org/project/academy/ (accessed 15 July 2019).

Mabizela, Mahlubi (2007) "Private Surge Amid Public Dominance in Higher Education: The African Perspective", *Journal of Higher Education in Africa* 5(2–3): 15–38.

Mbamalu, Williams O. (2014) "The Challenges of Theological Education in the Assemblies of God, Nigeria: A Critical Analysis", *Studia Historiae Ecclesiasticae* 40(2): 243–262.

McCain, Danny (2013) "Addressing Urban Problems Through Kingdom Theology: The 'Apostles in the Market Place' Model in Lagos, Nigeria", *Africa Journal of Evangelical Theology* 32(1): 61–80.

Moja, Teboha (2000) *Nigeria Education Sector Analysis: An Analytical Synthesis of Performance and Main Issues*, Washington, DC: World Bank.

Moland, Naomi A. (2015) "Nigeria: An Overview", in Emefie J. Takyi-Amoako (ed.) *Education in West Africa*, London: Bloomsbury, pp. 363–376.

NUC (2019a) "Private Universities", available at: https://nuc.edu.ng/nigerian-univerisities/private-univeristies/ (accessed 12 May 2019).

NUC (2019b) "Federal Universities", available at: https://nuc.edu.ng/nigerian-univerisities/federal-univeristies/ (accessed 12 May 2019).

NUC (2019c) "State Universities", available at: https://nuc.edu.ng/nigerian-univerisities/state-university/ (accessed 14 May 2019).

Obasi, Isaac N. (2015) "New Private Universities in Nigeria", *International Higher Education* (45): 14–15.

Odeyemi, Ezekiel A. (2009) "Rebranding Nigeria: Christian Education to the Rescue", *Redemption: A Monthly Publication of the Redeemed Christian Church of God* 13(6): 62, 78.

Rambla, Francesc X. and Margarita Langthaler (2016) The SDGs and Inclusive Education for All from Special Education to Addressing Social Inequalities, Briefing Paper, Austrian Foundation for Development Research (ÖFSE), No. 14.

Redeemer's University (2006) Programme, Redeemer's University Awards & Recognition Dinner, 7 October.

Redeemer's University (2015) "Ten Years of Extraordinary Grace", Vice-Chancellor's Speech Delivered at the 10th Anniversary and 7th Convocation of the Redeemer's University, 29 September, Ede, Osun State, Nigeria, p. 5.

Redeemer's University (2018) *RUN Student Handbook.*

Redeemer's University (2019a) "Mission, Policies and Regulations", available at: https://run.edu.ng/site/index.php?active=aboutus&pgcat=upolicies (accessed 28 May 2019).

Redeemer's University (2019b) "Redeemer's University Wins $1.54 Million Research Grant", available at: https://run.edu.ng/site/index.php?active=articles&pgcat=view&newsimg=front&newscid=22&catid=1 (accessed 28 May 2019).

Redeemer's University (2019c) "Redeemer's University, Others Get $80m From World Bank", available at: https://run.edu.ng/site/index.php?active=articles&pgcat=view&newsimg=front&newscid=40&catid=1 (accessed 28 May 2019).

Sahara Reporters (2012) "Northern Christians Cry for Justice and Religious Freedom", *Sahara Reporters*, 1 May, available at: http://saharareporters.com/2012/05/01/northern-christians-cry-justice-and-religious-freedom (accessed 14 May 2019).

Samoff, Joel and Bidemi Carrol (2003) *From Manpower Planning to the Knowledge Era: World Bank Policies on Higher Education in Africa*. Prepared for the UNESCO Forum on Higher Education, Research and Knowledge, Paris.

Teach for Nigeria (2019) "About Us", available at: https://teachfornigeria.org/about-us/ (accessed 15 May 2019).

Teferra, Damtew and Philip G. Altbachl (2004) "African Higher Education: Challenges for the 21st Century", *Higher Education* 47(1): 21–50.

Thaver, Beverly (2008) "The Private Higher Education Sector in Africa: Current Trends and Themes in Six Country Studies", *Journal of Higher Education in Africa* 6(1): 127–142.

The Task Force on Higher Education and Society (2000) *Higher Education in Developing Countries: Peril and Promise*, Washington, DC: World Bank.

Times Higher Education (2019) "Best Universities in Africa 2019", available at: www.timeshighereducation.com/student/best-universities/best-universities-africa (accessed 13 June 2019).

UNESCO (2015) *Education 2030: Incheon Declaration – Towards Inclusive and Equitable Quality Education and Lifelong Learning for All*, Paris: UNESCO.

UNICEF (n.d.) "Education", www.unicef.org/nigeria/education (accessed 4 April 2019).

uniRank (2018) "Top Pentecostal Universities in the World. 2018 uniRank University Ranking", available at: www.4icu.org/top-religious-universities/pentecostal/ (accessed 13 June 2019).

uniRank (2019) "Top Universities in Nigeria", available at: www.4icu.org/ng/ (accessed 13 June 2019).

University of Calabar (2019) "Vision, Mission & Philosophy", available at: www.unical.edu.ng/about-mission (accessed 22 May 2019).

University of Ibadan (2019) "Vision and Mission", available at: https://ui.edu.ng/content/vision-and-mission (accessed 22 May 2019).

5 Pentecostal healing and healthcare

Introduction

This chapter explores Nigerian Pentecostal approaches to healing and healthcare. The popularity of the Pentecostal practice of divine healing in Nigeria stems from its resonance with African traditional worldviews and the context of poverty in communities where access to affordable healthcare is restricted. Nigerian Pentecostal pastors with gifts of healing attract large followings. Increasingly, however, Nigerian Pentecostals are embracing a holistic model of healing that combines beliefs in divine healing with the use of modern medicine. Nigerian Pentecostals are also engaged in healthcare interventions in the wider community.

Health is recognized as an important component of the international development agenda. Adam Wagstaff and Mariam Claeson (2004) refer to the scale of death and ill-health in the world's poorest countries and its effects on development in relation to poverty levels, living standards, and economic productivity. Access to basic healthcare for all was declared as a fundamental human right by the 1978 Alma-Ata Declaration. The model adopted by Alma-Ata for providing healthcare services was "primary health care", which involved "community-based preventive and curative services" (Hall and Taylor 2003: 17). The MDGs, adopted in 2000 as the next generation of "health for all" goals, included three health-related goals: reduction in child mortality (Goal 4); reduction in maternal mortality and access to reproductive healthcare (Goal 5); and combating HIV/AIDS, malaria, and other diseases (Goal 6). Considerable progress was made towards the achievement of the health-related goals despite falling short of the MDG targets (WHO 2015; Buse and Hawkes 2015).

Health is also centrally positioned in the 2030 Agenda of the SDGs. One of the criticisms levelled against the MDGs was their focus on the poorest countries. The SDGs are broader in scope, encompassing both developing and developed countries. Migrants and minorities receive attention as groups vulnerable to greater ill-health and poorer access to quality healthcare than the wider national populations. The 17 SDG goals include one specific goal for health with 13 targets (SDG 3): "Ensure healthy lives and promote well-being for all at all ages" (WHO 2016: 3). The SDG 3 targets cover most major health topics, including reproductive, child and maternal health, infectious and non-communicable diseases, and mental health (WHO 2016). Health equity is at the centre of the 2030 Agenda, expressed in the concept of "leaving no one behind" and the call for "healthy lives for all at all ages" (WHO 2015).

The chapter begins by surveying the field of religion and health. Second, it sketches the landscape of health in the Nigerian context. Third, the chapter examines the health beliefs and practices of Nigerian Pentecostals, and discusses both the strengths and the weaknesses of Pentecostal approaches to healing and healthcare. Finally, the chapter explores Nigerian Pentecostal responses to three major health issues that assail the African continent: HIV/AIDS, maternal and reproductive health, and disability. The main focus of the chapter is the Nigerian context. However, it also examines Nigerian Pentecostal health practices in the diaspora.

Religion and health

The field of religion and health has produced a substantial body of literature from a wide range of disciplines, including medicine, psychiatry, nursing, psychology, anthropology, sociology, ethics, theology, and religious studies. Empirical evidence, based on quantitative and qualitative studies, suggests that involvement in religion and attendance at places of worship produces health-related benefits.[1] In the literature, the positive impact of religious participation on health outcomes is attributed to the effects of social support and religious coping on health behaviours and faith-related prescriptions of good health habits (Brewer *et al.* 2015). There are also an increasing number of studies on religious healing practices within different global contexts and religious traditions.[2]

Research on religious healing includes studies of divine healing within the Pentecostal and Charismatic traditions (Csordas 1997; Williams 2012; Alexander 2006; Brown (ed.) 2011). Recent studies have emphasized healing as the single most important category for understanding the expansion of Pentecostalism, especially in the Majority World (Brown 2011; Anderson 2013). While Pentecostal healing practices are prevalent in non-industrialized nations, Candy Gunther Brown (2011: 8) notes their persistence even in contexts where biomedical science "is the most sophisticated, convenient, and affordable". Most Pentecostals do not reject modern medicine, according to Brown (2011: 8), but "they do insist that God is able to heal even when medicine is unable to help". As Amos Yong (2011: 6) notes, "Pentecostals have always negotiated the tension between a robust belief in faith healing that repudiated medical technology entirely and the belief that faith healing and the use of medicine were indeed compatible." The appeal of Pentecostal healing beliefs and practices in many non-Western cultures is partly due to their resonance with indigenous conceptions of illness and healing. However, their popularity also stems from socio-economic conditions of poverty which predispose the poor to experiment with divine healing. Studies of African Pentecostalism refer both to continuities between traditional and Pentecostal cosmologies and to economic deprivation as factors behind the prevalence of divine healing practices (Ojo 2006; Maxwell 2006).

Faith communities are increasingly involved in public health interventions. As a field, public health addresses health-related issues at the level of community and populations rather than individuals. Research on religion and public health largely originates from the USA or Africa and other developing settings (Tomalin *et al.* 2019; November 2014). Linda Barnes (2011: 74) identifies three broad trends which tend to surface in relation to public health and religion. The first suggests that religious observance may pose health risks. The second argues that religious traditions may impede the growth of modernity. The third "targets religious convictions that may obstruct the implementation of biomedical healthcare delivery". As Barnes (2011: 74) notes, in each, a "common feature is the tendency to view religion as a problem".

Rather than employing a deficit approach to health, which focuses on what is lacking in particular contexts, recent research on religion and public health adopts an assets-based approach, which explores the health assets of faith communities and their role in reaching and changing behaviour of "hard to reach" groups. Studies in the United States have largely focused on the interventions of African American churches and their potential for reducing health inequalities among African Americans (Campbell *et al.* 2007; Thompson *et al.* 2009). The literature on religion and public health in Europe is more limited, although a number of studies have focused on the role of religious beliefs in shaping attitudes to health, health promotion and awareness interventions, overcoming barriers to accessing health services, and identifying religious health assets, especially among migrant religious communities (Tomalin *et al.* 2019). Among these are a handful of qualitative studies, which explore the multiple health practices of African, mainly Christian, migrants from a transnational perspective (Krause 2008; Onyigbuo, Alexis-Garsee, and van den Akker 2016).

Research on religion and public health in Africa has focused on the contribution of faith-based healthcare for achieving sustainable development (Olivier *et al.* 2015; Dilger 2009). Today we are seeing the re-emergence of faith-based healthcare provision in Africa, linked to the increasing fragility of state healthcare systems, the growing privatization of the health sector, the rise of the HIV/AIDS pandemic, and the influx of funds from international donors (Dilger 2009; Olivier *et al.* 2015). Of particular importance is the work of the International Religious Health Assets Programme, which grew out of the Africa Religious Health Assets Programme (ARHAP), founded in 2002 by James Cochrane and colleagues at the University of Cape Town (South Africa) and Emory University (USA). One aim of the programme was to enable faith communities to identify their "religious health assets" and to make them visible to the public health community (Cochrane 2006; Germond, Molapo, and Reilly 2007). The term "religious health assets" refers to the facilities and capacities that faith communities contribute to health outcomes. Related to this is the concept of "healthworlds", introduced by ARHAP researchers Germond and Cochrane (2010), in order to explore the empirical complexity of multiple ways of understanding health and plural health-seeking practices. The term "healthworld" refers to the way people construct their understandings of health and illness in the particular communities in which they are embedded. It relates to people's understandings of health and their health-seeking behaviour. The complexity of competing healthworlds is intensified in multicultural and transnational settings, where migrants come with multiple cultural beliefs and practices, including different understandings of illness and health as well as diverse health-seeking practices.

The idea of healthworld draws from Jürgen Habermas' notion of lifeworld elaborated in his theory of communicative action. Habermas (1987: 124) sees the lifeworld "as represented by a culturally transmitted and linguistically organized stock of interpretive patterns". It is a "reservoir of taken for granted, of unshaken convictions that participants in communication draw upon in cooperative processes of interpretation" (Habermas 1987: 124). Habermas distinguishes between the "lifeworld" characterized by "communicative action" (action oriented to consensus) and the system characterized by instrumental action (action oriented to outcomes). He argues that the system (the economy and the state) has increasingly come to "colonize" and dominate the lifeworld in advanced, capitalist societies in a process of progressive commodification and bureaucratization of society. As conceived by Germond and Cochrane (2010: 310), the healthworld is a "region" of the lifeworld "which has epistemic force, shaping what is known and how it is known with significant implications for health-seeking behaviour and the efficacy of health interventions". It is a way of knowing and acting in the world that is redemptive and oriented to a telos of comprehensive well-being. The health system is a region of the system concerned with health and includes the health economy/industry and the political organs of health (e.g. Department of Health). It colonizes healthworlds but is distinguished from the Western, biomedical healthworld, which is a region of the Western lifeworld (Germond, Molapo, and Reilly 2007). The notion of healthworlds is a helpful analytical tool because church members often hold strong theological and cultural convictions which shape their health-seeking behaviours. Healthworlds also reflect a transcultural reality with which healthcare providers have to come to terms, regarding them critically but also sympathetically.

The Nigerian context

A recent WHO analysis of the world's health systems ranked Nigeria 187 out of 191 member states in terms of health system efficiency (Uzochukwu 2017). According to Uzochukwu (2017: 5), "The health care system is largely public sector driven, with substantial private sector involvement in service provision." It is organized around three tiers: primary, secondary, and tertiary levels. Tertiary healthcare services are provided predominantly by the Federal Government through a network of teaching hospitals, specialist hospitals, and federal medical centres. Secondary healthcare is provided by general hospitals under the control of state governments. Primary health care (PHC), under the control of local government, is the foundation of the Nigerian health system and the entry point to healthcare services. At the primary level are health clinics and centres providing basic primary care services such as health education and promotion, diagnostic services, maternal and child care, immunization, and provision of drugs and supplies. Private medical practitioners also provide healthcare at this level. Primary healthcare was adopted in the National Health Policy in 1988 in order to improve health equity and access to basic health services (Aigbiremolen *et al.* 2014; Abdulraheem, Olapipo, and Amodu 2012).[3] However, as Abdulraheem, Olapipo, and Amodu (2012) note, the goal of accessible health for all has yet to be achieved in Nigeria, especially in rural areas where large proportions of the population reside. Reasons given for the failure to achieve universal health coverage include corruption within the Nigerian health system; increased demand due to population growth; insufficient and uneven distribution of human resources, exacerbated by low salaries and the exodus overseas of health professionals; poorly equipped health facilities; and low utilization of primary health services due to loss of confidence in PHC facilities (Uzochukwu 2017; Abdulraheem, Olapipo, and Amodu 2012).

Healthcare in Nigeria is financed through different sources. Following independence in 1960, the Nigerian government initially funded universal and free healthcare in public facilities through taxation and oil revenues. However, the global slump in oil prices in the 1980s and the introduction of the Structural Adjustment Programme in 1986 meant that the government could no longer provide free healthcare (Odeyemi and Nixon 2013). An important milestone was the creation of the National Primary Health Care Development Agency, set up in 1992 to support the National Health Policy as it relates to primary health care. The mandate of the agency included mobilizing resources for PHC programmes and promoting development of human resources for health. Current sources of healthcare financing include tax revenue, out-of-pocket payments, donor funding, and health insurance (Uzochukwu 2017). In 2013, the total government health expenditure as a proportion of GDP was 3.7 per cent, while out-of-pocket expenditure as a percentage of total health expenditure was 69.35 per cent (Uzochukwu 2017). Reliance on out-of-pocket expenses discourages healthcare consumption and exacerbates existing health inequities. The National Health Insurance Scheme (NHIS), which became operational in 2005, was intended as a strategy for overcoming barriers to accessing quality healthcare and protecting households from continuing health expenditure (Uzochukwu 2017; Odeyemi 2014). However, NHIS membership levels in Nigeria are low compared to some other African countries, with a pro-rich and pro-urban bias (Odeyemi and Nixon 2013).[4] Economic barriers to accessing biomedicine in Nigeria is one factor driving the pursuit of religious healing, including Pentecostal healing (Ojo 2006). It also explains why some Pentecostal churches offer free or subsidized healthcare to the urban and rural poor, as we will see later in the chapter.

The private sector provides healthcare to an estimated 60 per cent of the population and "serves as the first point of call for over 80 per cent of people" (Uzochukwu 2017: 23). Private healthcare providers include for-profit and not-for-profit private hospitals, maternity facilities, mobile clinics, pharmacies, medicine vendors, and traditional healthcare providers. FBOs represent a significant source of private healthcare provision in Nigeria. During the colonial era, the proliferation of Christian faith-based health services was fuelled by competition between Catholic and Protestant missions over territory. Following independence, mission churches continued to provide primary and secondary healthcare through a variety of institutions and initiatives including hospitals, PHC clinics, dispensaries, and maternity centres. Church-run facilities are numerous in Nigeria and tend to be distributed more evenly between rural and urban areas than public sector facilities (Alubo 2001). The majority are linked to mainline denominations such as the Catholic, Anglican, and Methodist churches but Pentecostal churches are increasingly contributing to faith-based healthcare provision. Ecumenical networks have also emerged as umbrella healthcare organizations. The most important is the Christian Health Association of Nigeria (CHAN), founded in 1973 by the Catholic Bishops Conference of Nigeria, the Protestant Christian Council of Nigeria, and the Northern Christian Medical Advisory Council of Nigeria.

Pentecostal healthworlds and health-seeking practices

Studies across the disciplines identify three dominant health paradigms within sub-Saharan Africa: African traditional healing (including herbal medicine), biomedical treatment, and faith healing (Scorgie 2007; Owoeye 2010). However, as Scorgie (2007: 57) notes, "the boundaries dividing these sectors are often blurred and porous", allowing for the cross-fertilization of ideas and practices. The Nigerian religious landscape is populated by a multiplicity of healthworlds and health practices. Cochrane (2006) distinguishes between tangible (visible) and intangible (invisible) religious health assets. What makes religious health assets different from other health organizations or structures, according to Cochrane, lies in what is internal to faith communities: the motivational and mobilizing capacities that are rooted in religious beliefs and behaviours. For Cochrane (2006: 117), the value of visible assets "depends upon understanding the less visible, intangible elements that help create 'best practices,' and transformative and empowering initiatives, particularly among the poor".

Nigerian Pentecostal churches possess a variety of tangible health assets such as social capital, human capital, financial resources, and buildings, as well as less tangible assets such as religious beliefs, values, and practices that encourage good health habits and motivate compassionate care towards others. However, religious understandings of illness and health can also discourage church members from seeking medical help and lead to abusive practices which place their health at risk. The "enchanted" worldview that underpins Nigerian Pentecostal approaches to illness and healing sometimes results in antipathy towards medical technology and recourse to rituals and behaviours detrimental to public health. For example, sufferers of mental health conditions and HIV/AIDS are vulnerable to stigmatization and accusations of witchcraft, which can lead to abusive practices and human rights violations as discussed below (Smith 2014; Fakoya *et al.* 2012; Thomas 2010).

Nigerian Pentecostal health practices are shaped by the Bible, their encounters with Western missions and global Pentecostalism, and their African indigenous heritage. They are also influenced by the contemporary political and socio-economic contexts. Pentecostal beliefs about sickness and health influence their health-seeking behaviours. Nigerian Pentecostals trace the aetiology of disease to three main sources. First, sickness is perceived as a product of a fallen and sinful world, as an enemy to be overcome by faith in Christ's redemptive work of salvation. An article entitled "Supernatural Health", written by Pastor Sam Adeyemi of Daystar Christian Centre, states:

> Sickness and diseases were never intended to be a normal part of human existence. They came as a result of sin and man's fall.... As believers, we need to change our thinking and refuse to accept sicknesses and diseases as being normal. When Jesus was on earth, He always ran illnesses out of people's bodies.... We are citizens of God's kingdom and so we should treat sicknesses as some of mankind's greatest enemies.
>
> (Adeyemi 2018)

This understanding of sickness and health encourages hope and agency in a context where access to healthcare is restricted and the costs of medical treatment are often prohibitive. Sickness is also explained as a direct consequence of immoral behaviour or the breakdown of social relations within families and communities. The Pentecostal tendency to moralize sickness and stigmatize sufferers as "sinful" can create barriers to accessing healthcare services, as in the case of AIDS (Smith 2014).

Second, Nigerian Pentecostals trace the aetiology of sickness to supernatural agents such as Satan, evil spirits, and witches. Nigerian Pentecostal publications refer to demons, "spirits of infirmity", and witchcraft as "agents of Satan" responsible for afflicting people with sicknesses such as cancer, epilepsy, arthritis, mental illness, and physical disabilities (Akoria 1992; Akinyemi 2011; Olukoya 2004). Invariably, these assertions are supported with reference to the Bible. Mysterious illnesses or sicknesses considered incurable by medical science are particularly susceptible to spiritual explanations of causality. Third, some Nigerian Pentecostals refer to biological and environmental causes of ill-health, such as poor nutrition, addictions, stress, high-risk behaviour, lack of exercise, inadequate health service provision, and poverty. These aetiologies of ill-health are not discrete categories but often overlap. For example, RCCG's Reproductive and Family Health Policy includes the following statement:

> Health connotes wholeness of a person's body, mind and spirit integrated and coordinated, and able to function creatively within the community.... Disease is everything that makes us less human, and diminishes the image of God in us. It comes from the devil, sin, ignorance, poverty and poor nutrition and is to be combatted with every means that God has given us.
>
> (RCCG 2008: 16)

Nigerian Pentecostal healthworlds are based on a holistic understanding of salvation which encompasses sin, sickness, demonic oppression, unemployment, poverty, and family relationships. This is reflected in the following excerpt from an interview with a pastor in Nigeria:

> Christ has come to bring healing to our spirits, healing to our minds, healing to our circumstances, even healing to our bodies.... So I would say that my main message is that the gospel of Christ is a holistic one. It should affect every area of human life.[5]

Nigerian Pentecostal theologies of health and healing suggest both continuity and rupture with African indigenous cosmologies. As noted in Chapter 1, ontological beliefs in a "spirit-filled" world permeate African societies and persist within African Pentecostalism. Ogbu Kalu (2008: 170) argues that Pentecostalism had grown in Africa "because of its cultural fit into indigenous worldviews and its response to the questions that are raised within the interior of the worldviews". Contrary to the attitude of the early missionaries, Pentecostals perceive a resonance between the Bible and African indigenous religions. In particular, Kalu (2008: 178–181) identifies a shared belief in the influence of an invisible spiritual world over the visible material world, the efficacy of words and prayer rituals for influencing the powers, and the salience of revelatory phenomena such as dreams and visions. The major contribution of Pentecostalism, according to Kalu, is how it addresses the continued reality of these forces, drawing upon the pneumatological resources of biblical theology (Kalu 2002: 130, 137).

Nigerian Pentecostals adopt multiple therapeutic strategies to combat ill-health. Most churches provide contexts for participants to receive prayer for healing (see Figure 5.1). In 2010, I attended a weekly healing meeting organized by Dunamis International Gospel Centre in Abuja. The church started in 1996 and has an estimated 20,000 members, largely attracted by the healing ministry of its senior pastor, former medical doctor Paul Enenche. During the meeting, Enenche delivered a series of detailed "revelations" concerning people who were being healed. This was followed by a flow of people coming to the front to testify about their healing. Various controversies have accompanied Pentecostal healing ministries in Nigeria. These have generally focused on the provenance of spiritual power and allegations over manipulation and counterfeit miracles. For example, in 2018, Chris Oyakhilome, pastor of Christ Embassy, was accused of performing "fake miracles" during a healing conference in South Africa (Udodiong 2018).

Pentecostal healing is closely associated with deliverance practices (Brown 2011). One Nigerian pastor who claimed a gift of deliverance told me:

> I have experienced many people bound by demons. They have been delivered, completely set free. Barren women have received children. Many who cannot be cured by medicine, after deliverance, they get there healing because they were oppressed by demon powers. Some people with mental

> problems have been set free. Some people with arthritis who could not be healed have been set free. Some people who have been paralysed have been made free by deliverance.[6]

Mountain of Fire and Miracles (MFM) has gained a particular reputation for its deliverance practices (Gifford 2014; Hackett 2003). MFM's General Overseer, Daniel Olukoya, believes that most diseases are caused by evil spirits and witchcraft (2004: 164; 1999: 23). One of his many publications, entitled *Prayers to Destroy Diseases & Infirmities*, is described as a "spiritual warfare manual specifically targeted at destroying diseases and infirmities". According to Olukoya, "[t]he only language the devil understands is the language of violence and resounding defeat", and he exhorts his followers to "fight until every foe is vanquished and Christ is Lord indeed" (Olukoya 1999: 9).

The Pentecostal preference for divine healing does not preclude the pursuit of biomedical interventions or the promotion of good health habits. All Christians Fellowship Mission's Statement of Faith includes the following: "Both human experience and Bible alike reveal the need for medical science as a means of alleviating human suffering and divine healing is not to be misconstrued as being opposed to medical science" (All Christians Fellowship Mission, n.d.: 26). A Pentecostal Bible study entitled "Divine Health and Healing" states,

Figure 5.1 Billboard for RCCG's 2010 Holy Ghost Congress, Lagos.

Source: author.

"He [God] may choose to heal us through the application of medicine, surgery or by His divine touch" (Redeemed People's Mission 1998: 34). Many Nigerian Pentecostals are former or practising health professionals and Pentecostal publications contain articles on health matters, including advice on healthy behaviours.

Some pastors have made health education and disease prevention a particular focus of their ministries. One example is Tony Akinyemi, senior pastor of The Shepherd's Flock International Church in Lagos and founder of the Rapha Healthy Living Institute (RHLI). RHLI courses address such topics as diet and nutrition, weight management, prevention and reversal of diabetes, infertility, hypertension, and eye health. Akinyemi regularly speaks on health matters to Christian audiences and uses print media, radio, and TV to raise awareness about health issues. His book *How to Regain your Health* (2011) contains chapters on "The aetiology of diseases", "The impact of our diet and lifestyle on our health", "How to get well and stay well", "A holistic and comprehensive health plan", and "Stress and your health". Akinyemi claims that his "healthy living principles" are "Bible-based, Science-supported, Time-tested, and People-proven" (2011: 2). In a talk delivered at the Elevation Church in Lagos, entitled "Modifiable risk factors", he identified three stakeholders that define health and longevity: God, government, and ourselves. According to Akinyemi, most diseases can be prevented if people adopt healthy lifestyles: "If you want to optimize your health, take charge of the things that are under your control, and put your absolute faith in the faithfulness of God to preserve you after you have done your part" (Akinyemi 2018).

The religious health assets of Nigerian Pentecostal churches include initiatives which seek to address health inequalities and obstacles to accessing healthcare services. Covenant Medical Fair, an annual event organized by Covenant Christian Centre in Lagos, offers free medical tests, screening, health education, counselling and referral services to members of the church and community (Covenant Christian Centre n.d.). RCCG's Women Arise medical team provides basic healthcare services free-of-charge to poorer communities in Lagos. Women Arise Initiative is a faith-based NGO founded by Siju Iluyomade, one of the pastors of RCCG's City of David parish. Another church engaged in health service provision is House on the Rock which operates a mobile clinic for delivering primary healthcare across Lagos. More surprising, given its emphasis on deliverance, is MFM's Hospital Healing Ministry which offers free healthcare to members of the church and community.

Pentecostal hospitals offering subsidized health services are a growing phenomenon, mirroring the hospitals and clinics set up by Christian missions in pre-independence Nigeria. These are usually established by Pentecostal megachurches, which have the necessary financial and human resources for such ventures. RCCG's City of David owns a hospital called Healing Stripes Hospital which provides in-patient and out-patient care, and specialist services in nephrology, cardiology, obstetrics and gynaecology, paediatrics, urology, dental and eye care, and general surgery. Another Pentecostal initiative is Nidus Aquilae

Hospital (formerly Grace Springs Medical Centre), established by the Fountain of Life Church in Lagos, which offers healthcare services to those unable to afford the costs of medical treatment in state-run hospitals (see Figure 5.2). The hospital is subsidized by a benevolent fund set up by the church to help pay the medical costs of less privileged patients.[7] Gilead Medical Centre was established by Winners Chapel to provide subsidized medical services for its church members. The church divides treatment in its hospital into three categories: poor health arising from "natural causes"; from "occupational exposure and hazards"; and from "unauthorised activities". Only those suffering poor health arising from occupational exposure and hazards are eligible for full reimbursement of their treatment costs, while anyone suffering poor health due to unauthorized activities, such as those living with HIV/AIDs, are denied the subsidy (Kuponu 2007: 65–66).

The transnational nature of Nigerian Pentecostalism allows for the cross-fertilization of health-seeking practices, creating complex landscapes of intermingling healthworlds. The continuing appeal of Pentecostal healing and deliverance practices to Nigerians in the diaspora is reflected in the crowds who flock to meetings in Europe and the United States presided over by Nigerian pastors such as Enoch Adeboye, Daniel Olukoya and David Oyedepo. Conferences I have

Figure 5.2 Signboard for Fountain of Life Church's Grace Springs Medical Centre, Lagos.

Source: author

attended in London follow a similar pattern to those in Nigeria with preaching interspersed with prayers for healing and deliverance. Publications produced by Nigerian diaspora churches contain articles on health education and good health habits similar to those back home. For example, Jesus House London's *Outflow* magazine has a regular column entitled "Your Health and You" which provides information about healthy living and different medical conditions such as hypertension, diabetes, and mental illness. Some of the larger Nigerian diaspora churches also offer free healthcare services, though on a smaller scale than their counterparts back home. In 2006, RCCG's Trinity Chapel in London organized a Community Health Open Day which offered free health checks, healthy living advice and leaflets, free medical counselling, dental check-ups, as well as information about the NHS and how to register with GPs (Trinity Chapel 2006: 7). Jesus House London has a healthcare team which conduct medical missions in African countries (including Nigeria), providing free health screening, dental checks, minor surgeries, and distribution of birthing kits to expectant mothers (Jesus House 2015).

The remainder of the chapter focuses on Pentecostal responses to three health issues which present particular challenges to populations on the African continent: HIV/AIDS, maternal and reproductive health, and disabilities. As we will see, Pentecostal therapeutic regimes combine divine healing practices with medical intervention, health education, and advocacy.

HIV/AIDS

Nigeria ranks among those countries with the highest incidences of HIV/AIDS in sub-Saharan Africa. Although HIV prevalence is much lower than other African countries such as South Africa and Zambia, the size of Nigeria's population makes the HIV epidemic there the second largest in the world (Avert 2017).[8] Many of those living with HIV are unaware of, or reluctant to disclose, their status due to the threat of stigmatization. This, together with low levels of access to antiretroviral treatment (ART) and inadequate numbers of HIV testing and counselling sites, means that there are still many AIDS-related deaths in Nigeria. Approximately 160,000 people died from AIDS-related illnesses in Nigeria in 2016 (Avert 2017; WHO 2017).

Combating HIV/AIDS, malaria and other diseases was addressed in Goal 6 of the MDGs. While substantial progress was made towards the achievement of Goal 6, HIV/AIDS remains a significant obstacle to development in sub-Saharan Africa. Within the health goal of the SDGs, target 3.2 requests that countries: "By 2030, end the epidemics of AIDS, tuberculosis, malaria and neglected tropical diseases and combat hepatitis, water-borne diseases and other communicable diseases." There is a growing body of literature on religious engagement with HIV/AIDS in sub-Saharan Africa, including Pentecostal responses (Prince, Denis and van Dijk 2009; Adogame 2007; Dilger 2007; Parsitau 2009; Smith 2014; Pfeiffer 2011; Attanasi 2008). Issues addressed include the intersection between religion, morality and risk behaviours, and the role of religious communities in facilitating or hindering the treatment and support of those living with HIV/AIDS. Some studies suggest that Pentecostal churches perpetuate the stigma associated with HIV/AIDS through their moralistic messages (Smith 2014), while others argue that Pentecostalism's promotion of abstinence and fidelity provides protection against risky behaviour. A number of studies discuss Pentecostal engagement in HIV education, prevention, counselling, care, and treatment (Prince, Denis, and van Dijk 2009; Parsitau 2009; Attanasi 2008; Adogame 2007).

In the case of Nigeria's AIDS epidemic, Daniel Smith (2014: 89) suggests that "Pentecostal Christianity has been at least as harmful as it has been helpful". The Pentecostal tendency to moralize the epidemic and stigmatize sufferers can create barriers by inhibiting testing and discouraging disclosure by those diagnosed as HIV positive (Smith 2014). By the early 2000s, Pentecostal churches in Nigeria began to revise their stance on HIV/AIDS. One catalyst behind this Pentecostal re-evaluation was the fragile government social services sector, which was clearly failing to cope with the catastrophe. Another catalyst was the increasing number of fatalities within their own ranks (Adogame 2007). Some Nigerian Pentecostal churches now provide diagnostic facilities, voluntary counselling, and training for sufferers and their families, free ARV (antiretroviral) drugs, and practical care for people living with HIV/AIDS. This has engendered hope and enabled some of those living with the disease to return to economically productive activity. However, the promotion of sexual abstinence outside marriage and the reluctance to recommend the use of condoms has contributed to Christian morality becoming increasingly visible in Nigeria's public space. In some churches, the emphasis on faith in relation to healing has deterred members living with HIV/AIDS from taking their ARVs. Pentecostal publications contain multiple testimonies from those who claim healing from HIV/AIDS at Pentecostal events.[9] Yet the quest for divine healing from HIV/AIDS does not necessarily preclude the use of medical therapy, as this testimony illustrates:

> I was tested HIV positive in October, 2003 and commenced the intake of anti-retroviral drugs which actually could not cure me. During the Healing and Deliverance Service of first January, 2008, I received a word of knowledge which addressed my condition. The Senior Pastor said, "There is somebody here who is HIV positive. God is cleansing your blood system right now! Go for another test, you are now HIV negative!" A new test conducted at Gwagwalada Specialist Hospital on the 9th of January, 2008, proved that I am now HIV negative.
>
> (Enenche 2008: 47)

The RCCG has adopted a holistic approach to the HIV/AIDS epidemic which includes spiritual and medical intervention (Adogame 2007; Ukah 2008). Spiritual intervention involves healing and deliverance rituals, which usually occur in communal settings such as cell groups, worship services, and conference events. RCCG literature contain testimonies of people healed of HIV/AIDS.

RCCG also runs the largest Pentecostal HIV/AIDS NGO in Nigeria, the Redeemed AIDS Programme Action Committee (RAPAC). RAPAC was established in 1997 to coordinate the RCCG's response to the HIV/AIDS epidemic (Ukah 2008).[10] Its stated aims are to increase access to support, counselling, and testing services among church members and host communities; to educate church leaders on HIV/AIDS issues and increase their capacity to provide effective pastoral care; and to foster behaviour change among church members (RCCG 2011). RAPAC programmes include sensitization and prevention workshops, anti-AIDS clubs in schools and universities, diagnostic and counselling services, free ARVs, the provision of home care and economic empowerment for people living with HIV/AIDS, and peer educator training.[11] Educational programmes are particularly directed at prevention strategies and the reduction of stigma. In its policy document, RAPAC identifies "unwillingness to make the required behavioural changes for prevention and transmission of HIV" and the belief by many RCCG pastors "that HIV infected persons are suffering the consequences of their sins" as the main factors limiting the impact of its programmes (RCCG n.d.: 7). RAPAC's prevention strategy favours abstinence and fidelity over condom use in keeping with its strong emphasis on the nuclear family and sexual morality. According to Pastor Laide Adenuga, the Director of RAPAC, addressing the issue of stigmatization through education and counselling is one of the most important tasks undertaken by RAPAC.[12] Some of its achievements listed in its publicity material include increased access to counselling and testing services, more open discussion of sexuality issues in the church, increased willingness among PLWHA to declare their status publicly, increase in adoption of abstinence among young people in the church, and evidence-based reports of divine healing of PLWHA (RCCG 2009).

RAPAC collaborates with national and international partners including the National Agency for the Control of AIDS (NACA), the Federal Ministry of Health, Family Health International, and the United States Agency for International Development (USAID). Much of its funding comes from the church, but also from international donors such as USAID and PEPFAR. Scholars refer to the moral narratives and conservative approach to AIDS prevention associated with some international donor organizations which have contributed to stigmatization (Smith 2014; Prince, Denis, and van Dijk 2009). There is also a transnational dimension to RCCG's fight against HIV/AIDS. In 2003, during the RCCG's Annual Convention held in Dallas-Texas, Enoch Adeboye and his wife Folu Adeboye led the "Walk for Africa" around Dallas to "raise awareness and financial assistance for HIV/AIDS victims in Africa" (Adogame 2005: 403). The same year, in collaboration with CitiHope International, RCCG's Africa Missions North America "donated AIDS drugs valued at $1.5 million to Nigeria for use in treating HIV-related complications" (Adogame 2016: 9). Publicity brochures advertising the work of RAPAC and requesting financial support are also available at RCCG conference events in the diaspora such as the Festival of Life in London.

Maternal and reproductive health

Two of the MDGs directly addressed child and maternal mortality: reducing under-fives mortality (Goal number 4) and improving maternal health and cutting maternal death rates (Goal number 5). Progress on achieving the targets of MDG Goals 4 and 5 was mixed. While there was a significant reduction in under-five mortality, there was no visible progress in maternal mortality reduction at the global level (Mojekwu and Ibekwe 2012). The SDG's health goal includes targets to reduce the global maternal mortality rate (3.1), to end preventable deaths of new-borns and children under 5 (3.2), and to ensure universal access to sexual and reproductive health care services (3.7).

Nigeria has one of the highest maternal mortality rates in the world, second only to India, and is the leading contributor to maternal death rates in sub-Saharan Africa (Mojekwu and Ibekwe 2012; Babalola and Fatusi 2009). Studies indicate that the main factors behind the high maternal mortality rates in Nigeria are barriers to accessing maternal health services, poor utilization of healthcare facilities, low levels of knowledge and insufficient health education of women, and low levels of skilled professional attendants (Babalola and Fatusi 2009; Harrison 2009). Literature on religion and reproductive health indicates that faith groups influence people's beliefs about sex outside marriage and decision-making about contraceptives, child-bearing outside marriage, and desired family size. Religious institutions may also influence the provision of reproductive healthcare services (Gaydos *et al.* 2010). Studies of reproductive health in Nigeria suggest that traditional and religious beliefs play major roles in maternal mortality and the utilization of medical healthcare services (Archibong and Agan 2010; Babalola and Fatusi 2009). As Babalola and Fatusi (2009) note, Nigerian women often "rate the services of traditional birth attendants as being of higher quality than medical healthcare practitioners, particularly with regards to interpersonal communication and relationships". Archibong and Agan (2010) suggest that churches can contribute to antenatal defaulting and a negative perception towards medical care.

Reproductive health is an issue of deep concern for Nigerian Pentecostals. This is reflected in the numbers of people, especially women, who attend Pentecostal events in their quest for children. Pentecostal publications are also replete with testimonies of "miraculous" births following prayer by Pentecostal pastors such as Enoch Adeboye and David Oyedepo. For example, a chapter entitled "Miracle Babies" in Oyedepo's book *Signs and Wonders Today* (2008) includes 30 testimonies of women healed or delivered from childlessness and miscarriages. Invariably the quest for children involves recourse to both medical and spiritual interventions, as the following testimony illustrates:

> After the delivery of our first child in 1998, there was no other issue. We waited on God, and not too long after, my wife took in; but there was a miscarriage. We visited several hospitals both in Lagos and Abuja, but all to no avail. Therefore, I decided that we would not go anywhere again, but wait

> and see the good work of God. My wife attended Shiloh 2001, where God's servant, Bishop David Oyedepo, declared that those looking for the fruit of the womb would go home with their Isaacs and Johns. In December 2002, my wife gave birth to a set of male twins.
>
> (Oyedepo 2008: 534)

Leke Sanusi, a London-based RCCG pastor, describes the process he and his wife underwent in their quest for a child in his book *None Shall Be Barren* (2004). Sanusi's account, which begins in Nigeria prior to his Christian conversion, demonstrates the experimental approach to religion among Nigerians. Despite seeking assistance from medical doctors in Nigeria and London, traditional *Babalawo* (priests), and Islamic priests, their problem remained unresolved until they became born-again Christians and began to engage in aggressive spiritual warfare. A turning point occurred in 1998 when Pastor Adeboye prayed for them during their ordination service in London. The following year his wife gave birth to a boy.

African Pentecostal perspectives on reproductive health are shaped by biblical and indigenous beliefs (Asamoah-Gyadu 2007). Nigerian Pentecostal narratives are filled with biblical references which associate childbirth with God's blessings. However, as stated above, Pentecostal perspectives are also influenced by indigenous cultural and religious norms. In Yoruba culture, for example, barren women are stigmatized and married men without children are expected to take additional wives (Pearce 1995; Koster-Oyekan 1999). According to Peel (2000: 91), a barren woman is unable to enjoy *alafia*, and "her desire for children was likely to surpass all other needs". Traditionally, high fertility was prized as a response to the socio-economic environment where enough children were needed to fill the necessary economic roles (Pearce 1995). In Yoruba indigenous thought, infertility can be caused by biological factors such as induced abortion and fibroids or spiritual factors such as witchcraft, evil spirits, and curses by ancestors and deities. Thus, treatment for infertility is sought from hospitals/clinics, traditional specialists in reproductive health, *babalawo*, *elewe omo* (herbalists), and Pentecostal churches (Koster-Oyekan 1999).

There are close affinities between indigenous and Pentecostal explanations for infertility in Nigeria. Oyedepo interprets childlessness as a spiritual issue that requires supernatural intervention:

> God is not responsible for your present predicament. He is not the one behind your frustrations, reproaches and shame. Rather He is there to help you. He created you and called you a joyful mother of children. The devil is the one behind your struggles with barrenness and miscarriages.
>
> (2008: 511–513)

In a book entitled *Ministering Deliverance* (1992: 71–79), Pentecostal Pastor Anthony Akoria lists biological, psychological, and spiritual causes ("family curses" and "demonic oppression") of childlessness. Asamoah-Gyadu (2007:

443) challenges the tendency for African Pentecostals to reinforce traditional worldviews of causality by alienating childless couples as "faithless victims of supernatural evil". He argues that this approach is pastorally deficient because it neglects the needs of those who may never have children, making their suffering ever more painful. A more balanced approach to childlessness, according to Asamoah-Gyadu, is to focus attention on the cross as a "symbol of trauma", and to work with childless couples so that they can feel the "empathy of Christ" (2007: 458). However, the testimonies of those who through persistent prayer are eventually able to conceive, encourages others to expect favourable outcomes if they follow similar prayer strategies. This approach also focuses on the cross, but as a symbol of victory over the forces of evil.

Some Nigerian Pentecostal churches combine spiritual and medical therapies for tackling childlessness and addressing reproductive health issues. One example is Christ Livingspring Apostolic Ministry (CLAM) in Lagos, founded in 1998 by Pastor Wole Oladiyun. Today, the church claims a regular attendance 6,000 members in its Sunday services. The church's weekly programme includes healing/deliverance services and prayer sessions for "pregnant women" and "waiting mothers". CLAM also counts the 50-bedded Soteria Maternity and Hospital, located in the church premises, among its religious health assets. According to Oladiyun, the hospital was built specifically to cater for poorer families in Lagos who struggle to afford the prohibitive costs of healthcare.[13] Pastor Oladiyun has strong transnational links with churches in Britain and the United States, where he is a regular conference speaker. One example is the Everlasting Arms Ministries in London which conducts an annual programme called "About This Time Next Year" featuring Pentecostal pastors (including Oladiyun) and medical doctors addressing issues around infertility from a spiritual and medical perspective.[14]

The RCCG is another church that combines medical and spiritual approaches to reproductive health. RCCG's Enoch Adeboye is renowned for his ministry of prayer for childless women, and RCCG parishes worldwide hold a monthly programme called Shiloh Hour specifically geared towards couples seeking the "fruit of the womb". The church also runs maternity clinics and hospitals in different locations across Nigeria. When I visited RCCG's maternity hospital in Lagos, I was introduced to six new mothers, one of whom had given birth during my visit. RCCG's approach to reproductive health is outlined in its Reproductive and Family Health Policy which is "set within the context of biblical teachings, the mission of the RCCG and the framework of the Nigerian national health policy". The document includes statements on family planning; adolescent reproductive health and high-risk behaviour; the implications of the HIV/AIDS epidemic on family health; maternal, neonatal, and childhood mortality; domestic violence and sexual abuse; gender-based harmful practices; inadequate services for infertility and limited access to reproductive health education programmes; and justice and human rights. While recognizing the reproductive rights of women, the RCCG's policy is at odds with the liberal human rights agenda when it comes to the issues of abortion and family planning. It opposes abortion and rejects the use of contraception by adolescents and unmarried young people (RCCG 2008).

Physical and mental disabilities

Physical disability and mental illness are major health hazards in sub-Saharan Africa, exposing sufferers to stigmatization, witchcraft accusations, and poverty (Groce and McGeown 2013; Asamoah, Osafo, and Agyapong 2014; Secker 2013). The inclusion of disability, mental health, and substance abuse in the sustainable development agenda represents a significant improvement on the MDGs where there was no mention of these conditions. Within the SDG health goal, two targets are directly related to mental health and substance abuse. Target 3.4 requests that countries: "By 2030, reduce by one third premature mortality from noncommunicable diseases through prevention and treatment and promote mental health and well-being." Target 3.5 requests that countries: "Strengthen the prevention and treatment of substance abuse, including narcotic drug abuse and harmful use of alcohol." Disability is referenced in several SDGs, especially those related to education (SDG 4), economic growth and employment (SDG 8), inequality (SDG 10), and accessibility to human settlements (SDG 11).

As with other healthcare problems, discussed above, sub-Saharan Africa has a long history of stigma and witchcraft accusations associated with physical and mental disability (Groce and McGeown 2013; Iheanacho *et al.* 2014). A common belief is that individuals are "born with or acquire a disability because they or a family member have sinned, violated a taboo or have aroused jealousy or anger in another" (Groce and McGeown 2013: 3). Modernization and advocacy around the UN Convention on the Rights of Persons with Disabilities (CRPD) have been credited with improving attitudes in Africa. However, in ethnic groups such as the Nigerian Yoruba, the link between disability and witchcraft remains deeply embedded. Traditionally, the focus of witchcraft accusations has been on the elderly and particularly elderly women. As Secker (2013: 24) notes, witches are usually thought to be possessed by evil spirits "which will force them to cause harm to other family and community members". The recent phenomenon of witchcraft accusations against children with disabilities in Nigeria is a deeply disturbing trend which has attracted attention from human rights activists, NGOs, media, and academic researchers (Secker 2013). Witchcraft stigmatization of children can lead to human rights abuses including discrimination, violence, imprisonment, forced starvation, and abandonment.

Despite the high number of people with physical and mental disabilities in Nigeria,[15] service provision is sparse. Nigeria is a signatory to international agreements and protocols such as the CRPD and the Salamanca Statement and Framework for Action on Special Needs Education (UNESCO 1994). The Nigerians with Disability Decree, introduced in 1993, provides legal protections for Nigerians with disabilities. However, the Nigerian government has lacked the political will to enforce the Act and to set in place strategies for education, free medical care, rehabilitation, and employment of people with disabilities (PWDs)

(Ajuwon 2017). Mental health service provision is also poor (Eaton and Agomoh 2008). Utilization of psychiatric services is low due to lack of accessible clinics, high costs of medicines, and lack of professionals. This is exacerbated by stigma and negative attitudes towards people with mental illness both in the general population and among medical professionals (Eaton and Agomoh 2008; Iheanacho *et al.* 2014).

Historically, Catholic and Protestant missions in Nigeria have provided specialized care and education for PWDs (Ajuwon 2017). Nigerian Pentecostal responses to PWDs are various, reflecting the diversity of the movement. In keeping with their "enchanted" worldview, most churches provide ritual contexts where PWDs can receive prayer, and Pentecostal publications contain testimonies of those healed or delivered from mental illness, paralysis, lameness, deafness, and blindness. Pentecostal beliefs about disability influence the type of treatment that is sought. Recent studies suggest that Pentecostal beliefs and practices compound the stigmatization of PWDs by associating disability with God's disfavour or by labelling them as victims of witchcraft and subjecting them to prolonged deliverance sessions (Groce and McGeown 2013; Secker 2013; Eaton and Agomoh 2008).

Some churches adopt a more holistic approach to disability. For example, Pastor Akoria of All Faith Revival Church lists poverty, abandonment by family, the effects of dangerous drugs, demonic attacks, birth defects, and guilt among the causes of mental illness (Akoria 1992). Pentecostal churches are also engaged in social ministry and advocacy on behalf of PWDs. God Bless Nigeria Church (GBNC), founded by Pastor Tony Rapu in 2006 as a church plant from This Present House, established the Deaf and Able Department to cater for disabled people who are audibly impaired. The church also has members who are wheelchair-bound. One of the GBNC pastors explained to me why Pentecostal churches are sometimes reluctant to engage in ministry to the disabled:

> I think it's because in the mind of the church, you think that your job is to heal them. So you are embarrassed to have a church with deaf people, blind people. You will think you have failed.[16]

In 2015, GBNC celebrated the International Day of People with Disability by holding a service to honour people living with disability. On its website, it posted the following message:

> We are calling on people across the world to identify and appreciate ability in disability. We all need to display the right attitude towards these people and jointly work towards the elimination of the various forms of stigmatization that goes with disability. This is a call on policy makers, lawmakers and the Government to work together in developing policies and practices that will strengthen integration and inclusion of people living with disability. Our goal is to help build a sustainable world for all living with disability. As a Church, our mandate is to empower them towards the fulfilment of their divine purposes. We are calling on well-meaning people

> around the world to support the work we are doing in empowering the Deaf and Able Community in Nigeria.
>
> (God Bless Nigeria Church 2018)

Tony Rapu is also involved in outreach to drug addicts through the Freedom Foundation, an NGO founded by This Present House. Drug addiction is a serious problem in Nigeria with significant economic and health implications, including HIV/AIDS and mental health issues (Azuike, Oni, and Dirisu 2012). Drug addiction is particularly rife among young men living on the streets but increasingly affects those from more affluent backgrounds. Freedom Foundation runs the House of Refuge, a drug and alcohol rehabilitation facility in Lagos State. House of Refuge adopts a holistic treatment regime which comprises medical, psychosocial, and spiritual services involving health professionals and volunteers. The spiritual component of the treatment model involves a daily routine of prayers, worship, Bible teaching, and counselling sessions, aimed at empowering participants to overcome their addiction (Azuike and Rapu 2011).

Another NGO addressing the growing problem of drug abuse in Nigeria is RCCG's Christ Against Drug Abuse Ministry (CADAM), which is recognized by Nigeria's National Drug Law Enforcement Agency and the United Nations Office on Drugs and Crime. Like the Freedom Foundation, CADAM adopts an integrative approach to healthcare, combining medical therapy with spiritual care (Adogame 2016). Some of the staff working in CADAM's residential houses as care-givers are former drug addicts who have been rehabilitated. One staff member, who had passed through the programme, told me that the key to CADAM's strategy is application of the "power of the gospel":

> Addiction means you are enslaved to something. When withdrawn from it you are empty. So you need something to replace it. We replace it with the gospel and Jesus, and Spirit baptism. It is believed that once an addict always an addict. But when one is genuinely born again, receive Christ, you may develop some inner strength to resist cravings.[17]

These words are mirrored in the publicity material on CADAM's website:

> We focus on faith in God as the primary source for addiction recovery. Drug abuse disconnects the addict from God. At CADAM, we therefore put into connection this disconnection that occurs with drug abuse and addiction because we believe that the power of God is stronger than the bonds of addiction.
>
> (CADAM 2019)

The Mental Health Foundation (MHF) is a Lagos-based NGO founded by Emmanuel Owoyemi, a psychiatrist and Pentecostal pastor of Souls Reapers International Missions. Owoyemi is a member of the Federal Ministry of Health's National Mental Health Action Committee and a graduate of the Institute for

National Transformation. The aim of the MHF is to promote mental health, prevent mental illness, reduce stigma, and advocate for the care of those living with mental illness. In order to achieve this, it organizes workshops, distributes free publications on mental health, conducts live interactive sessions on Nigerian TV, and raises mental health ambassadors. Owoyemi's public profile is such that his opinion on mental health issues is regularly solicited by the Nigerian press (*Guardian Nigeria* 2015). MHF is recognized by the Lagos State government and its network includes psychiatrists, clinical psychologists, educationalists, social workers, and religious leaders.[18]

Conclusion

Health is recognized as an important component of the international development agenda. This chapter has investigated the "healthworlds" and health-seeking practices of Nigerian Pentecostals, and discussed their contributions (or otherwise) to public health outcomes. Nigerian Pentecostal churches possess a variety of tangible health assets such as social capital, human capital, financial resources, and buildings, as well as less tangible assets such as religious beliefs, values, and practices that encourage good health habits and motivate compassionate care towards others. However, Pentecostal understandings of illness and health can also discourage church members from seeking medical help. The "enchanted" worldview that underpins Nigerian Pentecostal approaches to illness and healing sometimes results in antipathy towards medical technology and recourse to rituals and behaviours detrimental to public health.

As I have shown, the Pentecostal preference for divine healing does not preclude the pursuit of biomedical interventions and the promotion of good health habits. Increasingly, Nigerian Pentecostals are adopting holistic approaches to health that combine beliefs in divine healing with the use of modern medicine. They are also engaged in healthcare interventions which seek to address health inequalities and obstacles to accessing healthcare services in the wider community. The chapter explored the Pentecostal responses to three major health issues in Nigeria: HIV/AIDS, maternal and reproductive health, and disabilities. Pentecostal churches are sometimes criticized for perpetuating the stigma associated with HIV/AIDS, disabilities, and childlessness. However, the case studies discussed in this chapter show that some Nigerian Pentecostals are responding to these public health challenges by establishing ministries and NGOs which combine pastoral care with medical interventions, health education programmes, and advocacy.

Notes

1 For a review of the literature on religion and health, see Koenig *et al.* (2012).
2 For a review of the literature on religious healing practices within a range of religious traditions and ethnicities, see Barnes (2011).
3 The Nigerian National Health Policy of 1988 culminated directly from the Alma-Ata Declaration (Uzochukwu 2017).

4 In 2013, NHIS membership in Nigeria was 3.5 per cent, compared to 65 per cent in Ghana (Odeyemi and Nixon 2013).
5 Interview, Pastor Thompson Nwosu, Redeemed People's Mission, Jos, 31 August 2001.
6 Interview, Pastor Chuks Ogoalaji, Bread of Life Mission, Enugu, 23 May 2000.
7 Interview, Dr Ogunrinde, medical superintendent, Grace Springs Medical Centre, 17 December 2010.
8 In 2016, the estimated number of people living with HIV in Nigeria was 3,200,000 (WHO 2016).
9 For example, out of 59 testimonies of healing recorded in Oyedepo's book *Signs and Wonders Today* (2008), there are eight testimonies of healing from HIV/AIDS. Paul Enenche records six cases of healing from HIV/AIDS in his book *Divine Evidence Through the Ministry of Dr Paul Enenche* (2008).
10 According to its website, RAPAC runs HIV/AIDs activities in ten states across Nigeria, and employs 47 staff who are assisted by over 5,000 volunteers (RAPAC 2019).
11 Interview, Pastor Laide Adenuga, Director, RAPAC, 30 September 2011.
12 Interview, Pastor Laide Adenuga, Director, RAPAC, 30 September 2011.
13 Interview, Pastor Wole Oladiyun, Christ Livingspring Apostolic Ministry, Lagos, 7 December 2010.
14 Everlasting Arms Ministries was founded by Pastor Kayode Owolabi, formerly the pioneer pastor of Mountain of Fire and Miracles in the UK. It has branches in London, Glasgow, Reading (UK), Nigeria, and India.
15 In Nigeria, WHO estimates in 2008 put the number of people with disability at 19 million or approximately 20 per cent of the country's population (Amusat 2009). For Nigeria's national policy for mental health, see Federal Ministry of Health (2013).
16 Interview, Pastor Nneke, God Bless Nigeria Church, Lagos, 19 December 2010.
17 Interview, CADAM staff member, RCCG Redemption Camp, 15 December 2010.
18 Members of the Mental Health Foundation's advisory board include Professor Oye Nnom, head of the Department of Psychiatry (University of Ibadan), and Sam Adeyemi, pastor of Daystar Christian Centre.

References

Abdulraheem, B. I., Olapipo, A. R., and Amodu, M. O. (2012) "Primary Health Care Services in Nigeria: Critical Issues and Strategies for Enhancing the Use by the Rural Communities", *Journal of Public Health and Epidemiology* 4(1): 5–13.

Adeyemi, Sam (2018) "Supernatural Health", available at: https://daystarng.org/supernatural-health/ (accessed 2 September 2019)

Adogame, Afe (2005) "'A Walk for Africa': Combating the Demon of HIV/AIDS in an African Pentecostal Church – The Case of the Redeemed Christian Church of God", *Scriptura: International Journal of Bible, Religion and Theology in Southern Africa* 89(1): 396–405.

Adogame, Afe (2007) "HIV/AIDS Support and African Pentecostalism: The Case of the Redeemed Christian Church of God (RCCG)", *Journal of Health Psychology*, 12(3): 475–484.

Adogame, Afe (2016) "African Christianities and the Politics of Development from Below", *HTS Theological Studies* 72(4): 1–11.

Aigbiremolen, A. O., Alenoghena, I., Eboreime, E., and Abejegah, C. (2014) "Primary Health Care in Nigeria: From Conceptualization to Implementation", *Journal of Medical and Applied Biosciences* 6(2): 35–43.

Ajuwon, Paul M. (2017) "Disabilities and Disability Services in Nigeria: Past, Present and Future", in Roy Hanes, Ivan Brown, and Nancy E. Hansen (eds) *Routledge History of Disability*, London: Routledge, pp. 133–150.

Akinyemi, Tony (2011) *How to Regain and Retain Your Health*, Pittsburgh, PA: Dorrance Publishing.

Akinyemi, Tony (2018) "Modifiable Risk Factor", 21 March, Sermon Preached at Elevation Church, Lagos, available at: http://tsfchurch.com/sermon/modifiable-risk-factors/ (accessed 15 August 2019).

Akoria, A. O. (1992) *Ministering Deliverance*, Ibadan: God-Will-Do-It Publications.

Alexander, Kim E. (2006) *Pentecostal Healing: Models in Theology and Practice*, Blandford Forum, Dorset: Deo Publishing.

All Christians Fellowship Mission (n.d.) "Lesson 5: Our Statement of Faith", *Membership Bible Studies*, Abuja: All Christians Fellowship Mission.

Alubo, Ogoh (2001) "The Promise and Limits of Private Medicine: Health Policy Dilemmas in Nigeria", *Health Policy and Planning* 16(3): 313–321.

Amusat, N. (2009) "Disability Care in Nigeria: The Need for Professional Advocacy", *African Journal of Physiotherapy and Rehabilitation Sciences* 1(1): 30–36.

Anderson, Allan (2013) *To the Ends of the Earth: Pentecostalism and the Transformation of World Christianity*, New York: Oxford University Press.

Archibong, E. I. and U. Agan (2010) "Review of Policies and Programs for Reducing Maternal Mortality and Promoting Maternal Health in Cross River State, Nigeria", *African Journal of Reproductive Health* 14(3): 37–42.

Asamoah, Moses K., Joseph Osafo, and Isaac Agyapong (2014) "The Role of Pentecostal Clergy in Mental Health-Care Delivery in Ghana", *Mental Health, Religion & Culture* 6(17): 601–614.

Asamoah-Gyadu, J. Kwabena (2007) "'Broken Calabashes and Covenants of Fruitfulness': Cursing Barrenness in Contemporary African Christianity", *Journal of Religion in Africa* 37(4): 437–460.

Attanasi, Katy (2008) "Getting in Step with the Spirit: Applying Pentecostal Commitments to HIV/AIDS in South Africa", *Political Theology* 9(2): 193–208.

Avert (2019) "HIV and AIDS in Nigeria", available at: www.avert.org/professionals/hiv-around-world/sub-saharan-africa/nigeria (accessed 13 March 2019).

Azuike, Rose and Tony Rapu (2011) *Substance Abuse Treatment in Nigeria: Case Study of a Non-profit Rehabilitation Centre*, Lagos: Freedom Foundation.

Azuike, Rose, Alexander Oni, and Osasuyi Dirisu (2012) *Stakeholders' Views on Substance Abuse and the Development of Effective and Sustainable Interventions in Nigeria: Findings from a Consultative Forum*, Lagos: Freedom Foundation.

Babalola, Stella and Adesegun Fatusi (2009) "Determinants of Use of Maternal Health Services in Nigeria – Looking Beyond Individual and Household Factors", *BMC Pregnancy and Childbirth* 9(1): 1–13.

Barnes, Linda L. (2011) "New Geographies of Religion and Healing: States of the Field", *Practical Matters* 4: 1–82.

Brewer, Gayle, Sarita Robinson, Altaf Sumra, Erini Tatsi, and Nadeem Gire (2015) "The Influence of Religious Coping and Religious Social Support on Health Behaviour, Health Status and Health Attitudes in a British Christian Sample", *Journal of Religion and Health* 54(6): 2225–2234.

Brown, Candy G. (2011) "Introduction", in Candy G. Brown (ed.) *Global Pentecostal and Charismatic Healing*, Oxford: Oxford University Press, pp. 3–28.

Brown, Candy G. (2011) (ed.) *Global and Charismatic Healing*, Oxford: Oxford University Press.

Buse, Kent and Sarah Hawkes (2015) "Health in the Sustainable Development Goals: Ready for a Paradigm Shift?", *Globalization and Health* 11(13): 1–8.

CADAM (2019) "CADAM Rehab Facility", available at: https://cadam.org.ng/cadam-rehab-facility/ (accessed 11 October 2019).

Campbell, Marci K., Marlyn Hudson, Ken Resnicow, Natasha Blakeney, Amy Paxton, and Monika Baskin (2007) "Church-based Health Promotion Interventions: Evidence and Lessons Learned", *Annual Review of Public Health* 28: 213–234.

Cochrane, James R. (2006) "Conceptualising Religious Health Assets Redemptively", *Religion & Theology* 13(1): 107–119.

Covenant Christian Centre (n.d.) "Healing the Nations, One Person at a Time", *FaceUp @ C3. A Photo Compendium of Events at Covenant Christian Centre.*

Csordas, Thomas J. (1997) *The Sacred Self: A Cultural Phenomenology of Charismatic Healing*, Berkeley: University of California Press.

Dilger, Hansjörg (2007) "Healing the Wounds of Modernity: Salvation, Community and Care in a Neo-Pentecostal Church in Dar Es Salaam, Tanzania", *Journal of Religion in Africa* 37(1): 59–83.

Dilger, Hansjörg (2009) "Doing Better? Religion, the Virtue-ethics of Development, and the Fragmentation of Health Politics in Tanzania", *Africa Today* 56(1): 89–110.

Eaton, Julian and Ahamefula O. Agomoh (2008) "Developing Mental Health Services in Nigeria", *Social Psychiatry and Psychiatric Epidemiology* 43(7): 552–558.

Enenche, Paul (2008) *Divine Evidence Through the Ministry of Dr Paul Enenche*, Abuja: Destiny Publications.

Fakoya, I., A. Johnson, K. Fenton, J. Anderson, N. Nwokolo, A. Sullivan, P. Munday, and F. Burns (2012) "Religion and HIV Diagnosis among Africans Living in London", *HIV Medicine* 13: 617–622.

Federal Ministry of Health (2013) *National Policy for Mental Health Services Delivery*, available at: http://cheld.org/wp-content/uploads/2015/02/national_policy_for_mental_health_service_delivery__2013_.pdf (accessed 20 September 2019).

Gaydos, Laura M., Alexandria Smith, Carol J. R. Hogue, and John Blevins (2010) "An Emerging Field in Religion and Reproductive Health", *Journal of Religion and Health* 49(4): 473–484.

Germond, Paul and James R. Cochrane (2010) "Healthworlds: Conceptualizing Landscapes of Health and Healing", *Sociology* 44(2): 307–324.

Germond, Paul, Sepetla Molapo, and Tandi Reilly (2007) "The (Singular) Health System and the Plurality of Healthworlds", ARHAP International Colloquium, Cape Town, South Africa, 13–16 March, Collection of Concept Papers, pp. 65–70.

Gifford, Paul (2014) "Evil, Witchcraft and Deliverance in the African Pentecostal Worldview", in Clifton R. Clarke (ed.) *Pentecostal Theology in Africa*, Eugene, OR: Pickwick Publications, pp. 112–131.

God Bless Nigeria Church (2018) "International Day of People with Disability: God Bless Nigeria Celebrates Ability in Disability", available at: www.godblessnigeriachurch.org/international-day-of-people-with-disability-god-bless-nigeria-celebrates-ability-in-disability/ (accessed 25 September 2019).

Groce, Nora and Julia McGeown (2013) "Witchcraft, Wealth and Disability: Reinterpretation of a Folk Belief in Contemporary Urban Africa", Leonard Cheshire Disability and Inclusive Development Centre Working Paper Series: No. 30.

Guardian Nigeria (2015) "Improving Mental Healthcare Delivery in Nigeria", *Guardian Nigeria*, 30 December, available at: https://guardian.ng/features/improving-mental-healthcare-delivery-in-nigeria/ (accessed 24 September 2019).

Habermas, Jürgen (1987) *The Theory of Communicative Action, Vol. 2: Lifeworld and System: A Critique of Functionalist Reason*, Boston, MA: Beacon Press.

Hackett, Rosalind I. J. (2003) "Discourses of Demonization in Africa and Beyond", *Diogenes* 50(3): 61–75.

Hall, John J. and Richard Taylor (2003) "Health for All Beyond 2000: The Demise of the Alma-Ata Declaration and Primary Health Care in Developing Countries", *The Medical Journal of Australia* 178(1): 17–20.

Harrison, K. A. (2009) "The Struggle to Reduce High Maternal Mortality in Nigeria", *African Journal of Reproductive Health* 13(3): 9–20.

Iheanacho, Theddeus, Carla Marienfeld, Elina Stefanovics, and Robert A. Rosenheck (2014) "Attitudes Toward Mental Illness and Changes Associated with a Brief Educational Intervention for Medical and Nursing Students in Nigeria", *Academic Psychiatry* 38(3): 320–324.

Jesus House (2015) "Healthcare Mission: Bringing Care and Hope", *Jesus House Annual Report 2015*, pp. 50–51.

Kalu, Ogbu U. (2002) "Preserving a Worldview: Pentecostalism in the African Maps of the Universe", *Pneuma* 24(2): 110–137.

Kalu, Ogbu U. (2008) *African Pentecostalism: An Introduction*, Oxford: Oxford University Press.

Koenig, Harold D., Dana E. King, and Verna B. Carson (2012) *Handbook of Religion and Health*, New York: Oxford University Press.

Koster-Oyekan, Winny (1999) "Infertility Among Yoruba Women: Perceptions on Causes, Treatments and Consequences", *African Journal of Reproductive Health* 3(1): 13–26.

Krause, Kristine (2008) "Transnational Therapy Networks among Ghanaians in London", *Journal of Ethnic and Migration Studies* 34(2): 235–251.

Kuponu, Selome I. (2007) "The Living Faith Church (Winners Chapel), Nigeria: Pentecostalism, Prosperity Gospel and Social Change", PhD dissertation, University of Bayreuth, Germany.

Maxwell, David (2006) *African Gifts of the Spirit: Pentecostalism & the Rise of a Zimbabwean Transnational Religious Movement*, Oxford: James Currey.

Mojekwu, Joseph N. and Uche Ibekwe (2012) "Maternal Mortality in Nigeria: Examination of Intervention Methods", *International Journal of Humanities and Social Science* 2(20): 135–149.

November, Lucy (2014) "The Impact of Faith-based Organisations on Public Health and Social Capital", A FaithAction Review and Policy Paper, available at: www.faithaction.net/2014/09/26/faithaction-report-impact-faith-based-organisations-public-health-social-capital/ (accessed 4 August 2019).

Odeyemi, Isaac A. (2014) "Community-based Health Insurance Programmes and the National Health Insurance Scheme of Nigeria: Challenges to Uptake and Integration", *International Journal for Equity in Health* 13(1): 1–13.

Odeyemi, Isaac A. and John Nixon (2013) "Assessing Equity in Health Care Through the National Health Insurance Schemes of Nigeria and Ghana: A Review-based Comparative Analysis", *International Journal for Equity in Health* 12(1): 9–26.

Ojo, Matthews A. (2006) *The End-time Army: Charismatic Movements in Modern Nigeria*, Trenton, NJ: Africa World Press.

Olivier, J., C. Tsimpo, R. Gemignani, M. Shojo, H. Coulombe, F. Dimmock, M.C. Nguyen, H. Hines, E. J. Mills, J. L. Dieleman, J. L, A. Haakenstad, Q. Woden (2015) "Understanding the Roles of Faith-based Health-care Providers in Africa: Review of the Evidence with a Focus on Magnitude, Reach, Cost, and Satisfaction", *Lancet* 386: 1765–1775.

Olukoya, Daniel K. (1999) *Violent Prayers to Disgrace Stubborn Problems*, Lagos: The Battle Cry Christian Ministries.

Olukoya, Daniel K. (2004) *Prayer Warfare Against 70 Mad Spirits*, Lagos: The Battle Cry Christian Ministries.

Onyigbuo, Chineme C., Camille Alexis-Garsee, and Olga van den Akker (2016) "An Exploration of Health-Seeking Behaviours Among Nigerian Christians in the UK: Towards Enhanced Health Services Utilisation", *Mental Health, Religion & Culture* 19(1): 255–267.

Owoeye, Saibu A. (2010) "Healer-Prophets and Dynamics of Power", in David Ogunbile and Akintunde E. Akinade (eds) *Creativity and Change in Nigerian Christianity*, Lagos: Malthouse Press Limited, pp. 171–192.

Oyedepo, David O. (2008) *Signs & Wonders Today: A Catalogue of the Amazing Acts of God Among Men*, Lagos: Dominion Publishing House.

Parsitau, Damaris S. (2009) "'Keep Holy Distance and Abstain Till he Comes': Interrogating a Pentecostal Church's Engagements with HIV/AIDS and the Youth in Kenya", *Africa Today* 56(1): 44–64.

Pearce, T.O. (1995) "Women's Reproductive Practices and Biomedicine: Cultural Conflicts and Transformations in Nigeria", in F. D. Ginsberg and R. Rapp (eds) *Conceiving the New World Order: The Global Politics of Reproduction*, Berkeley: University of California Press, pp. 195–208.

Peel, John D. Y. (2000) *Religious Encounter and the Making of the Yoruba*, Bloomington: Indiana University Press.

Pfeiffer, James (2011) "Pentecostalism and AIDS Treatment in Mozambique: Creating New Approaches to HIV Prevention Through Anti-Retroviral Therapy", *Global Public Health* 6(sup2): 163–173.

Prince, Ruth with Philippe Denis and Rijk van Dijk (2009) "Introduction to Special Issue: Engaging Christianities: Negotiating HIV/AIDS, Health, and Social Relations in East and Southern Africa", *Africa Today* 56(1): v–xviii.

RAPAC (2019) "Who We Are", available at: www.rccgrapac.org/index.php?cat_id=138&item=201&dbSto=store_categories&dbItm=store_items&sprintell=#.XaIHJG5Fw3A (accessed 14 July 2019).

RCCG (2008) *RCCG Reproductive and Family Health Policy*, Lagos: RCCG/RAPAC.

RCCG (2011) *The Redeemed AIDS Programme Action Committee, RCCG/HIV/AIDS/STI Strategic Plan 2007–2011*, Lagos: RCCG/RAPAC.

RCCG (2009) *RAPAC 12th Anniversary Booklet*, Lagos: RCCG/RAPAC.

RCCG (n.d.) *RCCG HIV/AIDS Policy*, Lagos: RCCG/RAPAC.

Redeemed People's Mission (1998) "Lesson 11. Divine Health and Healing", *Redeemed Adult Sunday School Lessons*.

Sanusi, Leke (2004) *None shall be Barren: A Testimony of a Couple's Trials and Triumphs over Barrenness*, Enumclaw, WA: WinePress Publishing.

Scorgie, Fiona (2007) "Plural Health Systems", ARHAP International Colloquium, Cape Town, South Africa, 13–16 March, Collection of Concept Papers, pp. 55–64.

Secker, Emilie (2013) "Witchcraft Stigmatization in Nigeria: Challenges and Successes in the Implementation of Child Rights", *International Social Work* 56(1): 22–36.

Smith, Daniel J. (2014) *AIDS Doesn't Show Its Face: Inequality, Morality, and Social Change in Nigeria*, Chicago: University of Chicago Press.

Thomas, Felicity (2010) "Transnational Health and Treatment Networks: Meaning, Value and Place in Health Seeking amongst Southern African Migrants in London", *Health & Place* 16(3): 606–612.

Thompson, Elizabeth, Diane Berry, and Laura Nasir (2009) "Weight Management in African-Americans Using Church-based Community Interventions to Prevent Type 2 Diabetes and Cardiovascular Disease", *Journal of the National Black Nurses Association* 20(1): 59–65.

Tomalin, Emma, Joanna Sadgrove, and Roxanne Summers (2019) "Health, Faith and Therapeutic Landscapes: Places of Worship as Black, Asian and Minority Ethnic (BAME) Public Health Settings in the United Kingdom", *Social Science & Medicine* 230: 57–65.

Trinity Chapel (2006) "Community Health Check Day", *New Life Style* 5(10): 8.

Udodiong, Inemesit (2018) "Church Member Accuses Christ Embassy Founder of Performing Fake Miracles", *Pulse NG*, available at: www.pulse.ng/communities/religion/pastor-chris-oyakhilome-church-member-accuses-christ-embassy-founder-of-performing/3b98yyp (accessed 16 October 2019).

Ukah, Asonzeh F-K (2008) *A New Paradigm of Pentecostal Power: A Study of the Redeemed Christian Church of God in Nigeria*, Trenton, NJ: Africa World Press.

Uzochukwu, B. S. C. (2017) *Primary Health Care Systems (PRIMASYS). Case Study of Nigeria*, Geneva: World Health Organization.

UNESCO (1994) *Salamanca Statement and Framework for Action on Special Needs Education*, New York: UNESCO.

Wagstaff, Adam and Mariam Claeson (2004) *The Millennium Development Goals for Health: Rising to the Challenges*, Washington, DC: World Bank Publications.

WHO (2015) *Health in 2015: From MDGs to SDGs*, Geneva: WHO.

WHO (2016) *World Health Statistics 2016: Monitoring Health For the SDGs*, Geneva: WHO.

WHO (2017) "Nigeria HIV Country Profile: 2016", available at: www.who.int/hiv/data/Country_profile_Nigeria.pdf?ua=1 (accessed 28 September 2019).

Williams, Joseph W. (2012) *Spirit Cure: A History of Pentecostal Healing*, Oxford: Oxford University Press.

Yong, Amos (2011) *The Spirit of Creation: Modern Science and Divine Action in The Pentecostal-Charismatic Imagination*, Grand Rapids, MI: Eerdmans.

6 Pentecostals, human rights, and the family

Introduction

Kuramo Beach is situated on Victoria Island, a business hub of Lagos metropolis. Facing out to the Atlantic Ocean, it used to be a tourist attraction, but has now become an abode for child prostitutes, drug addicts, and criminal gangs. The beach is littered with discarded bottles and syringes. Shacks made out of cardboard, scrap wood, and tarpaulin are crammed together just above the high-tide zone. During the day, boys from Kuramo Beach go out on to the streets of Lagos to hustle and scavenge for food in an attempt to scrape a living, only to return to the beach at night because they cannot afford accommodation. Girls as young as 11 ply their trade as commercial sex-workers under the sway of pimps who profit from their exploitation.

Yet this is not the whole story. In recent years the streets and beaches of Lagos have become a focus for intensive religious activities. If one visits Kuramo Beach on a Sunday morning one is likely to encounter the ministry of Habitation of Hope, a social initiative started by a group of women belonging to the RCCG which seeks to rescue and rehabilitate street children. Already they have started a church on the beach and opened other branches in Lagos specifically to serve the needs of those living on the streets.

Street children and youth are a common feature of Nigeria's cities. Some have left home voluntarily in search of a better life; others have been abandoned by their families. Many are victims of internal human trafficking and child witchcraft accusations. This chapter investigates Pentecostal responses to human rights violations associated with women, young people, and children. The first part of the chapter discusses recent debates on religion, human rights, and development, especially as they impinge upon the experience of women and children in Africa. This is followed by an examination of Pentecostal interventions. Increasingly, Pentecostal churches are establishing "ministries" and NGOs in order to address the needs of street children, prostitutes, and victims of trafficking and domestic abuse. As I will show, these initiatives are shaped by Pentecostals' religious worldview, their conceptions of the family, and a theology of ministry that emphasizes healing, empowerment, and transformation.

Religion, human rights, and development

The relationship between religion, human rights, and development in Africa must be understood within the wider context of the global human rights movement. Human rights scholars and advocates agree that human rights and development are interdependent and mutually reinforcing (Tlakula 2004). The Universal Declaration of Human Rights (1948) sought to globalize human rights by declaring that "all human beings are born free and equal in dignity and rights". The notion of universal rights has been repeatedly challenged by proponents of cultural relativism, including African scholars, who question the applicability of the Western concept of human rights in countries from the global South (Ake 1987; Cobbah 1987; Deng 2004; Ilesanmi 1995). Cultural relativists argue that morality is culture-specific and human rights are culturally relative to different contexts. In debates on human rights in Africa, advocates of a uniquely African concept of human rights contrast the African emphasis on communal solidarity and interdependence with the individualism of the Western liberal human rights tradition. An important attribute of the notion of African human rights is the relationship between rights and duties: individual and communal rights are tied to obligations and responsibilities (Ibhawoh 2018).

Africa is only one of three regions, alongside Europe and the Americas, to have a regional human rights system. The central document of the African human rights system is the African Charter on Human and People's Rights (known as the Banjul Charter), which entered into force in 1986 and was ratified by all 53 members of the Organisation of African Unity (superseded in 2002 by the African Union). The African Charter recognized not only "first generation" (i.e. political and civil) rights but also "second generation" rights to economic, social, and cultural development (ACHPR, Article 22). It took as its point of departure the Universal Declaration of Human Rights. Unlike the latter, however, the African Charter stressed the importance of both individual and communal rights as well as the link between rights and duties (Mutua 1995; Zeleza 2007). Other African human rights instruments include the African Charter on the Rights and Welfare of the Child (1990) and the African Charter's Protocol on the Rights of Women in Africa (2003). Thus, Africa has a relatively robust position on human rights; they are not always upheld in practice, however, as it is dependent upon the political will of individual states to turn potential into reality.

In 1986, the United Nations Declaration on the Right to Development declared the right to development as an

> inalienable human right by virtue of which every human person and all peoples are entitled to participate in, contribute to, and enjoy economic, social, cultural and political development, in which all human rights and fundamental freedoms can be fully realized.
>
> (UN 1986 Article 1)

More recently, a rights-based approach to development, which incorporates the principles of equality, accountability, empowerment, and participation, has gained traction within development circles (Tomalin 2013). Such an approach "involves the pursuit of human rights as part of development as well as the adoption of human rights principles to guide development cooperation and programming" (Tomalin 2013: 129).

A common criticism levelled against universal human rights discourse is that it ignores the ways in which religion and culture shape social ethics, especially in the global south (Tomalin 2006). Debates about the relationship between religion and human rights often consider religion as problematic for the pursuit of human rights: there is a widespread tendency to associate religion with violence and intolerance. However, faith-based organizations are often at the forefront of human rights campaigns and initiatives. The challenge for development actors is to keep the destructive side of religion in check by developing its positive potential (Ter Haar 2011).

In order to understand Nigerian Pentecostal approaches to human rights, one must take account of their religious worldview. In contrast to secular approaches to human rights, religious approaches acknowledge "the existence of an invisible sphere distinct but not separate from the visible world that contains power to affect human life" (Ter Haar 2011: 313). As Ter Haar (2011: 305) notes, if a "spiritual dimension is deemed to be an essential part of the human condition, it means that this religious or spiritual aspect cannot be ignored in human rights debates". Religious practitioners and human rights actors are both concerned with the moral dimension of life, even if they may seek to combat evil in different ways. In African societies, religion is often the idiom in which popular perceptions of good and evil are expressed. As we will see later, alongside more conventional interventions such as advocacy, awareness campaigns, and rehabilitation programmes, Nigerian Pentecostals seek access to the "power of the Spirit" through prayer and spiritual warfare in order to combat evil forces deemed responsible for human rights infringements.

One of the tensions between religious and secular approaches to human rights is over the issue of rights versus responsibilities. Religious advocates of human rights are critical of the emphasis of secular liberalism on individual rights over duty to family and the wider religious community, as well as its failure to take account of the religious obligation to act according to divinely sanctioned laws (Tomalin 2013). Nigerian Pentecostals' emphasis on duties and responsibilities is manifested in a rehabilitation process that includes discipleship and empowerment programmes intended to turn street boys and girl prostitutes into responsible citizens who are able to make positive contributions to their families, churches, and the wider society.

Women, religion, and human rights

Gender discrimination and violence against women are major obstacles to sustainable development. Violence against women, particularly "intimate partner" violence (IPV), has previously been seen as a "private matter, a cultural and family issue, or at best, pertinent to social welfare policies" (Carrillo 1990: 28). In Nigeria, where there are high levels of IPV, women are reluctant to report episodes to law enforcement agents. There is a culture of silence surrounding such abuses, and a fear of stigmatization in a patriarchal society which commonly accepts the beating of wives as a form of discipline (Aihie 2009; Smith 2016). Many victims also suffer in silence because of their economic dependence upon men (Adebayo and Kolawole 2013). Despite the constitutional provision for the protection of women's rights in Nigeria, violence against women has continued unabated (Home Office 2016; Udobang 2018).

Violence against women was recognized in the Millennium Declaration of September 2000 in which the UN resolved "to combat all forms of violence against women and to implement the Convention on the Elimination of All Forms of Discrimination against Women" (UN 2005: 12, cited in WHO 2005: 2). Gender equality and women's empowerment were the focus of MDG Goal 3. However, they were addressed via a single target: to achieve parity between males and females in primary and secondary education (Fukuda-Parr 2016). Significantly, violence against women was not highlighted in the MDG targets or indicators. The SDG agenda is broader with respect to gender. The specific goal focusing on women and gender issues, Goal 5, calls upon countries to eliminate all forms of discrimination against women and girls (5.1), along with harmful practices such as violence against women and girls, including trafficking and sexual exploitation (5.2); forced marriage; and female genital mutilation (5.3).

A number of African regional human rights instruments include provision for women's rights. The African Charter recognizes and affirms women's rights but its provisions are largely seen as inadequate. Although it requires states to ensure the "elimination of every discrimination against women" and "protection of the rights of women", it upholds traditional values and practices that have long hindered the implementation of women's rights in Africa (Centre for Reproductive Rights 2006). The African Charter's Protocol on the Rights of Women in Africa, adopted in Maputo on 11 July 2003, has been an important resource for considering gender as a central component of development (Abusharaf 2011). It was ratified by 15 countries (including Nigeria), and entered into force in 2005. The Maputo Protocol provides broad protection for women's human rights by adding rights that were missing from the African Charter. It provides provisions relating to discrimination against women (Article 1); violence against women and trafficking in women (Article 4); harmful practices, including female genital mutilation (Article 5); marriage (Article 6); separation, divorce and annulment of marriage (Article 7); access to justice and equal protection of the law (Article 8); reproductive rights (Article 14); and the right to sustainable development (Article 19). In 2015, Nigeria enacted the Violence Against Persons Prohibition Act which aims to eliminate all forms of violence, including violence against women, and provide protection and justice for victims of violence.

Religion has played an ambivalent role in fostering gender justice and equality in Africa. Both foreign and indigenous religions are often seen as patriarchal and hostile to women's rights (Para-Mallam 2006). However, religious leaders are also playing a positive role in the "cultural transformation that the realization of gender justice entails" (Abusharaf 2011: 134–135). Studies of gender ideologies within African Pentecostalism have focused on the potential of Pentecostalism to be an agent of gendered social change (Van Klinken 2012; Lindhardt 2015; Burchardt 2018; Soothill 2010, 2015). Most scholars acknowledge that participation in Pentecostal/Charismatic religion, in some sense, offers women empowerment, both in private and in public (Soothill 2010; Lindhardt 2015). Recent research, however, highlights the ambiguities of Pentecostal gender ideologies and rhetoric. On the one hand, according to Burchardt (2018), the theological emphasis on charismatic gifts allows Pentecostal women access to positions of religious authority normally denied to them in traditional culture. Soothill (2015: 213) refers to Pentecostal beliefs about prosperity, victory, and success which "have encouraged women to participate in public spaces beyond the domestic sphere, in church leadership and in civil (sometimes political) society". On the other hand, as noted by Burchardt (2018: 113), "Pentecostal gender arrangements are organized around the paramount value of male headship, male domination and nuclear family norms."

Significantly, the African Pentecostal message of social change is also directed towards male behaviour considered harmful to women (Soothill 2010). Recent research on Pentecostal masculinities suggests that conversion to Pentecostalism brings about change in men's gender identities (Van Klinken 2012; Lindhardt 2015; Burchardt 2018). In the case of Zambian men, according to Van Klinken (2012: 235), Pentecostal conversion "entails a break with popular forms of masculinity in society that they associate with drinking, sexual aggressiveness, violence, absence from the family, and the oppression of women". This echoes official gender discourses within Nigerian Pentecostalism, which promote monogamy, marital fidelity, and the control of sexual behaviour, with equal stress placed upon the responsibility of men to love and respect their wives and the submission of wives to their husbands (Burgess 2008). Nonetheless, despite the rhetoric of radical change, gender inequality and patriarchy persist within Nigerian Pentecostalism, in both the domestic and the public spheres. Smith (2016: 53) refers to the reestablishment of the "patriarchal bargain" by Nigerian Pentecostal churches, in which women "acquiesce to men's authority in return for certain kinds of support", which favours the perpetration of violence against them. While IPV is officially proscribed, Pentecostal women continue to suffer domestic violence (Onoh *et al.* 2013), though this is more likely to occur at the hands of "unconverted" husbands.

Children, human rights, and development

In recent decades, children and youth have featured prominently in human rights discourse and development agendas. However, evidence of the limitations of international agreements, and the difficulties involved in their implementation, is reflected in the growing inequalities experienced by children and young people, especially in developing nations. Significant progress in child survival and development was made towards the MDGs in the areas of poverty reduction, access to healthcare and education, and gender equality (UNICEF 2010). Nonetheless, the MDGs have been criticized for "failing to prioritize inequality and gains for the poorest people" (Dornan 2017: 157). The SDGs advance a more comprehensive and child-inclusive agenda, building on the progress, and addressing the shortcomings, of the MDGs (Minujin and Ferrer 2016). The SDGs address issues related to children's rights such as health (SDG 3), education (SDG 4), gender equality (SDG 5), and violence against children (SDG 16.2).

The post-2015 sustainable development agenda encompasses the cluster of children's rights set out in the Convention on the Rights of the Child (CRC), which came into force in 1990. The CRC includes four guiding principles or categories of rights: non-discrimination between children (Article 2); the best interest of the child (Article 3); the right to life, survival and development (Article 6); and respect accorded to the views of the child (Article 12) (Ansell 2004). The Convention changed the consideration of children from "objects of compassion to subjects of rights" (Minujin and Ferrer 2016: 101). However, some scholars have criticized the CRC for its emphasis on the individual autonomy of the child and the "presumption of independent rights-bearing individuals, rather than social personhood embedded in larger social units – extended families, clans and villages" (Ansell 2004: 230).

The African Charter on the Rights and Welfare of the Child (ACRWC), ratified by 39 of the 54 African states, entered into force in 1999 in response to calls for a regime of children's rights informed by African cultural values (Kaime 2009). The African Children's Charter grants children the "right to express their opinions, but unlike the CRC, there is no requirement for children's opinions to be taken into account" (Ansell 2004: 231). It also specifies children's responsibilities to work for family cohesion and assist their parents and elders in case of need (Ansell 2004).

Nigeria ratified both the CRC and the ACRWC. In 2003, the Nigerian Federal Government enacted the Child Rights Act (CRA) in order to domesticate the principles enshrined in these international instruments under Nigerian law. The CRA incorporates the four guiding principles of the CRC, but also makes provisions for the specific needs of Nigerian children, including child betrothal and marriage (Articles 21–23) and child labour (Articles 28–30). Categories of child labour covered by the CRA include begging for alms, prostitution, domestic and sexual labour, slavery (including trafficking), and street-hawking (CRA 2003). In order to extend protection to all Nigerian children, however, the CRA needed to be passed into law at state level, and although 26 of the 36 states have done so, implementation remains a problem.

In the mid-1980s, UNICEF introduced the concept "Children in especially difficult circumstances" (CEDC) to refer to the minority of children who experience circumstances that are extreme (Ansell 2004). Current UNICEF priority areas include: street children, child labourers, children in armed conflicts, trafficked children, those without primary carers, and those who are subject to sexual abuse and exploitation (Ansell 2004). Many of these circumstances are addressed in Article 39 of the CRC.

Street children, prostitution, and trafficking

Street children and youth have been the focus of considerable academic interest and welfare concern, especially following the United Nations Convention on the Rights of the Child (1989). While most of the early literature focused on the Latin American context, there is a growing body of research on street children in Africa (Ennew 2003; Aderinto 2000; Edewor 2014; Aransiola *et al.* 2009). Studies have emphasized the size of the problem, explored the causes, characteristics, and consequences of a street lifestyle, and discussed various intervention strategies. Recently there has been a shift in the literature from a focus on the needs of vulnerable children to their human rights as citizens (Panter-Brick 2003).

The phenomenon of African street children is closely tied to issues surrounding the family. West African societies are generally organized around extended family networks and have high levels of polygyny compared to other sub-Saharan African societies (Orubuloye, Caldwell, and Caldwell 1991). This has implications for family stability. Where extended family patterns predominate, conjugal relationships are often fragile and prone to separation, divorce, and remarriage. This is especially the case in cities, where there are rising divorce rates and increasing numbers of one-parent families (Olubanke 2009; Orubuloye, Caldwell, and Caldwell 1991).

Research has shown the prevalence of mobility in most African societies (de Bruijn, van Dijk, and Foeken 2001). Early studies tended to equate mobility and migration with the breakdown of family and society. However, de Bruijn, van Dijk, and Foeken (2001: 2) suggest that some forms of mobility are "part of life and of making a livelihood, enabling families to establish connections and negotiate modernity". Rural-urban migration is perhaps the most common form of mobility in West Africa. In most countries in the decade following independence, employment opportunities attracted large numbers of migrants to the cities, resulting in high rates of urban growth. While rates are now declining in some areas due to increasing urban poverty, migration and urbanization remain important issues in the West African context (Tacoli 2001). In Nigeria, megacities such as Lagos or Ibadan are popular destinations for migrants seeking work or to further their education.

Children inevitably become caught up in these mobile networks. Child fostering, which is practised widely in West Africa, is one example of this. Fostering may occur following a crisis such as the dissolution of the family of origin by divorce, separation, or death of a spouse. Often children are sent away to homes where they can learn a trade or further their education. West African fostering is characterized both by its prevalence and by the early age at which it begins. It is practiced by both stable and unstable families, by rural and urban homes, and by wealthy and poor parents (Isuigo-Abanihi 1995). Thus, in many societies, fostering is an accepted means of raising children. As we will see later, it is also one pathway to their ending up on the streets.

Another symptom of family fluidity in West Africa is sexual networking, where spouses seek sexual partners outside the monogamous or polygynous family unit. This practice is quite common in West Africa, where it is widely assumed that most men must have sex with women other than their wives. According to Orubuloye, Caldwell, and Caldwell (1991), there are several reasons for this. There is a lack of social pressure for male sexual continence; the culture prescribes that wives are unavailable for sexual relations during pregnancy and its postpartum period; and there is a perception in a polygynous society that men need a variety of partners. Male extramarital relations may take place with single or married women, but also with prostitutes, who themselves are often separated wives with children to support.

In some studies, street children are depicted as either "throwaways", rejected by their families, or "runaways", seeking a better life away from home. Most writers concerned with African street children report family breakdown linked to poverty as the immediate precipitating push factor that prompts a child to leave home (Kilbride, Suda, and Njeru 2000). However, this tends to stigmatize impoverished families, blaming them for abandoning or discarding their children (Ennew and Swart-Kruger 2003). In the Nigerian context, a multi-level approach to causality is important. At the immediate level, a child may leave home to work on the street due to a sudden drop in income; a loss of support from a parent due to illness, death or abandonment; or an episode of domestic abuse. Sometimes a divorced or bereaved parent marries again and the child is rejected or maltreated by the new step-parent. In certain areas of Nigeria, children have been stigmatized as "witches" and abandoned to live on the streets by their parents (Secker 2013). On a second level, boys may be attracted to the freedom of life on the street compared to the discipline of family life. Sometimes girls are lured away from their family in the village with promises of education and employment only to end up in the city being forced into prostitution by a "foster parent", who may or may not be a blood relative. Finally, structural causes, such as rapid urbanization, economic adjustment programmes, and the failure of state welfare systems, have resulted in widespread poverty and a weakening of extended family ties, forcing some children into work on the streets (Aderinto 2000; Adepoju 2005).

Living on the streets is a precarious and insecure existence compared to being brought up in a stable nuclear family. In Lagos, children and young people are often found living under bridges, in taxi-parks, or on beaches. One discourse surrounding street children classifies them in terms of the risks to which they are exposed and the protective factors available to them, such as school, social networks, and caring adults. Apart from health risks, street children in Lagos are vulnerable to criminal gangs, physical abuse, theft and rape, as well as state violence. Street children and young people are also themselves regarded as risks. A particularly notorious group in Lagos are the so-called "area boys", who roam the streets threatening passers-by and extorting money from market women, businessmen, and bus drivers.[1] Nonetheless, many street children and young people are engaged in legitimate employment, for instance as street vendors, market porters, bus conductors, and shoe cleaners (Aderinto 2000; Olubanke 2009). They are often depicted as living outside the protective environment of their extended family, but they compensate by forming their own networks, groups and hierarchies which function as surrogate families and help to protect them from the police, from rival gangs, and from customers and passers-by on the street (Lalor 1999).

Street children are usually portrayed as victims, villains, or deviants, which influences the types of institutional intervention (Panter-Brick 2003). Thomas de Benitez (2003) distinguishes between reactive, protective, and human rights-based approaches. Reactive approaches regard street children primarily as a threat or potential threat to public order and safety. Politicians in particular are apt to regard the presence of street children as a danger to society. The criminalization of street children in Lagos, for example, has sometimes elicited violent responses from state security forces or led to attempts to "purify" the streets by relocating and/or rehabilitating them. Protective approaches are based on images of street children as victims or as social deviants. Here interventions focus on protecting children from the hazards of street life or rescuing them by placing them back with their family or at school. This may involve healthcare, welfare provision, participation in rehabilitation programmes, and education. For example, in Lagos, the Street Child Care and Welfare Initiative is an NGO that works in partnership with the government to provide shelter and education for children living on Kuramo Beach.

However, some studies question whether these approaches provide lasting solutions because they tend to disempower children by ignoring their own views, categorizing them as "children in need", and emphasizing their weaknesses and dependency (Panter-Brick 2003: 156). Recent approaches have focused on the rights of street children as citizens and their capabilities as agents of change (Thomas de Benitez 2003). A driving force behind this change has been the CRC, which emphasized the legal responsibility of governments towards street children. According to Thomas de Benitez (2003), a rights-based approach draws on images of children as human beings whose fundamental human rights have been violated. It seeks to empower street children by enabling them to gain access to their human rights and by including them in the planning and implementation of policy. Rather than attempting to reinsert children into mainstream society, this approach seeks to bring about structural reforms in educational, health, or welfare provision, and "to change perceptions of homeless children from delinquents or victims to individuals in difficult circumstances in need of empowerment" (Thomas de Benitez, 2003: 11).

Street children are particularly vulnerable to human traffickers, especially if they are orphans or have tenuous links with their natal homes (Adepoju 2005). Human trafficking has become a global industry driven by market forces of supply and demand. Nigeria is one of the leading sources of human trafficking where it has become the third most common crime after drug trafficking and economic fraud (Ofuoku 2010; Osezua 2013). There are two main types: trafficking in children, primarily for farm labour and domestic work; and trafficking in women and children for the sex industry both within and outside the region (Adepoju 2005). Poverty, persistent unemployment, poor education, rural-urban migration, corruption, and criminality have combined to create an environment for trafficking to flourish. Its prevalence is also connected to child fostering, which can be used to conceal practices that amount to trafficking (Adepoju 2005; Carling 2006). Internal trafficking of women and children occurs mainly from rural communities to cities such as Lagos, Ibadan, Kano, Kaduna, Calabar, and Port Harcourt (Ofuoku 2010). Those victims who are enticed into prostitution through internal trafficking networks work under the control "madams", often former sex-workers themselves. A recent development is the establishment of so-called "baby factories", often disguised as hospitals, clinics, or orphanages, where vulnerable women and girls are lured by the promise of good jobs or safe abortions and held until they give birth to babies that are subsequently sold to third parties (Huntley 2013).

International trafficking from Nigeria is a growing phenomenon, fuelled by emigration aspirations and limited opportunities for migrating to Europe or the United States (Carling 2006). Nigeria is listed as one of the countries with the largest number of trafficking victims overseas, especially in Europe but also in the United States, Saudi Arabia, and other African countries (Carling 2006; Osezua 2013; Pathfinders 2018a). Currently, there are an estimated 800,000 Nigerians male and female victims around the world engaged in forced labour and prostitution (Cummings 2017). The majority of Nigerians trafficked for prostitution come from Edo State (particularly Benin City), which has become an internationally recognized sex trafficking hub (Ofuoku 2010; Pathfinders 2018a). The victim's initial contact with a trafficking network is often through relatives or friends. Traffickers entice young women with offers of good jobs and a better life in Europe. The most important European destination for Nigerian trafficking victims is Italy, where prostitution has become a lucrative business. Other destinations include the Netherlands, Spain, Germany, Belgium, and Britain.

Scholars have referred to the role played by local religious traditions in prostitution-related emigration from Nigeria (Carling 2006; Osezua 2013). An important element in the dynamics of Nigerian trafficking is the so-called emigration pact, a religious ritual performed on behalf of the traffickers by an indigenous priest. The pact is regarded as a strongly binding agreement which obliges the victim to repay her "sponsor" the considerable debt incurred for the cost of travel documents (Carling 2006). Reports in the media and scholarly research also suggest the complicity of some Pentecostal churches in supporting human trafficking. Victims often attend Pentecostal churches, and Pentecostal pastors sometimes collude with traffickers by sanctioning the emigration pact through ritual prayers (Pemberton Ford 2017; Carling 2005; Igwe 2019). However, these pastors are by no means representative of the Nigerian Pentecostal community. The Pentecostal Fellowship of Nigeria has used the media to condemn the activities of pastors who offer prayers in support of traffickers (Ebegbulem 2018). As we will see later, some Pentecostal churches run rehabilitation programmes for victims of internal and international human trafficking networks.

Nigeria is party to most of the international human rights instruments combating human trafficking and protecting women and children. In 2003, it enacted the Trafficking in Persons (prohibition) Law Enforcement and Administration, which criminalizes offences related to human trafficking. It also set up the National Agency for the Prohibition of Trafficking in Persons (NAPTIP) to investigate, prosecute offenders, and rehabilitate victims of trafficking (Huntley 2013; Adepoju 2005). Despite these measures, however, levels of human trafficking remain high due to inadequate resources made available to NAPTIP and the lack of political will to prosecute perpetrators, including those within the ranks of the Nigerian military. Nigeria is currently categorized in Tier Two of the Trafficking in Persons Country List, compiled by the US government and Transparency International (Department of State United States of America 2019).

Pentecostal interventions

Alongside secular NGOs and other FBOs, Pentecostals are addressing human rights violations associated with street children and youth, commercial sex-workers, and trafficking victims. During fieldwork, I visited three Pentecostal churches working with street children and young people in Lagos. Fountain of Life Church conducts city mission outreaches that cater for children and young people living on the streets. The ministry began in an area of Lagos notorious for the activities of street gangs. The strategies adopted by the church include regular fellowship meetings in different locations, introduction to formal and vocational education, and medical support. In 2003, the church founded Grace Springs Home as a rehabilitation centre catering for street boys.[2] In 2015, the Lagos State Ministry of Youths and Social Development granted approval for the church to open a Reception Centre for young people willing to be rescued from the streets. The centre serves as the first point of contact where street boys and girls meet social workers and other professionals for counselling and family tracing exercises, selection interviews for rehabilitation, referral to other NGOs, and vocational training (Church Good Works 2018).

I have already introduced Habitation of Hope, which was started after a group of women belonging to the Redeemed Christian Church of God began to evangelize street children at Kuramo Beach. According to Grace Balogun, the pastor-in-charge of Habitation of Hope, the vision for the ministry came to her during prayer when she was instructed by God to go to Kuramo Beach. Within two months, about 500 young people had become Christians. In 2006, the women brought a group of newly converted boys to the RCCG's Redemption Camp ground for the church's annual Holy Ghost Congress. At the end of the week-long event, the boys refused to return to the beach and were temporarily housed in rented accommodation paid for by Pastor Folu Adeboye, the wife of the General Overseer. Since then, Habitation of Hope has opened a residential rehabilitation centre, close to the campground, which houses a chapel, a vocational skills centre, and Hope Academy, a school for former street boys (see Figure 6.1). Some of the residents have gone on to study at Redeemer's University.

Figure 6.1 Signboard for Habitation of Hope, Loburo, Ogun State.
Source: author.

Habitation of Hope has also opened several branches of the church, called "street parishes", specifically geared towards catering for the needs of children on the streets (This Day 2019).[3]

God Bless Nigeria Church (GBNC) is the outreach arm of Freedom Foundation. Every week a band of volunteers from the church, called Gideon's Army, evangelize those living on the streets and invite them to church. Some are then referred to the Freedom Foundation for inclusion in its rehabilitation programmes. GBNC's street ministry began when a group from the church ventured into the Lagos slums adjoining the city's main business district offering food and medical treatment to those living on the streets. Subsequently, small groups called "life centres" were established in different areas of Lagos. On a typical Sunday morning, GBNC is a hive of activity as street children and young people, transported to the church in a convoy of buses, are provided with food, clothing, and medical treatment before joining one of the discipleship classes. Significantly, approximately 80 per cent of church members are former area boys and prostitutes (God Bless Nigeria Church 2010b).[4]

Nigerian Pentecostals are also working with commercial sex-workers, trafficked women and girls, and victims of domestic abuse. Real Women Foundation (RWF) is a faith-based NGO founded by Nike Adeyemi, co-pastor of Daystar Christian Centre. In 1997, Pastor Nike began to visit brothels after encountering prostitutes on the streets of Ikeja local government, which has a high concentration of commercial sex-workers.[5] The Real Women Foundation started in 1999 with a series of seminars for the women and girls befriended by Pastor Nike and her co-workers. Pastor Nike also set up an outreach to prostitutes called the Lord's Angels. In 2002, RWF opened the Peace Villa, a rehabilitation centre for abused women between the ages of 13 and 25 years, including former prostitutes and trafficking victims (Real Women Foundation 2009: 5). The mission of Peace Villa is "To heal and develop abused ladies who will become responsible adults and helpful to others who may experience the same abuse like them in the society" (Real Women Foundation 2019c). When I visited the RWF's premises in 2011, I was told that most of the girls become Christians during the rehabilitation process but continue to have emotional problems which are addressed by trained counsellors and social workers.[6] Love Home Orphanage was set up in 2005 to cater for motherless, abandoned, and abused children. Its objectives as outlined in its publicity material are as follows:

> To bring up children in the way of God; to protect the rights of children; to reduce poverty among vulnerable children; to provide shelter, medical care, food and educational support for the less privileged children; to restore family values; to create and sustain healthy living in families and the community at large.
>
> (Love Home Orphanage n.d.)

RWF also runs a ministry called "For Girls Only", which conducts workshops for girls in public schools across Lagos aimed at teaching them "values and moral dignity" and preparing them for the future as "women, free of abuse and rejection" (Real Women Foundation 2019a). One of the obstacles to tackling trafficking and domestic abuse is the culture of silence surrounding such practices. RWF uses print media and television to publicize the ministry, create awareness, share testimonies of transformed lives, and provide a public forum for discussion of sensitive issues such as depression, rape, abuse, and incest.

Genesis House was founded in 2007 by the Freedom Foundation as a residential rehabilitation centre for commercial sex-workers, trafficked girls, and young women (aged 14 to 30 years old) (Nwabuoku 2010: 9). It started as a shelter for former commercial sex-workers before expanding to include other vulnerable girls and young women who have been sexually abused and trafficked. The majority of its clients came to Lagos in search of a better life or to escape an abusive family situation only to be forced into prostitution in order to survive. Members of God Bless Nigeria Church make regular visits to brothels in Lagos and conduct evangelistic "crusades" for those living on the streets. Some of the girls they encounter are as young as 12 years old. Once accepted as residents of Genesis House, they undergo a rigorous rehabilitation programme encompassing counselling, therapy, social and educational enrichment, vocational job training, and job placement assistance towards economic self-sufficiency (Freedom Foundation 2018).[7] Genesis House also engages in advocacy on behalf of trafficking victims in online blogs and on television. Recently, the Freedom Foundation received a grant from the United Nations Trust Fund for Victims of Human Trafficking to support its work on human trafficking (United Nations Office on Drugs and Crime 2019).[8]

My final example is Hope House, a shelter and rehabilitation centre for survivors of domestic and sexual abuse. Hope House was established by the Pastor Bimbo Odukoya (PBO) Foundation in 2008. Pastor Bimbo (1960–2005) was the first wife of Taiwo Odukoya, founder of Fountain of Life Church. Prior to her untimely death in an aircraft disaster,[9] she was well-known in African Pentecostal circles for her ministry to women and single people. The PBO Foundation was set up "with a mission to rescue, empower, and protect the rights of the woman and the girl child" (PBO Foundation 2015). Hope House provides healthcare, legal services, counselling, and vocational skills training for its clients. The PBO Foundation also runs a rape prevention programme for universities and advocacy projects teaching women and girls about their human rights.

In their ministries to children and young people, Pentecostal NGOs collaborate with Lagos State government agencies, such as the Ministry of Youths and Social Development, the Ministry of Women Affairs and Poverty Alleviation, and the Domestic and Sexual Violence Response Team. They also partner with the National Agency for the Prohibition of Trafficking in Persons (NAPTIP). Other partners and sponsors include local hospitals, schools, banks, and businesses as well as international donors and transnational corporations. They also collaborate with transnational FBOs and churches. For instance, Habitation of Hope uses RCCG networks in Britain and the United States to raise awareness of the plight of street children in Lagos, and its UK office helps to publicize its ministry among RCCG churches in the diaspora. Publicity material produced by Habitation of Hope UK invites donors to sponsor a child and to donate towards projects such as buildings and IT equipment.[10]

The Real Women Foundation partners with Pathfinders Justice Initiative (PJI), a USA-based NGO which seeks to eradicate sex trafficking in Nigeria and the Nigerian diaspora in Europe. The United States has taken a leading role in combating human trafficking, enacting the Victims of Trafficking and Violence Protection Act in 2000. PJI was founded by R. Evon Benson Idahosa, the eldest daughter of the late Archbishop Benson Idahosa, one of the pioneers of the post-independence Pentecostal revival in Nigeria. PJI also works with Church of God Mission International (CGMI), which was founded by Benson Idahosa in 1968. In 1998, Archbishop Margaret Idahosa succeeded her husband as General Overseer following his premature death. The CGMI headquarters is located in Benin City, Edo State, which has become the centre of international trafficking in Nigeria (Carling 2006). One of CGMI's outreach initiatives is the Christian Women Fellowship International (CWFI), which seeks to promote the dignity and development of women, and provide relief to widows, women, and girls in distress.

PJI initiatives in Nigeria include advocacy campaigns, free shelter, and legal representation for trafficking victims, trauma counselling, anti-sex slavery workshops, and vocational skills training (Pathfinders Justice Initiative 2018b). In August 2016, and in collaboration with the CWFI, it launched its first "Anchor" rehabilitation and safe-house centre in Benin City (Pathfinders Justice Initiative 2018b). In August 2018, Evon Benson Idahosa addressed the CWFI's women's convention, which attracts between 20,000–35,000 women annually in Benin City (Pathfinders 2018c). She also spoke at the 2018 edition of Covenant Christian Centre's The Platform event in Lagos. A former lawyer, Benson Idahosa serves as a consultant to the Office of the Senate President of Nigeria on migration and human trafficking, the UK Home Office, and the UN's Special Rapporteur on Trafficking.

Pentecostal interventions are shaped by images of street children and prostitutes as victims, not just of family breakdown or unscrupulous "relatives", but of Satan. For instance, one Pentecostal publication describes area boys as "lost, wandering" and as "ready tools in the hand of the devil" (God Bless Nigeria Church 2010a: 7). Pentecostal responses are also shaped by conceptions of the nuclear family. Despite (or perhaps in reaction to) the prevalence of polygamy in traditional Nigerian societies, and the incidence of sexual networking, Pentecostals emphasize monogamy, fidelity, and control of sexual behaviour. While they acknowledge the importance of extended family structures, they believe that the nuclear family should take precedence (Burgess, 2008). Thus, children who live outside their families, such as street children and prostitutes, are regarded as the deviant "other" in need of rescue, rehabilitation, and, if possible, restoration to their families of origin. This is reflected in the mission statement of the Pulpit in the Street Ministry, the outreach arm of Habitation of Hope: "to help street persons make Heaven; to help them become useful to the society; to raise evangelists out of street persons; to settle and reunite them with their family" (RCCG 2010: 6–7). While the focus on rescue and rehabilitation fits the profile of protective approaches to children and youth, the Pentecostal emphasis on empowerment and transformation suggests affinities with rights-based approaches, as we will see later.

Nigerian Pentecostal churches regard themselves as surrogate extended families, providing close-knit and supportive relationships for those "rescued" from the streets. This is achieved through establishing congregational worship centres which meet in different locations across the city where there are high concentrations of street children and youth. One Sunday morning, I accompanied RCCG's "Pulpit in the Street" ministry on a visit to Kuramo Beach's City of Refuge Parish. Before we set off, a team member called upon the "fire of the Holy Spirit" to "destroy the strong man of Kuramo", a prayer intended to sanctify the "satanic" spaces of Kuramo Beach. On our arrival, the team, equipped with Bibles and loudspeakers, moved amongst the dwellings inviting inhabitants to attend church. The worship service, attended by about 50 people, was standard Pentecostal fare with songs, prayers, preaching, and testimonies, ending with an altar call for salvation. Conversions and water baptisms are regular occurrences at these Pentecostal events. They function as "rituals of rupture", enabling street children and prostitutes to leave behind their former lifestyles. As one pastor told me, the primary aim of RCCG's "Pulpit in the Street" ministry is "bringing the street people to Christ … if they are not rooted in Christ they will go back to the streets".[11]

What sets these Pentecostal initiatives apart from government and other civil society initiatives is their emphasis on spiritual formation, empowerment, and equipping for ministry as evangelists to their former companions on the street. This is reflected in the Real Women Foundation's mission to bring "healing and empowerment" to girls and women affected by sexual abuse and trafficking (Real Women Foundation 2009: 1), and the PBO Foundation's aim to "protect the rights of women and the girl child, rescuing them from all forms of abuse and empowering them to attain to their full potential" (PBO Foundation 2015). God Bless Nigeria Church has an "empowerment" programme to socialize, empower, and mobilize new members. Here they receive physical and healthcare, and are taught spiritual disciplines such as prayer and Bible study (see Figure 6.2). They are also encouraged to be baptized in water and receive Holy Spirit baptism. The programme culminates in the "school of ministry" aimed at turning them into evangelists. Currently, its street ministry (Gideon's Army) comprises mainly former street children who have gone through the discipleship programme. It is felt that their familiarity with street life enables them to reach out effectively to those still living on the streets.[12]

Residential initiatives such as Genesis House and Habitation of Hope aim to help street children and prostitutes to make a clean break from their former life by temporarily removing them from the street environment. They also function as extended families, providing a protective covering from the rigours and risks associated with street life. Presided over by house parents, they involve a strict regime of rehabilitation, which includes school and vocational training as well as the inculcation of spiritual disciplines. Some who have passed through these

Figure 6.2 God Bless Nigeria Church's Empowerment programme for street children/young people in Lagos.

Source: author.

programmes have gone on to gain employment or to study at university; others have married and have children of their own. From a practitioner perspective, the success rate is high compared to government initiatives and other NGOs, although some clients leave because they miss the freedom of life on the streets. One reason for the success of residential initiatives is that they combine loving care with strict discipline and moral guidance characteristic of healthy families.

Despite the churches' role as alternative extended families, initiatives such as Freedom Foundation and Habitation of Hope encourage former street children and prostitutes to be reunited with their families of origin. The Real Women Foundation aims to empower "economically and socially disadvantaged women" to "positively affect their families and the society" (Real Women Foundation 2019b). This is consistent with the emphasis on duties and responsibilities to family and community in African conceptions of human rights. Some studies of African Pentecostalism suggest that the emphasis on rupture and autonomy associated with the born-again experience frees people from social obligations to kinship networks (see van Dijk 1992). However, in a recent study, Martin Lindhardt (2010: 242) suggests that Pentecostal Christians in Tanzania regard "the well-being of a person as being connected to and dependent on the maintenance of good relationships with one's family". While membership in Pentecostal communities does sometimes result in a rupture, at least temporarily, of family ties, in many cases it "enables converts to rework social relationships with family elders and heartily embrace socio-centric identities in new ways".

In the case of Nigerian Pentecostal initiatives, efforts are made to incorporate family networks into the rehabilitation process and to encourage the return of street children to their natal homes (God Bless Nigeria Church 2010b).

Conclusion

Nigeria has ratified several international human rights agreements fighting human trafficking and protecting the rights of women and children. It has also enacted laws to combat child abuse, human trafficking, and violence against women. Despite these measures, however, government implementation at state level remains a problem. In response, Pentecostal churches and NGOs are joining secular NGOs and other FBOs in addressing the needs of street children, prostitutes, and trafficking victims. As I have shown, these initiatives are shaped by Pentecostals' religious worldview, their conceptions of the family, and a theology of ministry that emphasizes healing, empowerment, and transformation. The dominant image adopted by Pentecostals is that of victims in need of rescue. However, their promotion of the stable nuclear family also leads them to regard street children and prostitutes as social deviants in need of rehabilitation and, if possible, restoration to their family of origin. From a practitioner perspective, the success rate of Pentecostal interventions is high compared to government initiatives and other NGOs. Part of their success rests on their function as surrogate extended families, combining a caring environment with a strict regime of rehabilitation. What sets them apart from government and other civil society organizations is their emphasis on spiritual formation, empowerment, and equipping for ministry.

Notes

1 The name "area boys" derives from the way they seek to control a defined locality in order to control the flow of goods and services to their advantage (Gore and Pratten, 2003).
2 Interview, Pastor Taiwo Odukoya, Fountain of Life Church, Lagos, 9 December 2010.
3 Interview, Pastor Grace Balogun, Habitation of Hope, 2 December 2010.
4 Interview, Pastor Nneke, God Bless Nigeria Church, Lagos, 19 December 2010.
5 Interview, Hephzibah Olaleye, Administrator, Real Women Foundation, Lagos, 7 October 2011.
6 Interview, Hephzibah Olaleye, Administrator, Real Women Foundation, Lagos, 7 October 2011.
7 The programme director of Genesis House is Chioma Dike, a gender specialist and human rights activist who obtained a Master's degree in Human Rights and International Relations from Roehampton University, London.
8 During its 2018–2010 funding cycle, the UNVTF funded 28 out of 183 proposals received from NGOs in 72 countries (United Nations Trust Fund for Victims of Human Trafficking 2019).
9 Sosoliso Airlines Flight 1145 crashed on 10 December 2005, resulting in the death of 108 of the 110 aboard.
10 For example, most of the funds for building Habitation of Hope's Hope Academy were raised by RCCG UK (Adedoyin 2010).

11 Interview, Pastor Grace Balogun, Habitation of Hope, 2 December 2010.
12 Interview, Pastor Nneke, God Bless Nigeria Church, Lagos, 19 December 2010.

References

Abusharaf, Rogaia M. (2011) "Gender Justice and Religion in Sub-Saharan Africa", in Thomas Banchoff and Robert Wuthnow (eds) *Religion and the Global Politics of Human Rights*, Oxford: Oxford University Press, pp. 129–156.

Adebayo, Abayomi A. and Taiwo Kolawole (2013) "Domestic Violence and Death: Women as Endangered Gender in Nigeria", *American Journal of Sociological Research* 3(3): 53–60.

Adedoyin, Ayo (2010) "RCCG – Habitation of Hope, Bringing Hope to the Hopeless", *Sunrise Magazine. Special Festival of Life Edition*, Autumn, pp. 44–45.

Adepoju, Aderanti (2005) "Review of Research and Data on Human Trafficking in Sub-Saharan Africa", *International Migration* 43(1–2): 75–98.

Aderinto, Adeyinka A. (2000) "Social Correlates and Coping Measures of Street Children: A Comparative Study of Street and Non-street Children in South-Western Nigeria", *Child Abuse & Neglect* 24(9): 1199–1213.

Aihie, Ose N. (2009) "Prevalence of Domestic Violence in Nigeria: Implications for Counselling", *Edo Journal of Counselling* 2(1): 1–8.

Ake, Claude (1987) "The African Context of Human Rights", *Africa today*, 34(1/2): 5–12.

Ansell, Nicola (2004) *Children, Youth and Development*, London: Routledge.

Aransiola, Joshua O., Olusina Bamiwuye, Akanni I. Akinyemi, and Lanre O. Ikuteyijo (2009) "Proliferation of Street Children in Nigeria: Issues and Challenges", *Journal of Social Work* 9(4): 371–385.

Burchardt, Marian (2018) "Saved from Hegemonic Masculinity? Charismatic Christianity and Men's Responsibilization in South Africa", *Current Sociology* 66(1): 110–127.

Burgess, Richard (2008) *Nigeria's Christian Revolution: The Civil War Revival and its Pentecostal Progeny (1967–2006)*, Carlisle: Paternoster.

Carling, Jørgen (2005) "Trafficking in Women from Nigeria to Europe", 1 July, Migration Policy Institute, available at: www.migrationpolicy.org/article/trafficking-women-nigeria-europe (accessed 2 July 2019).

Carling, Jørgen (2006) *Migration, Human Smuggling and Trafficking from Nigeria to Europe*, Research Series No. 23, Geneva: International Organization for Migration.

Carrillo, Roxanna (1990) "Violence Against Women: An Obstacle to Development", in Charlotte Bunch and Roxanna Carillo (eds) *Gender Violence. A Development and Human Rights Issue*, Rutgers, NJ: Center for Women's Global Leadership, pp. 23–46.

Centre for Reproductive Rights (2006) *The Protocol on the Rights of Women in Africa: An Instrument for Advancing Reproductive and Sexual Rights*, New York: Centre for Reproductive Rights.

Church Good Works (2018) "Grace Springs Rehabilitation Home", available at: http://churchgoodworks.org/projects/grace-springs-rehabilitation-home/ (accessed 20 October 2019).

Cobbah, Josiah A. M. (1987) "African Values and the Human Rights Debate: An African Perspective", *Human Rights Quarterly* 9: 309–331.

Cummings, Ed (2017) "Slaves on our Streets: Tracking the Route of Human Trafficking from Nigeria to Europe – And Back Again", *The Independent*, 29 September, available at: www.independent.co.uk/news/uk/crime/modern-day-slavery-nigeria-uk-human-trafficking-europe-investigation-lagos-slaves-on-our-streets-a7973366.html (accessed 2 October 2019).

De Bruijn, Mirjam, Rijk van Dijk, and Dick Foeken (2001) "Mobile Africa: An Introduction", in Mirjam de Bruijn, Rijk van Dijk, and Dick Foeken (eds) *Mobile Africa. Changing Patterns of Movement in Africa and Beyond*, Leiden: E. J. Brill, pp. 1–7.

Deng, Francis (2004) "Human Rights in the African Context", in Kwasi Wiredu (ed.) *A Companion to African Philosophy*, Malden: Blackwell Publishers, pp. 499–508.

Department of State United States of America (2019) *Trafficking in Persons Report*, June, available at: www.state.gov/wp-content/uploads/2019/06/2019-Trafficking-in-Persons-Report.pdf (accessed 15 October 2019).

Dornan, Paul (2017) "Children, Poverty and the Sustainable Development Goals", *Children & Society* 31(1): 157–165.

Edewor, Patrick A. (2014) "Homeless Children and Youths in Lagos, Nigeria: Their Characteristics, Street Life and Sexual Behaviour", *Mediterranean Journal of Social Sciences* 5(1): 537–545.

Ebegbulem, Simon (2018) "Edo CAN Places Curses on Pastors Aiding, Abetting Human Traffickers", *Vanguard (Nigeria)*, 14 April, available at: www.vanguardngr.com/2018/04/edo-can-places-curses-pastors-aiding-abetting-human-traffickers/ (accessed 21 October 2019).

Ennew, Judith (2003) "Difficult Circumstances: Some Reflections on 'Street Children' in Africa", *Children, Youth and Environments* 13(1): 128–146.

Ennew, Judith and Jill Swart-Kruger (2003) "Introduction: Homes, Places and Spaces in the Construction of Street Children and Street Youth", *Children, Youth and Environments* 13(1): 81–104.

Freedom Foundation (2018) "Genesis House", available at: www.freedomfoundationng.org/genesis-house/ (accessed 21 September 2019).

Fukuda-Parr, Sakiko (2016) "From the Millennium Development Goals to the Sustainable Development Goals: Shifts in Purpose, Concept, and Politics of Global Goal Setting for Development", *Gender & Development* 24(1): 43–52.

God Bless Nigeria Church (2010a) "Anything for the Boys?", *Urban Times: A Publication of God Bless Nigeria Church*, p. 7.

God Bless Nigeria Church (2010b) "Interview with Tenidola Awoyemi, Executive Director, Freedom Foundation. Freedom Foundation. Change has Come", *Urban Times: A Publication of God Bless Nigeria Church*, pp. 4–5.

Gore, Charles and David Pratten (2003) "The Politics of Plunder: The Rhetorics of Order and Disorder in Southern Nigeria", *African Affairs* 102(407): 211–240.

Home Office (2016) *Country Information and Guidance. Nigeria: Women Fearing Gender-Based Harm or Violence*, August, available at: www.refworld.org/docid/57b70ff44.html (accessed 4 October 2019).

Huntley, Svetlana S. (2013) "The Phenomenon of 'Baby Factories' in Nigeria as a New Trend in Human Trafficking", ICD Brief 3, October, International Crimes Database, available at: www.internationalcrimesdatabase.org/upload/documents/20131030T045906-ICD%20Brief%203%20-%20Huntley.pdf (accessed 21 September 2019).

Ibhawoh, Bonny (2018) *Human Rights in Africa*, Cambridge: Cambridge University Press.

Igwe, Leo (2019) "Mobilising Church Leaders Against Witchcraft Allegations in Nigeria", *Guardian Nigeria*, 20 October, available at: https://guardian.ng/sunday-magazine/ibru-ecumenical-centre/mobilising-church-leaders-against-witchcraft-allegations-in-nigeria/ (accessed 24 October 2019).

Isiugo-Abanihe, Uche C. (1995) "Child Fosterage in West Africa", *Population and Development Review* 11(1): 53–73.

Ilesanmi, Simeon O. (1995) "Human Rights Discourse in Modern Africa: A Comparative Religious Ethical Perspective", *The Journal of Religious Ethics* 23(2): 293–322.

Kaime, Thoko (2009) *The African Charter on the Rights and Welfare of the Child: A Socio-Legal Perspective*, Pretoria: Pretoria University Law Press.

Kilbride, Philip, Collette Suda, and Enos Njeru (2000) *Street Children in Kenya: Voices of Children in Search of a Childhood*, Westport, CT: Greenwood Publishing Group.

Lalor, Kevin J. (1999) "Street Children: A Comparative Perspective", *Child Abuse & Neglect* 23(8): 759–770.

Lindhardt, Martin (2010) "'If You Are Saved You Cannot Forget Your Parents': Agency, Power, and Social Repositioning in Tanzanian Born-Again Christianity", *Journal of Religion in Africa* 40(3): 240–272.

Lindhardt, Martin (2015) "Men of God: Neo-Pentecostalism and Masculinities in Urban Tanzania", *Religion* 45(2): 252–272.

Love Home Orphanage (n.d.) Information leaflet.

Minujin, Alberto and Mildred Ferrer (2016) "Assessing Sustainable Development Goals from the Standpoint of Equity for Children", *Journal of International and Comparative Social Policy* 32(2): 98–115.

Mutua, Makau W. (1995) "The Banjul Charter and the African Cultural Fingerprint: An Evaluation of the Language of Duties", *Virginia Journal of International Law* 35(339): 339–380.

Nwabuoku, Helen (2010) "Focus on Genesis House", *The TPH Review*, October, p. 9.

Ofuoku, A. U. (2010) "Human Trafficking in Nigeria and its Implications for Food Security", *International Journal of Rural Studies* 17(1): 1–6.

Olubanke, Akintunde D. (2009) "The Role of the Church in the Care of Street Children in Africa", *LUMINA. An Interdisciplinary Research and Scholarly Journal* 20(1): 1–8.

Onoh, R. C., O. U. Umeora, P. O. Ezeonu, A. K. Onyebuchi, O. L. Lawani, and U. M. Agwu (2013) "Prevalence, Pattern and Consequences of Intimate Partner Violence During Pregnancy at Abakaliki Southeast Nigeria", *Annals of Medical and Health Sciences Research* 3(3): 484–491.

Orubuloye, I. O., John C. Caldwell, and Pat Caldwell (1991) "Sexual Networking in the Ekiti District of Nigeria", *Studies in Family Planning* 22(2): 61–73.

Osezua, O. C. (2013) "Transmogrified Religious Systems and the Phenomenon of Sex Trafficking among the Benin People of Southern Nigeria", *AFRREV IJAH: An International Journal of Arts and Humanities* 2(3): 20–35.

Panter-Brick, Catharine (2003) "Street Children, Human Rights, and Public Health: A Critique and Future Directions", *Children, Youth and Environment* 13(1): 147–171.

Para-Mallam, Josephine O. (2006) "Faith, Gender and Development Agendas in Nigeria: Conflicts, Challenges, and Opportunities", *Gender & Development* 14(3): 409–421.

Pathfinders Justice Initiative (2018a) *Nigeria: Human Trafficking Factsheet*, 27 March, available at: http://pathfindersji.org/nigeria-human-trafficking-factsheet/ (accessed 24 September 2019).

Pathfinders Justice Initiative (2018b) "What We Do", available at: http://pathfindersji.org/what-we-do/ (accessed 24 September 2019).

Pathfinders Justice Initiative (2018c) "Pathfinders Sensitizes Over 20,000+ Women at CWFI Convention 2018", available at: http://pathfindersji.org/pathfinders-sensitizes-over-20000-women-at-cwfi-convention-2018/ (accessed 24 September 2019).

PBO Foundation (2015) *The Annual Report 2015*, available at: file:///G:/monograph_oup/human%20rights/primary/PBO%20Foundation%20Annual-report-2015-Impacting-Change-one-girl-per-time.pdf (accessed 28 September 2019).

Pemberton Ford, Carrie (2017) *Behind Closed Doors – Voices Against Gender-based Violence, Human Trafficking and Modern-day Slavery*, Cambridge: Churches Together in England & Cambridge Centre for Applied Research in Human Trafficking.

Real Women Foundation (2009) *The Real Woman: Ten Years Anniversary Special Edition.*

Real Women Foundation (2019a) "For Girls Only (FGO)", available at: http://therealwoman.org/home/for-girls-only/ (accessed 9 October 2019).

Real Women Foundation (2019b) "Our Mission", available at: http://therealwoman.org/home/our-statement/ (accessed 9 October 2019).

Real Women Foundation (2019c) "Peace Villa (Rehabilitation Centre)", available at: http://therealwoman.org/home/the-peace-villa/ (accessed 9 October 2019).

RCCG (2010) "The Pulpit in the Street Ministry", *Redeemed Christian Church of God, Habitation of Hope, Special Christmas and New Year Edition* 2(1): 6–7.

Secker, Emilie (2013) "Witchcraft Stigmatization in Nigeria: Challenges and Successes in the Implementation of Child Rights", *International Social Work* 56(1): 22–36.

Smith, Daniel (2016) "Modern Marriage, Masculinity, and Intimate Partner Violence in Nigeria", in Kersti Yllö and M. Gabriela Torres (eds) *Marital Rape: Consent, Marriage, and Social Change in Global Context*, Oxford: Oxford University Press, pp. 41–54.

Soothill, Jane E. (2010) "The Problem with 'Women's Empowerment': Female Religiosity in Ghana's Charismatic Churches", *Studies in World Christianity* 16(1): 82–99.

Soothill, Jane E. (2015) "Gender and Pentecostalism in Africa", in Martin Lindhardt (ed.) *Pentecostalism in Africa: Presence and Impact of Pneumatic Christianity in Post-colonial Societies*, Leiden: E. J. Brill, pp. 191–219.

Tacoli, Cecilia (2001) "Urbanisation and Migration in Sub-Saharan Africa: Changing Patterns and Trends", in Mirjam de Bruijn, Rijk van Dijk, and Dick Foeken (eds) *Mobile Africa: Changing Patterns of Movement in Africa and Beyond*, Leiden: E. J. Brill, pp. 141–151.

Ter Haar, Gerrie (2011) "Religion and Human Rights: Searching for Common Ground", in Gerrie ter Haar (ed.) *Religion and Development: Ways of Transforming the World*, London: Hurst & Co., pp. 295–314.

This Day (2019) "Habitation of Hope for the 'Unreachable'", *This Day*, 1 September, available at: www.pressreader.com/nigeria/thisday/20190911/281913069807114 (accessed 23 October 2019).

Thomas de Benitez, Sarah (2003) "Reactive, Protective and Rights-based Approaches in Work with Homeless Street Youth", *Children, Youth and Environments* 13(1): 1–16.

Tlakula, Pansy (2004) "Human Rights and Development", in Paul T. Zeleza and Philip J. McConnaughay (eds) *Human Rights, the Rule of Law and Development in Africa*, Philadelphia: University of Pennsylvania Press, pp. 109–119.

Tomalin, Emma (2006) "Religion and a Rights-based Approach to Development", *Progress in Development Studies* 6(2): 93–108.

Tomalin, Emma (2013) *Religions and Development*, London: Routledge.

Udobang, Wana (2018) "'We Are Brought Up to Think Suffering This Violence Is OK': Domestic Abuse in Nigeria", *Guardian*, 5 January, available at: www.theguardian.com/working-in-development/2018/jan/05/violence-domestic-abuse-nigeria-bullying-husbands (accessed 19 October 2019).

UN (1986) United Nations Declaration on the Right to Development, available at: www.un.org/en/events/righttodevelopment/declaration.shtml (accessed 13 September 2019).

UNICEF (2010) *Progress for Children: Achieving the MDGs with Equity*, New York: UNICEF.

United Nations Office on Drugs and Crime (2019) "Our Funded Projects Around the World", available at: www.unodc.org/unodc/en/human-trafficking-fund/human-trafficking-fund_grants-facility.html (accessed 21 September 2019).

United Nations Trust Fund for Victims of Human Trafficking (2019) "Human Faces & Success Stories Spotlight on NGO Freedom Foundation", *UNVTF Newsletter*, Issue 5.

Van Dijk, Rijk (1992) "Young Puritan Preachers in Post Independence Malawi", *Africa* 62(2): 159–180.

Van Klinken, Adriaan S. (2012) "Men in the Remaking: Conversion Narratives and Born-Again Masculinity in Zambia", *Journal of Religion in Africa* 42(3): 215–239.

WHO (2005) *Addressing Violence Against Women and Achieving the Millennium Development Goals*, Department of Gender, Women and Health Family and Community Health, Geneva: WHO.

Zeleza, Paul T. (2007) "The Struggle for Human Rights in Africa", *Canadian Journal of African Studies* 41(3): 474–506.

7 Pentecostals, violence, and peacebuilding

Introduction

In September 2001, I experienced first-hand a violent clash between Muslims and Christians while teaching in the northern city of Jos. For ten days, until the army intervened, staff and students were confined to the college campus while Muslim and Christian mobs rampaged across the city. As a deterrent to would-be attackers, students armed with machetes took turns to patrol the campus perimeter. Days and nights were disturbed by the sounds of intermittent gunfire, and from the vantage point of a hill overlooking the city we could see smoke rising from multiple locations. A few students ventured out into the neighbouring community, returning with reports of dead bodies on the streets and buildings destroyed.

The crisis began four days before the September 11th terrorist attacks in the United States but received little international media coverage despite extensive loss of life and destruction of property. The violence caught people by surprise because Jos was well-known for its cosmopolitan character and peaceful environment. Unfortunately, similar scenes repeated themselves at least four more times over the next ten years.

The focus of this chapter is on Pentecostalism's developmental role in relation to ethno-religious violence, conflict resolution, and peacebuilding. Violent conflict is a serious obstacle to sustainable development (Ter Haar and Ellis 2006; Poku, Renwick, and Porto 2007). In Nigeria, Islamic resurgence, combined with the growth of Pentecostal/Charismatic Christianity, have exacerbated existing religious tensions, resulting in escalating levels of ethno-religious violence and hindering development. Recent debate on the Nigerian context focuses on the implementation of sharia and the Boko Haram insurgency (Imo 2008; Ukah 2014; Ludwig 2008); the impact of Pentecostal evangelism and use of the media on inter-religious relationships (Akinade 2014; Hackett 2003); and the efficacy of interfaith dialogue and peacebuilding initiatives (Burgess and McCain 2015; Ojo and Lateju 2010). Ethno-religious violence is both a cause and an effect of Nigeria's underdevelopment. On the one hand, the involvement of youths in the violence is exacerbated by Nigeria's high unemployment rate and persistent poverty. On the other hand, successive waves of violence have had a devastating effect on development in terms of the loss of lives, forced migration, and the destruction of property (Abdullahi and Saka 2007; Hackett 2000).

Studies of Pentecostalism in Nigeria have suggested that the venture of Pentecostals into the public arenas of politics and the media to combat "Islamization", combined with their emphasis on evangelism and spiritual warfare, have exacerbated tensions between Christians and Muslims. This has led in turn to protests and retaliation by Muslim groups (Ojo 2007; Ukah 2009; Hackett 2000; Kalu 2008; Akinade 2014). A part of the Roman Catholic critique of Pentecostalism is that Pentecostal mission strategy, which favours evangelistic programmes over interfaith dialogue, militates against religious tolerance and exacerbates inter-religious tensions (Aihiokhai 2010). According to Marshall (2009: 226), the "increasingly aggressive presence" of Pentecostal evangelists in northern cities has "dramatically contributed to the degradation of interfaith relations". Ojo (2007) refers to the relationship of mutual mistrust between Pentecostals and revivalist Muslim groups fuelled by competition for souls, for dominance, and for access to state resources. Nigerian Pentecostals have also been criticized for their emphasis on prosperity theology and its tendency to divert attention from addressing the structural causes of poverty and sectarian violence. What is sometimes overlooked, however, is the capacity of Pentecostal Christianity to play a constructive role in building peace and addressing the social needs of victims of violence. As we will see later, some Pentecostal organizations in Nigeria are responding to ethno-religious conflict in their communities through peacebuilding initiatives.

The main location of my research was the city of Jos and its environs in the Middle Belt, which is roughly the lower half of northern Nigeria. However, the scope of my research also encompasses the core northern states where the violation of Christians' religious freedom is more pronounced. Although most of the interviews with Pentecostal leaders were conducted in Jos, some respondents had first-hand experience of visiting or living in the core northern states. Interviews were also conducted in London to explore the transnational dimension.[1] Jos is the capital of Plateau State, which has become one of the centres of ethno-religious violence in Nigeria over the past two decades. Pentecostalism has a strong presence in Plateau State reaching back to the 1940s when the Assemblies of God planted a church in Jos (1943). Currently, Plateau State has more than 1,000 Assemblies of God congregations (Pam 2013), as well as multiple neo-Pentecostal churches, including branches of RCCG, Deeper Life Bible Church, Winners Chapel, and Mountain of Fire and Miracles. Other important neo-Pentecostal denominations, which have branches in Plateau State, include All Christians Fellowship Mission, Redeemed People's Mission, and the National Evangelical Mission.

The chapter begins with a general discussion of the relationship between religion, conflict and development. It then examines the causes and effects of the violence and violation of religious freedom in northern Nigeria, with special attention given to Pentecostal explanations of the crisis in Plateau State. Third, it explores the diversity of Pentecostal responses to Islam and ethno-religious conflict. Finally, the chapter considers the transnational dimension of Pentecostal responses to violence in northern Nigeria. These include media use and visits to Europe and the USA to raise awareness among the international community, including the Nigerian diaspora.

Religion, violence, and peacebuilding

None of the MDGs specifically addressed the issue of violence. The past decade, however, has seen significant efforts on the part of the UN to develop a peacebuilding architecture and to foster "inclusive national ownership from a wide spectrum of domestic actors" (Shannahan and Payne 2016: 9). At global level, the UN established a Peacebuilding Commission, a Peacebuilding Support Office, and a Peacebuilding Fund. In 2015, promoting peaceful and just societies became Goal 16 of the Sustainable Development Goals. The first target of SDG 16 calls for a significant reduction in "all forms of violence and related deaths everywhere". Violence is also addressed in SDG target 5.2: "Eliminate all forms of violence against women and girls"; and SDG target 5.3: "End abuse, exploitation, trafficking and all forms of violence against children". In 2003, the African Union established the Peace and Security Council (PSC) with an African Peace and Security Architecture built around it, comprising a conflict prevention and resolution capability (Poku, Renwick, and Porto 2007). According to Shannahan and Payne (2016: 9), "Peacebuilding encompasses efforts to foster sustainable peace through measures that address conflict non-violently and tackle its root causes." They refer to the "local turn" within peacebuilding, reflected in the growing recognition of the key role played by local actors. This has important implications for faith-based peacebuilding, "much of which occurs at grassroots level and with hard-to-reach communities" (Shannahan and Payne 2016: 9). The dominant paradigm for those who take on the work of peacebuilding is "liberal peace", which stresses "human rights, democracy, free markets, and the central role of international institutions and state governments in building peace" (Philpott 2010: 4). Philpott (2010) contrasts this with strategic peacebuilding, which involves a far greater array of actors, activities, and levels of society, including religious actors.

Religion can either legitimize or discourage violence (Ter Haar 2005). As Haynes (2008) notes, religion is not necessarily associated with conflict, as it can also play a constructive role in building peace. According to Haynes (2008), when successful, religion's role in resolving conflicts is a crucial component in helping to achieve human development. Alongside studies on religious contributions to conflict and violence, there is a growing literature on religious or faith-based peacebuilding (e.g. Appleby 2000; Little and Appleby 2004; Haynes 2008; Powers 2010; Lederach 2015). Little and Appleby (2004: 5) define "religious peacebuilding" as the "range of activities performed by religious actors and institutions for the purpose of resolving and transforming deadly conflict, with the goal of building social relations and political institutions characterized by an ethos of tolerance and nonviolence". Religious peacebuilding activities are diverse, ranging from high-level mediation to grassroots peace initiatives. Lynch (2015: 600) suggests two primary reasons why faith-based actors are believed to provide "unique advantages to peacebuilding efforts". First, some religious communities are regarded as assets to peacebuilding because they have established roots in given societies. With these roots comes "trust on the part of local populations" and "decision-making authority". Second, religious communities often provide services not provided by governments, including healthcare, education, and basic needs such as food and shelter.

Violence often occurs in contexts where minority religious groups are subject to infringements of their rights to religious freedom. Although the UN recognizes religious freedom as a fundamental right,[2] "only a minority of people today enjoy the kind of liberties of conscience and belief called for in international covenants" (Hertzke 2012: 4). The international community has tended to resist religious interpretations of violence and the "religious persecution" discourse. According to Allen Hertzke (2004: 26), this "stems from a view that religion is a 'problem' – a contributor to intolerance, ethnic strife, and war". The main challenge to this secular discourse has come from the United States, where a new faith-based human rights movement emerged in the mid-1990s, consisting of a broad coalition of evangelicals, Catholics, Anglicans, Jews, and religious minorities. The movement exerted pressure on the US government to amend its foreign policy, culminating in the passing into law of the International Religious Freedom Act (1998) which has transformed the advocacy of religious freedom around the world (Hackett 2000; Hertzke 2004).

Causes and effects of violence and violation of religious rights

Northern Nigeria as a whole has a majority Muslim population. The Middle Belt has a large number of Christians while the "core north" has only a small percentage of Christians. While both religions have global missionary ambitions, Islamic leaders often state that their objective is to implement sharia, which has created considerable regional tension (Imo 2008). Plateau is a non-sharia state with a Christian majority. According to the 2006 Census, the population of Plateau State is 3.1 million. Accurate percentages of Muslims and Christians are difficult to obtain and are also politically contentious. Estimates are 60/40 or 70/30 per cent between Christians and Muslims (Ostien 2012). Jos, with a population between 800,000 and 1,000,000, is the state capital of Plateau State. Ownership of Jos is hotly contested by the three main indigenous ethnic groups (the Berom, Anaguta, and Afizere), on one side of the fight, and the descendants of Hausa-Fulani settlers (today known as the Jasawa), on the other. Other Plateau ethnic groups migrated to Jos either for commerce or for the tin mining industry. These were joined by people from the South, including the Igbo, Yoruba, Urhobo, Ibibio, and Tiv. The city of Jos has proved a favourable location for Western and indigenous Christian missions and is regarded as a bastion of Christianity in the north. Initially, it was a base for the evangelization of

Plateau peoples, but has since become the most important missionary centre for all of northern Nigeria. The presence of large southern populations has reinforced its orientation towards Christianity. After the introduction of sharia in some northern states and its attendant crises, the city experienced an influx of people from Kaduna, Kano, Bauchi, and Zamfara states seeking refuge (Higazi 2011). Episodes of mass killings and destruction occurred in Jos in 2001, 2002, 2008, and 2010. The violence has also affected rural communities surrounding Jos, most recently during the spate of attacks on Christians by Fulani herdsmen in 2018.

Indigeneity laws, sharia, and Boko Haram

Since the 1970s, there has been a resurgence of Islamic fundamentalist and reformist movements due to increased influences from abroad, which is further facilitated by oil money. These groups tend to be intolerant towards Christianity as well as towards more moderate forms of Islam. At the same time, this Islamic resurgence has coincided with the growth of Pentecostal and Charismatic expressions of Christianity. This movement is often characterized by conversion efforts, an antagonistic stance towards other religions, and a growing concern over perceived “Islamic resurgence”, which has exacerbated religious polarization in Nigeria (Ojo 2007; Ukah 2009; Hackett 2011). Haynes (2009) refers to competition between Christians and Muslims as the single most significant political issue in the country. According to Ojo (2007: 184), efforts to add sharia to the 1978 Constitution heightened Christian-Muslim tensions and “transferred the contest to the public arena”. Relations between the two faiths further deteriorated following the government’s decision in 1986 to join the Organisation of the Islamic Conference (OIC). From the late 1980s, Christian-Muslim violence became a common feature of life in northern Nigeria (Haynes 2009; Ojo 2007). Another significant development was the formation of ecumenical organizations, such as the Christian Association of Nigeria and the Pentecostal Fellowship of Nigeria, which have enabled evangelicals and Pentecostals to develop a united front in the face of perceived Islamization in the country (Akinade 2014).

The Nigerian Constitution provides for legal protections and extensive rights to all its citizens, including rights to freedom of religion,[3] and Nigeria is a signatory to several international human rights agreements. Nonetheless, these rights are not always enjoyed by religious and ethnic minorities in some areas of the country. Three interrelated issues have contributed to escalating violence and violation of religious freedom in northern Nigeria: the indigene-settler issue, the imposition of sharia, and the Boko Haram insurgency. Indigeneity laws in Nigeria declare certain ethnic groups in each state “indigenes” thus preventing members from other groups from formally being considered indigenes. The 1979 Constitution originally introduced the concept of “indigeneity” into public law to guarantee a fair regional distribution of power. One consequence, however, is that state governments tend to discriminate against non-indigenes in matters concerning land ownership, political participation, education, and employment (Human Rights Watch 2006). The issue of indigeneity is relegating many Nigerians to the status of second-class citizens in states other than their own (Ejobowah 2013). Despite the constitutional provisions guaranteeing citizenship rights, many states refuse to employ non-indigenes in their state civil services and deny them access to academic scholarships. Non-indigenes also face other discriminatory practices, such as in admission to state universities, barriers to political participation, and access to basic amenities. Such practices are made more harmful by the increasing levels of poverty throughout Nigeria, which create greater demand for civil service jobs normally not available to non-indigenes. In addition, discriminatory policies have served to aggravate interethnic animosity. The indigeneity issue has combined with other factors such as ethnic tensions, religious extremism, and poverty to push inter-communal relationships towards violence (Human Rights Watch 2006). As we will see later, indigeneity laws have had serious repercussions on Christian-Muslim relations in Plateau State.

Currently, sharia has been introduced in 12 northern Nigerian states: Zamfara, Sokoto, Kebbi, Katsina, Kano, Niger, Jigawa, Yobe, Borno, Bauchi, Kaduna, and Gombe.[4] Since its introduction, existing discrimination against indigenous and non-indigenous Christian minorities has increased. Sharia has existed in Nigeria for many years, but until 1999, it had only been applied to personal and domestic law. Democracy returned to Nigeria on 29 May 1999. In the core northern states, it met a traditional, hierarchical society, which had practiced Islam for hundreds of years. Because these states were overwhelmingly Muslim, they were able democratically to enshrine sharia into state criminal law, a move that was popular among many Muslims but opposed by Christians. Discontent among Christians led to public demonstrations, which were viewed as threatening by Muslims, who then responded with violence. Despite initial assurances that sharia would only apply to Muslims, non-Muslims are regularly subject to its structures. Since its introduction, Christian minorities in the core northern sharia states have endured violence at the hands of Islamic militants, greater restrictions on their rights to own land and establish places of worship, and increased levels of discrimination in employment, education, and access to public services. In some areas, abduction, forced marriage, and conversion of Christian women and girls are relatively frequent occurrences (Imo 2008; Ludwig 2008; Ukiwo 2003). In the Nigeria Survey (2011), only a small minority of Pentecostal/Charismatics agreed that Muslims should be free to establish sharia law in their country (9 per cent of Pentecostals and 7 per cent of Charismatics). In the interviews, some respondents regarded the extension of sharia as a violation of Nigeria's secular constitution. Others referred to the discrimination against Christians in sharia states.

Boko Haram is undoubtedly the most significant threat to religious freedom in Nigeria today (Mustapha 2014; Adesoji 2010). In 2016, the Institute of Economics and Peace ranked Boko Haram the deadliest Islamist group after ISIL in its annual Global Terrorism Index report (Institute for Economics & Peace 2016). Since its emergence in 2003, the group has "undermined national cohesion and led to the destruction of livelihoods of over six million residents in Borno, Adamawa and Yobe states" (Abubaka 2017: 33). Boko Haram (meaning "Western education is forbidden") is a Salafi-jihadi group which is seeking to eliminate all "Western influences" and create a "pure" Islamic state ruled by sharia. As well as attacking moderate Muslims and government institutions, the group targets Christian communities and churches in northern Nigeria. By 2009, it had set up a headquarters in the Borno State capital, Maiduguri, launching coordinated attacks in Bauchi, Yobe, Kano, and Borno states. Despite claims that its quarrel was with state officials and assurances that Christians would be safe, Boko Haram proceeded to kill several pastors, destroy over 20 churches and numerous Christian-owned businesses, and hold over 100 Christians hostage at its headquarters for use as human shields against federal forces. During the captivity, male hostages were given the choice to renounce their Christian faith or suffer beheading at the hands of the leader of Boko Haram, Muhammed Yusuf. This was the occasion of the much-publicized "martyrdom" of pastors Sabo Yakubu (Church of Christ in Nigeria), George Orji (Good News of Christ Church), and Sylvester Akpan (National Evangelical Mission). The Pentecostal Fellowship of Nigeria subsequently held a memorial for all the victims of the violence at the National Ecumenical Centre, Abuja (Eyoboka 2009a, 2009b).

Following the destruction of its headquarters and the alleged extrajudicial killing of its leader in July 2009, Boko Haram seemed to disappear. However, an attack in September 2010 on Bauchi prison that freed 100 alleged members, followed by bomb attacks in northern Nigeria, heralded its return. Since then, north-eastern Nigeria in particular has been subjected to a wave of bombings, attacks on church services and Muslim schools, and assassinations of government officials, members of law enforcement agencies, moderate Muslim clerics, and Christians (Christian Solidarity Worldwide 2011).

Some analysts view Boko Haram primarily as an armed response to government corruption, heavy-handed treatment by security forces, and widening economic disparity, especially in the Muslim north (Abubaka 2017; Iyekekpolo 2016; Campbell 2013). Some of my respondents, however, referred to religious as well as political and economic factors behind the violence. A Pentecostal pastor in Jos described Boko Haram's terrorist activities as a "religious war" inspired by the "devil" aimed at Islamization. Similar sentiments were echoed in a newspaper interview given by Pastor Ayo Oritsejafor, former Pentecostal President of CAN, when he urged Nigerians to regard the Boko Haram insurgency as religiously, rather than politically, motivated, with the ultimate goal of Islamizing Nigeria (Okonkwo 2014). The religious agenda of Boko Haram is reflected in its official name Jama'atu Ahlis Sunna Lidda'awati Wal-Jihad (People Committed to the Propagation of the Prophet's Teachings and Jihad), its declaration of jihad against Christians and the Federal Government, and its alleged links with Somalia's al Shabaab and Al Qaeda in the Islamic Magreb (Ajani 2014). In November 2013, the United States government formally designated Boko Haram, and its offshoot Ansaru, as Foreign Terrorist Organizations.

This affirmed US support for Nigeria's efforts to address its domestic terrorist threat and its belief that both organizations have links with Al Qaeda in the Islamic Magreb (US Department of State 2013).

In north-eastern Nigeria, Boko Haram is involved in a systematic campaign of "religious cleansing" through suicide bombings, violent attacks on church services, destruction of church buildings, murder of Christian businesspeople, assassinations of church leaders, and house to house killings in Christian suburbs (Christian Solidarity Worldwide 2013). Despite the government's declaration of a state of emergency in the north-eastern states of Borno, Yobe, and Adamawa in May 2013, and an increase in the campaign to defeat Boko Haram, there was an escalation of the group's activities. While many Christians from southern and eastern ethnic groups have fled to their home areas, the majority of Christians in the north are from indigenous communities and have no other home. To survive, many have been forced to relocate, leaving behind jobs, homes and ancestral lands (Human Rights Watch 2014).

Boko Haram insurgents have also attacked Pentecostal churches in northern Nigeria, including branches of the Assemblies of God, National Evangelical Mission, the Redeemed Christian Church of God, Deeper Life Bible Church, and Winners Chapel. In July 2009, suicide bombers attacked churches belonging to the Maiduguri division of the National Evangelical Mission, destroying buildings and killing church members. In 2014, Eliud Mshelizza, a pastor of Winners Chapel, was killed during a Boko Haram attack in Borno State. In July 2014, RCCG Pastor Taiwo Dokun was killed by Boko Haram insurgents in Borno State, and in July 2015, a suicide bomber attacked a RCCG congregation in Yobe State, killing six people (Pam 2013; Marama 2014; *Daily Post* 2015). The Boko Haram insurgency has forced some Pentecostal churches to close their branches in the areas worst affected by the violence.

Boko Haram has dominated the security discourse in Nigeria since early 2010, creating a climate of fear among both Christians and moderate Muslims throughout the nation but especially in the north. Several respondents referred to the failure of state governments to provide security for non-Muslims, prosecute perpetrators of violence, or compensate victims.

In December 2015, the newly elected president, Muhammadu Buhari, declared that Boko Haram had been defeated (Falode 2016). Sustained military action by the Nigerian government and neighbouring countries has forced Boko Haram to abandon territory it once controlled. However, it remains a significant threat to security in the region (Institute for Economics & Peace 2016). Despite the success of Buhari's counter-terrorism strategy, Boko Haram insurgents have continued to carry out attacks on communities in the north-east region, killing hundreds of Nigerians.

Plateau State and the Jos crisis

Since the Jos crisis started in September 2001, Plateau State has experienced successive waves of ethno-religious violence which have caused considerable anxiety and extensive loss of life. Analysts of the crisis have mainly focused on the indigene-settler issue and the politics of participation in government involving the "indigenous" Plateau peoples and the Hausa-Fulani "settlers" (Higazi 2011; Ostien 2009). In Plateau State, Hausa-Fulani Muslims tend to be defined as "settlers", whereas the mainly Christian Plateau peoples are recognized by the state government as "indigenous". There are also large Christian (mainly Igbo and Yoruba) populations from the South who have been settled in Jos for as long as the Hausa-Fulani and have also been excluded from the benefits of indigeneship. Unlike the Hausa-Fulani, however, they are not contesting with the indigenes for political control of Jos. When violence ensues, the Hausa-Fulani often count them with the indigenes, and communities from the south have incurred significant losses as a result (Ostien 2009). According to Adam Higazi (2011), the indigene-settler issue has served to exclude the Hausa-Fulani from government.

Pentecostal explanations of the crisis are various, reflecting the diversity of the movement (see McCain, Gaiya, and Korb 2014; Gaiya 2015). In the interviews, most pastors acknowledged the complexity of the problem and the entanglement of religious, political, and ethnic factors behind the violence. Some respondents emphasized religious causes, and especially the Islamist agenda of Muslim protagonists. Several pastors described the crisis as "religious persecution" perpetrated against Christians by local Muslims, by northern Muslim politicians, and by Boko Haram. Others referred to political and economic factors behind the crisis, such as competing claims by Plateau Christians and Hausa-Fulani Muslims over "ownership" of Jos and Christian resistance to perceived Muslim ambitions to rule Plateau State. Some pastors referred to ethnic issues and the competition for land between Plateau Christians, who are formally regarded as indigenes, and the settler Hausa-Fulani community. Connected to the issue of land ownership is the ongoing conflict between Muslim Fulani herdsmen and Christian farmers in Plateau State which has led to tit-for-tat killings. Finally, a number of pastors employed militant discourse, interpreting the conflict as a war against Christians. This perspective is represented by Jonas Katung, Pentecostal bishop of Maranatha Bible Church and a member of PFN's national advisory council, who described the crisis as a "war" perpetrated by "terrorists" rather than persecution against Christians.[5] Katung's viewpoint is consistent with the stance of Pastor Ayo Oritsejafor, former President of PFN and CAN, who described the 2011 Jos crisis as a "declaration of war on Christians" (Smith 2011).

Ethno-religious violence in Plateau State has had a significant impact on Pentecostal communities. One consequence of the violence has been the segregation of communities, an indication of deepening polarization in what were once genuinely mixed populations. The city of Jos has experienced increasing segregation along religious lines between Jos North, which is predominantly Muslim, and Jos South, which is predominantly Christian. There are now certain parts of the city that are off-limits for members of the "wrong" religion. One of the effects of the growing levels of distrust, as well as of Christian complicity in acts of violence against Muslims, is the difficulties churches now face in evangelizing their Muslim neighbours. Paradoxically, one respondent reported a rise in Muslim converts to Christianity during the crisis. He explained this in terms of a growing disillusionment with Islam because of its associations with violence against Christians, and the rise of Boko Haram, which targets moderate Muslims as well as Christians.[6]

Meanwhile, church members and pastors have lost houses, cars, and businesses, resulting in severe economic consequences. Families have found it difficult to recover financially, especially when no government compensation has been forthcoming. Muslim radicals have also targeted Pentecostal church buildings in Jos, sometimes in retaliation for Christian attacks on mosques. A pastor of Mountain of Fire and Miracles reported that Muslim militants attacked his church four times in 2011 (see Figure 7.1).[7] Another pastor explained how the Christ Apostolic Church headquarters in Kwararafa, Jos North, was burnt down and the pastor killed in 2011 in a reprisal attack by Muslims after indigenous Christians had attacked and killed Muslims in nearby Gada Biyu during their *salat* prayers.[8] Significantly, there were also accounts of Muslims protecting Christians and church buildings from attacks by fellow Muslims. Assemblies of God Pastor Kenneth Amadi described his experience during the 2001 Jos crisis: "When it started in Bukuru, my church was the first place they came to. They attempted to burn the church but my Muslim friends who were around me stopped them."[9]

The recurrent crises in Plateau State have resulted in thousands of lives being lost and many more injured. Most pastors referred to church members,

Figure 7.1 Concrete bollards and sandbags protecting Mountain of Fire and Miracles church in Jos from attacks by suicide bombers.

Source: author.

family members, and friends who had been injured or lost their lives either during Christian-Muslim riots or as a result of attacks by Boko Haram terrorists. One pastor said that four members of his church in Jos died and about 60 were injured following an attack by a Boko Haram suicide bomber. Another attack by Boko Haram on God's Chosen Church in Jos North resulted in two fatalities and 52 injured (Pflanz 2012). Pentecostal Pastor Comfort Padanu, who leads a social ministry for widows in Jos, said that during the previous few years about 800 widows have been added to the list of those they assist. Many are young widows whose husbands have been killed during these crises.[10]

Some pastors in Jos reported a significant decline in church attendance due to increased security measures on Sunday mornings, which make travel difficult; the killing of church members; the relocation of members to other parts of the city or to their homes in southern Nigeria; and fear of terrorist attacks. To some extent, this has been offset by church-planting strategies which have made branches more accessible and less vulnerable. For example, Shekinah Global Gospel Ministries, located in Jos North, claimed a membership of 500 in 2008. Following the 2008 Jos crisis, attendance dropped to less than 100. The church school was also affected, as enrolment fell from almost 700 to about 150. The church eventually opened a second branch in a more secure area of Jos South, and membership rose to about 200.[11]

The attacks by Muslims have often not gone unanswered. For example, in response to attacks by Hausa Muslims, some people from Christian communities lashed out against Muslim Fulanis in 2001. In the following years, Fulanis retaliated by raiding predominantly Christian villages and deliberately targeting women and children. The most notorious incident occurred in March 2010 with an attack on the Dogo Nahauwa, Zot, and Ratsat villages, which claimed an estimated 400 lives. This is widely believed to have been an act of retaliation following an attack by Christian mobs in January 2010 on the predominantly Muslim town of Kuru Karama, which killed at least 150 residents (Human Rights Watch 2010a, 2010b). Unfortunately, revenge and retaliation have become regular features of ethno-religious violence in Plateau State. While these attacks are partly motivated by land disputes between Muslim Fulani herdsmen and Christian farmers, some commentators suspect that Islamic extremists from outside Nigeria have aided and incited the Fulani.[12]

Pentecostal responses and development interventions

Pentecostal responses to ethno-religious violence are various, ranging from interfaith dialogue and peacebuilding initiatives to relief and rehabilitation programmes. Pentecostals have also used the media and transnational networks to raise awareness of violence perpetrated against Christians in northern Nigeria. To a large extent, their responses are shaped by the different narratives constructed to explain the crisis (McCain, Gaiya, and Korb 2014).

Dialogue and interfaith friendship

Interfaith dialogue is an important approach to conflict prevention and peacebuilding in northern Nigeria (Ojo and Lateju 2010; Akinade 2014). According to Hackett (2011: 137), a "deficit of dialogue" in conflict-ridden contexts is "a recipe for the manipulation of 'fault-lines' and historical memory, at times leading to violence". She suggests that religious leaders "have the capacity and authority to set the tone for (and mediate) reconciliation". In the literature, a distinction is made between high-level bodies and grassroots initiatives (Hackett 2000). Examples of national bodies in Nigeria engaged in interfaith dialogue include the Nigerian Supreme Council for Islamic Affairs, the Christian Association of Nigeria, and the Nigerian Inter-Religious Council.

The Pentecostal emphasis on evangelism and the tendency to demonize Islam in Pentecostal rhetoric exacerbates Christian-Muslim relations and militates against dialogue and conflict resolution. As Kalu (2008: 246) notes, the African Pentecostal combination of the uniqueness of Jesus' claims and urgency of mission hinders the development of interfaith dialogue. Kalu proposes that Nigerian Pentecostals overcome their fear of pluralism and "develop a concept of dialogue for the sake of a stable public space" (2008: 246). The Nigeria Survey shows high levels of mistrust among Nigerian Pentecostals and Charismatics: 80 per cent of Nigerian Pentecostals and 85 per cent of Nigerian Charismatics stated that they trust Muslims a little or not at all (Nigeria Survey 2011). A significant majority of Nigerian Pentecostal/Charismatics say that most or many Muslims are hostile towards Christians in their country (68 per cent of Nigerian Pentecostals and 80 per cent of Nigerian Charismatics) (Nigeria Survey 2011). Some of the Jos pastors emphasized the importance of building trust between Muslims and Christians through interfaith dialogue and establishing friendships with local Muslims, an example of bridging social capital. This approach is more likely to be adopted by those who downplay the religious factor and explain the crisis in terms of land ownership and interethnic tensions (McCain, Gaiya, and Korb 2014). However, several pastors expressed reservations about the value of dialogue because they felt that Muslims lacked sincerity. This response was quite common among respondents and suggests that deep mistrust persists between the two communities.

Doubts about the efficacy of interfaith dialogue are often based on bitter experience. The Interfaith Mediation Centre (IMC) in Kaduna was co-founded in 1995 by two former enemies: Assemblies of God Pastor James Wuye and Imam Muhammed Ashafa. Kaduna is the capital of Kaduna State in the north-western geopolitical zone. Both the city and the state have roughly equal populations of Muslims and Christians, who have co-existed for generations. However, the city has experienced major sectarian riots since the mid-1980s. In the aftermath of the 2000 sharia crisis in Kaduna, the IMC brokered a Muslim-Christian peace accord called the Kaduna Peace Declaration. This was followed three months later by another outbreak of violence associated with the Miss World controversy, which Christians blamed on Muslims. One pastor in Jos compared the efficacy of interfaith dialogue in Plateau and Borno states. During his years growing up and working in Borno State, relationships between Muslims and Christians were generally cordial. Today, however, he finds it difficult to trust Muslims because of their treatment of Christian minorities. In Jos, by contrast, where the balance of power between the two religious communities is more equal, and Muslims have also suffered as a result of the conflict, he believes that interfaith dialogue may be beneficial.[13]

Despite the mutual distrust that exists between the two religious communities, there is a willingness on the part of some Pentecostal pastors to engage with Muslims and work proactively with them to bring about peace. Several pastors are intentionally seeking to establish friendships with Muslims in their communities. For example, a pastor in Dadin Kowa, a religiously mixed area of Jos South which has remained relatively peaceful, said that he deliberately cultivated friendships with local Muslim leaders and engaged in dialogue with them.[14] Another pastor said that during the 2008 crisis his church members donated foodstuffs and clothing to poor Muslim families in the community, which helped them to develop interfaith friendships.[15]

Akintunde Akinade refers to this approach to inter-religious engagement as the dialogue of life, the daily encounter with the "existential realities" of those from other faiths. In the dialogue of life, "one relates to the Other with respect and attention in all of his or her Otherness" (Akinade 2014: 139–140). As Amos Yong (2008: 138) notes, practices of inter-religious hospitality are "key both to the flourishing of Nigeria as a nation and the reconciliation of its citizens across religious lines". Such a "stranger-centred" theology of hospitality

> opens up a "free space" where people of other faiths can enter, where strangers, even enemies, might be transformed into friends, where hosts do not dictate how guests must change but rather provide a safe forum for changes to occur.
>
> (Yong 2008: 132)

Community organizing and peacebuilding initiatives

Some Pentecostal leaders in northern Nigeria have moved beyond dialogue to engage in community organizing and peacebuilding across the religious divide. Since its inception in 1995, the Interfaith Mediation Centre has been involved in mediating religious conflicts in Kaduna, Jos, and Bauchi (Hackett 2011; Ojo and Lateju 2010). One of the IMC's aims is to encourage dialogue and promote a culture of mutual respect and acceptance of diversity by drawing on the faith traditions of both religions and using references from the Bible and the Quran (O'Connor 2013). The Centre trains interfaith mediators at the grassroots level in different communities and provides counselling and resettlement services to those affected by ethno-religious violence. Pastor Wuye and Imam Ashafa have faced opposition from some Muslims who regard all peace organizations as supported by Western institutions and therefore untrustworthy. They have also encountered resistance to the interfaith approach to conflict prevention from some Christian leaders. Pastor Wuye acknowledges that there is tension between the need to speak out publicly against violations of Christian rights in the north and the need for conciliatory language to promote peaceful resolution (Marshall 2011).[16]

The Young Ambassadors for Community Peace and Inter-Faith Foundation (YACPIF) was founded by Assemblies of God Pastor Yakubu Pam in Jos.[17] In December 2009, Pam gathered a group of Muslim youth who lived near his church to discuss peace principles. His efforts were put to the test in January 2010, when a major crisis broke out between Christians and Muslims in Jos. Significantly, some of the Muslim men he had trained protected his church when other Muslim youth from outside the area tried to destroy it. Soon after, he started the YACPIF.[18] Since then, Pam has organized a series of community-wide peace rallies involving Christian and Muslim youth. He has also opened a centre in a neutral area of Jos where both Christian and Muslim youth can meet together to watch films, develop friendships, build conflict resolution and leadership skills, and plan peace programmes in their respective areas (Pam and Korb 2011; McCain, Gaiya, and Korb 2014).[19] In 2011, the foundation's peace campaigns led to the establishment of the "Conciliation Group", a consultation forum involving political groups aimed at discouraging any recourse to violence for the settlement of political differences (*Sahara Reporters* 2011).

Through this foundation, some of the leading perpetrators of the violence have now become advocates of peace and reconciliation. Most of those involved in the violence are unemployed youth located on the margins of society. Many belong to street gangs and are engaged in various criminal activities in order to finance their drug habits. According to Rev. Pam, politicians on both sides of the religious divide are sponsoring the youth for their own political ends. In response, the foundation offers vocational skills training and loans to empower the youth and enable them to start their own businesses, making them less vulnerable to manipulation by unscrupulous politicians. Significantly, the foundation does not seek to convert Muslims who participate in its programmes. In fact, it is crucial for its approach to peacebuilding that Muslim peace ambassadors remain engaged with their religious communities, which would be difficult if they converted to Christianity. Rev. Pam claims that the strategy of engaging the youth as peace ambassadors has succeeded in reducing levels of ethno-religious violence in Jos, though his optimism is tempered by concerns over the threat posed by Boko Haram.[20]

Pentecostal women have also engaged in peacebuilding and community organizing. African women are often portrayed as passive victims of violent conflict. However, they have also played a key role in peacebuilding and conflict transformation despite their exclusion from formal peace processes (Alaga 2010; Ilesanmi 2017). Esther Ibanga is senior pastor of Jos Christian Missions International. In 2010, she founded an interfaith NGO called Women Without Walls Initiative (WOWWI) in response to the constant cycle of violence in Plateau State since 2001. Prior to founding WOWWI, Pastor Ibanga had organized a march of 100,000, mainly Christian, women through Jos in protest of the February 2010 Dogon-Nahawa crisis in Plateau State which cost many Christian lives, including women and children. Meanwhile, Muslim women led by Khadijat Hawaja organized their own protest march over the killings of Muslims in Jos. The protests "brought women's voices to the fore and also provided them with a platform for an active role in peace building" (Nwangwu and Ezeibe 2019: 178). After the marches, Pastor Ibanga reached out to Khadijat Hawaja and formed WOWWI (Anderson 2017; Ilesanmi 2017).[21] WOWWI describes itself as a "non-governmental, non-sectarian, all inclusive coalition, comprised of progressive Nigerian and international women from every facet of life formed to fight for and advance the cause of women-folk, youth and children, irrespective of ethnic, religious or political affiliation". Its vision is to "develop a non-violent, creative and inclusive approach for conflict resolution and transformation in Nigeria, through women who are natural agents for social and national change" (Women Without Walls 2018). The organization engages women across the religious divide in peacebuilding, trauma healing, advocacy, mediation, empowerment of women and youth, and development projects. WOWWI also joined the Bring Back Our Girls campaign that brought the world's attention to the plight of the Chibok schoolgirls kidnapped by Boko Haram in 2014 (Women Without Walls 2018).

Retaliation and self-defence

As previously noted, Christians in Plateau have sometimes deployed retaliatory and offensive tactics against Muslims. Some of the Jos pastors, however, made a distinction between genuine Christians and so-called "cultural" or nominal Christians, whose Christian identity is a mark of ethnicity rather than a sign of commitment to the Christian faith. Respondents blamed the latter for instigating revenge attacks. None of the Jos pastors said that they would encourage their church members to retaliate. When asked how he teaches his members to respond to the violence, one pastor replied: "With love. Because we preach love. Christ is love. I keep telling them. Inasmuch as we are committed to protecting and remaining here, we don't want to fight anybody. Our weapon is love and prayers."[22]

Responding to Boko Haram killings of Christians in northern Nigeria in 2012, leading Pentecostal pastors, including Ayo Oritsejafor, Enoch Adeboye, and David Oyedepo, issued a public statement insisting that their members would not embark on reprisal attacks (Joseph and Rothfuss 2012). Most pastors interviewed opposed the use of violence by Christians except in self-defence. Some said that they encourage their members to arm themselves with weapons to defend themselves because the government is failing to protect Christians and provide adequate security. Some churches also employ armed security guards who are usually church members.[23]

Pentecostal responses to ethno-religious violence and infringement of their religious freedom are inspired by a variety of biblical texts and themes. Some pastors referred to Jesus' teaching on loving and praying for one's enemies.

Several referred to Jesus' own example of non-resistance when confronted by his enemies. The theme of Christian persecution is another strand of biblical teaching and Christian tradition that has proved particularly poignant to Christians suffering the consequences of conflict and discrimination.

Social responses

Another Pentecostal response focuses on providing practical help to Christians and Muslims affected by the crisis. Pentecostal social programmes include relief work, rehabilitation programmes, ministries to widows and orphans, and microfinance funding of businesses. One example is the Macedonian Initiative, an NGO founded by Ladi Thompson, senior pastor of Living Waters Unlimited Church in Lagos and CAN's Special Adviser, Conflict Resolution & Matters Related to Terrorism. Thompson sent a team from his church to deliver aid to families in Kaduna city affected by the 2000 inter-religious riots following the introduction of sharia in the state. The Macedonian Initiative was launched in July 2000 as a collaborative venture involving Christian leaders from northern and southern Nigeria. It describes itself as a "faith-based strategy and policy institute that seeks to promote the effective establishment of enabling environments for people to co-exist peacefully, without any threat to their fundamental right to freedom of worship" (Macedonian Initiative 2015). As well as relief work, the Macedonian Initiative engages in the rehabilitation of victims of violence, the reconstruction of church buildings, research and advocacy, media awareness, and conflict resolution.

Another initiative is the Nehemiah Project, started by Prophet Isa El-Buba. El-Buba is a self-declared former Muslim radical and member of Jama'atu Nasril Islam (JNI),[24] who converted to Christianity in 1982 while residing in Maiduguri. Following his conversion, he relocated to Jos. El-Buba is the General Overseer of Evangelical Bible Outreach Ministry International, which combines as a church and prayer ministry. He is a close associate of former Plateau State governor, Jonah Jang, and served as his spiritual adviser while he was in office. One of the aims of the Nehemiah Project is to rebuild Christian communities affected by the violence along the lines of gated communities.[25] I visited one of its projects in a village outside Jos, which was attacked by Muslim Fulani herdsmen in 2011. The Nehemiah Project's building initiative included the construction of new houses, a school, an interdenominational church, a community centre, an indoor market, and a health centre. The village is adjacent to a Fulani settlement, where some of the perpetrators still reside.

Some Pentecostals have provided charitable relief to Muslims as well as Christians, which has helped them to build interfaith relationships of trust. One example is the Comfort Widows Ministry, an interdenominational NGO founded by Pentecostal Pastor Comfort Padanu in Jos, which provides food, clothing, medical drugs, skills training, and money for rent and children's school fees. While they encourage the Muslim widows to become Christians, they do not make this a condition of receiving aid.[26]

Ecumenical organizations, transnational networks, and international partnerships

Pentecostal responses are influenced by inter-church relations and transnational networks. Some of the Jos pastors hold senior positions in the Pentecostal Fellowship of Nigeria (PFN) and the Christian Association of Nigeria (CAN). Ojo (2006: 69) notes that the involvement of Pentecostals in CAN activities "indirectly helped Pentecostals to moderate their negative perception of Islam because of CAN's insistence on using dialogue to resolve disagreements with Muslims". Opinion is mixed regarding the role of Christian ecumenical organizations in relation to conflict prevention and promotion of peace. CAN has helped to foster good relationships with Muslim leaders at the national level through its participation in the Nigerian Inter-Religious Council. But some Nigerian Christians expressed concern about what they perceived as inflammatory public statements by the former CAN president, Pentecostal Pastor Ayo Oritsejafor, which sometimes exacerbated tensions between the two religious communities. Oritsejafor's immediate predecessor as CAN president, the Catholic Archbishop John Onaiyekan, tended to be more conciliatory in his remarks. Several informants commended the organization for its assistance of both Christian and Muslims victims of violence during the 2011 presidential elections, and its advocacy work reminding the government to live up to its responsibilities and counter the perceived bias in the media which tends to disregard the suffering of Christians. However, some pastors criticized CAN for its partisan support for and unwillingness to challenge the government; its failure to provide constructive advice to Christians in crisis situations; and its inability to speak with a single voice on behalf of the Christian community.

There is also a transnational dimension to Pentecostal responses to violence and violation of religious freedom in northern Nigeria. Some Pentecostals have visited other African countries, the United States, and Europe to raise awareness among the international community regarding the situation in northern Nigeria. In 2015, Esther Ibanga addressed the UN Security Council Counter-Terrorism Committee on the role of women in countering terrorism in Nigeria (Ibanga 2015). Pastor Wuye and Imam Ashafa have spoken about their approach to interfaith work at international conferences in Egypt, Kenya, Chad, Senegal, Germany, Britain, and the United States. In 2017, they were among five recipients of the "Intercultural Innovation Award", conferred by the United Nations Alliance of Civilizations and BMW. In 2002, the Macedonian Initiative sent a delegation to the British House of Lords to advocate for the reinstatement of 11 non-Muslim nurses in Bauchi State after they were sacked for non-compliance to sharia dress codes. MI was able to secure the collaboration of Baroness Caroline Cox, the President of Christian Solidarity Worldwide, who visited Bauchi in 2003. Her intervention finally led to the nurses' reinstatement.

Pentecostal NGOs have also established links with networks and organizations in other African countries as well as the United States and Europe.

The Interfaith Mediation Centre (IMC) has conducted training and mediation in Kenya, Uganda, Chad, South Sudan, and Sierra Leone. It is a member of the United Religions Initiative, a global grassroots interfaith network based in the USA, and the King Abdullah Bin Abdulaziz International Centre for Interreligious and Intercultural Dialogue. The IMC has also worked in partnership with Christian Aid to provide capacity-building of IMC staff and community members, community mobilization, and the production/distribution of educational material (Christian Aid 2014). In 2011, the United Nations Development Programme (UNDP) supported the Young Ambassadors for Community Peace and Inter-Faith Foundation (YACPIF) in its ongoing peace campaigns in Jos (UNCT Nigeria 2011). The Women Without Walls Initiative has collaborated with Women Without Borders, an international NGO based in Vienna, and the United States Institute of Peace.

Nigerian Pentecostals and Charismatics in the diaspora are also seeking to create awareness and mobilize prayer on behalf of victims of violence and human rights violations in northern Nigeria. One example is Love Justice (formerly Love Jos), a London-based organization which was started by a group of Nigerian Christians concerned about the escalating crisis in Plateau State.[27] Rather than replicate the work of organizations such as Open Doors and Release International, Love Justice seeks to mobilize members of the large Nigerian Christian community in Britain and persuade them to lobby their MPs and give charitable donations.[28] To fulfil its objectives, Love Justice organizes conferences and prayer meetings. The theme of its 2011 conference, which was held in the London premises of Matthew Ashimolowo's Kingsway International Christian Centre, was "Stand Up, Speak Out" and featured Christian speakers from Britain, Nigeria, and the Nigerian diaspora.[29] According to a flyer advertising the event, the aim of the conference was to "explore opportunities for advocacy, reconciliation, and how practical help might be offered to victims of persecution" (Love Jos 2011). Love Justice has also engaged in advocacy and awareness campaigns at RCCG's Festival of Life conference in London. Prayer is integral to the ministry of Love Justice because members believe that persecution has a spiritual dimension and is driven by demonic influences.[30] In January 2012, in collaboration with the Overseas Fellowship of Nigerian Christians, Love Justice organized a prayer vigil outside the Nigerian High Commission in London and presented a letter to the Nigerian High Commissioner protesting against the Nigerian government's failure to protect Christians in the north. Although it is a small organization, it uses print and electronic media to create awareness and mobilize Nigerian Christians in the diaspora. Recently, it launched the Loveback project, which aims to create awareness of the plight of Christians in northern Nigeria, engage in advocacy on their behalf, and change the narrative around violence and terror by telling the stories of those who have chosen to "fight back by loving back". The project's slogan is "Love is more violent than terror", and it advocates God's love (love for people and community) as the key to responding to violence (Love Justice 2019).

Conclusion

This chapter has investigated Pentecostal responses to violence and the violations of rights to religious freedom in northern Nigeria, where violent conflict has posed a serious threat to sustainable development. The combined effects of ethno-religious violence, the implementation of sharia in some states, and the Boko Haram insurgency have had a significant impact on Pentecostal communities in relation to economic status, participation in church activities, and civic engagement. Pentecostals have experienced discrimination in employment, restricted access to education and social amenities, barriers to political participation, the destruction of churches and personal property, and extensive loss of lives. To some extent, the venture of Pentecostals into the public arenas of politics and media to combat "Islamization", combined with their emphasis on evangelism and spiritual warfare, has exacerbated Christian-Muslim tensions. However, Pentecostal responses to violence and violation of religious freedom have included interfaith dialogue, peacebuilding initiatives, and programs that engage Muslim and Christian youth. Pentecostals are also involved in development projects that cater to both Christian and Muslim victims of violence. Church leaders and ecumenical organizations have used the media as well as their relationships with international partners to raise awareness of Christian persecution and marginalization. Unfortunately, retaliatory attacks on Muslim communities by some members of Christian communities in Plateau State have exacerbated tensions and prolonged the cycle of violence. The case studies discussed in this chapter show how insecurity, the perception of discrimination, and ethnic rivalry can become the breeding grounds for religious intolerance and human rights abuses.

Notes

1 Most of the research for this chapter was conducted during the Pentecostal and Charismatic Research Initiative. I also draw upon data collected during the Religious Freedom Project (RTP). I am grateful to Danny McCain, my co-researcher on the RTP, and to research assistants, Cosmas Wule and Gideon Yohanna Tambiyi, for carrying out some of the fieldwork.

2 Article 18 of The Universal Declaration of Human Rights (1948):

> Everyone has the right to freedom of thought, conscience and religion; this right includes freedom to change his religion or belief, and freedom, either alone or in community with others and in public or private, to manifest his religion or belief in teaching, practice, worship and observance.

3 The Nigerian Constitution includes a strong statement about freedom of religion:

> Every person shall be entitled to freedom of thought, conscience and religion, including freedom to change his religion or belief, and freedom (either alone or in community with others, and in public or in private) to manifest and propagate his religion or belief in worship, teaching, practice and observance.
>
> Federal Republic of Nigeria (1999)

4 Nine states have instituted full sharia. Three states (Kaduna, Niger and Gombe) have instituted sharia in areas with large Muslim populations.

5 Interview, Bishop Jonas Katung, Maranatha Bible Church, Jos, 18 May 2012.
6 Interview, Revd Kefas Tangan, Church of Christ in Nations, London, 17 July 2013.
7 Interview, Pastor Felix Oluwatayo, MFM, Jos, 10 May, 2012.
8 Interview, Pastor Bamidele Padanu, Christ Apostolic Church, Jos, June 2013.
9 Interview, Pastor Kenneth Amadi, Assemblies of God, Jos, 30 June 2013.
10 Interview, Pastor Comfort Padanu, Christ Apostolic Church, Jos, 22 June 2013.
11 Interview, Pastor Kenneth Amadi, Assemblies of God, Jos, 30 June 2013.
12 Interview, Dr Khataza Gondwe, Christian Solidarity Worldwide, London, 16 July 2013.
13 Interview, Revd Aaron Ndirmbita, Church of Christ in Nations, Jos, 18 June 2013.
14 Interview, Pastor James Sani, Christ Reaper's Assembly, Jos, 17 May 2012.
15 Interview, Pastor Yakabu Pam, Assemblies of God, Jos, 8 May 2012.
16 Interview, Pastor James Wuye, Assemblies of God, Kaduna, 4 July 2013. Pastor Wuye and Imam Ashafa have received several international awards for their work. Especially influential is the film "The Imam and the Pastor" which has been shown around the world. The IMC is affiliated to several national networks, including the Nigerian Supreme Council for Islamic Affairs, the Christian Association of Nigeria, and the Jama'atu Nasril Islam.
17 Revd. Pam is currently the chairman of CAN Northern Nigeria and Jos District Superintendent of Assemblies of God. He was formerly a pastor of a church located in a Muslim-dominated area close to Jos Central Mosque.
18 YACPIF's first trustees included the late Solomon Lar, former governor of Plateau State, and Alhaji Mohammed Maikarfi, former governor of Kaduna State.
19 Interview, Pastor Yakabu Pam, Assemblies of God, Jos, 8 May 2012.
20 Interview, Pastor Yakubu Pam, Assemblies of God, Jos, 8 May 2012.
21 Khadijat Hawaja is the Financial Secretary of the Women Without Walls Initiative.
22 Interview, Pastor Declain Onyebuchi, Assemblies of God, Jos, 20 June 2013.
23 Examples include Bishop Jonas Katung's Maranatha Bible Church and Prophet El-Buba's Evangelical Bible Outreach Ministry International.
24 The Jama'atu Nasril Islam was founded in 1964 as an attempt to unify Muslims in northern Nigeria. Two of the founding members were Sheikh Abubakar Gumi and former prime minister Ahmadu Bello (Loimeier 2011).
25 Interview, Prophet Isa El-Buba, Evangelical Bible Outreach Ministry International, Jos, 17 May 2012.
26 Interview, Comfort Padanu, Christ Apostolic Church, Jos, 22 June, 2013.
27 One of the founders of Love Justice is Fred Williams who was formerly a pastor in Jos.
28 Interview, Revd Tade Agbesanwa, Custom House Baptist Church, London, 2 July 2013.
29 Speakers included Baroness Caroline Cox (a former President of Christian Solidarity Worldwide), Matthew Ashimolowo (KICC), Anglican Bishop Michael Nazir-Ali, and Mark Lipdo (Stefanos Foundation).
30 Interview, Revd Tade Agbesanwa, Custom House Baptist Church, London, 2 July 2013.

References

Abdullahi, Ali A. and L. Saka (2007) "Ethno-religious and Political Conflicts: Threat to Nigeria Nascent Democracy", *Journal of Sustainable Development in Africa* 9(3): 21–36.

Abubaka, Dauda (2017) "From Sectarianism to Terrorism in Northern Nigeria: A Closer Look at Boko Haram", in Caroline Varin and Dauda Abubakar (eds) *Violent Non-state Actors in Africa: Terrorists, Rebels and Warlords*, New York: Palgrave Macmillan, pp. 17–48.

Adesoji, Abimbola (2010) "The Boko Haram Uprising and Islamic Revivalism in Nigeria", *Africa Spectrum* 45: 95–108.

Aihiokhai, Simonmary A. (2010) "Pentecostalism and Political Empowerment: The Nigerian Phenomenon", *Journal of Ecumenical Studies* 45(2): 249–264.

Ajani, Jide (2014) "Al-Qaeda Takes Over Boko Haram", *Vanguard*, 9 March, available at: www.vanguardngr.com/2014/03/al-qaeda-takes-boko-haram/ (accessed 21 September 2019).

Akinade, Akintunde (2014) *Christian Responses to Islam in Nigeria*, New York: Palgrave Macmillan.

Alaga, Ecoma (2010) *Challenges for Women in Peacebuilding in West Africa*, AISA Policy Brief 18. Pretoria: Africa Institute of South Africa.

Anderson, Becca (2017) *The Book of Awesome Women: Boundary Breakers, Freedom Fighters, Sheroes and Female Firsts*, Core Gables, FL: Mango Media Inc.

Appleby, R. Scott (2000) *The Ambivalence of the Sacred: Religion, Violence, and Reconciliation*, Lanham, MD: Rowman & Littlefield Publishers.

Burgess, Richard and Danny McCain (2015) "Christianity and the Challenge of Religious Violence in Northern Nigeria", in Timothy Shah and Allen Hertzke (eds) *Christianity and Freedom: Volume II: Contemporary Perspectives*, Cambridge: Cambridge University Press, pp. 306–338.

Campbell, John (2013) "Escaping Nigeria's Cycle of Violence", Expert Brief. Council on Foreign Relations, 15 May, available at: www.cfr.org/expert-brief/escaping-nigerias-cycle-violence (accessed 19 September 2019).

Christian Aid (2014) "Ten Years On: A Decade of Interfaith Work Promoting Good Governance and Sustainable Peace in Kaduna State, Nigeria", available at: www.christianaid.org.uk/sites/default/files/2016-11/ten-years-on-impact-of-interfaith-work-nigeria-report-december-2014.pdf (accessed 9 October 2019).

Christian Solidarity Worldwide (2011) "Nigeria: Religious Freedom", Unpublished Report, May.

Christian Solidarity Worldwide (2013) "Universal Periodic Review – 17th Session, CSW (Joint Submission) – Stakeholder Submission, Federal Republic of Nigeria", March: 1–8.

Daily Post (2015) "Boko Haram: Police Confirms Killing of Six in Yobe Church Attack", *Daily Post*, 5 July, available at: http://dailypost.ng/2015/07/05/boko-haram-police-confirms-killing-of-six-in-yobe-church-attack/ (accessed 19 September 2019).

Ejobowah, John B. (2013) "Ethnic Conflict and Cooperation: Assessing Citizenship in Nigerian Federalism", *Publius* 43(4): 728–747.

Eyoboka, Sam (2009a) "How Pastor Orji and I Were Captured by Boko Haram Operatives: Survivor", *Vanguard*, 4 September, available at: www.vanguardngr.com/2009/09/how-pastor-orji-and-i-were-captured-by-boko-haram-operatives-survivor/ (accessed 15 August 2019).

Eyoboka, Sam (2009b) "PFN Holds Service in Honour of Victims", *Vanguard*, 2 September, available at: www.vanguardngr.com/2009/09/boko-haram-pfn-holds-service-in-honour-of-victims/ (accessed 21 September 2019).

Falode, James A. (2016) "The Nature of Nigeria's Boko Haram War, 2010–2015: A Strategic Analysis", *Perspectives on Terrorism* 10(1): 41–52.

Federal Republic of Nigeria (1999) Federal Republic of Nigeria Constitution of 1999, Chapter IV, Section 38, available at: www.nigeria-law.org/ConstitutionOfTheFederalRepublicOfNigeria.htm (accessed 26 October 2019).

Gaiya, Musa A. (2015) "Charismatic and Pentecostal Social Orientations in Nigeria", *Nova Religio: The Journal of Alternative and Emergent Religions* 18(3): 63–79.

Hackett, Rosalind I. (2000) “Religious Freedom and Religious Conflict in Africa”, in Mark Silk (ed.) *Religion on the News Agenda*, Hartford, CT: The Leonard E. Greenberg Center for the Study of Religion in Public Life, pp. 102–119.

Hackett, Rosalind I. (2003) “Managing Or Manipulating Religious Conflict in the Nigerian Media”, in Sophia Marriage and Jolyon P. Mitchell (eds) *Mediating Religion: Conversations in Media, Religion, and Culture*, Edinburgh: T & T Clark, pp. 47–63.

Hackett, Rosalind I. (2011) “Nigeria’s Religious Leaders in an Age of Radicalism and Neoliberalism”, in Timothy D. Sisk (ed.) *Between Terror and Tolerance: Religious Leaders, Conflict, and Peacemaking*, Georgetown, WA: Georgetown University Press, pp. 123–144.

Haynes, Jeffrey (2008) *Development Studies*. Cambridge: Polity.

Haynes, Jeffrey (2009) “Conflict, Conflict Resolution and Peace-building: The Role of Religion in Mozambique, Nigeria and Cambodia”, *Commonwealth & Comparative Politics* 47(1): 52–75.

Hertzke, Allen D. (2004) *Freeing God’s Children: The Unlikely Alliance for Global Human Rights*, Lanham, MD: Rowman & Littlefield.

Hertzke, Allen. D. (2012) “Advancing the First Freedom in the Twenty-first Century”, in Allen D. Hertzke (ed.) *The Future of Religious Freedom: Global Challenges*, Oxford: Oxford University Press, pp. 3–30.

Higazi, Adam (2011) “The Jos Crisis: A Recurrent Nigerian Tragedy”, Discussion Paper 2, Abuja: Friedrich-Ebert-Stiftung.

Human Rights Watch (2006) “ ‘They Do Not Own This Place’: Government Discrimination Against ‘Non-Indigenes’ in Nigeria”, *Human Rights Watch* 18(3): 1–64.

Human Rights Watch (2010a) “Nigeria: Investigate Massacre, Step Up Patrols. Hundreds Killed by Mobs in Villages in Central Nigeria”, 8 March, available at: www.hrw.org/news/2010/03/08/nigeria-investigate-massacre-step-patrols (accessed 22 September 2019).

Human Rights Watch (2010b) “Nigeria: Protect Survivors, Fully Investigate Massacre Reports”, 23 January, available at: www.hrw.org/news/2010/01/22/nigeria-protect-survivors-fully-investigate-massacre-reports (accessed 2 November 2013).

Human Rights Watch (2014) “Nigeria: Boko Haram Attacks Cause Humanitarian Crisis”, 14 March, available at: www.hrw.org/news/2014/03/14/nigeria-boko-haram-attacks-cause-humanitarian-crisis (accessed 20 September 2019).

Ibanga, Esther (2015) *The Role of Women in Countering Terrorism in Nigeria*, Open Briefing Paper presented at the UN, 9 September, available at: www.un.org/sc/ctc/wp-content/uploads/2015/09/Open-Briefing-Statement-by-Pastor-Esther-Ibanga.pdf (accessed 15 August 2019).

Ilesanmi, Omotola A. (2017) “Women’s Agency in Nigeria’s Jos Crisis”, in Toyin Falola and Olajumoke Yacob-Haliso (eds) *Gendering Knowledge in Africa and the African Diaspora: Contesting History and Power*, London: Routledge, pp. 188–204.

Imo, Cyril (2008) “Evangelicals, Muslims, and Democracy: With Particular Reference to the Declaration of Shari’a in Northern Nigeria”, in Terence O. Ranger (ed.) *Evangelical Christianity and Democracy in Africa*, Oxford: Oxford University Press, pp. 37–66.

Institute for Economics & Peace (2016) Global Terrorism Index 2016. Measuring and Understanding the Impact of Terrorism, IEP Report 43, available at: http://economicsandpeace.org/wp-content/uploads/2016/11/Global-Terrorism-Index-2016.2.pdf (accessed 5 August 2019).

Iyekekpolo, Wisdom O. (2016) “Boko Haram: Understanding the Context”, *Third World Quarterly* 37(12): 2211–2228.

Joseph, Yakubu and Rainer Rothfuss (2012) "Threats to Religious Freedom in Nigeria", *International Journal for Religious Freedom* 5(1): 73–86.

Kalu, Ogbu U. (2008) *African Pentecostalism: An Introduction*, Oxford: Oxford University Press.

Lederach, John P. (2015) "Spirituality and Religious Peacebuilding", in Atalia Omer, R. Scott Appleby, and David Little (eds) *The Oxford Handbook of Religion, Conflict and Peacebuilding*, Oxford: Oxford University Press, pp. 541–568.

Little, David and Scott Appleby (2004) "A Moment of Opportunity? The Promise of Religious Peacebuilding in an Era of Religious and Ethnic Conflict", in Harold Coward and Gordon S. Smith (eds) *Religion and Peacebuilding*, New York: State University of New York Press, pp. 1–23.

Loimeier, Roman (2011) *Islamic Reform and Political Change in Northern Nigeria*, Evanston, IL: Northwestern University Press.

Love Jos (2011) Flyer advertising the Love Jos Conference "Stand Up, Speak Out", 24 September 2011.

Love Justice (2019) "The Loveback Project", available at: www.lovejustice.org.uk/index.php/the-loveback-project/ (accessed 20 November 2019).

Ludwig, Frieder (2008) "Christian–Muslim Relations in Northern Nigeria Since the Introduction of Shari'ah in 1999", *Journal of the American Academy of Religion* 76(3): 602–637.

Lynch, Cecilia (2015) "Religious Communities and Possibilities for Justpeace", in Atalia Omer, R. Scott Appleby, and David Little (eds) *The Oxford Handbook of Religion, Conflict and Peacebuilding*, Oxford: Oxford University Press, pp. 597–612.

Macedonian Initiative (2015) "Who We Are", available at: http://macedonianinitiative.org/who-we-are/ (accessed 15 April 2019).

Marama, Ndahi (2014) "RCCG Pastor Shot, Butchered in Borno", *Vanguard*, 18 July, available at: www.vanguardngr.com/2014/07/rccg-pastor-shot-butchered-borno/ (accessed 10 April 2019).

Marshall, Ruth (2009) *Political Spiritualities: The Pentecostal Revolution in Nigeria*, Chicago: University of Chicago Press.

Marshall, Katherine (2011) "A Discussion with Pastor James Wuye and Imam Muhammad Ashafa", Berkeley Center for Religion, Peace & World Affairs, 31 October, available at: http://berkleycenter.georgetown.edu/interviews/a-discussion-with-pastor-james-wuye-and-imam-muhammad-ashafa (accessed 15 August 2019).

McCain, Danny, Musa Gaiya, and Katrina Korb (2014) "Salt and Light or Salt and Pepper: Views on Ethno-Religious Violence and Peace among Pentecostals in Nigeria", *Pneuma* 36: 81–106.

Mustapha, Abdul R. (2014) "Understanding Boko Haram", in Abdul R. Mustapha (ed.) *Sects and Social Disorder: Muslim Identities and Conflict in Northern Nigeria*, London: James Curry, pp. 147–198.

Nwangwu, Chikodiri and Christian Ezeibe (2019) "Femininity is Not Inferiority: Women-led Civil Society Organizations and 'Countering Violent Extremism' in Nigeria", *International Feminist Journal of Politics* 21(2): 168–193.

Ojo, Matthews A. (2006) *The End-time Army. Charismatic Movements in Modern Nigeria*, Trenton, NJ: Africa World Press.

Ojo, Matthews A. (2007) "Pentecostal Movements, Islam and the Contest for Public Space in Northern Nigeria", *Islam and Christian-Muslim Relations* 18(2): 175–188.

Ojo, Matthews A. and Folaranmi T. Lateju (2010) "Christian–Muslim Conflicts and Interfaith Bridge-building Efforts in Nigeria", *The Review of Faith & International Affairs* 8(1): pp. 31–38.

Okonkwo, Oge (2014) "Ayo Oritsejafor: 'Boko Haram is a Religious Problem Not a Political One'", *Pulse NG*, 16 November, available at: www.pulse.ng/communities/religion/ayo-oritsejafor-boko-haram-is-a-religious-problem-not-a-political-one-id3276797.html (accessed 21 September 2019).

Ostien, Philip (2009) "Jonah Jang and the Jasawa: Ethno-religious Conflict in Jos, Nigeria", *Muslim-Christian Relations in Africa*, August: 1–42.

Ostien, Philip (2012) "A Survey of the Muslims of Nigeria's North Central Geo-political Zone", Working Paper No. 1, Nigeria Research Network, Oxford Department of International Development, January.

Pam, Yakubu (2013) "The Report of Religious Crisis in Jos and Northern Nigeria", October, available at: www.bgillott.org/2013/10-OCT/JosPERSECUTION.html (accessed 26 May 2016).

Pam, Yakuba and Katrina Korb (2011) *Fighting for Peace: Learning from the Peace Heroes Among Us*, Jos: FAB Educational Books.

Pflanz, Mike (2012) "Nigerian Churches Targeted in Sunday Attacks", *Telegraph*, 10 June, available at: www.telegraph.co.uk/news/worldnews/africaandindianocean/nigeria/9322998/Nigerian-churches-targeted-in-Sunday-attacks.html (accessed 15 August 2013).

Philpott, Daniel (2010) "Introduction: Searching for Strategy in an Age of Peacebuilding", in Daniel Philpott and Gerard F. Powers (eds) *Strategies of Peace: Transforming Conflict in a Violent World*, New York: Oxford University Press, pp. 3–18.

Poku, Nana K., Neil Renwick, and Joao G. Porto (2007) "Human Security and Development in Africa", *International Affairs* 83(6): 1155–1170.

Powers, G. F. (2010) "Religion and Peacebuilding", in Daniel Philpot and Gerard F. Powers (eds) *Strategies of Peace: Transforming Conflict in a Violent World*, New York: Oxford University Press, pp. 317–352.

Sahara Reporters (2011) "Something Good Out of Jos", *Sahara Reporters*, available at: http://saharareporters.com/2011/01/07/something-good-out-jos (accessed 8 October 2019).

Shannahan, Chris and Laura Payne (2016) *Faith-based Interventions in Peace, Conflict and Violence: A Scoping Study*, Coventry: Coventry University.

Smith, David (2011) "Church Bombings Are Declaration of War, Say Nigerian Christians", *Guardian*, 29 December, www.theguardian.com/world/2011/dec/29/church-bombings-nigerian-christians (accessed 18 September 2019).

Ter Haar, Gerrie (2005) "Religion: Source of Conflict or Resource for Peace", in Gerrie ter Haar and James. J. Busuttil (eds) *Bridge or Barrier: Religion, Violence and Visions of Peace*, Leiden: E. J. Brill, pp. 3–34.

Ter Haar, Gerrie and Stephen Ellis (2006) "The Role of Religion in Development: Towards a New Relationship Between the European Union and Africa", *The European Journal of Development Research* 18(3): 351–367.

Ukah, Asonzeh (2009) "Contesting God: Nigerian Pentecostals and their Relations with Islam and Muslims", in David Westerlund (ed.) *Global Pentecostalism: Encounters with Other Religious Traditions*, London: I.B. Tauris, pp. 92–114.

Ukah, Asonzeh (2014) "Born-Again Muslims: The Ambivalence of Pentecostal Response to Islam in Nigeria", in Akintunde Akinade (ed.) *Fractured Spectrum: Perspectives on Christian-Muslim Encounter in Nigeria*, New York: Peter Lang, pp. 43–62.

Ukiwo, Ukoho (2003) "Politics, Ethno-religious Conflicts and Democratic Consolidation in Nigeria", *The Journal of Modern African Studies* 41(1): 115–138.

United Nations Country Team Nigeria (2011) *UNDAF II (2009–2012) Mid Term Review Report*.

US Department of State (2013) "Terrorist Designations of Boko Haram and Ansaru", 13 November, available at: https://2009-2017.state.gov/r/pa/prs/ps/2013/11/217509.htm (accessed 21 September 2019).

Women Without Walls Initiative (2018) "WOWWI Program Report", available at: https://wowwi.com.ng/wp-content/uploads/2019/04/WOWWI-Program-Report.pdf (accessed 20 November 2019).

Yong, Amos (2008) *Hospitality & The Other: Pentecost, Christian Practices, and the Neighbor*, Maryknoll, NY: Orbis Books.

8 Pentecostals, migration, and development

Introduction

International migration is an important feature of our world and consequently has become a significant subject of social scientific research. The focus of migration studies has been on the social and economic determinants and consequences of population movements, and the specific contexts in which migration takes place. Migration scholars are especially interested in the role of social relations and economic considerations as factors influencing migration and incorporation into the host society (Brettel and Hollified 2000). Consequently, they have tended to neglect the role of religion in the migration process. Recently, however, the balance has been redressed with increasing attention given to the resources that religion provides in driving and sustaining migration (e.g. Adogame 2013; Hagan and Ebaugh 2003; Levitt 2001; Ter Haar 2001; Vertovec 2004). African Pentecostal churches are particularly important in this respect. Their function as social and religious support networks for their own members has been well documented (Adogame 2013; Ter Haar 2001; Harris 2006; Hunt 2002). What has been less explored is the significance for migration of their civic engagement in the wider society.

This chapter examines the nexus between Nigerian Pentecostalism, migration and development with a particular focus on Britain and the United States where some of the largest Nigerian diaspora communities are located. It begins by discussing the relationship between migration and development. It then reviews recent literature on immigrant religion and civic engagement. The remainder of the chapter investigates the contributions of Nigerian Pentecostal diaspora churches to immigrant incorporation, civic engagement, and international development.

Migration and development

Despite the importance of global migration for the contemporary world, it was omitted from the MDGs. The SDGs, by contrast, "incorporate migration explicitly into global development policy" (Piper 2017: 231). Although not referred to as a distinct domain, there are seven migration-related references in the

SDGs: education (SDG 4.b.), gender-based violence and trafficking (SDG 5.2), modern day slavery (SDG 8.7), migrant worker rights (SDG 8.8), safe migration (SDG 10.7), migrant remittances (SDG 10.c.), and trafficking of children (SDG 16.2). Formerly considered a problem for economic development, the "new mantra" is that migration can have a positive effect on development in countries of emigration (Faist 2008: 21).

The emergence of the migration-development nexus on the sustainable development agenda has resulted in three main foci: remittances, skilled migration, and diaspora involvement (Nijenhuis and Leung 2017). Discussions by academics and policy-makers have focused on the positive effects of financial remittances, the transfer of "highly-skilled" migrants from North to South and from West to East (so-called circular or temporary migration), and the training of diaspora organizations to contribute to development in the region of origin (Nijenhuis and Leung 2017; Glick Schiller and Faist 2010). In Nigeria, diaspora remittances represent a significant proportion of the country's GDP.[1] Recent attention has focused on the term "social remittances" which describes the transfer of knowledge, ideas and values, such as human rights, gender equity, and democracy (Page and Mercer 2010; Levitt 1998, 2001).

Some scholars have advocated a transnational approach to migration and development that encompasses both long-term migrants and those who engage in short-term mobility (Faist 2008; Glick Schiller and Faist 2010). Faist (2008: 27) refers to migrants as "transnational development actors" who form social spaces such as transnational families, hometown associations, and cross-border religious congregations. The Pentecostal churches discussed in this chapter fit the profile of Faist's transnational development actors. Their development activities are shaped by ongoing connections between home and host societies, facilitated by modern communication, information technology, and ease of travel.

Migrants are regarded as vital agents of international development by financial institutions such as the World Bank, international organizations from the United Nations, and NGOs (Glick Schiller and Faist 2010). However, in Europe and the United States, migrants are among the most vulnerable to poverty-related problems such as social exclusion, homelessness, and food insecurity, especially since the 2008 economic downturn (Glick Schiller and Faist 2010; Hadley, Zodhiates, and Sellen 2007; Busch-Geertsema *et al.* 2017; Pleace 2010; Fitzpatrick, Johnsen, and Bramley 2012). As we will see later, Nigerian Pentecostal churches in the diaspora are contributing to immigrant incorporation and welfare provision through a variety of social support mechanisms and initiatives.

Immigrant religion and civic engagement

Among scholars of religion and migration, there is a growing research interest in exploring the relationship between immigrant religion and faith-based civic engagement. Much of this research originates in the United States and encompasses Christian and non-Christian religious communities. Building on the work of Stephen Warner,[2] Ebaugh and Chafetz (2000) report the findings of the

Religion, Ethnicity and New Immigrant Research (RENIR) project, a comparative study across ethnic groups and religious faiths. The authors draw upon research in Houston, Texas, one of the largest immigrant ports of entry into the United States. The research studied 13 congregations, representing the major national origins groups and religions in Houston. Case studies included Catholic, Protestant, Buddhist, Islamic, and Hindu religious institutions. Only two case studies, a Pentecostal congregation and a Catholic church, included African immigrant members. Topics examined in the research included programmes to assist new immigrants, social services provided, ties with agencies and other outside groups, and transnational ties, all themes explored in my own research. In a subsequent edited volume, which focused on the transnational linkages of the Houston-based and country of origin religious institutions, Ebaugh and Chafetz (2002) refer to the bi-directional flows of financial resources, religious personnel, and influence once immigrant congregations acquire financial stability.

Other studies on immigrant religion and civic engagement in the United States have followed Ebaugh and Chafetz's ground-breaking work. Numrich and Kniss' *Sacred Assemblies and Civic Engagement* (2007) studied 16 immigrant congregations in the Chicago metropolitan region. Case studies included Catholic, Protestant, Orthodox Christian, Jewish, Muslim, Hindu, and Buddhist congregations that served immigrants from a variety of ethnic backgrounds. The authors examine how religious ideas, practices and identities affect members' civic engagement outside their congregations. Foley and Hoge's *Religion and the New Immigrants. How Faith Communities Form Our Newest Citizens* (2007) focuses on the role of worship communities among new immigrants in Washington, DC. Research included 20 ethnographic studies, encompassing Catholic, Protestant, Muslim, Hindu, and Sikh worship communities, and a quantitative survey of 200 worship communities. The demographic profile of the cases studies included congregations from African (including Nigerian), Chinese, Indian, Korean, and Salvadoran countries of origin. Foley and Hoge (2007: 12) identify three factors explaining the differing contributions of worship communities to immigrant incorporation and community engagement: differing circumstances of the immigrant communities themselves, organizational culture, and the role of religious tradition in shaping members' notions of obligations to the community. Stepick, Rey, and Mahler (2009) examine immigrant churches and civic engagement in Miami. The book is based on ethnographies of immigrant (Hispanic, Haitian, West Indian) and African American congregations and includes Catholic, mainstream Protestant, Pentecostal, and Seventh-Day Adventist churches. The relationship between immigrant religion and civic engagement, according to the authors, is influenced by four factors: denomination, immigrant generation, leadership, and context of reception (immigrants' treatment by American institutions and society).

In contrast to the United States, the literature on immigrant religion and civic engagement in Britain is less developed. Most research has focused on single, rather than multiple, religious traditions. A number of studies examine the civic engagement of Muslim minorities in Britain (McLoughlin 2005; Oskooii and Dana 2018; Peace (ed.) 2015). Another strand of literature focuses on African and Caribbean Pentecostal churches. Studies of Caribbean Pentecostals explore the role of black Pentecostal spirituality in identity construction, empowerment, and liberation in the face of racial oppression (Toulis 1997; Beckford 2011). Robert Beckford's work explores how a black Pentecostal political theology can challenge injustice in Britain (Beckford 2011). This political and liberative dimension is less pronounced in research on African Pentecostalism, probably because African immigrants have not encountered the same degree of racial discrimination as their Caribbean cousins. Scholars have focused on the social engagement of African Pentecostal churches as well as the flows of remittances and charitable donations from host to home country to support families, churches and NGOs (Adogame 2013; Fesenmyer 2016; Duffour 2012; Burgess 2009, 2011). A recent study by Cartledge *et al.* (2019) investigates the social engagement activities of five megachurches in London, including three Nigerian-led congregations (RCCG Jesus House, Kingsway International Christian Centre, and New Wine Church).

Migrant churches: social capital, holistic salvation, and empowerment

One reason for the appeal of African diaspora churches is the way their social and religious support networks assist African Pentecostals to negotiate the migration process. This is important in immigrant contexts in which people are separated from extended family networks. In the literature, African churches in diaspora are often referred to as "migrant" or "immigrant" churches due to their capacity to cater for the needs of African immigrants (Hanciles 2008; Währisch-Oblau 2009). As Gerrie Ter Haar (1998: 43) notes, diaspora churches "contribute significantly to the material and immaterial well-being of African migrants", especially those living in urbanized areas of Western Europe. Olupona and Gemignani (2007: 9) refer to the way African religious communities in the United States employ various formal and informal approaches "to improve the lives of immigrants, often aimed at both members and nonmembers". While African Pentecostal migrants hope for a better life, they often encounter difficulties, ranging from financial problems and unemployment to immigration difficulties and racial discrimination.

The function of migrant churches as social support mechanisms is often linked to theories of social capital (Adogame 2013; Foley and Hoge 2007). According to Adogame (2013: 109), "African Christian communities contribute enormous bridging, bonding and linking social capital, but also confront barriers to development and civic engagement." Churches provide contexts for communal worship and prayer as well as social interaction with those who share similar culture and customs, thus contributing to the stocks of social and cultural capital necessary for successful incorporation into host societies. Some congregations in Britain and the United States have ministries specifically geared towards assisting new immigrants to negotiate the migration process and settle in their local communities. Services provided include immigration information, careers guidance, and free legal advice.[3] As Adogame (2013) notes, African diaspora churches are places where vital information about travel, employment, education, housing, immigration, and healthcare is freely circulated. Nigerian churches organize seminars on such topics as business management, investment, immigration issues, marriage, and health awareness. Prayer in particular is considered an important resource for Nigerian migrants. Most churches have regular prayer meetings, which provide opportunity for people to receive prayer for particular needs, whether immigration issues, financial and health problems, or family relationships. Many congregations have house fellowships to provide pastoral care for members. They also have a variety of single interest groups to support different categories of people, including youth, women, men, lone parents, childless couples, and business people. Small groups also function as socialization mechanisms, inculcating Christian virtues and protecting adherents from the corrosive effects of Western liberal values deemed responsible for such societal vices as family breakdown, domestic abuse, sexual promiscuity, and youth crime.

Ralph Grillo (2001: 3) identifies three options for those migrants wishing to remain in the host society: assimilation ("here and the same"), integration ("here but different"), and enclavement ("here but separate"). To an extent, these are contingent upon the strength of transnational ties, weak and tenuous in the case of assimilation, and strong in the case of integration and enclavement. Most of the Nigerian churches in this study fall into the second category. In order to extend their social influence, they encourage their members to integrate into the host culture. However, their function as a social support network for Nigerian migrants, and their strong transnational ties, ensures that ethnic and cultural differences are maintained. As Stephen Hunt (2002) notes of Nigerian churches in Britain, although members may be integrated with other ethnicities and nationalities in the workplace and college setting, they maintain distance in their religious gatherings, taking refuge from potentially hostile and demanding circumstances. Ebaugh and Chafetz (2000) refer to this as selective assimilation, where individuals may be assimilated educationally, linguistically, and socially, but chose to continue participating in their ethnic congregations. By providing contexts in which migrants can socialize with others, immigrant religious institutions "serve as important sites for both ethnic reproduction and for immigrant adaptation to their new community" (Ebaugh and Chafetz 2000: 356).

Another characteristic of Nigerian Pentecostal churches is their holistic concept of salvation, which includes not only holiness, but healing, deliverance, and prosperity. The appeal of these theologies is obvious in a hostile economic environment like Africa, where access to medical facilities and to state funds is severely restricted, and adverse circumstances are often blamed on the activities of malevolent spirits. They are also popular among African migrants, who sometimes find it difficult to support their families, especially if they are students or low-paid workers without recourse to public funds. As Ogbu Kalu (2008: 288) reminds us, immigrants retain the spiritual worldview of their indigenous cultures and find Pentecostal churches "attentive to their deeply felt needs". One Nigerian pastor put it like this:

> We preach the whole gospel.... But at times African-based churches tend to sway towards success and prosperity because of our background ... maybe because we have been disadvantaged before; maybe because we have been poor before.... When you look at our congregations in the Western world, you discover the majority are migrants. So right now, they are struggling, so they need faith for them to come up.[4]

Perhaps more surprising is the continuing appeal of deliverance theology. Despite the influence of secularization, issues such as witchcraft continue to be a reality for Africans in the diaspora. Deliverance theology is popular in diaspora contexts because it is practical and progressive in orientation, enabling Africans to break free from social and religious ties considered a hindrance to personal development.[5] According to Olukoya (1999), the General Overseer of MFM, witchcraft is a global phenomenon, which manifests itself in diverse ways in different localities. Britain's liberal migration policy and multicultural society are sometimes blamed for allowing alien spirits from outside Europe to gain entry, resulting in ungodly behaviour such as homosexuality, gun crime, and terrorism. Thus, deliverance theology is promoted by MFM as essential if Christianity's decline in the West is to be reversed. African diasporic churches hold regular programmes, which provide ritual settings for the promotion of healing and deliverance. For example, MFM holds a monthly deliverance programme called "Power Must Change Hands" and RCCG's Victory House in London hosts an annual "Healing and Deliverance Week". Often speakers from Africa and the United States are invited to these events, reflecting the transnational nature of African Pentecostal churches. However, these meetings appeal mainly to African migrants. For example, during MFM's 2007 "Great Deliverance and Anointing Service" in London, which attracted over 3,000 people, the audience was overwhelmingly African, with only a few white people in attendance.

Pentecostalism's propensity to enhance socio-economic mobility is particularly appealing to African migrants. Economic deprivation is recognized as a factor preventing successful integration, and a key underlying source of tension undermining community cohesion in Britain (Singh 2007). Participation in Pentecostal networks provide Africans in Britain with opportunities to prosper financially, whether as an outcome of "faith" teaching, increased work ethic, or business acumen. Many African Pentecostals in Britain are highly educated professionals with a strong motivation to succeed, which makes them especially drawn to success-oriented theologies. Hunt (2002: 165) notes the way the RCCG in Britain has moved away from the sectarian and millenarian focus of traditional black Pentecostalism by inculcating some of the core values of Western society, such as materialism, success, careerism, and human potential. Congregational in-house magazines contain articles on financial issues and careers advice, and advertisements on behalf of financial advisers, mortgage advisers, and property consultants. African Pentecostals often regard financial accumulation as a means to an end: a way of financing evangelistic and social projects.

Nigerian Pentecostal churches are also committed to building members' capacity to influence society. This is reflected in some of the mottos adopted by individual congregations, such as "Empowering lives, influencing society for Christ" and "Manifesting expectations, impacting society", and their promotion of success-oriented theologies through sermons, conferences, magazines, and electronic media (Burgess 2011; Cartledge *et al.* 2019). As well as providing contexts for spiritual empowerment, churches organize seminars on business management, investment, marriage, job skills, and British culture. Some of the larger churches are able to mobilize considerable numbers of volunteers. For example, in 2009, Jesus House London had a volunteer workforce of around 650 members, serving in various departments in the church as well as in social engagement activities in the local community (Jesus House 2009).

Mission churches: church-planting and buildings

While transnational Nigerian churches function as social and religious support networks for African migrants, their rapid expansion is driven by a strong missionary agenda, fuelled by their metropolitan headquarters in Nigeria and the missionary ambitions of their pastors in the diaspora (Gornik 2011). Nigerian Pentecostals regard their churches as a significant social force with the potential to reverse the secularizing tendencies of the West. From their perspective, Nigeria is currently experiencing a Christian revival, which they hope to introduce into their host societies through a process of "reverse mission" (Burgess 2011). The predominant meaning of the term refers to the purported historic shift in the direction of mission. According to Paul Freston (2010: 155–156), this involves two main elements: a reversal in the geographical direction of mission and a reversal in the direction of "colonization", in other words an inversion of centre-periphery relations in Christianity, whereby the formerly colonized are now evangelizing the former colonizers. Most commonly it is used to refer to the emergence of African, Latin American, and Asian churches in Europe and the United States and their aspirations to re-evangelize the former heartlands of Christianity, which are regarded as increasingly secular (Ojo 2007).

The rhetoric of reverse mission adopted by Nigerian Pentecostals relies upon a particular self-representation and conception of the Other encountered in the host society. This often develops after their arrival in response to the perceived secularization and decline in Western Christianity compared to the religious vitality at home. Studies of contemporary international migrations have shown that the overwhelming majority are economically driven (Castles and Miller 2003). This was born out in my research which found that most Nigerian Pentecostals in Britain migrated either to study in order to improve their chances of gaining lucrative employment or to work, hoping to save money and improve their future prospects. However, many Nigerian Pentecostals in

Britain and the United States consider that God has given them a unique opportunity to bring the gospel back to those who originally provided it. As Olupona and Gemignani (2007: 8) note, the notion of "reverse mission" is "central to the way religion provides meaning and direction" for African Christians at different stages in the migration process.

Church-planting is an important strategy adopted by Nigerian Pentecostals to achieve their missionary ambitions. This is exemplified by the RCCG which has gained a global reputation for its church-planting activities. Included within its mission statement is the aim to "plant churches within five minutes walking distance in every city and town of developing countries and within five minutes driving distance in every city and town of developed countries" (RCCG 2019). The RCCG encourages members to plant churches wherever they are, thus fulfilling the divine promise given to its founder that the church would spread around the world before the Second Advent of Christ (Adedibu 2016). Acquiring a permanent place of worship is often a significant step in the process of integration and growth. Many Nigerian churches have to move from place to place, which seriously hampers their organizational structures, their numerical growth, and their capacity for community engagement (Burgess 2009). Invariably, financial constraints and planning regulations are the main obstacles to obtaining a building of their own. Once they do so, congregations are often left with heavy debts and the added financial burden of renovation and refurbishment.

Through church-planting, Nigerian Pentecostal churches have to engage with local social realities. This has a reciprocal effect of forcing local actors to take note of their presence, if only through the negotiations and permits needed to acquire or rent a building, the problems caused by the lack of parking spaces on Sunday, or the noise caused by all night prayer vigils. Several authors have shown how African Christian churches are instrumental in constituting the spaces and places of the African diaspora (Knibbe, 2009; Van der Meulen, 2009; Hunt, 2002; Harris, 2006). Typically embedded in "hard-to-reach" migrant communities, characterized by social inequalities, African diaspora churches represent largely untapped resources for social welfare interventions. In some areas of London, the religious landscape is littered with Nigerian churches, occupying a variety of secular and religious spaces including former industrial warehouses, office spaces, business centres, school halls, cinemas, and traditional church buildings. In the United States, Nigerian churches are mostly located in gateway cities such as New York, Washington, DC, Atlanta, and Houston, where there are large communities of African immigrants (Olupona and Gemignani 2007; Gornik 2011).

Community churches: social action and development practices

Studies of reverse mission sometimes measure success in terms of winning converts or adherents from indigenous communities and have consequently found migrant churches wanting (Freston 2010; Währisch-Oblau 2009; Hanciles 2008;

Ukah 2009). Yet Nigerian Pentecostals understand their mission in broader terms to include any activity that will change society for the better. This has driven some to embark on programmes of territorial expansion, not only through evangelism and church-planting but also by engaging in civic activity. Rather than reinforcing the image of Nigerians as economic migrants, or as prone to corruption and criminality, they are rebranding themselves as social activists contributing to the betterment of their neighbourhoods. Norris and Inglehart (2004) have noted the relationship between religious participation and civic engagement. They link this to theories of social capital which suggest that regular church-going encourages belonging to faith-based organizations and joining community groups in civic society.

Nigerian Pentecostal churches in Britain and the United States are engaged in a range of social initiatives, including soup kitchens for the homeless, feeding programmes for the poor, prison ministries, projects addressing crime and underachievement among young people, schools and educational programmes, healthcare initiatives, care for the elderly, pregnancy crisis centres, and international relief and development programmes. Some Nigerian congregations are involved in a wide spectrum of social engagement activities. Many are minimally engaged, however, either due to a particular theological orientation that favours evangelism over social action or because they lack the necessary human and material resources. Another variable is socio-cultural orientation. Those congregations whose main focus is the African diaspora have made limited headway in terms of church growth and civic engagement. Others that are cosmopolitan in character and more oriented towards British culture have fared better.

One congregation engaged in multiple social engagement activities is Jesus House London, RCCG's flagship parish in Britain. Jesus House's vision is to be a

> multicultural church made up of spiritually mature people of all ages living out their God-given purpose; a people who are passionate about social justice and committed to the spiritual transformation of society through the preaching of the complete message of Christ.
>
> (Jesus House 2017: 7)

Its mission and core values are informed by the scriptural text Matthew 22: 37–40.[6] Jesus House's social arm is called "Church Social Responsibility" (CSR), which consists of two strands: Community Action is the local expression of the church's social responsibility and CSR International is the international expression. Community Action initiatives include the Novo Centre (a drop-in centre for residents of a local housing estate), Jesus House Prison Ministry, the Manna Project (a food distribution centre), Abigail's Court (an outreach to the elderly), a Christians Against Poverty (CAP) debt counselling centre, and a Christmas homeless shelter (Burgess 2009). Jesus House tailors its social initiatives to meet the specific needs identified in the community either by buying into existing community franchises, such as the CAP debt counselling service and "Homeless in a Pack", or by developing its own projects (Adedoyin 2012). CSR International addresses problems associated with poverty, injustice, and conflict, and has collaborated with local churches and NGOs to fund projects in Africa, Asia, Latin America, and Eastern Europe. It also sends teams to visit and assist some of these projects (Irukwu 2012). Social engagement has enabled the church to gain public recognition, resulting in a number of high-profile visits from politicians and royalty, the most famous being those of the visit of the Prince of Wales in 2007 and of Teresa May, the former British Prime Minister, immediately prior to the 2017 general election. Jesus House also exports its social vision to other churches both at home and abroad through its annual "Heart & Soul" conferences which take place over three days in different locations.[7]

Several independent megachurches in London are also engaged in multiple social initiatives both at home and abroad. New Wine Church was founded in 1993 by former medical doctor Tayo Adeyemi. Before his untimely death in 2013, Adeyemi travelled the world as a conference speaker and church-planter.[8] The church's "Community Outreach" programme includes the John Wilson's Pantry, which provides food to people on low incomes; the Saturday Breakfast Club; an annual Christmas outreach to the homeless; financial empowerment workshops; a careers advisory service; an outreach to senior citizens called Cedar's Club; and a health and well-being initiative. The church is also engaged in international development activities in Africa, Asia, and Eastern Europe. In 2013, the Tayo Adeyemi Foundation was established by New Wine Church in memory of its founding pastor to further his legacy and provide a more robust structure for the church's humanitarian work (Cartledge *et al.* 2019). The foundation's goal is displayed on its website: "Empowering the poor, the vulnerable and less privileged for the purpose of alleviating poverty and promoting human dignity" (New Wine Church 2013). Kingsway International Christian Centre (KICC) is another independent church involved in multiple initiatives, including a befriending service to residents in homeless hostels, a prison ministry, a food bank, and the "Breaking Educational Barriers" programme which partners with universities to address educational inequalities within the black and minority ethnic community. KICC also runs an annual widows' empowerment programme in south-western Nigeria, which provides food, clothing and financial donations to Christian and Muslim widows (Cartledge *et al.* 2019).

Levels of social engagement among Nigerian Pentecostal churches in the United States also vary (Udotong 2010). One congregation which is heavily involved is RCCG's Kings Palace in Katy, Texas, which has two social arms: King's Justice Ministry and King's Touch Ministry. King's Justice Ministry consists of four outreach teams: "Governance and Politics", "Immigration and Social Integration", "Domestic Violence", and "Freedom Mission (Prison Outreach)" (RCCG King's Palace 2015a). King's Touch Ministry is an outreach to the homeless set up in response to the growing number of people from different ethnic, social, and religious backgrounds experiencing homelessness in America. Its vision statement is: "From the Streets to the Sanctuary, Transforming lives, Establishing Souls" (RCCG King's Palace 2015b). As a denomination, RCCG

North America has established a community initiative called "Hope for You" (HFY), headed by Dr Funmi Adeyemi, co-pastor of RCCG Lighthouse parish in Mansfield, Texas. HFY programmes include disaster relief, emergency shelter for the homeless, food assistance, poverty alleviation initiatives, health services, financial and employment counselling, and care for immigrants (RCCG North America 2019).

Poverty alleviation: homeless projects and foodbanks

Some Nigerian Pentecostal churches are addressing poverty-related issues such as homelessness and food deprivation. Homelessness is recognized as a significant problem in most developed countries, with higher rates of homelessness in the United States and Britain than elsewhere (Toro *et al.* 2007; Shinn 2010; Pleace 2010). In Britain, this is due in part to rising unemployment, inequality, social exclusion, and a reduction in social housing and homeless hostels. Migrant groups at risk include British citizens with a Black African or Caribbean ethnic origin, asylum-seekers and other undocumented migrants, and non-UK EU citizens (Pleace 2010; Busch-Geertsema *et al.* 2014; Fitzpatrick *et al.* 2012). During the 1990s, government initiatives introduced to tackle homelessness included the Rough Sleepers Initiative and the Homeless Action Programme and Rough Sleepers Unit. In April 2008, the Labour Government announced their intention to end rough sleeping by 2012. However, due to the impact of the economic downturn, long-term housing shortages, and cuts in social benefits, homelessness is again on the rise. Non-government organizations are also addressing the problem of homelessness. Alongside highly professionalized mainstream institutions, numerous smaller organizations, often poorly resourced and reliant on volunteers, provide homeless services such as soup runs and temporary accommodation (Johnsen, Cloke, and May 2005). The majority of basic services for the homeless are provided by FBOs, representing a range of religious affiliations including minority non-Christian faiths (Johnsen 2014).

Homelessness is also prevalent in the United States. Factors that have contributed to high rates of homelessness include social exclusion, housing discrimination, the experience of mental illness, the absence of a comprehensive social welfare system, and the existence of large numbers of people from minority ethnic groups. Among those over-represented among the homeless population are African Americans and Native Americans (Shinn 2010; Toro *et al.* 2007). Homelessness services are provided by government agencies and private non-profit organizations, including FBOs. The first major federal response to homelessness was the Stewart B. McKinney Homeless Assistance Act (now known as the McKinney-Vento Homeless Assistance Act), which was signed into law in 1987. It comprised a spectrum of initiatives, including provision of federal money for homeless shelter programmes and educational access for children and youth in homeless situations (Julianelle and Foscarinis 2003). The Act has been reauthorized over the years by the US Congress. The McKinney-Vento Homeless Education Assistance Improvements Act, aimed at ensuring the educational rights of homeless children and youth, was signed into law in 2001. Alongside secular non-profit institutions, FBOs have made significant contributions to homeless services in the United States, especially in the provision of food and shelter (Bass 2009; Toro and Warren 1999).

One of the first Nigerian Pentecostals to engage in ministry to the homeless was Ade Omooba, co-founder of the Christian Victory Group, a small Pentecostal church in Brixton, south London, which has a large African Caribbean community. Pastor Ade was born in Nigeria and brought up in the Anglican Church. In the mid-1980s, he relocated to London and began to attend a branch of the Christ Apostolic Church, one of the earliest Nigerian Pentecostal denominations to spread to Britain. Pastor Ade founded the Christian Victory Group in 1991. Christian Victory Group's "I Care" Homeless Project operates in Central London, supplying basic provisions such as food and clothing to over 100 people each week. It also provides a referral advice service to the homeless who require information about accommodation, welfare benefits, immigration, employment, and health. During the 1990s, Pastor Ade and his associates joined more established secular and religious organizations such as Oxfam, Shelter, the Salvation Army, and Crisis to lobby the government and persuade it to tackle the problem of "rough sleepers". More recently the focus of his work has shifted to politics and public policy engagement through the auspices of Christian Concern, a grassroots organization he co-founded in 2005 which seeks to empower Christians to engage in public life.[9]

Several RCCG congregations in Britain and the United States also run homeless programmes. Two examples will suffice. Croydon Tabernacle's "Heart of Compassion" in south London caters for homeless adults, including those with alcohol and drug addiction. Every Sunday, before the regular service, "Heart of Compassion" holds a separate worship service for "clients" who wish to attend. Church members also provide them with food and clothing. The church has formed a partnership with Alcoholics Anonymous and has attracted the attention of the local MP, who has visited on a number of occasions (Adedoyin 2009: 22).[10] Winners Assembly was founded by Raphael Adebayo in Dallas, Texas. The city of Dallas has a growing number of homeless people, with over 50 per cent from black and African American minority ethnic groups (McGee 2017). In 1995, Adebayo, a former Muslim, migrated to the United States in search of a better life. After his conversion to Christianity, while studying at the University of Texas, he joined RCCG following a visit to Nigeria where he attended RCCG's famous Lekki '98 Holy Ghost Service. Winners Assembly is located in inner-city South Dallas and most of its members are homeless or formerly homeless people. Every Tuesday night, the church serves meals to over 100 people. Despite its small congregation, it has purchased three houses where homeless people can live rent-free while looking for work. The church has also purchased land to build an outreach centre which will combine as a worship centre and a home for young pregnant women (Lyons 2014).

Some Nigerian Pentecostal churches are running food banks and other food assistance programmes. Emergency food banks have become a prominent, and politically controversial, feature of austerity measures in Europe and the United States (Garthwaite, Collins, and Bambra 2015). In Britain, where foodbanks are a relatively new phenomenon, food poverty presents a significant public health risk (Purdam, Garratt, and Esmail 2016). According to the Trussell Trust, which runs the largest network of food banks in Britain, food banks fed more than 1.3 million people nationwide between April 2017 and March 2018, a 13 per cent increase on the previous year (Trussell Trust 2019a). Trussell Trust is a Christian charity whose foodbank initiative is based on the premise that local foodbanks should be Christian-led projects. Its first foodbank in England was established in 2000 (Lambie 2011). By the end of 2018, the number of foodbanks supported by the Trussell Trust had grown to 1,200 (Trussell Trust 2019b). The stipulation that foodbanks are church-led initiatives taps into the Christian pre-disposition and commitment to engage in social action as well as the geographical reach of churches across the country (Lambie 2011).

Food insecurity is also a serious challenge facing families in the United States, especially since the 2008 recession (Gundersen *et al.* 2011; Weinfeld *et al.* 2014). In 2012, more than one in seven (17.6 million) US households experienced food insecurity, with rates of food poverty about twice as high among Black and Hispanic households (Weinfeld *et al.* 2014). The three largest federal food assistance programmes are the Supplemental Nutrition Assistance Program, the Special Supplemental Nutrition Program for Women, Infants, and Children, and the National School Lunch Program. Charitable food assistance programmes complement federal programmes. One of the largest is Feeding America, a nationwide network of 200 foodbanks and 60,000 food pantries and meal programmes. Foodbanks in the United States operate differently from Britain. In the United States, food banks act as warehouses, distributing food through a network of non-profit partner agencies like food pantries and other front-line organizations. In Britain, food banks hand out food parcels directly to clients. The majority of US partner agencies are faith-based or located in religious organizations. Other groups include secular non-profit organizations, Community Action Programmes, and government agencies (Weinfeld *et al.* 2014).

In Britain, Nigerian Pentecostal congregations collaborate with other churches to run food banks, sometimes hosting them in their church premises. In 2009, in partnership with the Trussell Trust, RCCG's Kingsborough Family Church started the Hillingdon Foodbank, the first of its kind in London. In 2011, the London Lighthouse (House on the Rock) opened Islington foodbank as part of its Touching the Community initiative. In April 2012, the church hosted the Trussell Trust's annual national Foodbank Conference, which was attended by representatives from across the country.[11] Other Trussell Trust foodbanks run by Nigerian-led Pentecostal churches in London include Jubilee Church's Enfield Foodbank, the Colindale Foodbank, which operates out of Jesus House's Novo Centre, and Haringey Foodbank, run by RCCG Living Spring Centre in collaboration with other churches in Tottenham.

In the United States, some Nigerian Pentecostal churches run food pantries in partnership with local food banks. One example is RCCG Strong Tower parish

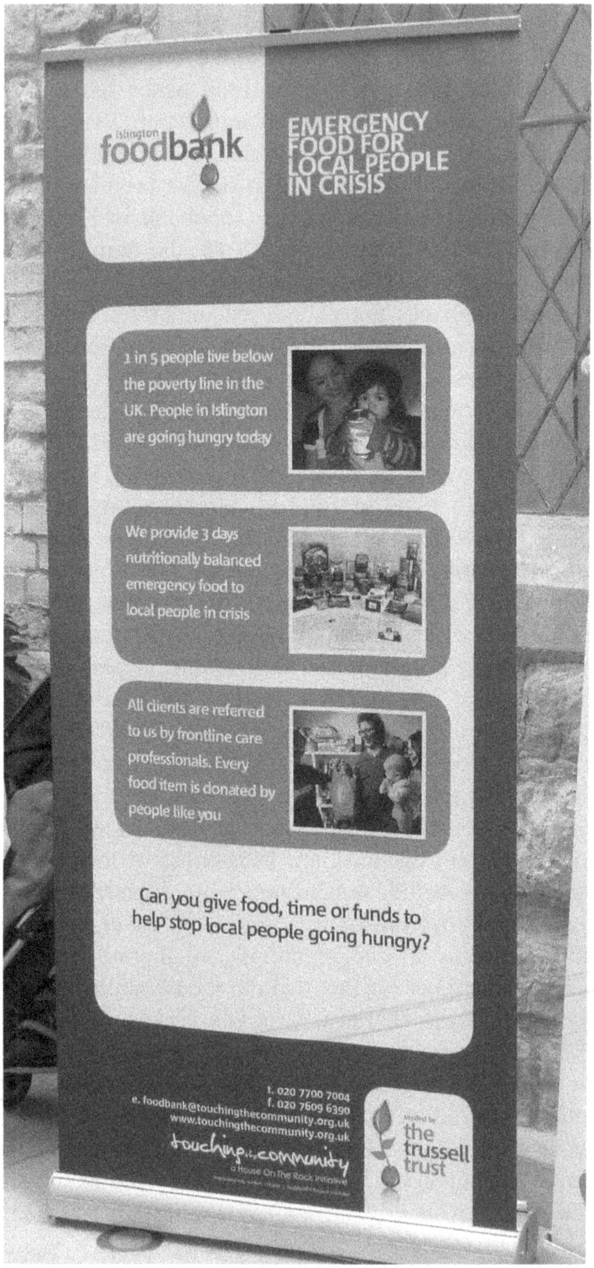

Figure 8.1 Banner advertising the Islington Foodbank in the foyer of House on the Rock, London.

Source: author.

in New Jersey. In 2011, Pastor Bunmi Oloidi founded the Benevolent Food Pantry, as a partner agency of South Jersey Food Bank. As well as supporting church members, especially those who had recently migrated to the United States, it distributes food to poorer members in the wider community (RCCG Strong Tower 2019). Another example is Restoration Chapel in Houston, Texas, which runs a food pantry in partnership with Houston Food Bank, an affiliate of Feeding America (RCCG Restoration Chapel 2019). The majority of Houston Food Bank's partner agencies are churches and other faith-based social service providers. However, it also works with secular non-profit organizations such as Target Hunger.

Tackling youth crime and gang violence

Nigerian Pentecostal churches in Britain are especially sensitive to the plight of black and minority ethnic (BME) children and young people, who often underachieve in Britain's educational system. BME underachievement is supported by research over the past two decades which has shown a close link between school exclusion, educational underachievement, unemployment, and involvement in the criminal justice system (Barn 2001; Graham and Robinson 2004). Some churches are engaged in ministry to young people involved in crime and street gangs. Here I focus on London, where there has been a surge of gun and knife crime involving youth gangs in recent years, raising serious concerns among the police and government policy-makers about how to tackle the problem.

In 2018, London's homicide rate reached its highest level in a decade, with 131 fatalities, including at least 75 stabbings and 13 shootings. Just over one third of victims were aged 16 to 24 (Dodd and Grierson 2018). As I write, reports in the media are referring to an epidemic of knife crimes and an escalation of fatalities involving young people (Dodd 2019). In London, an increasing number of African, including Nigerian, young people are joining gangs (Akomolafe 2016). The rise in crimes involving knives is partly blamed on cuts in community policing and youth centres. However, the growth of street gangs and youth crime is exacerbated by high levels of unemployment, parental neglect, and racial and ethnic tensions. Recent incidents, such as the murder of the Nigerian teenager Damilola Taylor in 2000, have "thrust violence perpetrated on and by black young people onto the public agenda" (House of Commons Home Affairs Committee 2007: 8). At the time of his murder, Damilola's family were members of Mountain of Fire and Miracles in Peckham, south-east London, which has the highest concentration of Nigerian immigrants in Britain. According to a recent House of Commons Home Affairs Committee report, young black people are more likely to be victims of violent crime (House of Commons Home Affairs Committee 2007). They are also disproportionately represented in the British criminal justice system (Pitts 2015). Crime is considered a viable alternative route to success for some young people, and gangs represent an alternative structure in which to achieve (House of Commons Home Affairs Committee 2007).

Some of the Nigerian pastors I interviewed in London expressed concern over the growing incidence of gun and knife crime and the number of young people from their churches who are joining gangs. One Pentecostal initiative specifically geared towards tackling youth crime in London is the Peace Alliance, founded by Nims Obunge, senior pastor of Freedom's Ark in the Borough of Haringey. Before its relocation to the former Tottenham Town Hall, Freedom's Ark was situated close to Tottenham's Broadwater Farm Estate where the notorious 1985 race riot took place.[12] In 2001, Pastor Nims launched the Peace Alliance in response to the growing levels of violent crime in Haringey. In an interview, he described how the Peace Alliance was started:

> There were young people being shot and stabbed in our community and I was being asked to bury young people who had never darkened our church steps. And the responsibility I felt was that we needed to do more work outside rather than inside the church.... So we developed material and held campaigns with the police and local council. And together with voluntary and community agencies, we said, we've got to do something about this. So Peace Alliance was part of that response.[13]

The Peace Alliance works in partnership with local churches, other faith groups, the Home Office, the Metropolitan Police, borough councils and local MPs to promote community safety and crime prevention. Since its inception, it has become a London-wide initiative involving all 33 boroughs. It also organizes the London Week of Peace, an annual event supported by the Mayor of London, the Metropolitan Police and the Home Office, which celebrates initiatives across the city that impact the community. In February 2007, Pastor Nims played a key role in galvanizing the church community in London to march against gun crime after the fatal killings of five young people. He is a regular visitor to 10 Downing Street and other corridors of power to give advice on young people, youth crime, and community safety. In the course of his work, he has held meetings with Prime Ministers Tony Blair, Gordon Brown, and David Cameron. In 2007, he was awarded an MBE in recognition of his services to community relations in Tottenham.[14] Pastor Nims believes that the current escalation of knife and gun crime in London makes it less safe than Nigeria for young people. In a recent interfaith conference on knife crime and youth violence, he expressed frustration about the lack of progress made towards alleviating the problem, despite the combined efforts of politicians and police. He believes that initiatives addressing youth crime need to be led by the community (including families and faith groups) rather than by the police (Obunge 2019). In 2019, Pastor Nims announced his intention to run as an independent candidate to be Mayor of London.

Another church addressing BME youth underachievement and crime in London is Salvation Proclaimers Anointed Church (SPAC) Nation, a transnational Nigerian Pentecostal church founded by Prophet Samuel Adegboyega in Ibadan, Nigeria. In 2008, his son Tobi Adegboyega co-founded a branch of

SPAC Nation in Peckham, south London. The church regularly attracts around 1,300 attendees to its Sunday worship services. Many of those who attend are young black African and Caribbean men and women who have previously been involved in criminal activities and youth gangs. However, church members also include property developers, city traders, doctors, and lawyers.

The five "pillars" or foundations of SPAC Nation are the Word of God, prayer, holiness, evangelism, and giving, reflecting its Pentecostal ethos (Olutoye 2019). Church services often last for hours and feature exuberant worship, sermons, altar calls for salvation, and prayers for participants to receive Holy Spirit baptism. Evangelism is critical to the growth of the church. The outreach team conducts street evangelism in various locations in London. One innovation is the establishment of TRAP ("Take Risk and Prosper") houses, which mimic the trap houses used by drug gangs. Here new converts find refuge from the rigours of street life and undergo a strict regime of Bible study and prayer. The church's strategy for rehabilitating and empowering young people is capacity-building through teaching, counselling, financial assistance, and mentoring (Akomolafe 2016). Pastor Tobi's ministry is supported by a cadre of young pastors who lead fellowship groups and disciple new converts. One of his mentors is Tunde Bakare, senior pastor of the Latter Rain Assembly in Lagos, who is a regular speaker at SPAC Nation events. Social media is used to publicize the church and testimonies of gang members turned business entrepreneurs are posted on the church's website. One of its flagship events is "Entrepreneurial Sunday" where young people from cities across Britain come together to pitch innovative businesses for investment opportunities. The SPAC Nation Foundation supports young black people from disadvantaged backgrounds by investing in start-up businesses, providing tuition fees, and mentoring. According to Pastor Tobi, the church provides former gang members and ex-offenders with alternative lifestyles and an extended family network, enabling them to prosper in their chosen professions.[15]

SPAC Nation has received media publicity due to its success in rehabilitating former gang members, its emphasis on prosperity and business entrepreneurship, and its distinctive style of worship which includes the use of hip-hop and "Gospel drill" music.[16] It has also been commended by politicians for its approach to tackling knife crime. However, the church is currently under investigation by the London Metropolitan Police and the Charity Commission over allegations of fraud and the exploitation of vulnerable young people. The church's senior leaders have refuted these allegations (Sabbagh and Gayle 2019; BBC 2020; Singh 2020).

Transnational development practices

There is also a transnational dimension to Nigerian Pentecostal development practices. Individuals and churches are engaged in a variety of practices, ranging from financial remittances and charitable donations, to short-term mission trips and development projects. Church members send remittances to support their families back home in Nigeria (Gornik 2011). Collective remittances are sent by churches to their Nigerian headquarters and to support social initiatives in Eastern Europe, Africa, Asia, and Latin America. Churches are also engaged in advocacy and awareness-raising on behalf of socially marginalized and economically disadvantaged groups through the use of media, conference events, and meetings with politicians. Media is also used to solicit charitable donations from church members. Most international development work is undertaken by large congregations with sufficient human and financial resources at their disposal. Here I focus on Pentecostal churches and FBOs in Britain and the United States engaged in multiple international development initiatives.

New Wine Church's Tayo Adeyemi Foundation has supported a number of international development projects, including an agricultural empowerment project in Tanzania, an HIV/AIDS programme in South Africa, and a building project for leprosy sufferers in India. It has also sponsored short-term mission trips to Papua New Guinea, South Africa, India, Tanzania, and Ghana (Cartledge *et al.* 2019). Another independent megachurch in London is Christ Faith Tabernacle (CFT), founded by Apostle Alfred Williams in 1989. CFT has branches in London, Birmingham, and Bristol, and internationally in the Republic of Ireland, Germany, India, and Nigeria. CFT's Jesus City Project is an ambitious development initiative aimed at alleviating poverty in Nigeria. Its motto is: "Help Africans build Africa. Transforming nations, one person at a time." So far, the church has purchased 430 acres of land at Ogere, Ogun State. The project comprises seven main areas: social housing, healthcare, agriculture, education, rehabilitation, recreation/leisure, and business. It also plans to build a 20,000-seater church auditorium. Although in its nascent phase, two projects are already underway: an agricultural project and a borehole project (Christ Faith Tabernacle n.d.).

Some of the larger RCCG congregations in Britain and the United States are also involved in international projects. In 2005, at the height of the Lord's Resistance Army insurgency in Uganda, Jesus House London sent a team to visited Pader, one of three districts most affected by the conflict. Following the visit, Jesus House partnered with local churches to finance the building of a shelter for displaced children of the war (Jesus House 2008). Jesus House also works with Solace Ministries in a region of Rwanda affected by the 1994 genocide. Solace Ministries is a Uganda-based ministry established in 1995 by a survivor of the genocide, Jean Gakwandi. The joint programme which kicked off in 2010 involved the purchase of livestock for every family in the community, and the training of families in livestock breeding, sales, and business management (Jesus House 2017). Jesus House has also donated emergency funds to support those affected by the 2004 Tsunami crisis, the 2010 Haiti earthquake, and the 2017 Sierra Leone flood. In 2017, it spent £92,730 on international projects (Jesus House 2017). RCCG congregations in the United States are also involved in international development work, though on a smaller scale than Jesus House London. For example, Jesus House Washington, DC runs Heritage International

Projects, which partners with NGOs in Nigeria, such as Trinity House's Heritage Homes Orphanage and Courage Educational Foundation, to provide educational scholarships, accommodation, transportation, food and clothing, microfinance, and skills development (Jesus House Washington, DC 2018).

RCCG churches worldwide support Africa Missions, an FBO founded in 1996 by Pastor Folu Adeboye, the wife of the General Overseer, to support RCCG missionaries and social welfare projects in Africa. Africa Missions works with other NGOs and uses RCCG's extensive global network of churches to reach underdeveloped, and often remote, communities. Its goal is to "Reach, Restore and Rebuild lives and communities in Africa and around the world" (Africa Missions Global 2019). Projects include the provision of church buildings, rehabilitation hostels, vocational centres, boreholes, medical institutions, schools, microfinance for small businesses, and emergency relief interventions. Organizationally, Africa Missions is divided into 11 chapters spread across countries in Europe, Canada, the United States, and Nigeria, each responsible for raising funds and executing projects in different regions of Africa. In keeping with RCCG's holistic approach to mission, Africa Missions combines social action with gospel evangelism. This is reflected in the three-fold mission of Africa Missions UK: "To promote the spread of the gospel and to alleviate poverty", "To promote the development of sustainable holistic programs", and "To provide services that will improve the quality of life of children, youth, families and aging people" (Africa Missions UK 2008).

Conclusion

This chapter has examined the relationship between Nigerian Pentecostalism, migration and development with a particular focus on diaspora communities in Britain and the United States. International migration is centrally positioned within the post-2015 sustainable development agenda, and migrants are regarded as vital agents of development by the international community. However, they are also vulnerable to poverty-related issues such as homelessness and food insecurity. Recent studies of immigrant religion have explored the contribution of faith groups to migrant incorporation and civic engagement as well as the transnational flows of financial resources, religious personnel, and influence between host and home countries.

The Pentecostal churches discussed in the chapter function as social and religious support mechanisms for African migrants, enabling them to negotiate the migration process and become incorporated into their host societies. Nigerian Pentecostals regard their churches as a significant social force with the potential to reverse the secularizing tendencies of Europe and the United States. From their perspective, Nigeria is currently experiencing a Christian revival, which they hope to introduce into their host societies through a process of reverse mission. As I have argued in the chapter, Nigerian Pentecostals understand their mission in broad terms to include any activity that will change society for the better. This has driven some churches to embark on programmes of territorial expansion, not only through evangelism and church-planting, but also by engaging in development activities in the wider community. The chapter examined a range of initiatives in Britain and the United States that address social issues such as homelessness, food insecurity, and youth crime. It also explored the transnational dimension and the contribution of diaspora churches to international development through individual and collective remittances, short-term mission trips, and development projects.

Notes

1 Nigerians in the diaspora sent an estimated US$25 billion in remittances to Nigeria in 2018, representing 6.1 per cent of its GDP. This figure translates to 83 per cent of the Federal Government budget in 2018 (Nevin and Omosomi 2019).
2 Warner's New Ethnic and Immigration Congregations Project studied immigrant religious communities across the United States. See Warner and Wittner (eds) (1998).
3 For example, RCCG Royal Connections parish, located in a predominantly white London neighbourhood, has an "Integration and career advisory team", and RCCG Kings Palace in Katy, Texas, has an "Immigration and social integration" team.
4 Interview, Pastor Ranti Oyewale, RCCG Covenant Restoration Assembly, Birmingham, 30 September 2010.
5 Interview, Pastor Ranti Oyewale, RCCG Covenant Restoration Assembly, Birmingham, 31 July 2011.
6 Matt 22: 37–40: "You must love the Lord your God with all your heart, all your soul, and all your mind. This is the first and greatest commandment. A second is equally important: 'Love your neighbour as yourself' " (New Living Translation).
7 For a detailed discussion of Jesus House London's social engagement activities, see Cartledge *et al.* (2019: 220–227).
8 New Wine Church has planted two branches in London and internationally in Nigeria, Uganda, South Africa, Canada, Luxembourg, and Bulgaria.
9 Interview, Pastor Ade Omooba, Christian Victory Group, London, 26 October 2010.
10 Interview, Pastor Ayo Ayeni, RCCG Croydon Tabernacle, London, 23 April 2008.
11 Interview, Pastor Michael Efueye, House on the Rock, London, 18 June 2012.
12 The background to the riot was the growing tensions between the predominantly white British and non-local police and the African-Caribbean community in Haringey.
13 Interview, Pastor Nims Obunge, Freedom's Ark, London, 5 August 2010.
14 Interview, Pastor Nims Obunge, Freedom's Ark, London, 5 August 2010.
15 Interview, Pastor Tobi Adegboyega, SPAC Nation, London, 14 March 2019.
16 Interview, Pastor Tobi Adegboyega, SPAC Nation, London, 14 March 2019.

References

Adedibu, Babatunde (2016) "Missional History and the Growth of the Redeemed Christian Church of God in the United Kingdom (1988–2015)", *Journal of the European Pentecostal Theological Association* 36(1): 80–93.

Adedoyin, Ayo (2009) "Croydon Tabernacle: Reaching Out With a 'Heart of Compassion' ", *Festival News*, March.

Adedoyin, Ayo (2012) "Impacting the Community", Paper presented at the Heart & Soul Conference, Jesus House, 6 July.

Adogame, Afe (2013) *The African Christian Diaspora: New Currents and Emerging Trends in World Christianity*, London: Bloomsbury.

Africa Missions Global (2019) "Our Vision", available at: http://africamissionsglobal.org/ (accessed 5 October 2019).

Africa Missions UK (2008) "Our Vision", *Africa Missions UK Newsletter* 2: 2.

Akomolafe, Femi (2016) *Black Damage: Why Africa and Black Communities Across the World Are Poor and Dysfunctional and the Ways Forward*, London: PublishNation.

Barn, Ravinder (2001) *Black Youth on the Margins: A Research Review*, York: Joseph Rowntree Foundation.

Bass, Ben G. (2009) "Faith-based Programs and Their Influence on Homelessness", *Family & Community Health* 32(4): 314–319.

BBC News (2020) "SPAC Nation: Church to be Debated in Parliament", 8 January 2020, available at: www.bbc.co.uk/news/uk-england-london-51034904 (accessed 11 January 2020).

Beckford, Robert (2011) *Dread and Pentecostal: A Political Theology for the Black Church in Britain*, Eugene, OR: Wipf and Stock Publishers.

Brettel, Caroline B. and James F. Hollifield (2000) "Introduction", in Caroline B. Brettell and James F. Hollifield (eds) *Migration Theory: Talking Across Disciplines*, London: Routledge, pp. 1–24.

Burgess, Richard (2009) "African Pentecostal Spirituality and Civic Engagement: The Case of the Redeemed Christian Church of God in Britain", *Journal of Beliefs & Values* 30(3): 255–273.

Burgess, Richard (2011) "Bringing Back the Gospel: Reverse Mission among Nigerian Pentecostals in Britain", *Journal of Religion in Europe* 4: 429–449.

Busch-Geertsema, Volker, Lars Benjaminsen, Masa F. Hrast, and Nicholas Pleace (2014) *Extent and Profile of Homelessness in European Member States: A Statistical Update*, Brussels: FEANTSA.

Cartledge, Mark J., Sarah Dunlop, Heather Buckingham, and Sophie Bremner (2019) *Megachurches and Social Engagement: Public Theology in Practice*, Leiden: E. J. Brill.

Castles, Stephen and Mark J. Miller (2003) *The Age of Migration: International Population Movements in the Modern World*, Basingstoke: Palgrave.

Christ Faith Tabernacle (n.d.) Brochure, Jesus City. Refuge for the Nations.

Dodd, Vikram (2019) "Knife Attacks on Teenagers Up By 93% In Five Years, Figures Show", *Guardian*, 4 March, available at: www.theguardian.com/uk-news/2019/mar/04/knife-attacks-teenagers-figures-east-london-manchester (accessed 6 October 2019).

Dodd, Vikram and Jamie Grierson (2018) "London Homicides Now Highest Annual Rate for a Decade", *Guardian*, 12 December, available at: www.theguardian.com/uk-news/2018/dec/12/london-homicides-now-highest-in-a-year-for-a-decade (accessed 6 October 2019).

Duffour, Amy (2012) "Moving Up and Moving Out? Cosmopolitan and Class Narratives in the Expansion of a London-based 'African Pentecostal' Church", in David Goodhew (ed.), *Church Growth in Britain. 1980 to the Present*, London: Ashgate, pp. 145–160.

Ebaugh, Helen R. and Janet S. Chafetz (2000) *Religion and the New Immigrants: Continuities and Adaptations in Immigrant Congregations*, Walnut Creek, CA: Altamira Press.

Ebaugh, Helen R. and Janet S. Chafetz (2002) "Prologue", in Helen R. Ebaugh and Janet S. Chafetz (eds) *Religion Across Borders: Transnational Immigrant Networks*, Walnut Creek, CA: Altamira Press, pp. vii–xvi.

Faist, Thomas (2008) "Migrants as Transnational Development Agents: An Inquiry into the Newest Round of the Migration–Development Nexus", *Population, Space and Place* 14(1): 21–42.

Fesenmyer, Leslie (2016) "'Assistance But Not Support': Pentecostalism and the Reconfiguring of Relatedness Between Kenya and the United Kingdom", in Jennifer Cole and Christian Gross (eds) *Affective Circuits: African Migrants to Europe and the Pursuit of Social Regeneration*, Chicago: University of Chicago Press, pp. 125–145.

Fitzpatrick, Suzanne, Sarah Johnsen, and Glen Bramley (2012) "Multiple Exclusion Homelessness amongst Migrants in the UK", *European Journal of Homelessness* 6(1): 31–57.

Foley, Michael W. and Dean R. Hoge (2007) *Religion and the New Immigrants: How Faith Communities form our Newest Citizens*, Oxford: Oxford University Press.

Freston, Paul (2010) "Reverse Mission: A Discourse in Search of Reality?" *PentecoStudies* 9(2): 153–174.

Garthwaite, K. A., P. J. Collins, and C. Bambra (2015) "Food for Thought: An Ethnographic Study of Negotiating Ill Health and Food Insecurity in a UK Foodbank", *Social Science & Medicine* 132: 38–44.

Glick Schiller, Nina and Thomas Faist (2010) "Migration, Development and Social Transformation", in Nina Glick Schiller and Thomas Faist (eds) *Migration, Development and Transnationalization: A Critical Stance*, New York/Oxford: Berghahn Books, pp. 1–21.

Gornik, Mark R. (2011) *Word Made Global: Stories of African Christianity in New York City*, Grand Rapids, MI: Eerdmans.

Graham, Mejada and Gil Robinson (2004) "'The Silent Catastrophe': Institutional Racism in the British Educational System and the Underachievment of Black Boys", *Journal of Black Studies* 34(5): 653–671.

Grillo, Ralph D. (2001) "Transnational Migration and Multiculturalism in Europe", Oxford: ESRC Transnational Communities Working Paper WPTC-01–08.

Gundersen, Craig, Brent Kreider, and John Pepper (2011) "The Economics of Food Insecurity in the United States", *Applied Economic Perspectives and Policy* 33(3): 281–303.

Hadley, Craig, Ariel Zodhiates, and Daniel W. Sellen (2007) "Acculturation, Economics and Food Insecurity Among Refugees Resettled in the USA: A Case Study of West African Refugees", *Public Health Nutrition* 10(4): 405–412.

Hagan, Jacqueline and Helen R. Ebaugh (2003) "Calling upon the Sacred: Migrants' Use of Religion in the Migration Process", *International Migration Review* 37(4): 1145–1162.

Hanciles, Jehu J. (2008) *Beyond Christendom: Globalization, African Migration, and the Transformation of the West*, Maryknoll: Orbis Books.

Harris, Hermione (2006) *Yoruba in Diaspora: An African Church in London*, New York: Palgrave Macmillan.

House of Commons Home Affairs Committee (2007) "Young Black People and the Criminal Justice System", Second Report of Session 2006–07, Volume 1, 15 June.

Hunt, Stephen (2002) "'Neither Here nor There': The Construction of Identities and Boundary Maintenance of West African Pentecostals", *Sociology* 36(1): 147–169.

Irukwu, Sola (2012) "Changing our World", Paper presented at the Heart & Soul Conference, Jesus House, 6 July.

Jesus House (2008) *Lending a Hand: Jesus House Annual Review 2008*, London: Jesus House.

Jesus House (2009) *Making a Difference: Jesus House Annual Review 2009*, London: Jesus House.

Jesus House (2017) *A New Dimension: Jesus House Annual Report 2017*, available at: www.jesushouse.org.uk/sites/default/files/jh-ar-2017-issuu.pdf (accessed 5 October 2019).

Jesus House Washington, DC (2018) "Community Outreach", available at: www.jesushousedc.org/project/community-outreach/ (accessed 15 August 2019).

Johnsen, Sarah (2014) "Where's the 'Faith' in 'Faith-based' Organisations? The Evolution and Practice of Faith-based Homelessness Services in the UK", *Journal of Social Policy* 43(2): 413–430.

Johnsen, Sarah, Paul Cloke, and Jon May (2005) "Transitory Spaces of Care: Serving Homeless People on the Streets", *Health & Place* 11(4) 323–336.

Julianelle, Patricia F. and Maria Foscarinis (2003) "Responding to the School Mobility of Children and Youth Experiencing Homelessness: The Mckinney-Vento Act and Beyond", *Journal of Negro Education* 72(10): 39–54.

Kalu, Ogbu U. (2008) *African Pentecostalism: An Introduction*, Oxford: Oxford University Press.

Knibbe, Kim E. (2009) "We Did Not Come Here as Tenants, But as Landlords. Nigerian Pentecostals and the Power of Maps", *African Diaspora* 1(2): 133–158.

Lambie, Hannah (2011) *The Trussell Trust Food Network: Exploring the Growth of Food Banks Across the UK*, Coventry: Coventry University.

Levitt, Peggy (1998) "Social Remittances: Migration Driven Local-Level Forms of Cultural Diffusion", *International Migration Review* 32(4): 926–948.

Levitt, Peggy (2001) *Between God, Ethnicity, and Country: An Approach to the Study of Transnational Religion*, Oxford: ESRC Transnational Communities Working Paper WPTC-01–13.

Lyons, Julie (2014) "Raphael Adebayo, a Former Muslim, Found His Calling on the Streets as Pastor to the Homeless", *Manna Express*, available at: www.mannaexpressonline.com/raphael-adebayo-a-former-muslim-found-his-calling-on-the-streets-as-pastor-to-the-homeless/ (accessed 5 October 2019).

McGee, Mike (2017) "Homeless in Dallas: Over Half Are Black", *The Dallas Examiner*, 19 March, available at: http://dallasexaminer.com/news/2017/mar/19/homeless-dallas-over-half-are-black/ (accessed 4 October 2019).

McLoughlin, Seán (2005) "The State, 'New' Muslim Leaderships and Islam as a 'Resource' for Engagement in Britain", in Jocelyne Cesari and Seán McLoughlin (eds) *European Muslims and the Secular State*, Aldershot: Ashgate, pp. 55–69.

Nevin, Andrew S. and Omomia Omosomi (2019) "Nigeria Economic Outlook. Top 10 Themes for 2019", available at: PricewaterhouseCoopers Nigeria, available at: www.pwc.com/ng/en/publications/nigeria-economic-outlook.html (accessed 6 October 2019).

New Wine Church (2013) "Tayo Adeyemi Foundation", available at: www.drtayofoundation.org/foundation (accessed 10 April 2019).

Nijenhuis, Geri and Maggi Leung (2017) "Rethinking Migration in the 2030 Agenda: Towards a De-territorialized Conceptualization of Development", *Forum for Development Studies* 44(1): 51–68.

Norris, Pippa and Ronald Inglehart (2004) *Sacred and Secular: Religion and Politics Worldwide*, Cambridge: Cambridge University Press.

Numrich, Paul and Fred Kniss (2007) *Sacred Assemblies and Civic Engagement: How Religion Matters for America's Newest Immigrants*, Piscataway, NJ: Rutgers University Press.

Obunge, Nims (2019) "Addressing the Challenges of Knife Crime and Youth Violence in London", Paper presented at the "Your Voice for a Noble Cause" Conference, KAICIID Dialogue Centre International Fellows Programme and Whitelands College (Roehampton University), London, 24 August.

Ojo, Matthews A. (2007) "Reverse Mission", in Jonathan Bonk (ed.) *Encyclopedia of Missions and Missionaries*, New York & London: Routledge, p. 380.

Olukoya, Daniel K. (1999) *Overpowering Witchcraft*, Lagos: MFM Ministries.

Olupona, Jacob O. and Regina Gemignani (2007) "Introduction", in Jacob O. Olupona and Regina Gemignani (eds) *African Immigrant Religions in America*, New York: New York University Press, pp. 1–26.

Olutoye, Funmi (2019) "SPAC Nation: A Church Transforming the Lives of Young People", *Keep the Faith*, available at: www.keepthefaith.co.uk/2018/06/21/spac-nation-a-church-transforming-the-lives-of-young-people-by-fungi-olutoye/ (accessed 29 September 2019).

Oskooii, Kassra A. and Karam Dana (2018) "Muslims in Great Britain: The Impact of Mosque Attendance on Political Behaviour and Civic Engagement", *Journal of Ethnic and Migration Studies* 44(9): 1479–1505.

Page, Ben and Claire Mercer (2010) "Diasporas and Development", in Kim Knott and Seán McLoughlin (eds) *Diasporas: Concepts, Intersections, Identities*, London, Zed Books, pp. 102–106.

Peace, Timothy (ed.) (2015) *Muslims and Political Participation in Britain*, London: Routledge.

Piper, Nicola (2017) "Migration and the SDGs", *Global Social Policy* 17(2): 231–238.

Pitts, John (2015) "Youth Crime and Youth Justice", *Youth & Policy* 114: 31–42.

Pleace, N. (2010) "Immigration and Homelessness", in E. O'Sullivan, V. Busch-Geertsema, D. Quilgars, and N. Pleace (eds) *Homelessness Research in Europe*, Brussels: FEANTSA, pp. 143–162.

Purdam, Kingsley, Elisabeth A. Garratt, and Aneez Esmail (2016) "Hungry? Food Insecurity, Social Stigma and Embarrassment in the UK", *Sociology* 50(6): 1072–1088.

RCCG (2019) "Mission and Vision", available at: http://rccg.org/who-we-are/mission-and-vision/ (accessed 6 October 2019).

RCCG King's Palace (2015a) "King's Justice Ministry", available at: www.rccgthekingspalace.org/index.php/template/pages/king-s-justice-ministry (accessed 10 February 2019).

RCCG King's Palace (2015b) "King's Touch Ministry", available at: www.kingstouchministry.org/en/ (accessed 10 February 2019).

RCCG North America (2019) "Hope for You Programs", available at: https://hopeforyou.org/who-we-are/programs/ (accessed 6 October 2019).

RCCG Restoration Chapel (2014) "Care Ministry", available at: www.rccgrestoration.org/i-connect/care-ministry (accessed 6 October 2019).

RCCG Strong Tower (2019) "Benevolent Food Pantry", available at: https://rccgstrongtower.org/project/food-pantry/ (accessed 6 October 2019).

Sabbagh, Dan and Damien Gayle (2019) "Tory-Supporting Church 'Asks Young Members to Hand Over Thousands'", *Guardian*, 12 November, available at: www.theguardian.com/politics/2019/nov/12/spac-nation-church-asks-young-members-to-hand-over-thousands (accessed 14 November 2019).

Shinn, Marybeth (2010) "Homelessness, Poverty, and Social Exclusion in the United States and Europe", *European Journal on Homelessness* 4: 19–44.

Singh, Arj (2020) "SPAC Nation: MPs Call for Action to Stop Church 'Exploiting' Young People While it is Investigated", *Huffington Post*, available at: www.huffingtonpost.co.uk/entry/spac-nation-commons-debate-mps_uk_5e165c0bc5b6b32c72bcac75 (accessed 11 January 2020).

Singh, Darra (2007) *Our Shared Future: Final Report of the Commission on Integration and Cohesion*, London: Commission on Integration and Cohesion.

Stepick, Alex, Terry Rey, and Sarah J. Mahler, (2009) "Religion, Immigration, and Civic Engagement", in Alex Stepick, Terry Rey, and Sarah J. Mahler (eds) *Churches and*

Charity in the Immigrant City: Religion, Immigration and Civic Engagement in Miami, New Brunswick, NJ: Rutgers University Press, pp. 1–40.

Ter Haar, Gerrie (1998) *Halfway to Paradise: African Christians in Europe*, Cardiff: Cardiff Academic Press.

Ter Haar, Gerrie (2001) *African Christians in Europe*, Nairobi: Acton Publishers.

Toro, P. A., C. J. Tompsett, S. Lombardo, P. Philippot, H. Nachtergael, B. Galand, N. Schlienz, N. Stammel, Y. Yabar, M. Blume, and L. MacKay (2007) "Homelessness in Europe and the United States: A Comparison of Prevalence and Public Opinion", *Journal of Social Issues* 63(3): 505–524.

Toro, Paul A. and Melissa G. Warren (1999) "Homelessness in the United States: Policy Considerations", *Journal of Community Psychology* 27(2): 119–136.

Toulis, Nicole R. (1997) *Believing Identity: Pentecostalism and the Mediation of Jamaican Ethnicity and Gender in England*, Oxford: Berg.

Trussell Trust (2019a) "What We Do", available at: www.trusselltrust.org/what-we-do/ (accessed 15 September 2019).

Trussell Trust (2019b) "Mission and Vision", available at: www.trusselltrust.org/mission-and-vision (accessed 15 September 2019).

Udotong, William (2010) "Transnational Migration and the Reverse Mission of Nigerian-Led Pentecostal Churches in the USA: A Case Study of Selected Churches in Metro Atlanta", PhD Thesis, Asbury Theological Seminary.

Ukah, Asonzeh F-K. (2009) "Reverse Mission or Asylum Christianity? A Nigerian Church in Europe", in Toyin Falola and Augustine Agwuele (eds) *Africans and the Politics of Popular Cultures*, Rochester: University of Rochester Press, pp. 104–132.

Van der Meulen, Marten (2009) "The Continuing Importance of the Local: African Churches and the Search for Worship Space in Amsterdam", *African Diaspora* 1(2): 159–181.

Vertovec, Steven (2004) "Religion and Diaspora", in Peter Antes, Armin W. Geertz, and Randi R. Warne (eds) *New Approaches to the Study of Religion*, Berlin: Verlag de Gruyter, pp. 275–303.

Währisch-Oblau, Claudia (2009) *The Missionary Self-perception of Pentecostal/Charismatic Church Leaders from the Global South in Europe: Bringing Back the Gospel*, Leiden: E. J. Brill.

Warner, Stephen and Judith G. Wittner (eds) (1998) *Gatherings in Diaspora: Religious Communities and the New Immigration*, Philadelphia: Temple University Press.

Weinfeld, N., G. Mills, C. Borger, M. Gearing, T. Macaluso, J. Montaquila, and S. Zedlewski (2014) *Hunger in America: National Report Prepared for Feeding America*, Chicago, IL: Feeding America.

Conclusion

This study has investigated the relationship between religion and development through the lens of Nigerian Pentecostalism. Taking its cue from the 2030 sustainable development agenda, expressed in the SDGs, Pentecostal development practices were studied broadly in relation to the intersecting spheres of economics, governance and democracy, education, healthcare, human rights, and peacebuilding. It also explored the transnational dimension by examining the nexus between Nigerian Pentecostalism, migration, and development with a particular focus on Nigerian diaspora churches in Britain and the United States. This concluding chapter begins with a summary of my findings from the churches studied and their key practices of development. It then examines various factors that account for the heterogeneity of African Pentecostal approaches to development. The remainder of the chapter considers some of the challenges hindering positive engagement between African Pentecostals and the development sector, and suggests ways that these challenges can be overcome in order to enable mutual understanding and foster collaboration.

Nigerian Pentecostalism represents one of the most vibrant expressions of global Christianity, and Nigeria is home to some of the largest Pentecostal churches in the world with multiple national and international branches. There is also a multiplicity of smaller Pentecostal congregations and denominations which exert significant social and religious influence on their members and the wider society. Nigerian Pentecostalism is a heterogenous movement consisting of churches with a variety of theological and social orientations. Most of the churches, networks, and individuals discussed in this book belong to an emergent sector which has become increasingly active in development since the mid-1990s. As I have shown, this shift in orientation is driven by a variety of contextual and cultural factors, including Pentecostalism's encounter with Islam. In Nigeria, an important feature of this emergent movement is a focus on nation-building and national transformation through diverse forms of social, economic, and political engagement. Leaders associated with the movement include some of the most influential Nigerian Pentecostal pastors alongside academics, business entrepreneurs, politicians, and social activists. One explanation for this new emphasis, I have argued, is a reaction against an overdependence on miracles, which has failed to deliver its promises of economic prosperity for the vast majority of church members, coupled with a new understanding that the purpose of wealth is for it to be used for the common good rather than for personal enrichment. Another factor is the influence of "kingdom" theology which was introduced into Nigeria by Sunday Adelaja, founder of the Embassy of God in the Ukraine. However, from a participant point of view, an important factor driving this new movement is the church's response to the biblical mandate to love one's neighbour by addressing the spiritual, physical, and social needs of the wider society.

In Chapter 1, two main types of Nigerian Pentecostal development organizations were identified. Many are informal "ministries" run by church congregations and denominations as part of their corporate social responsibility. However, some Pentecostal churches and individuals in Nigeria have established FBOs of the NGO variety. Pentecostal NGOs often start out as informal ministries but assume more formalized structures in their quest for recognition and partnership with state agencies and donor organizations. Most Pentecostal NGOs are founded by pastors and maintain links with their congregations of origin, but others are established by lay church members as independent, free-standing organizations. Pentecostal development programmes cover a range of areas including education, healthcare, charitable relief, rehabilitation, economic empowerment, human rights, politics, and peacebuilding. However, the majority of Pentecostal NGOs focus on the following four areas: education, economic empowerment, rehabilitation and human rights, and healthcare. Some Pentecostal churches and NGOs partner with government agencies, international donor organizations, transnational corporations, and other faith-based NGOs, especially in the areas of HIV/AIDS and human trafficking. They also use transnational religious networks to appeal for funds and to publicize their development activities.

Pentecostal beliefs impinge upon the economic domain, alternatively motivating or discouraging the pursuit of wealth and its employment for the benefit of others. One of the questions discussed in Chapter 2 is whether churches help to build some of the economically significant beliefs and behaviours that can be loosely described as the Protestant ethic. Some Nigerian Pentecostal pastors have rightly been criticized for using prosperity teaching for personal enrichment. However, others are intentionally seeking to implement a reformation of culture by inculcating values such as hard work, integrity, discipline, and altruism. Significantly, some pastors are defining Africa's economic predicament in terms of social and political structures, recognizing that collective prosperity will be achieved only if the structural causes of poverty and inequality are addressed. The chapter examined various Pentecostal programmes geared towards economic empowerment. Business enterprise is recognized as an important development partner by the international community. Nigerian Pentecostal churches and NGOs are increasingly involved in building the capacity of the SME sector through microfinance initiatives, business schools, and entrepreneurship education, including programmes geared towards the economic empowerment of women entrepreneurs. Business entrepreneurship has also become an important occupation for Nigerian Pentecostals in the diaspora, sometimes involving border-crossing entrepreneurial activities facilitated by transnational social and religious networks. In Britain, Nigerian Pentecostal churches run seminars and conferences which provide contexts for members to engage in prayer for financial success and receive practical advice on business management and wealth creation.

In Chapter 3, we considered the intersection between Pentecostalism and politics in Nigeria. Good governance and the building of democratic institutions are essential for achieving sustainable development. The study identified various political strategies employed by Nigerian Pentecostals, ranging from electoral politics and public expressions of political protest to more implicit strategies such as prophecy and prayer. Pentecostals have a mixed record in the move toward democratization. They played an active role in the politics of transition during successive military regimes, but their susceptibility to state co-option during Nigeria's Fourth Republic has tainted their record of critical activism. Nonetheless, Tunde Bakare's Save Nigeria Group marked a significant departure for Pentecostal political engagement; pastors have used the media to call for free and fair elections; and programmes have emerged to prepare Pentecostals for civic responsibilities. Chris Okotie's unsuccessful incursion into politics shows the dangers of seeking routes to office without preparation and training. And while only in their nascent phase, organizations and churches such as Governance 500, AFREG, the Institute for National Transformation, and Daystar Christian Centre offer a more long-term potential of transforming Nigeria's political culture.

Pentecostal engagement in education and healthcare builds on a long tradition of Christian social action in Nigeria reaching back to the early colonial era when schools and hospitals were established as instruments of evangelization and social change. In Chapter 4, we considered Pentecostal educational initiatives and their contribution to development in Nigeria. Education is recognized as an important contributor to development and a key driver in achieving the SDGs. Pentecostals are responding to the perceived collapse of morality and declining standards in Nigeria's educational system by engaging in capacity-building programmes in public schools, establishing educational NGOs, and opening private schools and universities. One perspective is to regard Pentecostal educational institutions as driven by market concerns to generate economic capital, similar to secular-based private institutions. However, Pentecostal discourse on education is usually framed in ethical terms as an expression of the church's social responsibility. Like education, healthcare is a key component of the 2030 sustainable development agenda. Our discussion of Pentecostal approaches to healing and healthcare in Chapter 5 examined the influence of theology, culture, and context on Pentecostal health-seeking practices. Increasingly, Nigerian Pentecostals are adopting holistic approaches to health that combine beliefs in divine healing with the use of modern medicine. They are also engaged in public health interventions which seek to address health inequalities and obstacles to accessing healthcare services by offering free or subsidized healthcare and opening clinics and hospitals. However, Pentecostal understandings of illness and health can also discourage church members from seeking medical help. The "enchanted" worldview that underpins Nigerian Pentecostal approaches to illness and healing sometimes results in antipathy towards medical technology and recourse to rituals and behaviours detrimental to public health. It can also perpetuate the stigmatization of people living with conditions such as HIV/AIDS, physical and mental disability, and childlessness.

Recently, a rights-based approach to development has gained traction within development circles. In Chapter 6, we discussed Nigerian Pentecostal responses to human rights infringements against women, young people, and children. Nigeria has ratified several international human rights agreements fighting human trafficking and protecting the rights of women and children. It has also enacted laws to combat child abuse, human trafficking, and violence against women. Despite these measures, however, government implementation at state level remains a problem. In response, some Pentecostal churches and NGOs are joining secular NGOs and other FBOs in addressing the needs of street children, commercial sex-workers, and trafficking victims through charitable relief, medical intervention, and rehabilitation programmes. One of the distinctive features of these programmes, which sets them apart from government and other civil society initiatives, is their focus on spiritual formation, empowerment, and equipping for ministry. Born-again conversion, deliverance, and Holy Spirit baptism are regarded as essential "rituals of rupture" enabling clients to make a clean break from their former lifestyles and addictions. Discipleship programmes and other church activities function as socialization mechanisms, turning former gang members, drug addicts, and prostitutes into worship leaders, pastors, and evangelists to their former companions on the street. Pentecostalism has played an ambivalent role in fostering gender justice and equality in Nigeria. On the one hand, participation in Pentecostal religion offers women empowerment, both in private and in public. On the other hand, Pentecostal gender arrangements, which favour male domination and nuclear family norms, can encourage the perpetuation of violence against women. More disturbing are media reports and scholarly research that suggest the complicity of some Pentecostal pastors in child abuse associated with witchcraft accusations and human trafficking.

Violent conflict is a serious obstacle to development, and promoting peaceful and just societies is one of the UN's Sustainable Development Goals. Religion can either legitimize or discourage violence. In Chapter 7, we considered Pentecostal responses to violence and the violation of the rights to religious freedom in northern Nigeria. The combined effects of ethno-religious violence, the implementation of sharia, and the Boko Haram insurgency have had significant impact on Pentecostal communities in relation to economic status, participation in church activities, and civic engagement. Pentecostals have experienced discrimination in employment, restricted access to education and social amenities, barriers to political participation, the destruction of churches and personal property, and extensive loss of lives. To some extent, the venture of Pentecostals into the public arenas of politics and media to combat "Islamization", combined with their emphasis on evangelism and spiritual warfare, has exacerbated Christian-Muslim tensions. However, some pastors have intentionally sought to establish friendships with their Muslim neighbours through acts of inter-religious hospitality. Pentecostal responses to ethno-religious violence are various, ranging from interfaith dialogue and peacebuilding initiatives to relief and rehabilitation programmes. Pentecostals have also used the media and transnational networks to raise awareness of violence perpetrated against Christians in northern Nigeria.

International migration is centrally positioned within the 2030 sustainable development agenda, and migrants are increasingly regarded as vital agents of development. However, in Europe and the United States, migrants are among the most vulnerable to poverty-related problems such as social exclusion, homelessness, and food insecurity. In Chapter 8, the nexus between Pentecostalism, migration, and development was investigated with a particular focus on Britain and the United States. Nigerian Pentecostal churches in the diaspora are contributing to immigrant incorporation and welfare provision through a variety of social support mechanisms and initiatives. They are also addressing social issues in the wider society such as homelessness, food insecurity, and youth crime. These initiatives are influenced by a "reverse mission" discourse and aspirations to re-evangelize the former heartlands of Christianity which are regarded as increasingly secular. Nigerian Pentecostals understand their mission in broad terms to include any activity that will change society for the better. This has driven some churches to embark on programmes of territorial expansion, not only through evangelism and church-planting but also by engaging in civic activity. Some of the churches fit the profile of Faist's transnational development actors (Faist 2008). Their development activities are shaped by ongoing connections between home and host societies, facilitated by modern communication, information technology, and ease of travel. Individuals and churches are engaged in a variety of transnational practices, ranging from financial remittances and charitable donations, to short-term mission trips and international development projects.

Nigerian Pentecostalism's contribution to successful development outcomes is difficult to determine. Most of the churches and NGOs discussed in this book represent only one strand of Nigerian Pentecostalism, albeit a growing and increasingly influential one. In Nigeria, they are clearly having an impact at the local level through their economic empowerment programmes, healthcare initiatives, educational institutions and NGOs, rehabilitation programmes, community development projects, and peacebuilding initiatives. At the national level, this emerging movement is having less visible impact despite its evident growth and the ambitions of its leaders. Much will depend upon whether its influence is able to spread to other sectors of Nigerian Pentecostalism. Another factor is the inter-religious dimension and the disruptive influence of Christian-Muslim conflict. In Britain, Nigerian Pentecostal churches are gradually becoming a social force to be reckoned with: they are expanding, finding new ways of engaging with society, and are shaping the self-conception of their members as valuable members of their host society. They represent a challenge to the notion that religion is losing its social significance in public life. Nonetheless, despite their cosmopolitan agenda, they have generally failed to make incursions into the indigenous population and remain predominantly Nigerian in composition. They are also facing a critical moment in their history in terms of retaining second and third generation African members brought up in Britain.

A plurality of African Pentecostal approaches to development

One of the issues discussed in the literature is whether Pentecostal responses to development challenges are distinctive compared to those of other faith groups and secular NGOs (Freeman 2012; Haustein *et al.* 2015). Haustein *et al.* (2015: 258) question whether it is feasible or even sensible to treat Pentecostalism as a "distinct or unified entity" when considering its role in development discourse and practice. One reason for this is the diversity of the movement due to its multiple origins and variety of expressions in different cultural and regional contexts. Another is the influence of Charismatic movements on mainline churches, which makes it difficult to distinguish between Pentecostals and other Christian actors in the development sector.

Owing to the heterogeneity of African Pentecostalism, there is a plurality of African Pentecostal approaches to development. Various factors account for differences in the nature and scope of African Pentecostal development activities. I present here some preliminary observations based on the churches and individuals examined in the book. One layer of diversity is theological orientation. Beyond a common emphasis on the experience of the Holy Spirit and the practice of spiritual gifts, and a shared focus on empowerment and transformation, there is considerable diversity of theological emphasis within contemporary Nigerian Pentecostalism. African Pentecostalism has long been associated with individual transformation, and Pentecostals commonly consider conversion as the key to social change. This can sometimes divert Pentecostals from addressing the social and structural causes of poverty and underdevelopment. However, some Nigerian Pentecostal churches and NGOS are intentionally seeking to bring about social transformation in their communities. This is evident in the language used in their mission statements and publicity material. It is also reflected in an emphasis on national transformation and initiatives geared towards reforming cultural values and practices deemed inimical to economic development. This new social awareness is encouraged by an emerging "kingdom theology", the failure of the state to deliver on its promises of economic development, and a disappointment with the results of contemporary Pentecostalism (McCain 2013).

An important Pentecostal distinctive is the prosperity gospel, which links faith and prayer with the expectation of individual prosperity and success.

There is a tendency to make generalizations when studying Pentecostal prosperity churches and to regard them as an obstacle to Africa's development. A more nuanced approach needs to take account of the different meanings attached to prosperity in different contexts. As noted above, some Nigerian pastors have used the prosperity gospel for personal gain, growing rich at the expense of their churches' impoverished members.[1] Others have adopted a different understanding of prosperity: the purpose of wealth is for the common good rather than for personal enrichment. Another trend is a shift away from a miraculous approach to prosperity to an emphasis on work and entrepreneurial skills. Significantly, influential pastors such as Tony Rapu, Sam Adeyemi, and Tunde Bakare are defining Africa's economic problems in terms of social and political structures. In church sermons, conference talks, and political speeches, they are challenging government economic policies and institutional arrangements that they consider to be incompatible with positive development outcomes.

African Pentecostals do not separate religion from development. This is in keeping with their holistic doctrine of salvation which includes material, physical, and spiritual redemption. Development is not conceived of exclusively in materialist terms but includes reference to an invisible world of spirits. This "enchanted" worldview is sometimes regarded as a hindrance to development, encouraging a culture of fear and distrust, and diminishing human responsibility. However, levels of "enchantment" vary between different strands of African Pentecostalism. This is reflected in the diversity of Nigerian Pentecostal approaches to healing and healthcare. As I have already noted, the Pentecostal tendency to trace the aetiology of illness to supernatural agents, such as demons or witches, can result in antipathy towards scientific medicine and encourage recourse to rituals and behaviours detrimental to public health. Increasingly, however, Nigerian Pentecostals are adopting holistic approaches that combine faith-healing practices with healthcare services such as subsidized medical care, primary health education, health clinics, and hospitals. The plurality of African Pentecostal approaches to development is also reflected in the range of political theologies and practices adopted by Nigerian Pentecostals. An "enchanted" approach to politics, which emphasizes spiritual causality, holds demons responsible for adverse political circumstances. One of the consequences is that corrupt and incompetent politicians are not held to account for their poor performance. Nonetheless, some Nigerian Pentecostal leaders are encouraging their members to get involved in the political process by voting in elections, joining political parties, and seeking political office. Finally, the diversity of Pentecostal theologies of religions has resulted in a plurality of responses to ethno-religious violence. The demonization of Islam associated with the Nigerian Pentecostal emphasis on spiritual warfare has contributed to the deterioration of Christian-Muslim relations. However, some Pentecostal organizations in Nigeria, which have embraced a more conciliatory approach to other religions, are playing a constructive role in building peace and addressing the social needs of victims of violence.

Another layer of heterogeneity which influences African Pentecostal churches' approaches to development is their organizational culture. The ecclesiological structures of Nigerian Pentecostal churches are diverse, ranging from independent churches characterized by charismatic leadership styles to denominations where leaders are appointed on the basis of constitutional guidelines rather than personal charisma. The ability of Pentecostal churches to play a constructive role in development depends to a large extent upon the competence and social orientation of their leaders. Pastors who have embraced a transformational model of leadership, which encourages lay participation, have tended to foster churches with a strong sense of social responsibility. Equally important for Nigerian Pentecostal engagement in development are networks of like-minded church leaders, such as Church for Change and Apostles in the Marketplace. Their relatively flat and flexible ecclesiology and their focus on leadership training enables the mobilization and empowerment of the laity for engagement in different spheres of public life. They also allow more space for creativity and innovative practices outside the constraints of denominational structures. Nonetheless, the Pentecostal emphasis on charismatic power has also encouraged the elevation of "powerfully anointed" leaders who use their position as power-brokers for personal gain rather than to serve the needs of the poor and marginalized. As Yong (2012: 116) notes, this "not only minimizes the role of the laity but also undermines the structures of accountability so important for successful charismatic leadership".

A final layer of heterogeneity relates to the size and socio-economic status of Pentecostal organizations. A small, independent Pentecostal church in a poor neighbourhood in Lagos, where members struggle to survive, will have a very different approach to development from a rich megachurch which has a predominantly educated and upwardly mobile membership. Most Nigerian Pentecostal development work is undertaken by large congregations with sufficient human and financial resources at their disposal. Megachurches such as Daystar Christian Centre and Fountain of Life Church in Lagos, and RCCG Jesus House in London, are capable of mobilizing significant numbers of volunteers for development activities. They are also able to generate considerable financial resources due to their emphasis on prosperity teaching, mandatory tithing, and the generosity of their more prosperous members. This has enabled some churches to build schools, universities, hospitals, and rehabilitation centres. Small congregations, by contrast, often have to share space with other faith groups or rent space in secular buildings which seriously hampers their capacity for civic engagement. This is more common among diaspora churches in Britain because of limitations of worship space in urban environments. Transnational religious networks also provide significant resources for international development through remittances, charitable donations, and short-term mission teams who volunteer their time and expertise for development projects. Partnerships with local and international donor organizations are another important resource for Pentecostal development activities. Pentecostals are more likely to receive funding from donor organizations if they have established FBOs of the NGO variety.

African Pentecostalism and the development sector

This study has shown that some Nigerian Pentecostals are engaging with development discourse and the international development agenda, though further research is needed to assess the extent of this engagement. The remainder of this chapter considers some of the challenges hindering positive engagement between African Pentecostals and the development sector, and suggests various ways that these challenges can be overcome in order to foster collaboration.

African Pentecostal churches face a number of challenges in their engagement with the development sector, which are related to their mixed track record of development activity and their adherence to certain beliefs and practices. There is a perception among some African Pentecostals that state agencies and development actors doubt the competence of religious institutions to undertake development initiatives. Pentecostals are also put off by what they perceive as the excessive bureaucratic processes involved in establishing collaborative partnerships with state agencies and external donors.[2] Pentecostalism's "enchanted" worldview, associated with a miraculous approach to prosperity and a tendency to explain national poverty in spiritual terms, also poses a challenge to positive engagement with the development sector. One aspect of this is the predominance of individualistic and unaccountable Pentecostal leaders, which results from the focus on the pastor's "anointing" and the excessive emphasis on charismatic power. Another obstacle is the merging of development with evangelism, which has the potential to bring Pentecostal churches and NGOs into conflict with secular donor organizations, NGOs, and state agencies.

In order to encourage positive engagement and collaboration, development actors need to gain a better understanding of African Pentecostal spirituality and to treat it on its own terms. A number of scholars have drawn attention to the necessity for higher levels of religious literacy within development circles in order to contribute positively to the relationships between religions and international development (Tomalin 2013; Clarke 2015; Haustein *et al.* 2015). As Tomalin (2013: 237) notes, this involves "not only enhancing one's knowledge of the importance of religions in people's lives in developing countries but also learning about the beliefs and practices embodied within different religious traditions". A major critique of engagement of international development actors, according to Tomalin (2013: 235), is that it has "tended to be instrumental, using religion where it can help meet pre-defined and western-oriented development goals rather than thinking through how religions themselves contribute towards people's understanding of what counts as development". African Pentecostal approaches to development are holistic, encompassing the physical, material, moral, and spiritual aspects of people's lives. This needs to be taken into account when seeking development partnerships with Pentecostal churches and NGOs. Recent research has shown the points of contact and areas of overlap between Pentecostalism and mainstream development theory. Clarke (2015) refers to the common ground that exists between Pentecostals and development actors in respect to improving human well-being, particularly their practices of participation and transformation. Both practices are prominent features of the Pentecostal development activities examined in this book. It is hoped that this glimpse into the life of one particular strand of African Pentecostalism will contribute to a better understanding of the movement's distinctive spirituality and its influence on Pentecostal development approaches and practices.

One of the ways that Pentecostal and development actors can increase their understanding of each other's approaches to development is through sustained dialogue. As Haustein *et al.* (2015: 260) note, dialogue "not only brings together various perspectives, it also shapes and alters them". Dialogue between Pentecostal organizations and their members, development practitioners, and academics is already taking place in different contexts.[3] However, more "forums for exchange" are needed to improve development work among Pentecostals, collaboration between Pentecostals and other development actors, and scholarly awareness of relevant issues (Haustein *et al.* 2015: 260). African Pentecostal churches and organizations represent a significant, if largely untapped, resource for development. Increased information about African Pentecostal development activities and perspectives in different regional contexts will contribute to this knowledge exchange and provide opportunities for collaborative initiatives between the development sector and African Pentecostal churches and NGOs.

Notes

1 A recent list of Africa's ten richest pastors includes seven Nigerian Pentecostals: David Oyedepo (Winners Chapel), Enoch Adeboye (RCCG), Ayo Oritsejafor (Word of Life Bible Church), Chris Oyakhilome (Christ Embassy), T. B. Joshua (Synagogue Church of All Nations), Matthew Ashimolowo (KICC), and Lazarus Muoka (Lord's Chosen Charismatic Renewal Movement). See Lists.ng (2018).

2 See Daniel Akhazemea's contribution in Haustein *et al.* (2015). Akhazemea is an ordained pastor in the Redeemed Christian Church of God (UK) and Principal of RCCG's Christ the Redeemer College (London).

3 One example is the 2014 GloPent conference on "Pentecostalism and Development" held at the School of Oriental and African Studies (SOAS), which brought together academics and practitioners. Some of the conference papers were subsequently published in a special edition of the journal *PentecoStudies* (2015).

References

Clarke, Matthew (2015) "Friend or Foe? Finding Common Ground Between Development and Pentecostalism", *PentecoStudies* 14(2): 156–175.

Faist, Thomas (2008) "Migrants as Transnational Development Agents: An Inquiry into the Newest Round of the Migration–Development Nexus", *Population, Space and Place* 14(1): 21–42.

Freeman, Dena (2012) "The Pentecostal Ethic and the Spirit of Development", in Dena Freeman (ed.) *Pentecostalism and Development: Churches, NGOs and Social Change in Africa*, London: Palgrave Macmillan, pp. 1–38.

Haustein, Jörg, Carole Rakodi, Daniel Akhazemea, Mike Battcock, Rick James, and Claudia Währisch-Oblau (2015) "Roundtable–Pentecostalism and Development Practice", *PentecoStudies* 14(2): 241–260.

Lists.ng (2018) "Top 10 Richest Pastors in Africa 2019", available at: https://lists.ng/top-10-richest-pastors-in-africa-2019/ (accessed 23 November 2019).

McCain, Danny (2013) "The Metamorphosis of Nigerian Pentecostalism: From Signs and Wonders in the Church to Service and Influence in Society", in Donald Miller, Kimon Sergeant, and Richard Flory (eds) *Spirit and Power: The Growth and Global Impact of Pentecostalism*, Oxford: Oxford University Press, pp. 160–181.

Tomalin, Emma (2013) *Religions and Development*, London: Routledge.

Yong, Amos (2012) "What's Love Got to Do with It? The Sociology of Godly Love and the Renewal of Modern Pentecostalism", *Journal of Pentecostal Theology* (21): 113–134.

Index